Bankrupting the Enemy

BANKRUPTING *the* ENEMY

The U.S. Financial Siege of Japan
before Pearl Harbor

EDWARD S. MILLER

NAVAL INSTITUTE PRESS
Annapolis, Maryland

Naval Institute Press
291 Wood Road
Annapolis, MD 21402

First Naval Institute Press paperback edition published in 2023.

ISBN: 978-1-68247-897-4 (paperback)

ISBN: 978-1-61251-118-4 (eBook)

The Library of Congress has cataloged the hardcover edition as follows:

Miller, Edward S.

Bankrupting the enemy : the U.S. financial siege of Japan before Pearl Harbor / Edward S. Miller.

p. cm.

Includes bibliographical references and index.

ISBN 978-1-59114-520-2 (alk. paper)

1. Economic sanctions, American—Japan—History—20th century. 2. United States—Foreign economic relations—Japan. 3. Japan—Foreign economic relations—United States. 4. Japan—Economic conditions—1918-1945. I. Title.

HF1602.15.U6M55 2007

940.53'113—dc22

∞ Print editions meet the requirements of ANSI/NISO z39.48-1992 (Permanence of Paper). Printed in the United States of America.

31 30 29 28 27 26 25 24 23   9 8 7 6 5 4 3 2 1

First printing

CONTENTS

Photographs follow page 180

ILLUSTRATIONS

Figures

Endsheets

Charts

Tables

PROLOGUE

War Plan Orange

The American perception of Japan's economic and financial vulnerability dated back to a time thirty-five years before Pearl Harbor. President Theodore Roosevelt grew concerned after the victory over Russia in 1905 that Japan would seek to dominate China in contravention of the U.S. Open Door policy, which championed independence and free trade for China. Japan would perceive that policy, and U.S. bases in the Philippines and Hawaii, as barriers to building an empire. Roosevelt asked the U.S. Navy for a plan to fight Japan, if and when necessary.

The result, War Plan Orange, was fundamentally an economic strategy in both origins and outcome. (Japan was code-named Orange, the United States Blue.) The godfathers of the plan, Admirals George Dewey and Alfred Thayer Mahan, had served as young officers enforcing the Union's Anaconda Plan against the Confederacy, an "island" vulnerable to economic blockade. They and later disciples in the War Plans Division of the Navy demonstrated a fierce mindset favoring vigorous action, a mindset echoed by civilian bureaucrats who advocated a nonviolent economic and financial "war" against Japan in the crisis years before Pearl Harbor.

While U.S. military planners assumed Japan's war aims would be limited—a surprise attack, victory in naval battle, and a negotiated peace ceding dominance of East Asia—their aim was a crushing defeat of the enemy, an aim demanded by an aroused public. They understood that Japan, an island nation poor in natural resources, depended on overseas trade for the sinews of war and its very economic life. The Japanese Empire produced food enough, but industrialization and conquests led to voracious needs of metals and fuels. The planners designed a strategy of siege. After initial losses, Blue forces would fight back island by island, sink the enemy fleet, seize bases near Japan, starve it of vital imports, and ultimately force it to capitulate. Japan's financial destitution would be ensured by "coercive pressure" on world lenders to deny funds such as Wall Street provided during the Russo-Japanese War. Plans rang with confidence that the United States could enforce "final and complete commercial isolation" (1906), leading to "eventual impoverishment and exhaustion" (1911) and "in the end . . . economic ruin" (1920). As air power came of age, bombing of industry and transportation intensified the siege plan. In 1941 Plan Orange morphed into global Plan Rainbow Five, and in 1942–45 it was executed in most major respects. The Pacific war culminated in unconditional surrender after devastation of Japan's economy, including, at the end, the deployment of atomic bombs.[1]

In the 1930s peaceable internationalist governments in Tokyo gave way to military-dominated regimes. The anticipated violations of the Open Door unfolded in the invasion of China and designs against colonies of the Western powers. The helplessness of Japan, if isolated economically and financially, evolved into an axiom at a time when the U.S. government was averse to fighting a war. When national policy to deter Japanese aggression took root, the United States gradually deployed its vast economic and financial powers to strangle Japan by means other than ships and bombs. It was a Plan Orange strategy in peacetime.

The story now turns to the U.S. strategy of achieving the nation's foreign policy aims, without combat, by bankrupting Japan.

SOURCES AND TECHNICAL NOTES

The focus of this book is the United States' financial and economic sanctions against Japan before Pearl Harbor, reconstructed primarily from official U.S. sources. Many histories have been written about the run-up to the Pacific war, largely by diplomatic historians, understandably in view of the centrality of the Department of State in U.S.-Japanese negotiations and that department's voluminous, well-organized files, which were declassified long ago, some as early as 1943, supplemented by forty volumes of congressional hearings of 1946 about Pearl Harbor and precursor events.[1]

Financial and economic records, however, were far less accessible until fifty years after World War II. Not until 1996 did the National Archives, at the prompting of a U.S. interagency group on Nazi assets, declassify and make more readily available the worldwide papers of the Treasury Department's Office of the Assistant Secretary of International Affairs, established on 25 March 1938 and directed by Harry Dexter White.[2] These records contain a trove of U.S. assessments of Japan's financial problems, and U.S. proposals to exploit them, that have not appeared in other histories. A similar wealth of information is in the records, first opened to the public in 1996–97, of the Division of International Finance of the Board of Governors of the Federal Reserve system, primarily from 1935 to 1955. The Federal Reserve Bank of New York voluntarily sent to the National Archives those of its records "that relate to the activity in accounts for foreign governments" in the same era.[3] The files of the U.S. Alien Property Custodian, which include the 1880–1942 records of Japanese bank branches in the United States seized in 1941, were closed until fifty years after seizure to researchers lacking special permission and were inconveniently located until transferred to the National Archives II in 1995–96 and "bulk declassified." The records of the Tariff Commission (now the U.S. International Trade Commission), with a wealth of studies on specific Japanese products, were open but not properly described and arranged until 1992.[4] The planning records of the Administrator of Export Control, the office that led the drive for sanctions against Japan during the crucial months of September 1940 to May 1941, were difficult for researchers to use until recently, when they were rearranged and a finding aid was prepared at the National Archives. That office was subsumed in September 1941 into the vast wartime bureaucracy of the Foreign Economic Administration, which in turn was reorganized three or four times during the war. Its boxed records extend 3,817 cubic feet and weigh seventy-five tons. A comprehensive catalogue of all international records of the era, which are mostly located at National Archives II in College Park, Maryland, was completed in 1999 under the direction of Greg Bradsher and is available online at http://www.archives.gov/research/holocaust/finding-aid.

The main Japanese sources are the excellent historical data published in bilingual tables by the Japan Statistical Association, and Japanese commercial and diplomatic studies published in English. Most of Japan's official records of 1931 to 1945 were burned in the two-week interval between the surrender and the occupation in 1945 in anticipation of war crimes trials. However, economic information for the last prewar decade was reconstructed in detail and published by the U.S. Strategic Bombing Survey and by investigators of the Supreme Commander of the Allied Powers during the postwar occupation.

Japanese financial and trade statistics are usually presented for fiscal years beginning 1 April, so that, for example, "1940" means the twelve months beginning 1 April 1940 and ending 31 March 1941. U.S. statistics are usually given for calendar years, making some comparisons awkward. Physical trade units are stated here in U.S. measures such as ounces, tons, or yards, or occasionally in metric measures. Some Japanese figures have been converted from metric units or the ancient weights and measures then used in trade.

Money figures are stated in U.S. dollars, the dominant world currency then and now. The 1935–41 dollar was worth about $10 in 2007 dollars if measured by an average of U.S. prices of goods, or about $25 if measured by average U.S. wages. In exchange markets the yen was worth 49 to 50 cents from 1899 until devalued on 14 December 1931. It dipped as low as 20 cents in 1932–33, then stabilized at 28.3 cents until 24 October 1939, when it was devalued to 23.4 cents. There was no organized exchange market after 25 July 1941; fragmentary trading in China suggests that in late 1941 the yen's gray market value was much lower, perhaps 11 or 12 cents.[5] After a devastating wartime and postwar inflation, the yen was stabilized at 0.28 cents (360 per dollar). It subsequently has risen to almost 1 cent (100 per dollar).

The U.S. economy is roughly 150 times larger than in 1935–40 in unadjusted dollars and about 10 times larger adjusted for price inflation. The Japanese economy is about 500 times larger in unadjusted U.S. dollars and about 50 times larger adjusted for U.S. inflation. The prewar Japanese economy was about 8 percent the size of the American. In 2006 it was about 40 percent as large. Japanese foreign trade is now about seven hundred times greater in nominal value, $1.1 *trillion* versus $1.5 *billion* before the war, of which half was within the "yen bloc." (Both figures are unadjusted for inflation.) To grasp the relative significance in twenty-first century terms of $100 million in 1941, a very large fraction of Japan's international liquidity at the time, the reader may wish to multiply by a factor of one thousand.

ACKNOWLEDGMENTS

Sixteen years before publication of this book, I wrote *War Plan Orange: The U.S. Strategy to Defeat Japan, 1897–1945*, also published by the Naval Institute Press. That book reflected my interest in the era before World War II and the American strategy for fighting Japan if and when war came. I was fortunate that key documents had been declassified from secret status. shortly before I began my research, so that my work disclosed information unavailable to, or sometimes ignored by, other historians of the period. This effort is in many ways parallel to my earlier one. I again address U.S. strategy developed in the prewar era, but now the *peacetime* strategy to deter Japan from war. Again, I was fortunate that hitherto classified documents were opened to view about the time I began my research. However, the projects differ in that my credentials as a historian of naval strategy were negligible at the time, whereas this book reflects a knowledge of international finance and trade that I gained in a thirty-five-year career with one of America's largest mining and resource companies, culminating in becoming its chief financial officer, and as a director of an aluminum joint venture with Mitsui and Company, a major Japanese trading firm. I have tried to put this experience to good use in interpreting the deployment of U.S. financial power. The two books differ in another profound aspect: The United States successfully launched Plan Orange to win the war in the Pacific, but the prewar bankrupting of Japan failed in its purpose of deterring Japan from attacking.

I wish to acknowledge the assistance and encouragement given by my friend of sixty years, David Kahn, the doyen of cryptologic history and fellow historian of World War II. I enjoyed valuable help from the learned archivists at the National Archives in College Park, Maryland: Tim Nenninger; Greg Bradsher, who catalogued the formerly secret financial records; and the long-serving John Taylor, who is a national treasure. Most of the other research was done at the Library of Congress in Washington, D.C. I was astonished to calculate that I had worked in eleven of the library's eighteen reading rooms: Business and Economics, Science, Geography, Newspapers and Government Documents, Manuscripts, Microforms, Prints and Photographs, Asian, Rare Books, Law, and, especially, Humanities and Social Sciences. Among many dedicated librarians, I wish to thank Dr. Steven Elisha James, David Kelly, and Kathy Woodrell for their help in finding information in that vast storehouse of knowledge. Will O'Neil thoughtfully sent voluminous scanned documents. In Japan, Professor Yasuhiko Doi kindly supplied data not easily available here, and Seiichiro Satoh of Shinchosa, Limited urged me onward toward publication there. I was fortunate to receive comments and criticism, which I put to good use in rewriting the manuscript, from two eminent historians of the era of U.S.-Japanese conflict, Dr. Mark R. Peattie, Research Fellow of the Hoover Institution, and Dr. Michael Barnhart, Distinguished Teaching Professor at Stony Brook University of New York. Thanks also to the Naval Institute Press for supporting and encouraging this project, notably former editorial directors Paul Wilderson and Mark Gatlin. The Institute took a chance on me as a rookie historian the first time around. I hope they are as satisfied this time. Finally, I acknowledge the love of my family, all of whom suffer, along with me, the urge to write: Joyce, my patient, tolerant spouse of fifty-five years; my daughter-in-law Kris Waldherr, who provided the imaginative cover art; and my children Susan Elizabeth and Thomas Ross, to whom I dedicate this book.

INTRODUCTION

Bankruptcy

The judgment of history is that Japan attacked Pearl Harbor and launched the Pacific War to thwart American resistance to its designs of imperial conquest in East Asia. U.S. opposition included diplomatic pressure, military preparations, and, above all, economic sanctions. Historians have emphasized the de facto embargo of oil as the most deadly sanction because Japan's navy and army depended on U.S. exports of fuel, a situation the military leaders effectively in control of Japanese policies perceived as an intolerable weakness. But the U.S. action of 26 July 1941 was not just a trade embargo. It was an emasculation of Japan's laboriously accumulated international money reserves, imposed by President Franklin D. Roosevelt by invoking an obscure 1917 law, the Trading with the Enemy Act.

I propose that the most devastating American action against Japan was the financial freeze. Money mattered. In 1941 war had congealed the financial systems of other great powers, rendering their currencies inconvertible. Abroad, the yen itself was illiquid, that is, not acceptable for payments outside the Japanese Empire. The United States stood in the extraordinary position of controlling nearly all the world's negotiable money resources. It applied its extraordinary power to "bankrupt" Japan.

Bankruptcy is a condition imposed by a court of law to compel settlement of debts. A bankrupt person or company that is judged insolvent lacks sufficient assets to pay. A sovereign nation, however, is not subject to a court's jurisdiction, and in any case, on 25 July 1941, Japan held ample liquid assets—dollars in U.S. banks and gold bars in Tokyo vaults—to purchase vital imports and service its relatively small international debts. Japan was not insolvent, then or later. On 26 July, however, a stroke of the pen rendered it

illiquid. The freeze isolated Japan economically from the outside world, void-
ing its monetary assets, both sums on hand or obtainable in the future.
Consent to buy strategic goods in the United States, or in any country that
exported for dollars, was withheld by the United States in conjunction with
parallel freezes by the British and Dutch empires. Japan's commercial sphere
shriveled to the "yen bloc" of its colonies and conquered regions in East Asia.

Midlevel officials of the U.S. government applied the monetary freeze with
devastating effect. Financial strangulation was not the intended policy of
Roosevelt or his cabinet secretaries or Congress. It was a weapon honed by
staff aides who were thrust suddenly into positions of power due to their
expertise. They opportunistically seized the reins to drive a U.S. policy
"designed to bring Japan to its senses, not its knees" toward a warlike confrontation.[1]

"Bankrupt" and "impoverished" are terms often used interchangeably.
Japan's international illiquidity would, beyond doubt, have impoverished the
nation within a couple of years. The U.S. freeze presented Japan with three
choices: suffer economic impoverishment, accede to American demands to
yield its territorial conquests, or go to war against the United States and its
allies. Unfortunately for Japan, it chose the latter.

Rarely before had illiquidity—equivalent to bankruptcy in foreign affairs—
presented such a Hobson's choice to a powerful nation. Nor is it likely to hap-
pen again. The world of the twenty-first century is awash in liquid funds that
migrate freely across borders, beyond the command of any nation seeking to
control the financial destiny of another.

1

Trading with the Enemy

I n the autumn of 1937 Franklin Delano Roosevelt brooded about deterring foreign military dictatorships from attacking peaceful nations. On 5 October, thirteen weeks after Japan invaded China, the president delivered his famous "quarantine" speech. Likening the spreading aggressions to an epidemic disease, he suggested that law-abiding countries ought to quarantine the aggressors. When pressed by reporters, he denied that he meant economic sanctions, calling sanctions "a terrible word to use." "There are," he said, "a lot of methods in the world that have never been tried yet."[1] Roosevelt was not sure what he meant until December, after Japanese bombers sank a U.S. gunboat in China. He turned to his energetic secretary of the treasury, Henry Morgenthau Jr., for a "modern" weapon to wield against Japan. Treasury experts unearthed the perfect device: a relic of the First World War known as Section 5(b) of the Trading with the Enemy Act (TWEA), a single paragraph that empowered the president to paralyze dollars owned by foreign countries, whether enemy or not. Denial of U.S. dollars, a key reserve currency of the world and indispensable to Japan for waging war, could dissuade Japan from belligerence. That surviving section of the act had arisen from an obscure spat in 1917 between government agencies that foreshadowed the bureaucratic graspings for power in Washington during 1937–41 as the United States groped toward invoking its great financial powers to render Japan effectively bankrupt in the world.

Sanctioning to impose a nation's will on others in peacetime was hardly a novel concept. International law governing trade relations among sovereign states had been laid down by the European jurists Hugo Grotius and Emeric de Vattel in the seventeenth and eighteenth centuries in the wake of dreadful destruction of the Thirty Years' War. They held that nations had the absolute right to decide what and from whom to import. Refusal to export was also a sovereign right, although Vattel considered extreme actions such as withholding food in time of famine might be construed as acts of war.[2] In 1807–9 President Thomas Jefferson applied the Embargo Acts, drastic trade sanctions to protest by means short of war the violations by Britain and France against U.S. shipping and trade and British impressments of American seamen. The acts outlawed incoming and outgoing trade with those empires. Lack of American cotton nearly wrecked the British textile industry, and the Royal Navy suffered shortages of masts from the tall white pines of American forests. Nevertheless, the European powers did not deem Jefferson's embargo a *casus belli*, in part because of smuggling and evasion, and the embargo ended in failure.[3] In 1812 America had to fight a real war to restore its maritime rights. Money, however, had not been a coercive tool in those early episodes, nor could it be an option of U.S. foreign policy for another century until the United States rose to financial supremacy during and after World War I.

When the United States declared war on Germany on 6 April 1917 it had no legal mechanism for restricting economic dealings with the enemy other than publishing lists of contraband goods under the common law. At the urging of Secretary of State Robert Lansing, Congress added to an espionage bill of 15 June some export restrictions as a stopgap measure. Lansing, in testimony before a House of Representatives committee, noted that although the rules applied to all international trade, they did not cover financial transactions.[4] A committee of officials of the State, Commerce, Treasury, and Justice Departments set about drafting a more comprehensive Trading with the Enemy Act focusing on physical trade. Lansing showed little further interest, presumably viewing war measures as outside his diplomatic realm and certainly not expecting any restrictions to outlive the war.

In June and July 1917 Secretary of Commerce William C. Redfield, a strong advocate of regulations, described to the House of Representatives how the proposed TWEA avoided the meddlesome English system of approving or disapproving each and every foreign transaction. By limiting controls to dealings with enemy countries, it preserved as much as possible the U.S. tradition of noninterference in commerce. Although not within his authority, Redfield urged regulation of financial dealings as well, because, he said, "we are now the world's purse," having "the greatest present source of credit in the world."[5] Redfield's deputy, Edward E. Pratt, agreed that "the most important aspect of the whole thing is the financial and credit transactions that might take place." Although the British blockade had shrunk Germany's substantial transatlantic trade to a trickle, international transactions were complex proceedings that could be routed through neutrals such as Spain. Most congressmen agreed that "this war is to be won as much by dollars as it is by men and guns."[6] Redfield proposed that his Commerce Department administer both trade and financial dealings involving enemy states.[7] The House agreed. Its bill and the subsequent Senate versions included a variety of controls on international financial dealings. Some were exhaustively detailed as matters to be settled after the war.[8]

Control of physical commerce was straightforward in the draft TWEA. It restricted trade with an enemy nation (Germany) and its citizens and businesses; with "allies of an enemy," for example, Austria-Hungary, that were not yet at war with the United States; and foreign states and entities that might try as middlemen to circumvent the act. Direct or indirect enemy trade, if any, would be authorized only under licenses granted by the authority of the president. The Department of Commerce, the agency whose customs houses granted clearances to cargoes aboard vessels and trains entering and leaving the United States, would enforce the act.[9] The House bill contained no indication that the act was other than a temporary war measure that would lapse when peace returned. The bill passed and moved to the Senate.

During deliberations, Secretary of the Treasury William Gibbs McAdoo had been absent promoting Liberty Bond sales. McAdoo was an influential, practical-minded presence in Washington: a former electric railroad executive, an early supporter of President Woodrow Wilson—he married Wilson's daughter Eleanor in 1914—and an architect of the Federal Reserve system.[10] Upon returning to Washington to testify before the Senate Subcommittee on Commerce, he wholeheartedly supported financial regulations but demanded that the Treasury and Federal Reserve Board, not the Commerce Department, must wield the levers of control. Every transaction, he argued, involved both a physical movement of goods and a money settlement. Shipment of gold abroad was clearly a movement of "money," not of a commodity. Most elusive were foreign-owned bank deposits that were transferable from a distance by letter or telegraphic wire. To block Germany from obtaining dollars to spend in the United States or in third countries, McAdoo argued that German bank accounts in the United States must be frozen and sale or mortgaging of Germany's large investments in U.S. factories and securities must be prohibited.[11]

A bureaucratic dogfight erupted. While Secretary Redfield conceded the Treasury's authority over financial controls and acknowledged the bank-regulating expertise of the Federal Reserve system established four years earlier, he insisted that the definitive authorization of a regulated transaction must be an export or import license granted by the Department of Commerce.[12] In response, McAdoo unleashed Milton C. Elliott, general counsel of the Federal

Reserve Board. Elliott, a handsome young Virginia attorney who sported the pince-nez eyeglasses worn by the president, typified the midlevel Washington bureaucrat of this narrative: expert, clever, aggressive, and determined to magnify the power of his agency and his superiors. After a stint as lawyer for the comptroller of the currency, he came to McAdoo's attention, traveling with him as secretary of a barnstorming mission in 1914, a bit of political theater aboard a lavish private train steaming around the country to organize the regional Federal Reserve banks. He was named counsel of the Federal Reserve Board in 1915, a post he held until after the war, when he returned to private practice.

Elliott's clever innuendos and bizarre explanations ran rings around bumbling Commerce Department spokesmen in the hearings. His arguments were both genuine, such as providing the Federal Reserve's banking know-how, and trivial, such as the storage space for confiscated gold in sub-Treasury vaults. Redfield, forced to retreat, conceded a cosmetically joint system whereby Commerce-approved merchandise movements would be deemed automatically licensed by the Treasury. McAdoo and Elliott bridled, demanding coequal status: authorized deals were to be licensed by *both* Commerce and the Treasury acting independently.

At a key moment in the proceedings Elliott submitted an amendment authorizing the Treasury, assisted by the Federal Reserve, to regulate and license *all* international financial transactions with *all* countries. It ultimately emerged, word for word, as Section 5(b) of the TWEA.[13] In relevant part, the section read:

> That the President may investigate, regulate, or prohibit . . . by means of licenses or otherwise, any transactions in foreign exchange, export, or earmarkings of gold or silver coin or bullion or currency, transfers of credit in any form . . . and transfers of evidences of indebtedness or of the ownership of property between the United States and *any foreign country, whether enemy, ally of enemy or otherwise,* or between residents of one or more foreign countries, by any person within the United States (emphasis added).[14]

A great mystery surrounds how and why Section 5(b)'s sweeping applicability to all nations at all times appeared in the Trading with the Enemy Act. According to a congressional study sixty years later, the act's history was "short and sketchy."[15] There is no record of debate or discussion in Congress on 5(b). Elliott may have inserted it to ensure interception of enemy dealings through neutrals, or to dictate postwar settlements of financial and property claims or, as a good attorney, merely to confer maximum powers on his client without thought of the long-term future. McAdoo had in his pocket the blessing of

President Wilson. He prevailed with the help of friendly senators. Congress passed the Trading with the Enemy Act on 6 October 1917. President Wilson signed the bill on 23 November. All financial elements of controlling "enemy" financial dealings were lodged in the Treasury Department. The power over modern economic warfare passed from who controlled shipping, as in Jefferson's day, to who regulated the money. McAdoo designated the Federal Reserve Board as subagent of the Treasury to administer financial controls. The permanent powers of Section 5(b) apparently escaped everyone's notice. In February 1918 an authoritative 485-page manual published by a Stanford University law professor as legal guidance to the TWEA merely reprinted 5(b) without comment except a technical cross-reference to shipping.[16]

Section 5(b) accomplished two things. First, it awarded dominion over licensing financial transactions to the Treasury Department as agent of the president not subject to challenge by other agencies, not even the diplomats of the State Department. Second, it added the fateful words *"any foreign country, whether enemy, ally of enemy or otherwise."* Therefore, it endured long after the war ended and no enemy existed, unlike other provisions of the TWEA concerned only with enemies that lapsed after the peace treaties of 1921.[17] But 5(b) was not limited to an "enemy" in "time of war." It continued to empower presidents to regulate financial dealings of Americans with *all* foreign countries and entities, conferring on them enormous unilateral powers over international finance in a world where the dollar would come to reign supreme.

The TWEA, amended for a few minor details, lay largely unused until 4 March 1933. Immediately upon his inauguration as thirty-second president, Franklin D. Roosevelt invoked it to declare a "bank holiday," temporarily shutting down the nation's failing banking system. On 9 March Congress passed, in eight hours, with no hearings and little debate, and even before the bill was in print, "An Act to provide relief in the existing national emergency in banking, and for other purposes." The president immediately signed it. Congress validated the existence of a serious national emergency and endorsed all the president's actions in his first five days "pursuant to the authority" of 5(b). It also amended the TWEA so that its provisions could be handled through any agency he designated "during time of war or during any period of national emergency declared by the President." It added to the definition of covered transactions "transfers of credit between or payments by banking institutions," astonishingly removing a bar against regulation of purely *domestic* banking transactions by invoking a foreign emergency. Absolute control of money dealings, foreign and domestic, thereafter required not an act of Congress but only a national emergency as a president saw fit to declare.

Roosevelt invoked Section 5(b)'s transcendent powers later in 1933 for executive orders directing the Treasury to regulate all foreign exchange transactions, to forbid exports of gold, and in 1934 to sponsor legislation to prohibit Americans from possessing gold (other than jewelry, rare coins, tooth fillings, and such). Gold bars and ordinary gold coins had to be sold to the government. Gold ownership, except specially licensed firms such as mining companies, became subject to criminal penalties.[18]

The TWEA, a relic of the Great War, evolved into the ultimate U.S. weapon of financial power over foreign nations in time of peace, but not until 1940–41.[19] In the 1930s lesser schemes of economic control were put into play, focusing on denying specific products to Japan's army and navy, which did not inhibit much of Japan's international trade or injure its civilian economy. None packed the awesome power of a monetary blockade. Except for a brief moment after Japan launched its attack on China, financial sanctions were not seriously explored. In the late 1930s U.S. financial experts believed that the war would drive Japan into self-imposed bankruptcy (chapter 5). To understand that development, which helped delay imposition of Section 5(b) against Japan until 1941, it is helpful to explore how Japan historically acquired dollars, through exporting to the United States and accumulating reserves of gold, and the crises it faced as its sources of dollars withered away.

The 1930s

FINANCIAL POWER SLUMBERING

In the 1930s the American people and their government worried about foreign events that might again involve them in a war. Three totalitarian powers—Germany, Italy, and Japan—pursued imperial ambitions by annexation and invasion in an era when democracies favored Wilsonian ideals of settlement by negotiation and treaty. In 1931 Japan seized Manchuria by military coup, established the puppet state of Manchukuo, and, in 1932, bombed Chinese cities. In 1933 Hitler rose to power. Germany rearmed, occupied the Rhineland in 1936 in violation of the Versailles Treaty, and by the end of the decade had absorbed Austria and Czechoslovakia into the Third Reich. Mussolini attacked Ethiopia in 1935, and from 1936 to 1939 Spain's civil war engaged the forces of several European powers. In 1937 Japan launched an all-out attack on China. The League of Nations denounced the aggressions but proved helpless to stop them.

The United States, not a member of the league, chose to adopt laws and policies to reduce risks of commercial and financial dealings with countries at war. The actions were of two kinds: embargoes of exports of war-related goods (chapters 6 and 7) and restraints on financial dealings, which are the subject of this chapter. In the case of Japan, embargoes scarcely affected its war in China. Until late 1940 the United States was unready to impose stringent trade controls. Until the summer of 1941 it was unprepared to deploy financial sanctions. The primitive financial testings of the 1930s were mere slaps on the wrist.

Closing the Capital Market

An early shift in financial relations with Japan came about as a consequence of the Great Depression, not by deliberate national policy. Until 1931 Wall Street had opened its coffers to the Japanese government. From 1924 to 1930 Japan sold in the United States $284 million (face value) of bonds of the Imperial government and of entities guaranteed by it. Banking syndicates headed by J. P. Morgan and Company underwrote $150 million for reconstruction after the 1923 Tokyo earthquake; $63 million for electric power in Yokohama, Tokyo, and Taiwan; and $71 million again in May 1930 for the central government. U.S. investors eagerly subscribed, reflecting Japan's good credit standing and, not least, interest yields as high as 6.5 percent compared with 3.5 percent or 4 percent for U.S. Treasury securities.[1]

With the onset of the Depression, hundreds of millions worth of other foreign bonds collapsed into default and became worthless. Congress investigated whether foreign government paper of abysmally poor credit rank, especially South American and central European bonds, had been foisted onto ordinary citizens. (The average purchaser had invested $3,000.) Public disgust and the paralysis of capital markets brought overseas lending to a halt. Foreign bond issuance in the United States plunged from an average of $693 million in 1919–30 to $62 million in 1931–39, the latter mostly Canadian. Although Japan scrupulously paid interest and principal on all its debts and sought to borrow for industrial development of Manchukuo and other purposes, the global crisis ruled out new loans.[2]

If capital had been available, the U.S. government could have applied an unofficial mechanism to discourage loans to Japan after the takeover of Manchuria. Ever since 1920 when President Warren G. Harding asked investment bankers, they had quietly disclosed to the State Department proposed issues by foreign governments. According to Thomas W. Lamont of J. P. Morgan and Otto Kahn of Kuhn Loeb, the department would respond, "We do not desire to interpose any objection," meaning it had no *political* complaint. (It objected only twice, on loans supporting cartels in European potash and Brazilian coffee.) In 1931 Senate Finance Committee interrogators investigated whether shady bond salesman had lied to naïve customers that creditworthiness of foreign governments had been certified and that U.S. "moral authority" backed the bonds. Despite Japan's impeccable credit record, the State Department could have vetoed new borrowings by informal objections.[3]

In March 1932 Congress briefly considered a credit embargo to put teeth into the State Department's feeble protests against Japan's seizure of Manchuria. Congressman Morton D. Hull, a Republican industrialist from Illinois, introduced Joint Resolution 317 empowering President Herbert Hoover to declare that, if "conditions of international conflict exist in violation, or threatened violation, of the general pact for the renunciation of war [the 1928 Kellogg-Briand Pact]," he could prohibit "the granting of any loan or the extension of credit" by American banks or people. Hull made clear that the resolution was aimed at Japan, a signatory to the pact, as the aggressor against China. The House Foreign Affairs Committee heard testimony from Harold G. Moulton, president of the Brookings Institution, who had recently published an analysis of Japan's international financial condition. Moulton advised that cutting off loans would be effective. Japan had exhausted its foreign exchange reserves, had suffered a shrinkage of its gold reserve from $431 million to $234 million in 1931 alone due to a flight from the yen by Japanese investors as abandonment of the gold standard loomed, and was suffering a boycott of exports to China. Hence Moulton felt Japan could not finance war operations much longer without foreign credit. Congressman Hull conceded that a loan embargo would fail unless all creditor countries joined together, but he felt that it would be more feasible than a multinational trade embargo, even one limited to munitions. The isolationist Representative Hamilton Fish III angrily retorted that enforcing the Kellogg-Briand Pact was not an obligation of the United States. In any case, Hull's resolution was not adopted. Oddly, he had not noticed the president's authority to restrict foreign loans under Section 5(b) of the Trading with the Enemy Act, probably because such power was unclear until Congress amended the 1917 act, on Roosevelt's first day in office in 1933, to accommodate the president's declaration of a banking "holiday" to halt a crisis of bank failures.[4]

The Johnson Act, 1934

The Johnson Act of 1934, the first punitive financial legislation between the wars, was an act of spite against friendly powers, not aggressors. Public opinion had come to regard involvement in World War I as a tragic mistake. Senator Gerald Nye chaired a committee that disclosed the enormous profits manufacturers and bankers had earned before the United States entered the war. *Merchants of Death*, a popular book, pilloried international arms dealers, and revisionist historians absolved Germany of war guilt. Pacifistic citizens' groups and members of Congress sought to avoid commercial entanglements that might lure the country into another war.

In 1915–16 Britain and France had borrowed $950 million from U.S. investors through bond issues arranged by J. P. Morgan and Company. Isolationists later accused the bankers of pressuring Washington to declare war on Germany to protect their shaky investments when the Allies appeared to be losing. After declaring war in April 1917, the U.S. government loaned huge sums to Britain, France, Italy, and smaller Allies—there were no Lend-Lease gifts of materiel in that war—amounting to $11.9 billion (including interest and postwar relief). The Allies used some of the money to repay the private loans. During the 1920s the debtor countries repaid very little to the U.S. government, even though it scheduled repayments over sixty-two years at interest rates of 1 to 3.3 percent. Upon onset of the Depression they defaulted, one after another. President Herbert Hoover granted a temporary repayments moratorium in 1931. When the Lausanne Agreement of 1932 practically abolished German war reparation payments to the Allies, Britain, the largest debtor, declared it would repay only one-tenth of that year's liability to the United States. After December 1933 neither Britain nor any other country (except Finland) paid any of their obligations to the United States. Taxpayers felt swindled.[5]

In a blunt retaliation, Congress passed the Foreign Securities Act of 1934, better known by the name of its sponsor, Senator Hiram Johnson of California. Johnson was a fierce isolationist who "almost single-handedly" kept the country out of the League of Nations. He deplored the cheating of small investors who had bought foreign bonds, but politically he could retaliate only against former Allies who defaulted on U.S. government loans.[6] Although a legislator rather than a bureaucrat, Johnson nevertheless exemplified how a strong-willed midlevel operator could inflict his biases on national policy. FDR bowed to isolationist pressures and signed the bill. The Johnson Act prohibited any nation that had defaulted on war debts from borrowing money or selling new securities in the United States and imposed criminal penalties on U.S. citizens or firms that tried to buy them. It closed the U.S. long-term capital market to most European countries but, ironically, not to Germany and Japan.[7]

The Neutrality Act Amendment, 1936

On 29 February 1936 Congress extended provisions similar to the Johnson Act to any country at war, by amending a neutrality act of the prior year that prohibited munitions sales to them (chapter 5). The amendment barred governments and companies of *any* belligerent country from obtaining long-term loans or selling securities in the United States, directly or through intermediaries. The action at the time had no bearing on Japan, which was at peace—and anyway, the U.S. capital market was moribund—but it made clear that Wall Street could not again finance a foreign war with long-term credit as it had lavishly done for Japan in the Russo-Japanese War of 1904–5. Congress, however, authorized the president to allow belligerents temporary credit "of a character customarily used in normal peace-time commercial transactions" for purchase of civilian goods. Short-term trade credit was not regarded as a war trap, as even the pacifistic Secretary of State William Jennings Bryan had agreed in 1915, because it self-extinguished upon deliveries to the buyers, leaving no risks to U.S. banks. It was an important exception for Japan, which regularly financed sales of raw silk to the United States and purchases of U.S. cotton with credit from the New York money market (chapters 3 and 5).[8]

Roosevelt Considers Financial Action

During the summer and fall of 1937 Franklin D. Roosevelt chafed over his inability to pressure Japan to halt the invasion of China. He had no intention of dispatching U.S. military forces to fight Japan, yet he was impatient with the idealistic "moral suasion" protests of Secretary Cordell Hull's cautious Department of State. Roosevelt had declared that the Neutrality Act, a 1935 law inhibiting armaments exports to nations at war, did not apply to China, a weak slap at Japan. (Japan's factories and shipyards were largely self-sufficient in arms production.) Although Japan's military forces and segments of its economy relied on raw materials bought primarily from the United States, a U.S. embargo alone would be futile unless all trading nations acted in concert, an unlikely prospect because Germany, Italy, the Soviet Union, and most small nations could not be counted on.

On 5 October 1937 the president, speaking in Chicago, delivered his historical "quarantine" speech. The aggressions in China, Ethiopia, and Spain were like epidemics. He suggested that peaceable nations uphold international law by "quarantining" aggressors. How this might be done he left unspoken.[9] Norman Davis, his hand-picked delegate to an international conference in Brussels, tried to sound out British diplomats about an economic boycott of Japan.[10] Hull's noninterventionist policy and negative public opinion stifled the gambit. Roosevelt quietly let the quarantine trial balloon deflate.

When Japanese naval aircraft attacked and sank the U.S. gunboat *Panay* in the Yangtze River on 12 December 1937, Roosevelt contemplated retaliation against Japan by financial sanctions. The United States was Japan's principal trading partner, and the latter conducted much of its international trade in dollars. To finance purchases of war commodities it sold gold from the reserves of its central bank, the Bank of Japan, to the U.S. Treasury, the only significant buyer of gold in the 1930s. Roosevelt turned to his secretary of the treasury,

Henry Morgenthau Jr., with a question: How much gold and foreign exchange did the Japanese government hold in the United States and what steps might be taken to deny Japan use of its money?

The Treasury Department

Overseas relations, including trade, were the bailiwick of the Department of State. Foreign financial relations, however, by longstanding custom, were the province of the Department of the Treasury. Morgenthau, the son of a Democratic party supporter and diplomat of German-Jewish origins, had been a well-to-do apple farmer in the Hudson Valley near Roosevelt's family home in Hyde Park, New York. The two men grew close, personally and in politics, the president being somewhat of a father figure. When FDR gained the White House, he put his friend in charge of the Farm Credit Administration (FCA), a New Deal agency helping distressed agriculture and rural banks. In January 1934, when Secretary of the Treasury William Woodin resigned in ill health, Roosevelt appointed Morgenthau to the post. (He served eleven years, longer than anyone but Andrew Mellon.) The president rejected Undersecretary of the Treasury Dean Acheson, who had resisted his program of buying gold to reflate the currency. Acheson left government service until 1941. From Morgenthau, Roosevelt got what he wanted: a "devoutly loyal" supporter and practical administrator who got things done for his domestic anti-Depression programs. Morgenthau ardently opposed the totalitarian powers. He arranged to buy silver from China to bolster its financial condition in the face of Japanese pressures. From 1937 onward he prodded Roosevelt toward strong antidictatorship policies, in contrast to the cautious State Department.[11]

Morgenthau, not a financial expert, surrounded himself with a "little brains trust" in echo of FDR's famous New Deal brains trust. He chose aides on foreign matters who were superbly educated experts, articulate, practical, and assertive in exercising Treasury authority. They typified the midlevel activists coming into positions of influence to play a decisive role in flexing U.S. financial power in the world. Professor Jacob Viner, a special adviser from the University of Chicago, was a renowned authority on economic theory, balance of payments, and international trade, said by Professor Irving Fisher (an iconic architect of modern economics) to be one of only eighteen economists who "understand the real meaning of money." Viner did not dwell in the ivory tower but sought real-world solutions to Treasury problems. A disciple of Viner from Chicago and fellow Harvard Ph.D., Harry Dexter White, arrived for a special study on exchange rates. In 1937 Morgenthau created for him the permanent title of director of monetary research. White shared Morgenthau's antipathy to

Germany and Japan. Brilliant and practical but abrasive in manner, he became the secretary's chief adviser on foreign matters. Archie Lochead, manager of a dollar stabilization fund, kept an eye on market developments. (He even had a ticker tape machine in his office.) The Treasury did not usually work closely with the staffs of other agencies. An exception was L. Werner Knoke, a vice president of the Federal Reserve Bank of New York, a former commercial bank officer and knowledgeable on foreign exchange and currencies as supervisor of the bank's foreign functions. Morgenthau summoned him to conferences for his practical knowledge of the money markets. An exception to the hard-driving adventurous staff, Assistant Secretary C. Wayne Taylor glumly warned that financial sanctions might cause a war.[12]

Morgenthau interpreted FDR's query as a signal to investigate the powers he and the president might invoke to punish Japan financially. The Treasury staff believed Japan held abroad $55 million of liquid assets—bank deposits and securities, most presumed to be within the United States—but no gold.[13] On 14 December 1937 FDR asked him for a Treasury lawyer to advise on his authority to seize assets of the Japanese government, companies, or citizens as payment for the bombing damage to the *Panay*. Morgenthau chose Herman Oliphant, general counsel of the Treasury Department. Oliphant was another product of Chicago academics, but in law, not economics. Morgenthau first met him at FDR's inauguration then promptly recruited him to the FCA and, soon afterward, to the Treasury post. Hard working and imaginative, the "greatest single source of new ideas," which Morgenthau "kept pushing to produce,"[14] Oliphant inspired a team of lawyers who at times acted as an informal legal workshop for Roosevelt. He vigorously opposed the rising Axis powers, advocating financial cooperation with Britain and France and later joining Professor Viner in recommending clever but ultimately futile notions of imposing punitive duties on imports from Germany and Japan by manipulating obscure sections of tariff law. If he had not died in 1939, Oliphant might well have played a key role in developing financial sanctions against Japan.

Offered Oliphant, FDR said, "Swell." Writing in secrecy behind drawn blinds with two aides, Oliphant produced a memo asserting that Roosevelt could exercise unlimited authority over financial transactions with foreign nations by invoking the Trading with the Enemy Act of 6 October 1917, specifically Section 5(b).[15] Although Roosevelt had applied that section on his first day in office in 1933, to suspend the U.S. banking system, he exclaimed, "My god, I completely forgot about it."[16]

Morgenthau and his team pelted Oliphant with questions, including some raised by Roosevelt. Oliphant felt an emergency proclamation to invoke TWEA controls against Japan would be justifiable to forestall a crisis by "quarantining a war situation dangerous to the peace" and to provide an indemnity for U.S. injuries and costs. His draft order would bar Americans from banking and foreign exchange dealings in yen with the Japanese government, directly or indirectly, except as licensed by the Treasury after vetting by the Federal Reserve. The severity of punishment would depend on how rigorous or lenient were any licensed exceptions, and whether Japan could deal through the foreign currency markets of London or Paris because the yen was inconvertible, that is, not acceptable for payments outside the yen bloc of the Japanese Empire. Notably, there was no suggestion of a role for other agencies.[17] Oliphant coolly shot down Viner's contrary notion to regulate trade with Japan through vessel clearance procedures of the Commerce Department at the ports. No such authority existed under the TWEA, as Viner should have known.

At a Cabinet meeting on 17 December 1937, Roosevelt brandished Herman Oliphant's draft for imposing Section 5(b) financial constraints on Japan by proclaiming an emergency. Morgenthau was enthusiastic. If the United States didn't make Japan behave, he declared, "it's only a matter of five or ten years before we'll have them on our neck." Roosevelt taunted Cordell Hull about the weakness of his diplomacy and scoffed at an old-fashioned belief that sanctions meant war, whereas he proposed merely "quarantines." The president even mused of a blockade line of U.S. Navy cruisers across the Pacific in concert with the European democracies. Morgenthau phoned Sir John Simon, his British counterpart, to probe the idea, without much success.[18] That evening he learned that the notoriously fickle FDR had "cooled off on this thing" and was in no great hurry until a naval representative conferred in Great Britain.[19] He dispatched Capt. Royal E. Ingersoll, the director of the Naval War Plans Division, to London to explore with the Admiralty the mounting of a sea blockade of Japanese shipping by U.S. Navy patrol lines from the Aleutians to Samoa and Royal Navy lines extending to Singapore. It was a bizarre notion, far beyond the capabilities of the two navies and totally out of sync with the American public's aversion to deploying military force. Ingersoll reported the results of his conference to be of no importance.[20]

Credit Warning, June 1938

The only concrete outcome of the flirtation with financial sanctions against Japan was a mild admonition. Because Japan was not deemed to be at war, it maintained full access to strategic raw materials and to normal bank credit for all imports and exports. In June 1938, however, the Commerce Department served notice that because of the "increasing severity with which exchange restrictions in Japan were being enforced, it appeared advisable that exporters in the United States should have a confirmed irrevocable credit in their hands before accepting orders for shipments to Japan." A letter of credit was a bank document guaranteeing that an American exporter would be paid by a bank, which usually held title to products in transit as collateral. Commerce cited no instances of nonpayment, but Tokyo was rationing dollars to its importers. The advice, without force of law, mattered little. Japan held ample supplies of dollars in U.S. banks to pay for both peaceful and martial articles, and it encountered no trouble financing exports of its major product, raw silk, considered prime loan collateral, through U.S. lending markets.

After Roosevelt's retreat from his "quarantine" inspiration, U.S. official staffs turned away from excited ideas of a financial assault on Japan and turned instead to studying Japan's monetary position, which was precarious due to its war expenditures in China. Their studies raised hopes that Japan would go bankrupt and obviate the need for U.S. financial sanctions. Before describing their investigations, the narrative now turns to examining how Japan acquired dollars, essential for buying American raw materials, by exporting silk and manufactures. Penetration of U.S. markets had historically gained the needed currency, yet its prospects of maintaining those earnings were fragile at its time of extraordinary need.

3

Hanging by a Silken Thread

The international economic fate of Japan had dangled by a silken thread for eighty years. Since its emergence as a trading nation in the 1860s, Japan had derived most of its earnings of dollars from the export of raw silk for fashionable women's clothing. The prosperous trade had been an engine of Japanese growth and power. At its peak in 1929, sericulture afforded a livelihood to 2.2 million Japanese farm households. Raw silk exports, nearly all to the United States, enriched the nation's coffers by $363 million that year. Imports of raw silk, nearly all from Japan, constituted America's largest import by value and supplied the material for a great manufacturing industry. But Japan's silk road to the United States had been pitted by dilemmas of low quality, high price, substitution, and shocks of fashion that exposed it to ruin time and again. With diligence and innovation in both countries, however, the silk trades weathered the threats and prospered. The Great Depression diminished but did not destroy the primacy of silk as a source of dollars. At the end of the 1930s, however, the business that was Japan's dominant source of dollars faced an irrevocable collapse within a few years.[1]

A word about dollars. Before 1939 it mattered little where, outside the yen bloc, Japan exported its goods because the major currencies were convertible into dollars in foreign exchange markets (unlike the yen, an inconvertible currency that only Japan's colonies and the occupied areas of China could use to buy Japanese goods). Until then, the British, French, and Dutch colonies of Asia and the Pacific, all of them large markets for Japanese manufactures, might pay in sterling, francs, or guilders, and China in silver, but Japan's receipts were changeable into U.S. dollars, the currency it coveted for procuring metals, oil, and other strategic raw materials from the neutral United States. The outbreak of war in Europe forced the belligerent countries to impose exchange controls. Japanese exporters to them and their colonies were paid with blocked currencies, barred from conversion into dollars and spendable only for the products of the walled-in currency blocs, which had few of the strategic commodities Japan needed.

This had not been true in earlier days. Before 1914, in the heyday of the gold standard, Japan's trade pattern was triangular. Surplus earnings from trade with the United States were spent in Europe, especially Britain, for steel, capital equipment, and warships, products in which the United States was not yet a principal competitor. In the interwar years, trade with the United States was more balanced, dominated by the two-way movements of raw silk and raw cotton, while foreign exchange markets continued to function adequately even though the international gold standard expired in the early 1930s. When the world crisis erupted in 1939 and free convertibility of major nondollar currencies came to an end, exporting to the United States (and to a small degree to other dollar-bloc territories—Canada, South America, and the Philippines) became crucial for financing Japan's aggressive empire-building policy.

Success in Sericulture

Newly emerging economies usually depend on exports of unique commodities, but none was so vulnerable to whims of the marketplace as Japanese raw silk. In the nineteenth century the Meiji oligarchy's wish to shape a modern nation required exporting to pay for machinery and armaments. Inviting overseas investors into Japan was anathema for fear of foreign dominance or even colonization. But what commodities could Japan offer in return? It manufactured nothing of international value. The islands lacked minerals. Land and climate were unsuited for commercial plantations; the 15 percent of land that was arable yielded barely enough grains to feed the people. Yet Japanese farm families were hard working and dexterous at crafts. By harnessing their energy to raise specialty crops, nonperishable goods of high value that could be shipped across oceans, Japan paid its way in the world.

Raw silk was by far the most important Japanese export. Farmers raised silkworm cocoons throughout old Japan but especially in impoverished Nagano province, north of Tokyo. They planted mulberry trees on hillsides and field borders, clipped the tender green leaves, and scattered them onto bamboo trays to feed *Bombyx mori L.*, the silkworm moth. A mature worm extruded a filament half a mile long to wrap itself into a cocoon the size and shape of an unshelled peanut. Haru Reischauer, wife of a later U.S. ambassador, wrote, "No one who has heard the sound will ever forget the low, all-night roar created by the munching of thousands of voracious silkworms in a Japanese mountain farmhouse."[2] When the insects finished spinning, the farmers heated the cocoons to kill the worms and sold the dried cocoons to filature plants, which unwound and twisted the strands into skeins of raw silk.

As the Japanese entered world trade they planted more and more land in fast-growing mulberry trees. Meiji authorities encouraged scientific sericulture. They recruited former samurai as commercial managers. From 1890, when good statistics were first available, to 1929, mulberry acreage rose 157 percent to 1.5 million acres, covering a remarkable 10 percent of the arable land. Chemical nitrogen fertilizer supplanted the manures of plants, animals, and humans. Summer and fall cocoon raising supplemented the spring crop. Government agencies and trade associations built sanitary cocoon warehouses, bred improved worms to spin more and better silk, and ruthlessly destroyed diseased worms. Cocoon productivity per acre of mulberry rose 271 percent in the four decades up to 1929. In the countryside hundreds of filature plants housed young women in dormitories, toiling to earn for their families and, as legend has it, for marriage dowries. At work they dropped cocoons into basins of hot water to loosen the natural sericin glue and unwound three, six, or more cocoons simultaneously, twisting the strands onto reels to form the multifilament yarn known as raw silk. Their skills improved with training. Soon reels powered by water wheels and engines replaced hand-turned reels. By 1929 a cocoon yielded 40 percent more silk than one of 1890.

Exports of raw silk commenced in the 1860s to France and Italy, where a worm disease had ravaged sericulture until Dr. Louis Pasteur found a cure. Haulers lugged skeins of raw silk down mountain trails to Yokohama. There, merchant companies inspected and packed them into "picul" bales of 132.3 pounds. Steamers freighted the bales to San Francisco, Seattle, or Vancouver, where speedy, super-clean trains highballed them to importing firms in New York, the warehousing and financing hub near the textile mills of Paterson, New Jersey, "the Lyons of America." Exports surged from 6 million pounds in 1900 to 70 million in 1929. In the 1890s the United States surpassed France as the leading customer. At the turn of the century Japan surpassed China as the world's dominant supplier. In the 1920s Japan supplied two-thirds of world commercial output. It had successfully monetized its first-class work force and second-class land into a foreign exchange generator that underwrote its destiny of *fukoku kyōhei*, "rich country, strong military."

The Beginnings of Silk in America

Japan's success was due to an equally phenomenal growth of silk textile manufacturing in the United States, where wealthy and middle-class women han-
kered for stylish clothing. Before World War I the nation purchased 80 percent
of Japan's silk exports, during the war 90 percent, and in the late 1920s 95
percent. Raw silk was never subjected to tariffs because sericulture failed in
the United States for lack of peasant labor. Instead, U.S. manufacturers developed unique machinery and marketing systems adaptable to capricious fashion
fads. "Throwing" mills cleaned and twisted raw silk into fine yarn and dyed it.
(Hollow silk filaments absorb colors thirstily.) Silk thread, stronger than steel
wire of similar diameter, was prized for stitching clothing and boots. In the
1870s Swiss entrepreneurs established fabric weaving mills in New Jersey and
Pennsylvania, where French weavers trained workers. Laying warp (lengthwise)
threads on looms was an expensive hand-labor chore, whereas the filling
(crosswise) threads were inserted by machine, so the mills wove "narrow
goods" (ribbons) less than eighteen inches wide. Women ornamented their hair
and hats with silk ribbons, their gowns with *passémenterie* fringes and tassels,
and wore the wider ribbons as scarves and sashes. But only talented seam-
stresses could craft whole garments of narrow silk. In the 1880s improved
looms began to weave bolts of "broad silk." Shielded by tariffs, broad silk manufacture grew exponentially. In 1899, 76 percent of U.S. yardage was broad.
The takeoff arrived at a crucial moment for Japan, which in the 1880s had
practically exhausted its monetary reserve, primarily of silver. Without the
broad silk boom in the United States it is unlikely that Japan could have purchased the British warships that sank the Chinese and Russian navies in the
next two decades.

Women's clothing always accounted for about 90 percent of U.S. demand.
(Men wore silk neckties and suit linings, rarely silk shirts and socks.) Raw silk
cost five times more than wool and twenty times more than raw cotton. Silk
was more difficult to weave, and productivity was lower because of frequent
breaks in naturally irregular silk yarn. Nevertheless, bolts of broad silk thirty
and thirty-six inches wide, piece-dyed or printed, enabled ordinary seam-
stresses and home sewers to cut and stitch entire garments. The mills wove
taffeta, a simple over-and-under pattern suited to mass production. Satin, an
easy weave with a shiny finish from reflected light, ranked second. Ribbed fabrics rounded out the line. Velvets were consumed for furniture and drapes and
some gowns. By 1920 only "fancies," comprising 3 percent of consumption,
were imported from Europe. Japanese silk "tissues," as the term was translated, did not sell well in America due to poor quality and tariffs of 45 to 60

percent, except minor yardages of *habutae*, a low-grade homespun for lining suits and dresses.

Broad silk marketing grew into a huge business. Department stores, another American innovation, stocked rainbows of broad silks. A ready-made clothing industry blossomed into mass production. Garment factories at first produced standardized shirtwaists (blouses) of a few sizes and colors. Jewish immigrants in New York City opened "cutting up" shops to manufacture dresses, suits, and coats using electric cutting and sewing machinery. Improved broad silks forty-eight to fifty-four inches wide were ample enough to cut the body of a dress from one panel. Inexpensive ready-to-wear garments transformed Japanese silk into an article "for the masses, not the classes."

Old-Time Silks

The silk boom rode the ups and downs of women's fashions (chart 1). The creations of Paris couturiers illustrated in U.S. women's magazines dictated elegance. In the 1880s stylish women wore floor-sweeping skirts of ten or fifteen yards circumference at the hem over corsets and layers of petticoats, covered with overskirts swagged like theater curtains, their outfits cut from ten square yards of fabric. Skirts billowed behind into fishtail trains or swooped over bustles jutting a foot or two to the rear. Cultural historians have debated the meaning of such extreme modes. Some claim that fashion emphasizes erogenous zones in cycles so that exaggeration of buttocks was merely a shift from a focus on breasts and waists in earlier decades. An average woman, however, owned one "grandmother" gown of silk taffeta, stiffly weighted by black metallic dye and frequently restyled, that rustled as she walked. In the 1890s straight-draping skirts of the "Gibson Girl" years "really used the material" in creases and folds that cascaded to the floor. In 1907 French designer Paul Poiret introduced supple messalines and other silks gaudily colored by brilliant aniline dyes from Germany. The hobble skirt and lampshade silhouettes of 1910–14 were also long and full, and two-piece outfits, suits, and sportswear of silk came into vogue.

During the prosperity of World War I American women demanded ever more silk for all occasions. Japan enjoyed a market bonanza in spite of the loss of French markets, shipping shortages, and labor and coal bottlenecks at U.S. weaving mills. Costly financing of raw silk shipments by British banks or by rapacious New York commission houses eased when the Federal Reserve system coaxed U.S. banks into low-cost "bankers acceptance" financing secured by silk bales as collateral. A fashion design industry took root in New York, promoting black and white fabrics until an American aniline industry sprang up to

CHART 1 **U.S. Women Employed, 1870–1940, and Samples of Dresses in Sewing Pattern Books by Square Yards of Fabric Required**

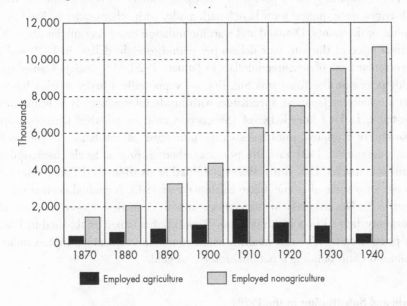

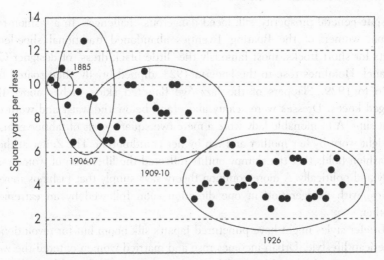

Department of Commerce, U.S. Women Employed, *Historical Statistics of the United States on CD-ROM*, Part D. Yardage from a random sampling of fifty-six patterns in *The Deliniator: A Journal of Fashion, Culture and Fine Art* (London, Butterick), *Designer and the Woman's Magazine* (New York: Designer Publications), and *American Modiste*, various dates.

replace German dyes. American women appreciated the wartime fashions, skimpier to save fabric, for their informality and comfort.

Price instability was a perennial risk for operations in both countries. Raw silk prices were quoted for a benchmark grade, with other grades at fixed premiums or discounts. Demand and wartime inflation drove raw silk far above its normal price of three to four dollars per pound to eight dollars in 1919 and a spectacular peak of seventeen dollars in January 1920. U.S. traders blamed the giddy prices on the Yokohama Silk Bourse, supposedly a hedge market but in fact a casino for Japanese speculators with inside information; U.S. firms were amateurs, lacking knowledge of the cocoon crop or whether filatures were hoarding or dumping, until bales came "into sight" at Yokohama. In the postwar recession of 1921 raw silk prices crashed to prewar levels, bankrupting many overstocked U.S. firms. Prices stabilized at six to seven dollars per pound except for a spike after the Tokyo earthquake of 1923. A gradual decline set in after 1925. Nevertheless, silk operations in both countries enjoyed a decade of prosperity, helped by a legitimate New York Silk Exchange established in 1928 for price hedging. The silk wealth was instrumental in financing Japan's industrialization and building a national reserve of gold.

Style and Substitution in the 1920s

Despite general prosperity, silk faced dangerous challenges. In a fashion revolution, women of the Roaring Twenties abandoned traditional shoe-length skirts for short frocks, most famously the "little black dress" of designer Coco Chanel. Hemlines rose to the knee in 1923, dipped briefly, then soared from 1926 to 1929. Flappers of the Jazz Age flaunted skirts inches above their rouged knees. Dresses were scanty above and below the waist and worn over light slips. A fashionable lady wore a mere two square yards of fabric versus six or eight worn by her mother and ten by her grandmother. The Zeitgeist theory of fashion holds that the skimpy outfits reflected the liberation of women, sexually and politically. A more common theory says simply that fashions move in cycles, with exaggeration in one direction soon followed by an extreme in another.

Briefer styles might have punctured Japan's silk boom but for revolutions in American lifestyle. Urban incomes rose and married women entered the workforce en masse. In the 1920s, twice as many women worked outside the home as in 1900. Women drove cars, patronized sporting events, speakeasies, and tea dances, and they bought outfits for active lifestyles. Ready-to-wear clothing, scarcely an industry before 1900, soared to 163 million dresses in 1929, four units per adult woman, worth $810 million wholesale. Manufacturers also cut

$642 million of suits, coats, and undergarments. Of course, only a fraction of the garments were of silk or silk blended with other fibers. (The United States imported almost no clothing because of high tariffs, and aside from a minor vogue for kimonos as beach coverups, Japanese designs were unpopular.)

Both countries' silk industries had to cope with quality problems. Raw silk was naturally flawed: tangles, off color, cocoon debris, and, most distressingly, bad "running quality" due to random thicknesses of yarns. Silkworm extrusions are 30 percent thicker in the middle than at the ends. Filature girls could not consistently blend away the variations as they reeled several strands together. Machinery stoppages during throwing and weaving to knot the broken ends together exacerbated the problem. Dressmakers knew how to disguise imperfections in heavy taffeta, but when unskilled factory hands sewed sheer goods, streaks and bumps showed up in the garments. Mill owners demanded that the Japanese adopt scientific quality testing. Japanese merchants insisted that the trained eye of the inspector in Yokohama could best sort raw skeins into dozens of grades, from elegant Crack Double Extra down to shabby Number One, which yielded, respectively, one visible flaw per linear foot of fabric versus one flaw per inch. (Lowest grade Number Two silk went to the Japanese domestic market.) U.S. mills also lobbied for branding by the filatures. Japanese exporters labeled their bales with exotic "chops" (logos) such as "Peach," "Five Girls," and "Lobster," but in reality they continued to blend silk from dozens of filatures of varying quality. Negotiating teams sailed back and forth across the Pacific to no avail. A partial solution emerged when U.S. throwsters adopted a French technique of twisting silk thread seventy-five turns to the inch into coiled, springy yarns for weaving crêpe Georgette and crêpe de Chine. Crêpe fabrics were comfortably stretchy with a pebbled appearance that hid flaws. In the 1920s crêpes came to dominate stylish ready-made clothing. Japan welcomed the 5 to 12 percent of extra silk in hard-twisted yarn.

Japanese silk weathered the fashion challenges because women bought silk outfits for all occasions, more than offsetting scantier yardage per garment. Raw silk swelled into America's largest commodity import by value, feeding one of its largest manufacturing industries. In the peak years of the 1920s raw silk bales (95 percent to America) comprised 38 percent of Japan's global exports and an even larger 45 percent of net "domestic exports," defined as exports minus foreign materials contained in them. Including silk textiles and filature waste, silk in all forms comprised a stunning 54 percent of Japan's domestic exports to the world. The U.S. silk craze contributed hugely to financing earthquake reconstruction as well as the electrification and industrialization of Japan.

Broad silk, however, faced another and more ominous threat: competition from rayon. Artificial silk—"art silk," as it was labeled until the Federal Trade Commission put a stop to it—had been a perennial quest of chemists. Since the 1890s low-quality rayon had been manufactured from wood pulp. When dissolved in a chemical slurry and squirted through nozzles, it hardened into strands resembling silkworm extrusions. Rayon yarn was uniform, shiny, and took dyes well. Although it lacked the strength and resilience of silk, it could be blended with stronger fibers. In the 1920s viscose rayon, a superior variety, came into production in Great Britain and soon in all industrial countries. (Japan itself became a major rayon producer in the 1930s.) Flawless rayon textiles could be woven on high-volume cotton looms. The price of rayon, once higher than silk, fell steadily, to $1.50 per pound versus $6 for thrown silk. Rayon gained niches at first in inexpensive underthings and casual garments, but it was intrusion into elegant outerwear that alarmed silk men. By the end of the decade U.S. rayon production was 50 percent greater by weight than raw silk imports. Nevertheless, U.S. silk consumption held its own as prosperity rolled on, soaring to a peak of eighty-seven million pounds in 1929, 70 percent above the early 1920s.

The Depression, Broad Silk, and Stockings

The world Depression that struck the United States in late 1929 (and Japan in 1927) destroyed the broad silk industry. U.S. incomes shrank drastically. Demand for luxury clothing plunged. Women shifted down market to rayon or cotton garments, or did without. The collapse was devastating for Japan. U.S. broad silk production shriveled from 47 million pounds in 1929 to 6 million in 1939, while rayon fabrics surged from 29 to 335 million pounds (chart 2). Silk clothing, the glory of fashionable women throughout history, virtually disappeared from store racks. Rarely has a large industry imploded so suddenly and completely. Japanese raw silk collapsed to $1.27 per pound in 1934, hovered around $1.50 to $2.00 the next few years, and inched above $3.00 only in 1939–41. One and a half million Japanese households still tried to support themselves, at least in part, by sericulture, but destitution and malnutrition stalked rural Japan, fertile breeding ground for fanatical nationalists recruiting boys for the army.

One last miracle, however, rescued Japanese sericulture for a final decade: the full-fashioned silk stocking. Modes that hid female legs throughout history owed more to ugly stockings than to prudery. Only stockings of a knitted fabric, sheer and stretchy, flattered the leg. (In knitting mills, yarns are looped around one another rather than criss-crossed as in weaving.) But machine-knitted stockings around the turn of the century were straight, ill-fitting tubes,

CHART 2 **U.S. Production, Broad Silk vs. Silk Hosiery, 1919–1939**

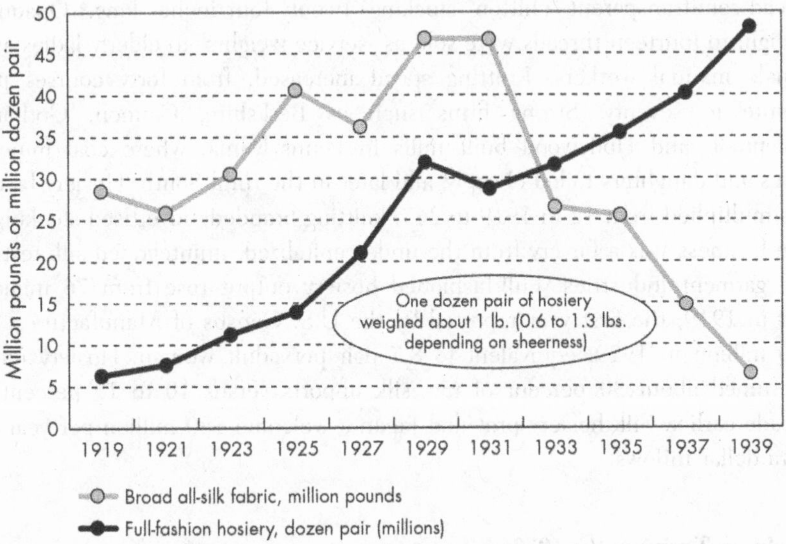
Million pounds or million dozen pair
50
45
40
35
30
25
20
15
10
5
0
1919 1921 1923 1925 1927 1929 1931 1933 1935 1937 1939
One dozen pair of hosiery weighed about 1 lb. (0.6 to 1.3 lbs. depending on sheerness)
Broad all-silk fabric, million pounds
Full-fashion hosiery, dozen pair (millions)

Department of Commerce, Census of Manufactures (for silk and related goods), 1919–39.

and rayon hosiery, baggy at the knee and glossy, was relegated to children's wear and bargain counters. Only the rich could afford hand-sewn silk hosiery. "Silk stocking district" became a metaphor for wealth. Most women preferred long skirts and high-buttoned shoes.

Silk yarn was ideal for knitting stockings. It could stretch 20 percent and "kick back" to original length immediately. The vogue for short skirts coincided with the development of knitting machinery adapted to fine yarns for mass production of long silk stockings that clung snugly to legs and feet yet yielded at knees and ankles. Factory workers knitted the boot (leg) on a legger machine as a trapezoid of fabric, narrowing from wide thigh to slender ankle. Skilled workers machine-stitched the boot panel into a tapered knee-high cylinder about twenty inches long and joined it to the foot, which was knitted on a footer machine of cotton for durability. Customers preferred sheer stockings, dyed in flesh tones with trade names like nude, peach, and suntan, to complement peek-a-boo and slit skirts and knee-high hemlines. A dark seam sewn up the back of the leg was considered alluring; men glanced admiringly as women leaned over to straighten them. Women wore pumps with vampish high heels or sandals. Flappers rolled stockings down to the knee to show a flash of thigh. Some fashion theorists claimed that legs had become the "pathway" to previously taboo erogenous zones.

By the end of the 1920s, forty-two-gauge machines knitted four- and five-thread semitransparent "chiffon" stockings twenty-four inches long.[3] Opaques of eight to fourteen threads were sold as "service weights" to elderly ladies and female manual workers. Knitting speed increased, from forty courses per minute to seventy. Strong firms such as Berkshire, Cannon, Gotham, Holeproof, and Hollywood built mills in Pennsylvania, where coal miners' wives and daughters toiled cheaply, and later in the rural South. Hosiery factories multiplied from 92 in 1919 to 263, knitting branded, advertised stockings. The business was a far cry from the undercapitalized, unintegrated silk textile and garment industries. Full-fashioned hosiery output rose from 76 million pair in 1919, the first year reported by the U.S. Census of Manufactures, to 360 million in 1929, equivalent to 8.7 pair per adult woman. Hosiery mills consumed about 30 percent of raw silk imports versus 10 to 15 percent a decade earlier. Silk hosiery provided Japan a welcome $80 million per year of extra dollar inflows.

Stockings Thrive in the 1930s

The depressed 1930s were surprisingly good years for silk stockings. Demand rose while other luxury markets slumped. Hollywood glamorized movie stars' silken legs. Although hemlines dropped below midcalf in 1931 (another example of Zeitgeist?), they rose again to the knee after economic recovery began in 1934. The hosiery industry struggled to overcome raw silk irregularities that caused unsightly flaws. Japanese exporting firms culled the best raw grades to meet standards imposed by the New York Silk Exchange, and throwsters improved their techniques, but the two most nagging problems were finally solved by knitting innovations. Irregular yarn thickness showed up as dark circular rings in the boot. In 1934 machines that drew alternately from three spools of yarn dissipated the ring to invisibility. In 1937 an all-in-one machine knitted hosiery entirely of silk, eliminating the ugly lower seam where foot and boot joined and lowering costs by knitting twenty-four stockings simultaneously. Since women no longer had to inspect for flaws at the hosiery counter, stockings were packaged in sealed cellophane bags. But the fragility problem remained. Sheer stockings tore or snagged into unsightly "ladder" runs. There were reweaving shops, but usually a snagged stocking was ruined forever. Some stores sold three to a box to provide a spare. Mills improved durability by knitting springy crêpe-twisted yarns, which also lent a fashionably dull finish. Elasticized welts (upper thigh portions) and longer stockings that rose close to the girdle's connector tabs reduced strains on the fabric. Manufacturers offered thigh-highs, twenty-eight to thirty-three inches long with proportionally tapered boots. Nevertheless, sheer hosiery was and remains fragile.

American women of the 1930s came to regard sheer hosiery as a necessity. Retail prices fell to a range of 79 cents to $1.35 per pair, due largely to low wages and, especially, productivity gains rather than to cheaper Japanese silk because a pair contained only 15 to 20 cents of raw silk. Hosiery counters contributed to 10 percent of department store sales at lush 30 percent profit margins. Chain stores and drug stores sold bargain stockings. Working girls skipped lunches to afford them. Wives of the unemployed peddled hosiery door to door. By 1939, two- to four-thread ultrasheers held 80 percent of the market. Women bought an average of eleven pairs of silk stockings in 1939, their most frequently purchased item of apparel. Retail hosiery prices in the Depression were equivalent to about $10 in year-2000 dollars, adjusted for price inflation, or $25 adjusted for wage levels, far more expensive than excellent $5 nylon-spandex pantyhose of the twenty-first century.

In spite of the vogue for silk stockings, Japanese sericulture suffered severely in the early and mid-1930s. Raw silk exports declined 30 percent by weight from peak 1920s years, and 75 percent in dollar value. U.S. imports slumped from $427 million in 1929 to a low of $72 million in 1934, then stag-

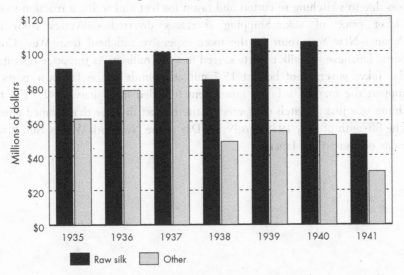

CHART 3 **U.S. Imports from Japan, Raw Silk vs. Other, 1935–1941**

Department of Commerce, Foreign Commerce and Navigation of the United States, 1936–42.

nated at just under $100 million for the next five years as rayon destroyed the broad fabric market (chart 3). U.S. hosiery mill takings dropped briefly in the Depression then recovered to thirty-three million pounds of raw silk in 1936 and thirty-eight million in 1939. By 1939 American hosiery, nearly all of it women's full-fashioned, accounted for 81 percent of U.S. silk consumption— 90 percent in 1941—and 60 percent of *total* world silk consumption. In July 1937 a Japanese commission sought to steady the markets under a Raw Silk Price Stabilization Law.[4] In 1939 the market turned more favorable for Japan. The U.S. economy improved, hemlines rose—skirts were the shortest since 1929 (Zeitgeist again?)—and hosiery demand surged. As mills fearful of war disruptions stockpiled raw silk, Japanese exports rose to $128 million. In the fourth quarter of 1939, as war broke out in Europe, raw silk tipped up to $4.00 per pound in early 1940 before settling back to around $3.00, still the highest price in a decade. The Japanese government Silk Commission felt confident enough in July to buy buffer stocks to ensure a floor price of $2.55 per pound.[5] During the price boomlet Tokyo even encouraged firms to buy from filatures in occupied Shanghai and Canton for local currency and reexport for dollars, but in September 1940 it halted the practice.[6] Despite losing its minor market in Europe, the Japanese silk trade had apparently weathered the war crisis.

The recovery, however, petered out. U.S. hosiery mill takings in 1940 dropped to 28 million pounds, the lowest since 1934. Two-thirds of the drop was due to switching to cotton and rayon for feet and welts, a reaction to the higher price of silk. Shipping shortages diverted deliveries from the Panama–New York route to the more expensive rail haul from West Coast ports. Japanese raw silk exports sagged to $104 million. As the price retreated, the Tokyo government bought 15.7 million pounds at the Japanese ports to support the market, a failed experiment it ended in January 1941.[7] But the slump was just a twitch compared to the market disaster that loomed ahead. The fifteenth of May 1939 was Nylon Day at the New York Worlds Fair. It was a day of disaster for Japan.

4

Japan's Failed Quest for Dollars through Manufacturing

The drastic shriveling of income from raw silk in the 1930s prodded Japanese businesses and government to explore possibilities of earning dollars by exporting other products to the United States (and to other dollar countries, although their markets were relatively inconsequential). In the 1930s Japan launched a drive to sell processed and manufactured goods wherever it could.[1] Raw silk historically had enjoyed a privileged status in U.S. markets. It was the raw material of a major industry that employed hundreds of thousands and provided articles of high-end consumer satisfaction that did not compete seriously with American cotton and rayon textiles (and not at all after the collapse of broad silk in the 1930s). Thus it encountered no restrictive tariffs or quotas. Conversely, most other products Japan attempted to sell in the United States attracted the hostility of U.S. industrial competitors. They lobbied Congress to legislate protective tariff rates and the independent Tariff Commission that recommended higher duties whenever Japan appeared to score gains by dumping below cost. Their trade associations demanded negotiations of import quotas with Japanese firms that were fearful of even higher tariffs if they did not acquiesce. Although such barriers were not erected as a matter of U.S. policy to punish Japan's aggressions in Asia, an unintended result was to encourage Japanese expansionists who pressed for economic advantage by military conquests.

During the Depression the world fragmented into narrow trade and finance blocs. Germany and the Soviet Union negotiated bilateral deals with smaller neighbors in Eastern Europe, in effect bartering. The British Empire withdrew into semi-isolation under the Ottawa agreements of 1932, which enforced preferential trade access among members of the sterling area. Other industrial countries raised tariffs exorbitantly. The U.S. Smoot-Hawley Tariff Act (known by the names of Republican sponsors Sen. Reed Smoot of Utah and Rep. Willis C. Hawley of Oregon and signed by President Herbert Hoover in 1930) imposed historically high duties on imports of almost every product grown or made in the United States. Although U.S. tariff policy did not overtly discriminate among nations, that is, identical products incurred the same duty regardless of country of origin, the complex rates of Smoot-Hawley in fact discriminated ferociously against processed and manufactured articles made uniquely by Japan.

As noted previously, until the autumn of 1939 most markets outside the yen bloc were equally desirable to Japan because foreign currencies earned in trade were convertible each to the other. Upon the outbreak of war on 3 September 1939, however, Great Britain erected a fence of controls around the "fortified sterling area." Japanese firms selling to customary markets in India, Australia, New Zealand, Malaya, and British Africa thereafter received payment in "blocked sterling" in London bank accounts. Without special permission, they or fellow Japanese firms could spend the money only within the sterling bloc, which, being at war, had few strategic commodities to offer after supplying Britain's needs. The colonial governors of the Dutch East Indies and French Indochina, isolated from their mother countries, also imposed exchange controls. Only the United States freely sold metals, machine tools, and large volumes of crude and refined petroleum. With other currencies inconvertible, exporting to the United States became an acute challenge for Japan, just as nylon began to pinch off its prime source of dollars. If Japan could not sell manufactures to Americans it would have to liquidate its monetary gold or do without strategic imports.

Japan normally exported to the United States about $50 million per year of nonsilk goods, worth only 40 to 50 percent of its raw silk sales to America. The array of such articles was extraordinarily diverse. The U.S. Tariff Commission calculated that in 1940 Japan sold to the United States 138 different products (as defined in tariff schedules) worth at least $50,000 each, another 85 worth between $25,000 and $50,000, and many others of lesser value. Only about a dozen products, however, amounted to $1 million or more per year.[2] Most Japanese offerings clung to market toeholds, hemmed in by tariffs and quotas or in some cases by inferior quality. Japan was unable to sell to America its rayon textiles or the mass-produced footwear, bicycles, and other consumer wares it marketed throughout East Asia. Industrial machinery and chemical firms could not compete for U.S. orders. Japanese businesses, instead, exported more readily marketable low-value specialty wares, hoping not to arouse the ire of U.S. competitors and provoke a backlash of antidumping actions and quotas. They probed for niches of two varieties: semiluxury items of good quality in which Japan had advantages of low-cost labor, management skills, or local materials, and consumer specialties so cheap that U.S. producers could not or would not match their prices. Japan's campaign to diversify dollar earnings failed, however, primarily because of deliberate U.S. barriers.

Cotton Textiles

In the 1930s Japan pinned its hopes for earning dollars on its largest export industry, cotton textiles. Since Meiji times spinning and weaving mills around Osaka had supplied Japanese home demand. With modern textile machinery from abroad, and later designed in Japan, their durable, low-priced fabrics and diligent salesmanship won markets in the underdeveloped world, displacing the output of the British Lancashire district. Japanese workers, mostly young and female, tended fewer spindles or looms and lagged behind in productivity, but they earned one-tenth of Western wages and benefits. Mill labor comprised only 20 to 25 percent of fabric cost, however, whereas imported raw cotton made up 50 to 60 percent. (The remainder included freight, supplies, and capital.) Japan grew no cotton, and the yen bloc grew too little to export. Japanese mills purchased American raw cotton, desirable for its longer staples (fibers), which provided strength, for about half their needs. For the rest they blended cheap short-staple cotton from India.

By the late 1920s the textile industry employed nearly three million, 40 percent of all Japanese manufacturing workers. A slump had forced small firms to rationalize into efficient giant syndicates that bought raw cotton in quantity when bargains appeared and mastered the technology of blending all grades. Hedging on the New York Cotton Exchange afforded protection against volatile price and currency fluctuations, and crucial for Japan, the exchange's low-cash-margin hedge contracts did not tie up scarce dollars. In the 1930s Japan surged to second largest world producer of cotton textiles, behind the United States. Half its production was sold abroad, the other half retained for the domestic market. In December 1931 exporters got a lift from a yen devaluation. In 1933 Japan surpassed Britain as the largest cotton textile exporter. By 1935, however, the devaluation boost had played out while U.S. raw cotton prices rising from Depression lows squeezed profits. Japanese industrialists turned their eyes to the billion-dollar U.S. fabric market.[3]

Americans consumed an enormous quantity of cotton goods, some nine billion square yards in the late 1930s (seventy yards per person), 98 percent of it woven domestically. Because of heavy-handed lobbying in Washington, mills were sheltered by tariffs and other import protections. The Smoot-Hawley Tariff Act extended an already complicated array of duties. In general, the finer the weave, the higher the duty; only a few elegant European and English fabrics surmounted the tariff wall. The duties on medium-grade cloth, Japan's specialty, were 38 to 42 percent. Because half the duty was, in effect, imposed on foreign raw cotton, the burden on value added in Japan was twice as high, about 80 percent.[4]

Bleach Cloth

During the early New Deal era the National Industrial Recovery Act (NIRA) restricted domestic textile competition in hopes of raising both factory wages and the ruinously low prices received by cotton farmers. It levied a processing tax on U.S. factory output but not on imported textiles. Powerful Japanese trading companies, including Mitsui and Mitsubishi, spotted an opportunity. In late 1934 they began massive shipments of broad cotton cloth, thirty to fifty count (threads per inch) bleached pure white, into the New York textile market. The fabrics, woven of finer yarns, were 15 percent lighter than American goods, excellent for inexpensive women's nightgowns, children's and women's underwear, and handkerchiefs, items not subject to rough wear and tear. Using forty-four- and fifty-two-inch-wide Japanese bolts, the factories cut nightgowns across the width with less wastage than when they cut thirty-six-inch U.S. cloth lengthwise. Typical Japanese fabrics entering at 5.7 cents per square yard including duty emerged as nightgowns sold for 25 to 39 cents in bargain basements and five-and-dime stores. Heavier 10-cents-per-yard U.S. goods wound up in nightgowns costing 49 to 79 cents and sold in upscale stores. The Japanese also sold lightweight "print cloth" fabrics dyed in light hues and ready for printing of patterns. Cotton textile exports to the United States, previously a minuscule one million square yards, jumped in 1934 to seven million and in 1935 to thirty-six million square yards, the latter barely half of 1 percent of the U.S. cotton fabric market but 12.6 percent of the grades in which it competed.

U.S. mill operators howled in protest. They made common cause with activists advocating boycotts because of Japanese treatment of the Chinese. They drowned out the voices of farmers' advocates who well understood that Japan bought 32 percent of U.S. raw cotton exports in the mid-1930s, in fact, 16 percent of the entire U.S. crop, especially from south Texas and other impoverished regions far from the weaving mills of the Carolinas. The political uproar dampened any impulse the administration might have had to negotiate with Japan the sort of treaty authorized by the Reciprocal Trade Act of 1934. Such treaties empowered the president to cut tariff rates on a country's products by up to half, and to extend the cuts to other countries under the "most favored nation" doctrine. (Only a few such treaties were negotiated before World War II, none with Japan or with countries from which treaties could have benefited Japan.) A "scientific" study by the U.S. Tariff Commission determined that Japanese costs of the popular textile grades were below those of domestic mills and recommended tariff increases of 10 to 14 percentage points. Roosevelt so ordered in 1936.

The action did not slow Japan's market invasion. By vigorous salesmanship and processing low-cost cotton purchased earlier, and despite tougher competition after the Supreme Court killed the NIRA and the processing tax, Japanese exports to America doubled in 1936 to 77 million square yards. Ultimately the textile onslaught was curbed by a "gentlemen's agreement" crafted by a consortium of U.S. mill operators with government blessing. Claudius T. Murchison, president of the Cotton Textile Institute and a former senior officer in the Commerce Department, led a five-man team across the Pacific to negotiate with the Japanese textile cartel. The parties agreed to a quota allowing doubled imports of 155 million yards in 1937 but a reduced quota of 100 million in 1938, which was subsequently extended into 1939 and 1940. Acquiescence of the Osaka exporters was no doubt due to the generous concession—a measly thirty-six-million-yard quota had been rumored—and to anticipation that Tokyo would soon restrict textile production in order to shift labor, machinery, and foreign exchange to war needs.[5]

Cotton Specialties

Accepting quotas on basic cloth but hungry for hard currency, Japan turned to higher value labor-intensive goods, hoping to wring more than the 4 cents per square yard (before duty) it received from processing imported raw cotton into standard cloth. Japanese velveteen, a shoddy imitation velvet suitable only for bedroom slippers, picture frames, and jewelry box linings because its pile shed when rubbed, sold for 15 cents per yard. Japan supplied 40 percent of the U.S. demand and 100 percent of the very lowest quality velveteen. For upscale customers Japan sold up to $1 million a year of decorative table-top wares at 45 cents per yard or more: damask table cloths, napkins, place mats, and "Japanese blue print" table runners. Demand firmed when the war halted British competition. Cotton fishing nets were another labor-intensive Japanese specialty. On the other hand, Japan made no headway in 50 percent–dutied knitted gloves and socks or in hemmed sheets and towels. "Hit or miss" rag floor rugs were worth eight or nine cents a square yard but, hammered by a 75 percent tariff, brought in less than half a million dollars per year. At the extreme downscale end, Japan exported penny-a-yard bundles of torn-up kimonos and underwear, used as wiping rags for machines and locomotives. The volume, an astonishing thirty million pounds in 1937, was twice the weight of all new textiles exported to America. For reasons unknown, shipments ended in 1940.

Textiles a Poor Dollar Earner

What did Japan gain from its cotton textile push into the United States? Not much. Bleach and print cloth sales worth $3 million in 1935 provoked tariff and quota retaliation. Under the gentlemen's agreement Japan sold $11 million worth in 1937, even though cloth prices dropped one cent per yard during the U.S. recession. Thereafter it shipped no more than 64 percent of its lowered quota. From 1938 to 1941 Japan's share of bleached and print cloth demand stalled at 5 percent of the market, earning $6 million annually. Higher-value specialties rarely exceeded half a million dollars each. Textile sales campaigns in other dollar countries met with little success outside Argentina and Chile. Canada, tied to British imperial preference, remained loyal to Lancashire. In the tropical American republics and in the Caribbean and the Philippines the United States held a relationship edge in exporting textiles because it bought their coffee, sugar, and bananas and Japan did not. Given that raw cotton constituted 50 to 60 percent of the cost of plain cloth (but much less for specialties) and that Japan necessarily bought American raw cotton for strength, the two-way cotton trade resulted in a net deficit in dollars.

After the outbreak of war with China, Tokyo converted textile labor and factories to war uses. It restricted raw cotton imports to the quantities needed to weave fabrics for export under the so-called link system, soon rendered more stringent by limiting raw cotton intake to cloth sold strictly for hard currency. Japanese consumers, accustomed to a plentiful fifty square yards of cotton textiles per capita, had to make do with shabby rayon staple cloth. Cotton fabric exports continued to earn some nondollar hard currencies, but Japan spent more U.S. dollars for raw cotton than it earned from link trade. The futility was painfully evident in 1940. Japan sold $8 million of cotton textiles to the United States but spent $30 million for American raw cotton. Although far below the pre–China war purchases of $90 to $100 million (due to link restrictions, and switching to more Indian cotton, and to some Brazilian payable in dollars), the total dollar outlay far exceeded textile sales to the dollar area. The proud cotton textile industry, bellwether of Japan's surge into world industrial prominence, had become a burden the nation could ill afford.[6]

A Miscellany of Wares

The decaying fortunes of silk and cotton energized Japanese business and government to promote other dollar-earning exports, with mixed but usually disappointing results. Raw silk and all textiles (including minor yardages of rayon and wool) together comprised 75 percent of sales to the United States. The other 25 percent consisted of a variety of wares worth $40 million per year on average, a useful sum exceeding half the value of empire gold production as well as a beacon of hope for diversification and commercial survival. The products, though individually small earners, required almost no foreign raw materials and gave employment to hundreds of thousands of Japanese. Modest successes attended sales of a few traditional articles upgraded by modern processing and the exploitation of niche markets for premium seafood, plant extracts, ceramic tablewares, and hat-making materials that did not compete directly with American producers. Tariffs of 20 to 50 percent were relatively benign for that era. By 1940 such products had gained or at least maintained U.S. markets, and the outlooks were promising. On the other hand, Japan fared poorly in expanding exports to America of small industrial components like zippers and miniature electric light bulbs because of terrible quality and of extremely cheap plastic novelties for adults and children that could not surmount punitive duties of 100 percent and higher. By 1940 these once-promising exports had shriveled nearly to zero.

At first glance U.S. tariff schedules did not appear to discriminate (chart 4). In 1935 Japanese products were subject to an average of 14.3 percent duty, compared with 30 percent average on products of the seven most important European industrial countries, because raw silk entered duty-free. Japan's average burden on dutiable articles (that is, everything except raw silk) at 49 percent was not much worse than the 44 percent average on dutiable European articles and slightly less than on those from Britain, the largest supplier of manufactures to the United States. Japan was hugely disadvantaged, however, by duties levied on "Miscellaneous products," one of the ten broad product categories in U.S. tariff schedules, mostly small consumer and household novelties. The average charge of 71 percent against Japan was far higher than against European and British miscellaneous products that paid an average of 43 percent. Only Switzerland's highly engineered, high-priced goods were close, at 65 percent duty (chart 5).[7]

CHART 4 **U.S. Tariff Rates on Imports from Eight Industrial Countries, 1935 (ad Valorem Equivalent, Percentage of Value)**

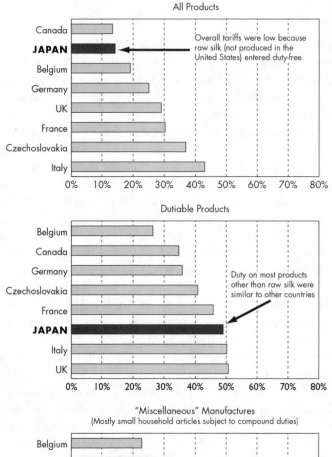

All Products

Overall tariffs were low because raw silk (not produced in the United States) entered duty-free

Duty on most products other than raw silk were similar to other countries

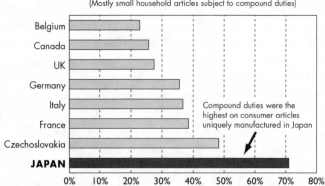

"Miscellaneous" Manufactures
(Mostly small household articles subject to compound duties)

Compound duties were the highest on consumer articles uniquely manufactured in Japan

Tariff Commission, *Computed Duties and Equivalent ad Valorem Rates.*

CHART 5 **U.S. Tariff Rates on Selected Japanese Imports, 1935**

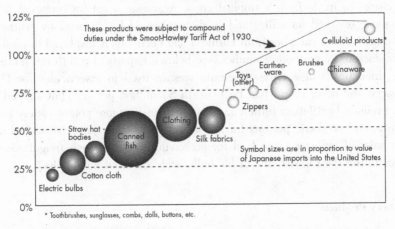

Tariff Commission, *Computed Duties and Equivalent ad Valorem Rates.*

Agricultural and Natural Specialties

Japan was the principal supplier to the United States of native plant and forest products worth, in total, $10 to $12 million per year. Green tea had once been Japan's largest export, but it had fallen victim to changes in consumer preference. In the 1870s and 1880s tea shipments of around $5 million per year had constituted 15 to 25 percent of Japan's meager exports, increasingly sold to the United States, where green tea (and later delicate oolong from Formosa) was popular. Both governments enacted purity laws to prevent the adulteration that plagued Chinese green tea. In the 1890s, however, the hearty black tea of India and Ceylon (from the same plant but fermented by a different process) won over English and European consumers. Americans remained loyal to the delicate Japanese brew, perhaps because they drank coffee prodigiously and relished a milder cup of tea at supper, green tea having one-fourth the caffeine of coffee and half that of black tea. After the turn of the century two lifestyle changes persuaded Americans to drink black tea: tea bags for convenience and iced tea for hot weather. Subtle green tea was too delicate for either purpose. Sales plummeted. In the 1920s Japanese advertising promoting Vitamin C in green tea came to naught. By 1940 Japan's remaining $3 million in tea sales, mostly for oriental restaurants, constituted a mere 2 percent of its exports to the United States.[8]

Japanese plant extracts for U.S. industry also faced adverse conditions in the 1930s. Menthol, a peppermint aromatic used for medicines and flavored cigarettes such as Kool brand, struggled against competition from synthetic oil of citronella made from a tropical grass. Agar-agar, a gelatin extracted from Japanese seaweed for jellies and medicines, could be replaced by synthetic gelatins. Natural camphor from Formosa had been largely displaced in plastics manufacture by synthetic camphor (see below). Exports of pyrethrum flowers, the dried heads of a chrysanthemum species used in insecticides for U.S. tobacco and other crops, had been worth $2 million per year but slipped to $0.4 million by 1940 in futile competition against a more potent variety from Kenya, and synthetic poisons for household spray guns. Japan also eked out tiny sales of creosote, a coal oil for preserving wood, through freight advantages to the West Coast, and of lily bulbs and farm-bred mink pelts.[9]

Fishery Products

Japan's brightest prospect appeared to lie in high-value marine products. The Japanese fishery, the world's largest, employed 1.4 million workers full and part time, mostly aboard three hundred thousand small boats in coastal and empire waters. They harvested four million tons worth $200 million per year, primarily sardines and other small fry for food, cooking oil, and fertilizer. Large motor vessels netted the most valuable 5 percent of the catch favored by Americans, from distant waters of Siberia, the North Pacific, and even the North Atlantic. Fishing consumed only a little foreign exchange for fuel oil, hemp for nets, and tin-plated steel canning sheet. When Tokyo rationed fuel oil after 1937, it treated the deep-sea fishery more liberally than inshore fishing. By the end of the 1930s, as U.S. incomes rose and seafood prices firmed when foreign competition disappeared due to war, Japan delivered $8 to $9 million in ocean products to the United States, second in dollar trade earnings only to silk.

Americans had grown fond of king crabs from northern waters, and Japan provided 80 percent of the U.S. supply. Japanese fishermen trapped, deshelled, cooked, and canned the crabs aboard factory vessels, or at shore stations in Russian Kamchatka, for sale mostly to America. King crab was a pricey delicacy at 36 cents per pound wholesale, so the 15 percent duty was no impediment, nor was tin plate at 3.5 cents per pound once Japan became self-sufficient after 1936. The tariff served no protective purpose because American crabbers caught different-tasting blue and Dungeness crabs, packed in unsealed tins too perishable for inland sales. Japanese appeals failed to reduce the tariff (which was, oddly, increased to 22.5 percent in September 1941 after all trade had ceased). Nevertheless, crabmeat sales to America doubled in the 1930s to more than ten million pounds, yielding Japan nearly $4 million per year in 1939 and 1940. Further growth was likely as the U.S. economy strengthened and Russian competition vanished.

U.S. consumers took a liking to canned tuna fish in the 1920s. Demand grew fivefold from 1923 to 1940. In 1932 Japan's deep-sea fishery began delivering to the United States. By the end of the decade it supplied 60 to 75 percent of the light-meat albacore, which constituted the most lucrative 10 percent of the U.S. tuna market. Albacore canned in cottonseed oil, at 16 to19 cents per pound wholesale, was a semiluxury preferred by upscale consumers. Lower-income Americans and the Japanese themselves ate dark bluefin tuna. During the Depression complaints by U.S. fishermen led to a tariff of 45 percent. Japanese attempts to negotiate a "voluntary" quota in lieu of the tariff failed. The always-erratic tuna catch yielded Japan about $1.5 million per year, including 20 percent sold as inexpensive fresh and frozen tuna, but with demand rising the canned tuna market looked favorable for growth.

Japan delivered other premium seafood to America. At Boston, Japanese vessels landed frozen Atlantic swordfish, a contra-seasonal delicacy subjected to a duty increase in 1936. On the Pacific Coast scallops and other shellfish, and in Hawaii canned salmon, entered duty-free. Canned clams, however, encountered a lawsuit in 1934 that led to a very high duty on its trivial $130,000 of sales, which soured relations with Japan because duties against Canadian clams were reduced. Japan also supplied $1 million of decidedly nonpremium, 2-cents-per-pound scrap and meal from fish processing plants, sold by the ton to poultry farms and fertilizer mixing plants.

In the vitamin-conscious United States oils pressed from fish livers provided vitamins D and A for humans and animals. Imports were welcomed duty-free because American fishermen could not meet the demand. Until war interrupted cod liver oil from Norway Japan had been a negligible source. Although synthetic substitutes for human nutrition seemed economically viable, livers harvested by Japanese vessels, primarily from tuna, yielded oils suitable for poultry. In 1940 prices tripled to 33 cents per pound. Imports from Japan jumped from almost nil to more than $2 million, about one-third of the vitamins fed to poultry. The future looked bright.[10]

Hat Materials

In 1939 adult Americans didn't venture outdoors bareheaded in the summer. U.S. factories turned out $44 million in summer hats for men and women. In Japan thirty thousand workers toiled constructing hat bodies, two-thirds sold to U.S. plants for finishing and trimming. Japan earned $2 million per year with no outlay for imported materials. It supplied "pedaline," strips of tinted cellophane braided around hemp string, for forming hats, and "toyo" hat bodies of twisted rice paper coated with celluloid plastic for so-called harvest hats. The tariffs of 36 to 45 percent were taxes on low-income Americans because neither product could be made in the United States due to labor cost, lack of natural materials, and Japan's advantage in celluloid. (Japan did not export felt bodies for winter hats because of a 110 percent duty and lack of local wool.) Women's hat demand seemed positive as a bareheaded fad reversed, and men's demand, too, as flat "boaters" gave way to dapper "Panama" hats.[11]

Shabby Parts

Japanese failures in selling manufactures to the United States were not always due to tariffs and quotas. Poor quality relegated some products to toehold niches in the cheapest items, sold for a few pennies apiece. Metal slide fasteners, or zippers, came into widespread use in the 1930s. In 1934, after a key patent expired, dozens of Japanese firms began exporting to America. Their low-wage advantage overcame a 45 percent duty and even a 66 percent rate imposed in 1936 when U.S. firms claimed dumping, although Japan had garnered only 5 percent of the market. Japan sold metal-toothed zippers at two cents per unit. Other patents barred it from locking-type zippers worth ten cents. But the greatest problem was poor quality—a jammed zipper ruined an entire sweater or suitcase. In the late 1930s Japanese exporters sold less than five hundred thousand dollars' worth of zippers per year, only 3 percent by value of a rapidly growing market.[12]

Japan made headway, after some patent expirations, exporting miniature electric light bulbs to America, for cheap flashlights, toys, and Christmas tree decorations, at a fraction the price of U.S.-made bulbs. For the big market in automobile instrument bulbs, Japanese quality was too unreliable, a reason the Tariff Commission declined to raise a 20 percent duty as demanded by American factories. Japan maintained exports, including some large bulbs, at around $1 million. Its market share of miniatures in 1938 of 21 percent by volume was only 3 percent by value.[13]

The Blight of Compound Duties on Housewares and Notions

Japanese workshops could surmount "ordinary" U.S. tariffs but several of their most promising lines failed to penetrate markets because of extravagant and unusual Smoot-Hawley tariffs. A longstanding principle of American tariff policy, intended to protect factory workers and investors, decreed that tariff rates should rise with degree of manufacture. Basic commodities not produced in America faced zero to moderate duties. Finished articles for the consumer faced the highest rates, typically 50 percent or so. Historically, the United States had levied two kinds of tariffs. *Ad valorem* duties were set at a fixed percentage of invoiced price. Their burden was countercyclical, diminishing when prices fell in depressions and rising with prices in prosperous times. *Specific* duties, usually applied to simple commodities, were levied as a fixed number of cents per pound, bale, gallon, or square yard. In depressions their effective rates rose as a percent of value as prices declined, and fell in good times. Specific duties punished foreign sellers when they were most vulnerable. They were especially punitive when applied to cheap, multipiece manufactures, leading to astonishingly high rates on small articles of uniquely Japanese origin. An unwritten U.S. tradition of capping duties at 90 percent, on the sensible notion that an industry unable to cope at twice foreign costs did not deserve protection, succumbed in the Great Depression.

Until 1930 Japanese consumer novelties encountered only ad valorem barriers. Rates were high but some could be surmounted because of low labor costs and in some cases Japanese materials or skills. The Smoot-Hawley Act, however, selectively imposed *compound* duties, a heavy-handed combination of ad valorem and specific rates. Congress voted very few compound duties, and those almost exclusively on items imported entirely from Japan. A Japanese product, say, a painted porcelain knick-knack landed at four cents, might pay 50 percent ad valorem *and* two cents per unit specific duty, a combined 100 percent tariff. In the Depression some duties rose far above 100 percent, sometimes to several hundred percent. Among the approximately twenty-one thousand rates that Congress legislated item by item under Smoot-Hawley, a search for manufactured consumer articles amounting to at least fifty thousand dollars' worth of imports from all countries in 1931 that incurred effective duties of 100 percent or more turned up only a few classes of pottery, celluloid goods, buttons, and the like, uniquely Japanese, with tariff burdens of 110 to 164 percent. (A rare non-Japanese category was men's silk opera hats from Europe at 121 percent. Even the wealthy suffered.) It is hard to fathom such malicious discrimination against Japan. Smoot-Hawley was fashioned during the summer of 1929, before the Depression, and signed in June 1930 before Japan's aggression in Manchuria angered Americans. Japan was America's second largest supplier of goods (after Canada) and third largest international customer (after Canada and Britain). Its raw cotton purchasing was a godsend to poor sharecroppers, white and black alike. Cheap Japanese wares did not compete against American labor. In a few cases Japanese workshops managed to cope by shifting upscale to middle class customers. For the most part, however, their wares for low-income consumers and children simply fell away by 1940.[14]

Ceramics

Japanese workmen and women crafted excellent china and porcelain table-wares from local clays in the Nagoya area, including the famous brands Noritake and Amari. Their elaborately hand-decorated pieces were unlike anything else available at affordable prices. (French Limoges and English bone china, made in part from calcined animal bones, sold for ten times the Japanese price.) Japanese porcelain was slender, translucent, and decorated with geometric and floral patterns that charmed customers. America's large pottery industry mass produced only thick, heavy earthenware or stoneware dishes, sold glazed but undecorated for home tables and as semiglazed "white-ware" for hotels and restaurants. During the 1920s exports to America earned Japan $4 million per year. About half the sales were fancies and miniatures—delicate tea sets, condiment dishes, salt and pepper shakers, vases, and figurines such as the Cinderella slipper glazed in gold and sky blue that adorned my childhood shelf. Nevertheless, one or two U.S. firms lobbied so vociferously that Congress added to the 70 percent ad valorem rate (in effect since 1922) a compound duty on decorated pottery of ten cents per dozen pieces. The burden was extraordinary. Tea sets landed at ten to fifteen cents per dozen pieces incurred duties of 140 to 170 percent. The importing firm Morimura Brothers voiced the disappointment of families wanting something finer than stoneware and explained U.S. noncompetitiveness as being due to high labor cost. Its appeal was futile.

Japanese producers survived by shifting to larger items suited to U.S. lifestyles, for example, ninety-six-piece dinner services for twelve (twice the pieces in American stoneware sets), including large plates, covered meat platters, and coffee cups and saucers. A specific duty of 10 cents per dozen was more bearable on sets worth 50 to 60 cents per dozen than on table notions and bric-a-brac. The strategy held the duty to a barely tolerable 90 percent. Japan clung to an export business of $3 million annually through 1940, 30 percent of the U.S. tableware market. Glass tablewares, novelties, and lenses added half a million dollars.[15]

Celluloid and Camphor

The saddest articles of Japanese failure were celluloid novelties. Although Japan never earned many dollars from them, the plight of this diverse industry vividly demonstrated the hopelessness of salvaging dollar earnings to offset silk's decline. In the 1920s Japan had risen to world leadership in pyroxylin, the first commercial plastic, commonly known as celluloid. The basic raw material, nitrocellulose "gun cotton," was produced by treating raw cotton with nitric and other acids. An addition of refined camphor, a "plasticizer" oil of the terpene family, reduced it to a gelatinous mass easily rolled at steam temperature into sheets—for example, clear cellophane or photography film—or precipitated as crystals for hot molding into intricate shapes of any color. Japan gained an early advantage from distilling the plasticizer from the branches of a laurel tree called Japan camphor that grew almost exclusively in Formosa. In 1899, four years after seizing Formosa from China, a Japanese government monopoly took control of camphor exports.

Production of celluloid articles blossomed in the United States, Europe, and Japan. The "artificial ivory" was fashioned into piano keys, billiard balls, cutlery handles, cigarette holders, combs, hairbrushes, dolls, and toys. But Japan's advantage faded when German chemists learned to distill synthetic camphor from wood turpentine. The United States kept duties low because it did not manufacture synthetic camphor until 1934, when demand for automobile safety glass enticed the Du Pont company into its production behind a higher protective tariff. (Safety glass consisted of a tough celluloid membrane laminated between two sheets of glass that prevented flying shards in an accident. Synthetic camphor was preferred because the celluloid did not discolor.) Nevertheless, Japan supplied about 40 percent of U.S. camphor demand until the late 1930s, especially to Kodak for photo and movie film, but earning only $1 million per year, a fraction of the earlier peak.[16]

Celluloid Articles

In small workshops and in homes Japanese workers mass produced hundreds of household articles molded of colored celluloid and assembled and decorated, extraordinarily cheap items sold to children and low-income families through low-priced chain stores. The five-and-dimes, pioneered by Frank W. Woolworth in the nineteenth century and popular in rural and urban America, were ideal outlets because they shopped the world for bargains and bought opportunistically in great quantities. In 1929 U.S. imports of Japanese celluloid goods reached $2.5 million despite a 60 percent ad valorem tariff. The outlook was strong until the Smoot-Hawley Act imposed punitive compound duties. Secretary of State Henry Stimson sent to the Senate, without comment, pitiable appeals by Japanese exporters, joined by Woolworth, to no avail.[17] Three product lines illustrate the devastation of Japanese hopes.

Toothbrushes

Celluloid toothbrushes, molded in vivid colors and inset with Chinese hog bristles, were a Japanese specialty, as were toothbrush handles for brush completion in U.S. factories. Prospects were good as awareness of oral hygiene flourished in the 1920s. A Japanese toothbrush landed at 2.5 cents plus 60 percent ad valorem duty had provided a generous profit margin to five-and-dime chains retailing at 10 cents. The 1930 act imposed a specific duty of 2 cents a brush plus 50 percent ad valorem, effectively 125 percent. The cost rose beyond Woolworth's ability to sell for 10 cents, a price point it never broke as a matter of policy. (Not until the eve of World War II did it sell articles for 25 cents.) In 1934 the Tariff Commission investigated competition from imports but mercifully recommended no further increases. Nevertheless Depression-era compound duties that rose as high as 129 to 142 percent squeezed Japan out of the market. Peak sales of ten million units earning Japan barely $300,000 dwindled by 1940 to two million units. The 10-cent child's toothbrush disappeared, leaving the field to domestic 25-cent brushes sold in drugstores. Similarly thwarted by duties, Japanese hair brushes and combs also dwindled to insignificance.[18]

Sun Goggles

Another item demonstrating Japanese nimbleness in catching a fad, to no avail, was sun goggles, as sunglasses were known. Reacting to suave images from Hollywood, demand took off. In 1933 twenty-one U.S. firms produced thirteen million pair. The following year production rose 57 percent despite high costs mandated by the NIRA code. The profitability amazed the Tariff Commission. A pair with glass lenses worth 13 cents wholesale (only 20 percent of the cost being labor) sold for well over 25 cents retail. Japanese firms spotted a low-end opportunity. In 1933 they began exporting goggles stamped out of black celluloid sheet and sporting wire ear pieces. Landed at 3.5 cents plus 70 percent ad valorem (and no specific duty because they had been unknown in 1930), they were wildly popular in Woolworth's at 10 cents retail. In the spring season of 1934 Japan delivered 1.1 million pair to capture 10 percent of the market by number, although far less by value. The Tariff Commission, in accordance with NIRA objectives, recommended a "voluntary" restraint of 2.1 million pair under threat of higher duty, but the order soon expired with the NIRA itself. Pressure for restraint remained, however. Imports peaked at about 6 million pair in 1937, earning Japan a meager $300,000. Thereafter taste migrated upscale to designer glasses made in small lots, an arena in which Japan was uncompetitive. By 1940 Japan exported almost no sun goggles to Americans.[19]

Toys

The tariff on celluloid toys was most brutal of all. Japanese workshops made very small toys for very small children: rattles, pinwheels, and tiny dolls a few inches long with movable arms and legs. Woolworth's also sold miniature 1-cent celluloid knick-knacks for Christmas stockings and candy box prizes. (The flammability of cellulose apparently did not trouble parents in those days.) In 1929 Japan exported $2.3 million of plastic toys to America. Then Smoot-Hawley slapped a 1-cent-per-piece levy on top of 60 percent ad valorem. The formula devastated multipiece sets—soldiers for boys and doll families for girls. U.S. factories making larger and better 87-cent celluloid dolls had no intention of competing in "the small stuff." U.S. importers pleading to Congress at hearings displayed toys bearing 200 percent duty, as well as trinkets and Christmas decorations at 600 to 800 percent, presumed to be the highest duty in American history. A few senators expressed shock at penalizing the poorest toddlers but refused to act. Japanese celluloid toy sales withered away to almost nil. In the 1930s some Japanese firms upgraded to higher-priced rubber and metal toys dutiable at "only" 70 percent but drew lawsuits against their shameless imitations of U.S. packaging and logos. The drive failed. Toy sales to America of $1.7 million in 1935 dwindled to $0.9 million in 1940.[20]

Anticipating Japan's Bankruptcy, 1937–1940

When Japan invaded China on 7 July 1937, U.S. government financial experts reckoned the aggressor could not wage a long war because it lacked hard currency to purchase essential commodities abroad. As Herbert Feis, the economic adviser of the State Department, wrote, "Warfare requires many vital raw materials which Japan does not possess at all or in sufficient quantities, and which must by purchased with foreign exchange." Therefore, the "ability of Japan to carry on a protracted war depends ultimately upon her actual and potential foreign exchange resources."[1]

The Japanese Empire was singularly deficient in metals: iron and steel, copper, lead, zinc, and alloying elements for toughening steel. The home islands and colonies contained insignificant petroleum deposits and had inadequate capacity to refine imported crude oil into fuels for the sea and air forces and the civilian economy. Japan also imported wool and leather for uniforms, lumber for construction, chemicals, and even foods. Although it produced textile machinery, it lacked the know-how to build complex machine tools for metal working. Japan fashioned its first-class warships, aircraft, and munitions with imported machine tools—lathes, grinders, drills, forgers, millers, and the like.

Could Japan sustain a long campaign so dependent on foreign supplies? The yen was a "soft" currency, inconvertible, unwanted by foreign exporting firms, and useless for buying outside the empire. Japan financed its non-empire imports with hard currency earned by exporting, but the balance was precarious. Its export earnings were sure to shrivel as it diverted labor and capital to war. Raw silk, historically Japan's big earner, was a luxury product suffering from weak demand and low prices during the Depression. The heroic

CHART 6 **Japan's Foreign Trade Deficit by Principal Trading Areas, 1937–1941**

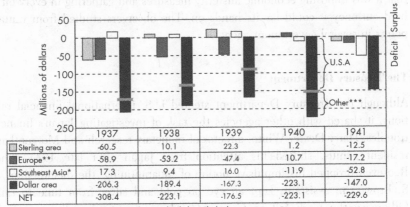

	1937	1938	1939	1940	1941
☐ Sterling area	-60.5	10.1	22.3	1.2	-12.5
■ Europe**	-58.9	-53.2	-47.4	10.7	-17.2
☐ Southeast Asia*	17.3	9.4	16.0	-11.9	-52.8
■ Dollar area	-206.3	-189.4	-167.3	-223.1	-147.0
NET	-308.4	-223.1	-176.5	-223.1	-229.6

* Netherlands East Indies, French Indochina, Thailand
** Mainly Germany, 1937–39
*** Latin America, Canada, Philippines

Composite drawn from Japan Statistical Association, *Historical Statistics of Japan*, Table 10-5-a, converted to dollars.

push to export cotton textiles met success in some markets in the 1930s, but every dollar of cloth contained fifty cents of cotton purchased with hard currency, whereas silk was 100 percent of domestic origin. Even rayon fabric, another successful export innovation, was manufactured from imported wood pulp and salt. Japan's other manufactures sold well in East Asia, but the U.S. market for its consumer goods was shrinking.

U.S. economists correctly predicted that Japan's merchandise trade balance outside the yen bloc would plunge into deficit (chart 6). As to invisible (non-merchandise) earnings, ocean shipping, a longstanding source, would evaporate as Japan converted its merchant marine to war duty. Since its weak credit standing and political antagonisms abroad ruled out foreign loans, Japan would have to cover the trade deficit by spending its reserves of gold and hard-currency assets. The drain, economists thought, would soon render Japan internationally bankrupt. Even if the United States and other democracies did not curtail their commerce with Japan, the attack would bog down for lack of financial resources. For the next three years Washington's response to Japan's financial plight was watchful observation and detective sleuthing, not interference.

From the summer of 1937 through the summer of 1940 U.S. government experts assessed and reassessed Japan's financial staying power in war. Despite

Tokyo's lowering of a veil of secrecy over economic data, it became evident that it was imposing economic austerity measures and gathering in every bit of hard currency it could lay its hands on. The observers studied from vantage points in several government agencies.[2]

The Treasury Department

Although the Treasury Department steered U.S. international financial relations, it shared with other agencies the task of investigating Japan's financial troubles. Harry Dexter White, director of monetary research and Morgenthau's resident genius, shifted his attention from Japan after late 1937, when Roosevelt dropped his impulsive notion of "quarantining" the dictatorships. P. S. Brown, an assistant, kept an eye on gold and silver from time to time. Otherwise the work fell to George C. Haas, the veteran director of the Division of Research and Statistics, not White's subordinate. Haas, an agricultural economist who came to the Treasury from the Farm Credit Administration with Morgenthau in 1934, watched market trends on a ticker-tape in the office.[3] In 1938–39 White relied on Harold Glasser, an assistant, who departed in 1940.[4] White then hired a dubious choice, twenty-eight-year-old V. (for Virginius) Frank Coe, as assistant of his Division of Monetary Research to replace Glasser. But Coe (who later succeeded White as division chief) focused on China more than Japan. His public service career ended bizarrely after the war.[5] Toward the end of 1940 the Treasury Department recruited Andrew M. Kamarck, a twenty-six-year-old Harvard Ph.D. in economics, from a post with the Federal Reserve Board of Governors. Kamarck independently analyzed Japan's financial resources.[6] In February 1941 the Treasury further focused on Japan in response to the discovery of a secret Japanese dollar cache and the proddings of a newly appointed assistant secretary of state, Dean Acheson. W. H. Taylor, an aide to White, assembled information from other agencies and public sources into an elaborate study, which White summarized for Morgenthau.[7] However, Treasury experts, despite the department's potent authority, were not the most frequent investigators of Japan's presumed money crisis.

The Federal Reserve

The most talented experts in actual money transactions around the world worked in the Federal Reserve system. Among the first economists to analyze Japan's finances, at the time of FDR's quarantine scheme in late 1937, was

Emanuel A. Goldenweiser, one of the twentieth century's most brilliant economists. Goldenweiser had emigrated from Russia as a youngster, studied at Cornell University, and joined the Bureau of the Census as a statistician. He came to the Federal Reserve Board of Governors in Washington in 1919. As director of research and statistics, and economist to the Fed's Open Market Committee, he pioneered famous economic measurements such as the index of industrial production. International finance was not his forte, however, and after his initial work analyzing Japanese assets, he moved to the Federal Reserve Bank of New York (FRBNY).[8] Not until 1940 did the Federal Reserve Board of Governors engage Joseph Burke Knapp, a twenty-eight-year-old banker whose Oxford degree was in literature but who had five years' experience with Brown and Harriman, investment bankers, in London. Knapp compiled and critiqued information about Japan from other government agencies.[9]

But the primary center of expertise in matters of foreign exchange lay in the Federal Reserve Bank of New York at Thirty-three Liberty Street, a few blocks from America's financial capital on Wall Street, where nearly all U.S. trading in securities and currencies took place. The FRBNY was the most important of the twelve regional Reserve banks. In addition to bank regulation and currency management in the Second Federal Reserve District, comprising New York State and nearby parts of New Jersey and Connecticut, the "desk" in New York City executed the system's open market trading in government bonds and foreign exchange on behalf of all U.S. agencies. Its data on banks and bank accounts were highly important. Foreign banking offices, and foreign bank correspondent relationships with U.S. banks, were concentrated in New York. Among them were the Yokohama Specie Bank, the conduit for Japan's dollar dealings and holder of its dollar positions. Officers of the New York Fed, as bank examiners, could contact local Japanese executives for information unencumbered by diplomatic protocols that the State and Treasury Depart-ments faced. Japanese gold sales to the U.S. Treasury were publicly known to all, but the FRBNY was by far the agency best situated to observe opaque movements of Japan's dollar reserves.

Unlike political appointees in cabinet jobs, the management and senior staff of the FRBNY were generally independent, long-serving professionals. President George L. Harrison, a lawyer who was formerly counsel to the Federal Reserve Board of Governors in Washington, was mainly concerned with the banking crises of the Depression.[10] He left most foreign matters to Allan Sproul, his first vice president. Sproul, who had started his career as a research and analytical economist at the San Francisco Fed, impressed Benjamin Strong, Harrison's powerful predecessor. In 1930 Sproul moved to

New York to serve in the foreign department. He rose rapidly, attended monetary conferences abroad, and beginning in 1938 supervised the open market
desk. On 1 January 1941 he superseded Harrison as president (a post he held
until 1956).[11] Sproul lent stature to the bank's international research, but the
key agent for the bank's sleuthing in regard to Japan was assistant vice president L. Werner Knoke. In 1931, Knoke, a commercial banker with the Irving
Trust Company, joined the New York Fed. At the beginning of 1937 he was
elevated to a vice presidency with direct supervision of international functions,
including foreign exchange dealings. He maintained friendly relations with the
Treasury, for example, by attending conferences at Morgenthau's request
(whereas Sproul continuously fought against what he perceived as Treasury
encroachments on formulation of Fed monetary policy).[12]

A succession of unusually young economists, holding doctorate degrees
from prestigious universities, reported to Knoke on Japan's foreign exchange
situation. Emilio G. Collado, a brilliant, twenty-seven-year-old Harvard-trained
analyst who was serving briefly in New York between jobs in the Treasury and
the State Departments, wrote several studies of Japan's specie and foreign
assets in 1937–38.[13] In 1939 Oscar E. Moore brought practical banking experience to Japan watching. He had taken a five-year sabbatical from his
FRBNY job to work at Bankers Trust Company in New York and Paris, and at
the Bank for International Settlements in Switzerland, then returned as chief
of the Foreign Research Division.[14] Next up was a talented thirty-year-old academic, Frank M. Tamagna. Italian born but educated in the United States,
including a Yale doctorate, with commercial banking experience, Tamagna
took over analysis of Japanese foreign assets in 1940–41.[15] Assisting him was
Walter H. Rozell Jr., age thirty, a career officer educated in banking studies
who moved up as manager of the Foreign Department.[16] The young, highly
trained FRBNY staff provided dispassionate research, generally free of political bias. That their forecasts of Japan's financial plight were often wrong was
due not to lack of talent but to absence of data, occasionally naïve assumptions about Japan's financial policies, and, ultimately, Japanese deceit in hid-
ing dollars.[17]

Other Officials

Other agencies attempted financial investigations from time to time. The
Department of State set *economic* policy in overseas relations; Secretary Cordell
Hull especially favored treaties on trade with friendly countries. Herbert Feis,
his senior adviser on international economic affairs, was also a prolific writer on

diplomatic history (including a postwar book on U.S.-Japan stresses leading to the war). Although Feis was the de facto contact with the Treasury, he focused on tariffs and the stockpiling of strategic materials.[18] Analysis of Japan's gold and dollars fell to George Francis Luthringer, a thirty-six-year-old former Princeton economics professor and author of works on gold and credit, who was recruited to Feis's staff in 1938 and worked there until 1941.[19] Otherwise, the State Department's expertise on *financial* matters was slim.

Army and Navy intelligence staffs looked at Japanese problems of strategic raw materials and shipping in relation to war needs, but they lacked expertise in finance. A rare exception was Lt. Norman E. Towson, assistant treasurer of a bank in Washington, D.C., and a military intelligence reserve officer, whose independent study for Army G-2 of Japan's problems in March 1941 stressed its vulnerability in foreign exchange. His paper ran afoul of criticism from competing divisions of the State Department for offering political opinions. Nevertheless, Morgenthau recruited him into the Treasury Department later in the year to work for John W. Pehle, an assistant to the secretary, who thought highly of him.[20]

Forecasts of Bankruptcy

The many U.S. government experts calculated that Japan was trending toward absolute depletion of its gold and hard-currency foreign assets. Several boldly projected dates when Japan's vaults would stand empty and, by inference, the war in China would halt (see chart 7):

- December 1938: E. F. Lamb, a New York Fed analyst, estimated that at recent rates of drain Japan would exhaust all foreign exchange resources in thirty-eight weeks, that is, by September 1939.[21]
- August 1939: Oscar Moore of the FRBNY calculated that at 1939 gold liquidation rates Japan would deplete its gold reserves in ten months, that is, by June 1940, if it were willing to ship every last ounce. Further, "it is not clear how Japan can carry on at the present rate of devisen [foreign exchange] expenditures for more than another year." Tighter austerity might gain it only six additional months.[22]
- January 1940: Luthringer of the State Department and Rozell of the New York Federal Reserve projected that at the 1939 rate of drain gold would be exhausted by the middle of 1941.[23]

- March 1940: Towson, then with Army Intelligence, joined in agreement with Stanley K. Hornbeck, the State Department's adviser on political relations, to declare, "I emphasize I contemplate *complete* exhaustion of all assets capable of being converted to foreign exchange at the end of 1940 or March 1941."[24]

CHART 7 **U.S. Forecasts of Japan's International "Bankruptcy," 1937–1941**

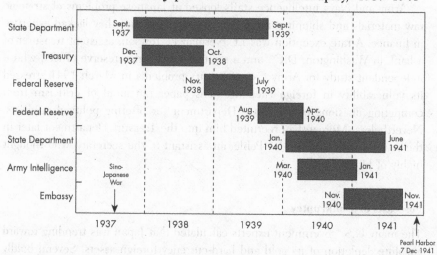

EA (Herbert Feis, economic adviser), Japan's Ultimate Foreign Exchange Resources, 20 September 1937; George C. Haas to Morgenthau, Japan's Foreign Exchange Resource, 13 December 1937, File Japan Foreign Exchange Position, Box 21, RG 56, Office of Assistant Secretary for International Affairs, Records of Department of the Treasury, NA; E. F. Lamb to Knoke, Japan: International Assets, 28 December 1938, File Japan International Position 1937–46; O. E. Moore, "The Effect of the War with China," 18 August 1939, File Japan International Position 1937–46, Box 50, International Subject Files, 1907 to 1974, International Finance Division and predecessors 1907–1974, Records of the Federal Reserve Board, RG 82, NA; G. F. Luthringer, "Japanese Gold and Foreign Exchange Resources at the End of 1939," 23 January 1940, File 894.51; Norman E. Towson, "The Economic Position of Japan: Current Estimate," 26 March 1940, File 894.50/119 1/2, Roll 11, State Department microfilm LM-68, RG 59, NA; Report from Embassy Tokyo cited in Rozell to Knoke, Japan's Financial Position vis-à-vis the United State, 23 January 1941, File Japan Finance 1922–51 (1), Box 50, FRBNY.

Two trends of these "doomsday" forecasts stand out. First, the analysts tended over time to broaden the definition of Japan's gold and hard-currency resources by teasing out information from dwindling public sources and from semisecret diplomatic reports. Their conclusions tended to diverge over time because some narrowly counted only gold, while others included foreign exchange and/or foreign investments. Second, and more important, each new analysis pushed the deadline of "bankruptcy" further into the future. American experts were continually surprised that Japan somehow came up with more gold and foreign exchange for war than they anticipated. Doomsday always lay a year or more in the future. To be sure, they cautioned that Japan could stretch its funds by draconian cuts of civilian imports, even though by 1939 it was believed that Japan had slashed food and fiber imports by 50 percent and other consumer articles even more. From the New York Federal Reserve, Oscar Moore wondered if a further lowering of the standard of living was feasible "even in such a disciplined nation as Japan."[25] But George C. Haas, director of the Research and Statistics Division of the Treasury Department, felt the people could bear the burden if its leaders believed national existence to be at stake. Other analysts speculated on energetic Japanese initiatives such as achieving raw material self-sufficiency in the yen bloc, export drives to overcome trade barriers and boycotts, or barter with Germany and Italy. They speculated on hidden reservoirs of credit (nonexistent) and wondered if Japan would default on paying its foreign debts or sell Imperial family treasures (it didn't).[26]

The Americans were duped. Not until late 1940 did they learn that Japan had hidden, right under their noses, a reserve of dollars large enough to postpone doomsday years into the future, perhaps to 1943 (chapter 8). Only then did senior U.S. policy makers understand that they could not count on imminent Japanese bankruptcy. Only then did they turn to serious contemplation of freezing Japan's international assets to block their expenditure for war.

Gold Before the China War

U.S. agency staffs peered through a unique window. Japan held almost all of its official monetary reserves in the form of gold bars in Tokyo at the Bank of Japan, the government central bank analogous to the Federal Reserve or the Bank of England. In the late 1930s the United States Treasury controlled the world gold market, uniquely so after September 1939. It stood ready, by law, to buy and sell from foreign governments unlimited quantities at thirty-five dollars per troy ounce, a policy facilitated by U.S. government ownership ultimately of 80 percent of the world's monetary gold, and by the universal liquidity of the dollar.[27] To cover its yawning trade deficits Japan regularly shipped gold bars to the United States, sold them to the Treasury, and deposited the dollar proceeds in U.S. bank accounts. The analysts suspiciously watched every ounce and every dollar.

Gold had been a key element of Japan's climb to world stature. During its centuries of isolation before the 1860s, mining of sparse ore veins by primitive methods yielded little gold. Instead, abundant silver deposits supplied the specie for feudal coinages. In 1871, three years after the Meiji restoration united the country, the government launched the silver yen, a national currency unit worth about one U.S. dollar. During their first years of world trade, subject to "unequal treaties" restricting tariffs, the Japanese binged on imported novelties like sugar, tobacco, and cotton textiles. The imbalance frustrated leaders' hopes to import equipment for industrialization and arms under their policy of "rich nation, strong military." Japan had little to offer the world in return: just green tea, fish, silkworm cocoons, low-grade silk—and silver. By 1881 Japan had been sucked dry of its silver coin patrimony, probably amounting to $300 million.

In the 1880s and 1890s Japan was oddly fortunate that vast silver discoveries in the western United States flooded world markets. Silver prices plummeted. Continental Europe and soon the United States abandoned silver-backed currency to join Great Britain on the gold standard. The silver crash depreciated the silver-linked yen by 50 percent, to 50 U.S. cents per yen, a serendipitous devaluation that promoted exports and discouraged imports. Devaluation, along with the austerity policies of Finance Minister Masayoshi Matsukata, tamed the lopsided trade deficit and rebuilt monetary reserves. It enabled the Imperial Navy to purchase British cruisers that defeated China in the Sino-Japanese War of 1894–95. Under the Treaty of Shimonoseki, Japan extracted from China a gold indemnity of $187 million, a treasure enabling it to join the gold standard in 1897 with the yen fixed at 0.75 grams of gold, equal to U.S. 48.9 cents. The navy spent part of the windfall on modern battleships that sank the Russian fleet in the war of 1904–5. Japan, newly creditworthy, was then able to borrow abroad at reasonable terms. During the Russo-Japanese War, Japan sold $408 million (face value) of bonds in the United States, Britain, and Germany to finance over half the cost of the war. But postwar interest payments strained the balance of payments and delayed further accumulation of gold reserves.[28]

In World War I, Japan, like most countries, suspended the gold standard, meaning it embargoed private dealings in gold. It did little fighting but it prospered by selling ships and other products to the Allies, and silk to prosperous Americans at inflated prices. Meanwhile, imports lagged due to shortages of foreign goods and shipping. By 1920 trade surpluses piled up $1.1 billion of gold reserves, six times the prewar reserve, in the Bank of Japan. Then a post-war slump, return of global competition, and reconstruction costs of the 1923 Tokyo earthquake plunged Japan back into trade deficits. Yet the country was fairly prosperous and its credit was sound. The national and colonial governments, industrial and electric utility companies, and city governments floated $718 million of bonds in New York and London in the 1920s.[29] In 1930 Japan still retained a $500 million gold cache (at the world price of $20.67 per ounce). Japanese leaders felt strong enough on 31 December 1929 to place the yen back on the gold standard at the prewar value of 48.9 cents.

The timing was disastrous. The worldwide Depression had just begun. The price of raw silk collapsed by 80 percent, and the brutal Smoot-Hawley tariff ravaged other exports to America. Japanese banks, businesses, and investors fled the overvalued yen into gold and foreign currencies, some scandalously dealing on inside information. Desperate attempts to shore up the yen drained half the national specie reserve in less than a year. On 30 June 1931 the Japanese government capitulated, abandoning the gold standard and ordering companies and individuals to surrender their gold to the Bank of Japan for yen. Tokyo officially linked the yen to the pound sterling at a rate of one yen to one shilling tuppence, equivalent to U.S. 28.5 to 29.0 cents, but it plunged as low as 20.0 cents in the exchange markets before stabilizing at the official level in 1934, still 40 percent lower than the previous 48.9 cents.[30]

In 1934 the United States devalued the dollar by raising the price of gold, from its historical value of $20.67 per ounce to $35.00, in hopes of fighting the Depression through exporting. Thereafter—until 1972—the U.S. Treasury stood ready to purchase unlimited quantities of gold from foreign central banks at the new official price. Gold markets in other world financial centers maintained prices within 25 or 30 cents (the costs of physically shipping, insuring, and assaying gold bars and interest for an average of twenty days' transit) of $35 by arbitrage operations, but their capacity was small.[31]

Japan's seizure of Manchuria in September 1931 in violation of League of Nations strictures made it a pariah among nations. It lost access to international long-term lending and investment markets, which in any case lay moribund during the Depression. Yet the Japanese managed their problem deftly in the early 1930s. The government fostered heavy industry, stepped up military spending, and promoted exports of manufactured goods that held up in price better than agricultural exports. By 1933 Japan was pulling out of the Depression sooner than other countries. The gold drain halted and reserves recovered a bit.

Mobilizing Gold for War

History had taught the Japanese that they were strongest when they were strong in gold. Bullion (gold bars and coins) served as backing for the paper currency. The volume of yen currency notes issued by the Bank of Japan was limited by law to the value of its gold at the old price of $20.67, plus 1 billion yen. The gold "cover" of the yen was respectable among national currencies. At the beginning of 1937 the Bank of Japan reported it owned 13.2 million troy ounces,[32] worth at least $398 million and perhaps as much as $469 million. (U.S. analysts were uncertain about the price the bank assumed for valuation, the status of gold held by the semiofficial Banks of Taiwan and Korea, and other discrepancies.[33])

In March 1937, after a lapse of several years, the Bank of Japan resumed selling gold to the U.S. Treasury.[34] A test of other markets was found wanting when it offered a trifling $4 million of gold in London and realized only $34.17 per ounce.[35] Thereafter Japan sold only to the U.S. Treasury, typically in lots of two hundred thousand ounces (six or seven tons) delivered by fast steamer to San Francisco, where the bars were assayed and immediately purchased through the Federal Reserve Bank of that city as agent for the Treasury. Japanese officials notified U.S. agencies whenever a cargo sailed.[36] During the spring of 1937 Japan delivered about $15 million of gold per month. American officials paid little heed. Japan needed extra dollars because prices of commodities it bought were rising and its earnings normally lagged until the spring silk crop sailed. On 23 June 1937 Allan Sproul, first vice president of the New York Fed, was assured by Mr. Araki, New York agent of the Bank of Japan, that Tokyo was not abandoning its faith in gold but merely settling an adverse trade balance and supporting the yen.[37] There was no reason for suspicion. Japan had no hidden agenda.

The situation changed abruptly after 7 July, when Japan invaded China. On 25 August 1937 the Bank of Japan announced drastic steps to mobilize gold for war. It revalued its bullion cache closer to the $35 per ounce world price, which created a bookkeeping surplus of $136 million not legally required for backing the currency. It assigned the notional gain to a Gold Fund Special Account, supposedly to act as a balance wheel for trade, for example, to be run down in the first half of a year and replenished in the second half to counteract seasonal receipts for silk and payments for cotton. In fact, the Gold Fund Special Account was a war reservoir. Japan rapidly drained it to buy war commodities (chart 8). From 25 August to 31 December 1937, a period when Japan ought to have enjoyed a seasonal trade surplus, gold exports, entirely from the new fund, accelerated to as much as $40–45 million per month.

CHART 8 **Bank of Japan Special Gold Account, 1937–1941**

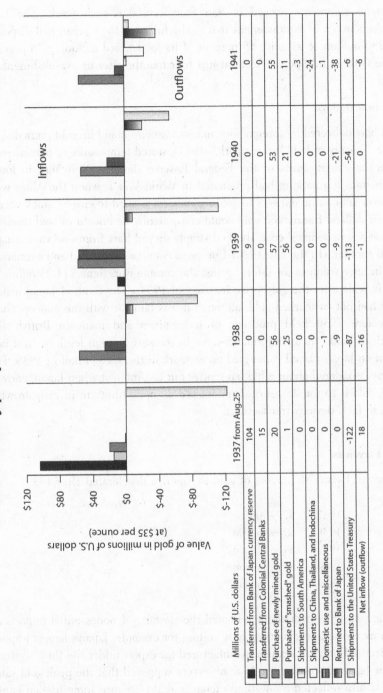

Value of gold in millions of U.S. dollars (at $35 per ounce)

Millions of U.S. dollars	1937 from Aug.25	1938	1939	1940	1941
Transferred from Bank of Japan currency reserve	104	0	9	0	0
Transferred from Colonial Central Banks	15	0	0	0	0
Purchase of newly mined gold	20	56	57	53	55
Purchase of "smashed" gold	1	25	56	21	11
Shipments to South America	0	0	0	0	-3
Shipments to China, Thailand, and Indochina	0	0	0	0	-24
Domestic use and miscellaneous	0	-1	0	0	-1
Returned to Bank of Japan	0	-9	-9	-21	-38
Shipments to the United States Treasury	-122	-87	-113	-54	-6
Net inflow (outflow)	18	-16	-1	0	-6

Survey of the Gold Fund Special Account, c. August 1945, File Japan Gold and Silver, Box 21, OASIA.

Nineteen shipments arrived in San Francisco, one each week. The U.S. observers noted in astonishment that in the full year 1937 Japan had disposed of $250 million of its gold, 55 percent of its total hoard including 76 percent of the Gold Fund Special Account just four months after its establishment.[38]

Gold into Dollars

Gold bars delivered by foreign government agencies could be sold immediately to the Treasury or held "on earmark," that is, stored temporarily or permanently in the basement vaults of the Federal Reserve Bank of New York in lower Manhattan. Earmarking had originated in World War I, when the Allies worried over submarine dangers to gold cargoes yet wished to ensure quick access to their dollars. Earmarked gold could conveniently be bought or sold immediately at a few pennies' cost; the Fed simply moved bars from one vault chamber to another. (In the late 1930s European countries both sold and earmarked gold in huge volumes for safety against the coming war, some $11.25 *billion* in the six years after the gold price increase of 1934.) The Bank of Japan historically had not earmarked gold, although it was familiar with the concept, having before 1930 held proceeds of indemnities and loans in British and American banks as an informal reserve to reassure foreign lenders. In a rare exception Japan placed some gold on earmark in the second half of 1939. Fed analysts wondered about a hidden motive but lost interest when Japan, early in 1940, sold it to the Treasury. They missed an opportunity to investigate what were, in fact, devious transactions.

Gold Forecasts

As shown, Japan's shipments of gold to America decelerated after 1937:

1937	$264 million
1938	$169 million
1939	$166 million
1940	$112 million
Total	$711 million[39]

The year-by-year declines reflected the slashing of nonessential imports as Japan moved to a war footing. Raw cotton, for example, Japan's largest import, was licensed only for textiles manufactured for export under the "link" system, not for Japanese consumers. U.S. observers supposed that the peak gold sales of 1937 also reflected a one-time exchange drain because some foreign banks declined to renew short-term trade financing due to concerns about Japan's credit standing.[40] Some in Washington believed that by 1939 Japan had achieved most of its objectives in China and was scaling down operations, reducing its need for war materiel.[41]

CHART 9 **Japan's Gold and Dollars Assets, 1937–1941**

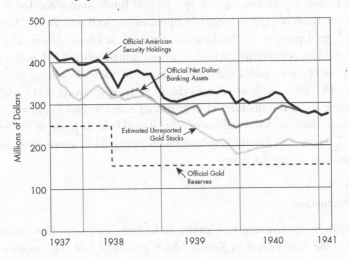

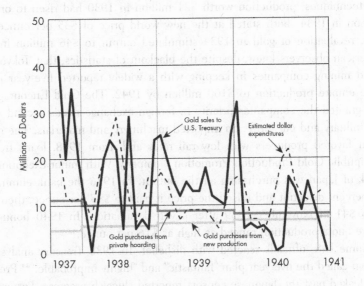

FRBNY, chart, 13 February 1941, File Japan Gold and Silver 1928–1954, Box 50, International Subject Files, 1907 to 1974, Federal Reserve Board of Governors, International Finance Division and Predecessors 1907–1974, RG 82, NA.

On 13 July 1938, after exhaustion of the Gold Fund Special Account, Japan enacted a second law to mobilize its gold for war. It placed $95 to $98 million (the value depending on the exchange rate assumed) in the Special Fund for Foreign Exchange, which was intended for conversion into overseas currencies, ostensibly to smooth out peaks and valleys in foreign transactions due to timing. Operations of both special gold funds were shrouded in secrecy, unlike the Bank of Japan's continuing publication well into World War II of its "official" gold position for backing the currency at home. American observers called the two mysterious caches, endowed initially with $231 million, "unreported" or "secret" gold funds and guessed at their dwindling size as time passed. The 1937–40 gold sales to the U.S. Treasury worth $711 million had been *three times* the quantity of gold placed into the two funds and substantially more than the $462 million of official gold held in Japan at the beginning of 1937. Japan had clearly acquired much new gold in those years (chart 9). U.S. analysts wondered how.[42]

Gold Production

The Japanese government was known to be bending every effort to mine gold in the home islands and in Korea, which produced half the empire's gold in the 1930s. Success had been elusive. Despite the introduction of modern mining techniques, production worth $21 million in 1930 had risen to only $29 million in 1934 (both stated at the new world price of $35 per ounce). The U.S. revaluation of gold in 1934 stimulated output to $46 million in 1936. American observers knew, despite the blackout of statistics, that Tokyo subsidized mining companies in keeping with a widely reported five-year plan to raise empire production to $100 million by 1942. The Gold Encouragement Act granted the companies priority in foreign exchange needs second only to the military and cut tariffs on imported machinery and materials. The government favored producers with low rail rates and, from 1938, loans from the semipublic Gold Production Promotion Company. With minor exceptions, the Bank of Japan was purchasing all the output. In 1936 the bank eliminated a 21 percent discount and raised the price it paid to $35 per ounce, then raised it to $41 in November 1939 after a yen devaluation. In 1940 bonuses for above-quota production ranged as high as $16 per ounce.[43]

Some U.S. officials reacted with disbelief. In 1938 Treasury analyst P. S. Brown called the five-year plan "fantastic" and "highly improbable."[44] Press stories leaked past the Japanese censors reported sluggish progress. For example, mining subsidies paid were a mere $3 million in 1940 and $6 million in

1941.[45] American skeptics reckoned deliveries to the Bank of Japan at not more than $58 million per year, far below the slope of the five-year plan. Independent estimates by the U.S. Mint, the Bank for International Settlements in Switzerland, and metal trade associations were similarly low. The Japanese minister of finance acknowledged that production was disappointing.[46] American guesses about Manchukuoan production ranged from a low of $4 or $5 million to a figure well advanced toward a rumored goal of $50 million in 1942.[47] But rumors of a giant ore discovery on Formosa were not credible, and in China not much gold was acquired despite lurid reports of extortion and looting.[48] Some analysts thought that smugglers in Korea and Manchukuo skimmed off gold that never reached the bank.[49] Some gold was legitimately resold to Japanese industries and arts, which consumed $13 million worth annually before the invasion of China, for manufacturing spinnerettes (nozzles for squirting the chemical slurry that hardened into rayon thread), fountain pen nibs, watches, ornaments, gold leaf, and for dentistry. Some U.S. analysts ignored the internal consumption and some suspected small reductions, but the Treasury correctly assumed a 75 percent cut in use due to reduced rayon output and laws that forbade new golden ornaments. The actual four-year average consumption of $6 million went mostly into "public health," that is, dentistry.[50]

Although they discounted extreme rumors, most U.S. evaluators were unduly impressed by Japanese gold production ambitions. In 1937 and 1938 their guesses centered on $60 million of output per year, which was close to the truth. However, as embassy attachés and commercial travelers forwarded gossip of energetic efforts, they escalated to a consensus of $72 million. League of Nations reports were similarly inflated. A few U.S. experts, frustrated by the inexplicably large gold deliveries to the U.S. Treasury, grasped at estimates as high as $84 to $92 million in 1940 and a four-year 1937–40 total production of $300 million. In their perplexity they missed the negative factors. Labor, materials, and technicians were in short supply. Mines waited two years for machinery and electric motors. Indeed, new mines in Korea stalled while electric power lines were strung and sixty thousand laborers were recruited. In the home islands 40 percent of all gold was recovered as a byproduct of copper mining, which failed to expand much.[51] Harry Dexter White, the most senior prewar analyst, wrote a memo for Morgenthau early in 1941 that assumed Japan's 1937–40 gold output at $269 million, or $67 million per year, and projected $78 million in the current year.[52] The facts, discovered after World War II, reveal that Japan fell short. From 1937 to 1940 output in Japan and the colonies averaged $58.5 million per year, peaking at

$63 million in 1939. Manchukuo produced negligible amounts.[53] The Americans had overestimated empire production by $35 to $65 million, or up to one year's output.

A word about silver. U.S. money analysts correctly viewed it as unimportant. In 1935 the Japanese government sold in London $64 million of silver to offset a trade deficit, but it was a one-time disposition of coins that had been replaced by base-metals coinage and perhaps some silver acquired in China. Empire silver production (half of it byproducts of base metals, and a bit from Korea) was only $3 to $5 million in most years, part of which was consumed by domestic industries and only a small amount exported.[54]

Smashed Gold

Curiously, the inflated American assumptions of gold-mining success were offset by underestimates of an unusual second source of gold: the private treasures of the Japanese people for melting, or "smashed gold" as the term was translated into English.[55] In 1937 Tokyo began exhorting citizens and foreigners to turn in coins, rings, jewelry, and plate in exchange for yen. (Exempted were rayon spinnerettes, fountain pens, badges, monograms, medical needles, and articles hard to extract gold from, including teeth.)[56] Three to 4 million people owned some gold, according to censuses. Many responded patriotically; 1.2 million Japanese surrendered gold in the summer of 1939 alone.[57] Jewelry disappeared from shop windows. The U.S. embassy called it a "pseudo collection actually a confiscation of holdings cloaked in patriotic garb," but although the laws prohibited private sales of gold, they stopped short of actual seizure.

The results were secret. U.S. onlookers were slow to credit success. They reckoned old coins hoarded by the public since gold standard days at $10 million and scrap generated by arts and industries at $5 or $6 million a year. But as collection of smashed gold got under way a U.S. consular officer guessed it might reach $30 million by the end of 1939. In 1940 reports filtering back upped the Treasury's guess to $45 million. By late 1940 cumulative estimates zoomed to $71 million. In the end a "confidential source" cited by the Federal Reserve that reported $122 million was closest to the truth, although analysts dismissed the source's belief that another $200 million of gold vessels remained in private hands. Some officials wondered if currency-backing bullion transferred by the Bank of Japan to the two special funds for foreign trade was replaced by artistic treasures that were not actually melted down. In fact, the Japanese government acquired $103 million of smashed gold altogether, 7 percent of which was from the colonies. Suspicions to the contrary, very little was collected in China. In 1941 it rounded up a further $8 million, and $8 million during the war when it was not needed. The smashed gold harvest was $30 to $50 million above typical U.S. guesses. Fortuitously, the American exaggeration of mine output was offset by the underestimation of treasure collection. Nevertheless, gold acquisitions did not fully explain Japan's financial resilience. Intelligence gatherers had to look elsewhere.

Foreign Securities

Among possible sources of hard currency for war were the foreign securities owned by Japanese banks, companies, and individuals.[58] Since 1933 the Ministry of Finance had required them to report holdings. U.S. observers expected Tokyo to sequester the securities, sell them overseas, and compensate their owners with yen. Sequestration was a common practice among nations preparing for and waging World War II.[59] How much hard currency Japan might realize was far from clear, however. The Japanese had not historically invested much in portfolios of foreign marketable securities.

Federal Reserve officials attempted to assess holdings from Japanese reports and their own guesses at liquidation values. In 1934 a survey published by the Diet in Tokyo had reported that the Japanese owned $152 million of foreign securities. In April 1937 the figure rose to $197 million, largely bonds of foreign governments and government-controlled entities, with lesser amounts of other bonds and stocks. Results thereafter were kept secret. The published censuses did not, however, distinguish holdings by currency or country of issue. U.S. experts squabbled over the sum Japan might actually realize by selling whatever securities it might commandeer. George C. Haas of the Treasury calculated $80 million realizable by arbitrarily assuming lower holdings than reported and forced sales that would garner only 50 percent of quoted market prices. Later E. F. Lamb of the New York Fed accepted full Japanese figures and assumed discounts of only 20 to 33 percent to arrive at an extravagant $145–154 million realizable. In May 1939 the State Department's George Luthringer split the difference and guessed at $120 million realizable.

The analyses were far off the mark. Tokyo's Department of Finance figure of $197 million "was said to exclude" Chinese and Manchukuoan paper, a doubtful assumption in view of the big increase from 1934 to 1937, when Japan invested heavily in those regions and not much elsewhere. The officially stated holdings were translated at the pre-1931 yen exchange value of 49.8 cents. At the new rate of 28–29 cents the nominal value would have been closer to $120 million. Finally, the assumed market discounts were far too sanguine. New York Fed economist Emilio G. Collado, seeing no transactions reported there or in London, observed that large sales would have shown up in Japanese bank balances abroad. As no such buildup was evident, he surmised that most Japanese holdings were not truly liquidatable, especially in prevailing weak markets.

U.S. analysts also attempted to tabulate Japanese ownership of U.S. securities directly. (Investments in European and other non-yen-bloc issues were thought to be small because trade with Japan was relatively small.) The U.S. Bureau of Foreign and Domestic Commerce estimated in June 1937 by a sampling survey that the Japanese held $48 million of American securities. But most bonds of that era were issued as anonymous "bearer" certificates that could be resold through brokers and dealers to anonymous new owners not registered on the books of the issuing governments or companies. In December, Harry White and Archie Lochead, technical assistant to Morgenthau, threw up their hands after consulting Treasury bond subscription lists, corporate registries, tax returns of Japanese branches in the United States, and Commerce Department data, and guessed wildly that the Japanese held somewhere between $55 and $125 million U.S. securities. They contemplated sending Internal Revenue Service auditors to branches of Japanese banks and firms but feared triggering a sudden flight out of dollars into sterling. Adding to the bafflement, in 1939 Japanese bank branches bought $66 million U.S. Treasury bills but sold them by October 1940.

On 25 February 1941 White took a fresh look and reported to Morgenthau that in 1937–39 Japan had liquidated $17 million of American issues (bought $50 million, sold $67 million). He concluded, "It is therefore not unlikely that Japan has recently divested itself entirely of holdings in American securities." He was almost right. A special census of foreign investments in the United States later in 1941 disclosed that on 14 June Japanese bank agencies in the United States held U.S. securities worth only $11.7 million (including a small amount held in custody for non-Japanese), of which $7 million were U.S. Treasuries and $4 million were stocks. The figures were virtually identical to Japanese assets seized after Pearl Harbor. By October 1941, when the census data were fully tabulated, it no longer mattered because Japanese assets in the United States had been frozen. No definitive estimate of dollars raised by Japan from liquidating securities was made by U.S. analysts. The likely sum may have been between $36 million (the 1937 Commerce Department survey of $48 million less $12 million left behind) and White's minimum 1937 guess of $55 million.

Japanese Foreign Currency Bonds

Another class of hard-currency securities seemed potentially an even larger dollar source but was in reality of slight value to Tokyo's war chest. These were bonds denominated in foreign currencies that Japanese governments and companies had sold abroad before 1931 that had been repurchased by the Japanese.[60] In 1936 Japanese investors owned registered holdings of $275 million par value of bonds denominated in dollars, sterling, or French francs that had been floated by their own government to finance the Russo-Japanese War, earthquake reconstruction, colonial development, and other purposes, and by cities, utilities, corporations, and banks. It was "fairly well known" that unreported holdings were also large. In the 1930s Japanese investors, fearing further yen devaluations but restricted by laws from buying foreign securities, had snapped up the bulk of such hard-currency bonds from overseas owners. Press stories, considered accurate, reported that $220 million worth had passed into Japanese hands between 1930 and 1936. These bonds appealed especially to the Japanese when they fell in price after Japan's ostracism from foreign investment circles following the seizure of Manchuria. Issues bearing 6 to 7 percent interest coupons traded at cheap prices to yield 11 percent or more per annum to buyers in an era when U.S. and British bonds yielded about 3 percent. It was a handsome return even though Japanese buyers had to surrender their semiannual hard-currency interest coupons for yen.

In theory Tokyo could have sequestered the old external bonds from its banks and citizens and resold them overseas. Fifteen such issues were quoted on the New York Stock Exchange and some on the London, Paris, or Berlin exchanges. But trading volume was negligible. By late 1937 small trades were executed only rarely in New York, at discounts of 50 to 77 percent from par value. In 1938 minor lots in London sold at a 36 to 50 percent discount. In the view of the State Department's George Luthringer, forced sales in quantity might fetch only 20 or 25 percent of par value, still a significant number approaching $70 million. Haas of the Treasury scoffed. Surreptitious sales might gradually raise $25 million, he thought, a mere 6 cents per dollar of par value, but large volumes would destroy prices altogether. Luthringer later accepted the $25 million guess. In December 1938 Lamb of the Federal Reserve deemed any realization whatsoever "questionable" and eliminated Japanese external securities from his calculations. Harry Dexter White did likewise in his February 1941 summation to Morgenthau. Japan's war chest gained no discernible dollars from remarketing ancient bonds.

Business Investments Abroad

Japanese direct investments in the United States, although more visible than portfolio holdings, were minor and of little help to the Japanese war chest.[61] Unlike the American manufacturing and real estate interests of British and European firms, Japanese companies had merely established branch banks and shipping offices to assist their foreign trade. To a lesser extent, they opened small wholesale and retail operations serving the emigrant communities in Hawaii and California. Japanese enterprises accounted for only 1.5 percent of foreign direct investments in the United States. (Investments in other non–yen-bloc countries were considered insignificant by American analysts, and in any case not convertible to dollars after 1939.) In 1937 the Commerce Department evaluated Japanese-owned U.S. businesses at $41 million. The Treasury widened the range to $25 to $50 million because of uncertainties, but in fact, the Commerce number was accurate. The special U.S. census of June 1941 reckoned the capital of firms that were at least 25 percent Japanese-owned at $35 million. This included $19 million in subsidiaries and branches of large trading houses, $11 million in branches of five banks, and $5 million in shipping and miscellaneous businesses and hundreds of small wholesalers and retailers. In 1942, after the businesses were seized, the U.S. Alien Property Custodian valued their assets at $61 million, a figure close to the prewar range of estimates because it did not deduct liabilities to report net worth.

U.S. watchers felt untroubled at prospects of Japan raising liquid dollars by divesting American businesses. In May 1940 Herbert Feis, the State Department's economic adviser, recommended controlling repatriations of Japanese capital in retaliation for similar controls imposed on American operations in Japan. But the narrowly specialized Japanese branch operations were of no value to others and, in any case, the U.S. government would learn soon enough of any dispositions if it wished to intervene. In a rare exception, two long-established insurance companies, Tokio Marine and Meiji Fire, sold their American branches to U.S. insurers in September 1940. Repatriation to Japan of their free surplus, $5 million after conservative reserves for losses, drew no U.S. opposition until a final $1 million remittance was held up on 9 July 1941 at State Department suggestion and later trapped by the freeze.

Devisen

Japan's most elusive external foreign assets were its bank deposits in foreign money centers. Bank deposits and short-term liquid securities were known as *devisen* (a German word from old French for "dividing line"). Demand deposits in banks were extremely fluid, subject to withdrawal or transfer at a moment's notice, hard to trace, and easily disguised by convoluted transactions and false names. Balances gyrated day to day in response to movements of trade and gold. Deposits could be invested at a moment's notice in Treasury bills or short-term commercial paper and just as quickly resold for cash or pledged as collateral for loans. Japanese devisen operations confounded U.S. observers, who wondered why their doomsday forecasts failed to materialize year after year.

Japan's devisen were centralized in the Yokohama Specie Bank, nominally a privately owned institution but in fact subject to government dictates. Founded in 1880, the Specie Bank maintained a web of branches in Japanese ports, Far Eastern trade centers, and financial capitals in the Americas and Europe. Its agency branch at 120 Broadway in lower Manhattan was established the same year it was founded. Other branches and subbranches did business in Los Angeles, Seattle, San Francisco, and Honolulu. The latter two operated as locally chartered banks offering personal checking accounts and services to Japanese immigrants and others—the Honolulu branch with deposits of $10 million was Hawaii's second largest bank—and interest-bearing time deposits for U.S. businesses, including the movie industry. The San Francisco branch assisted administratively in moving Japanese gold bars from arriving ships through the assay procedure at the U.S. Mint. But Japanese West Coast branches, having total deposits of only $5 to $7 million, were irrelevant to Japan's massive financial mobilization. Japanese commercial banks, notably the Sumitomo Bank, maintained seven branches on the West Coast and in New York, but they too played insignificant roles in management of Japan's devisen.

Although Japan was a pariah to long-term lenders after 1931, short-term trade finance was another matter entirely. Japanese commerce outside the yen bloc floated on a sea of hard-currency acceptance financing, a credit technique ideally suited for goods that moved across broad expanses of space and time and were quoted on commodity exchanges. Before World War I Japan had financed 75 percent of its foreign trade through London. War turmoil induced a shift to New York. The Federal Reserve Act of 1913 had, fortuitously, authorized American banks to "accept" bills of exchange, that is, to promise to honor commercial obligations generated by foreign trade. In those days a seller prepared the instrument of payment, the draft. (In modern open-account sales a buyer prepares the payment by check or electronic transfer.) Major American banks that "accepted" drafts ensured ready financing of foreign trade at interest rates as low as 3 percent per annum and bank fees as low as one-quarter of 1 percent. Bales of raw silk, for example, unloaded at Seattle or Vancouver, were whisked by super-clean express trains to East Coast warehouses and ultimately delivered to the hosiery mills of New Jersey and Pennsylvania. Control of the bales passed successively to common-carrier shiplines, railroads, and warehouse companies, whose documents provided excellent collateral for bankers. Take the following example. A Japanese trading firm, say, Mitsui Bussan Kaisha, loaded raw silk it bought from up-country filatures aboard a vessel in Yokohama. Mitsui drew a draft at "ninety days usance" on its American customer, say, the trading firm of E. Gerli and Company in New York. It attached the steamship bill of lading and presented all the papers to the Specie Bank's home office in Yokohama, which forwarded them to its New York agency by fast steamer or, after mid-1935, by Pan American flying boat. The Specie Bank agency in New York then presented the draft to Gerli, who wrote "accepted" across the face and signed it, obligating it to pay dollars to Mitsui in New York when it matured ninety days after it was created. When the silk arrived in New York, it was consigned to a bonded warehouse. Gerli executed a "trust receipt," in effect legally acting as trustee for the Specie Bank agency. The bank allowed him access to the bales for testing their quality and delivery to the ultimate customer, a hosiery mill, which paid Gerli thirty days after it received the silk. When the ninety-day draft matured, Gerli paid the Specie Bank agency in New York, which credited the account of Mitsui's U.S. branch for the benefit of Mitsui's home office, completing the transaction.

The Yokohama Specie Bank in New York, however, was not capitalized amply enough to finance three months of U.S. raw silk imports, about $30 million, nor did Mitsui in this example wish to finance U.S. importers or knitting mills. In practice the Specie Bank agency accepted the draft, pledging to honor it at maturity, which transformed it from Gerli's IOU into a "bankers acceptance," albeit of less than stellar quality and not readily saleable at the best price as it was not a major U.S. bank. Therefore the Specie Bank agency requested a prominent New York bank, say, the National City or Chase, to add its own acceptance. For a small fee, the large bank converted the instrument into a triple-A rated prime bankers acceptance (still backed by the bales as collateral), which could be sold immediately for cash at a small discount in the New York money market.

The three-month-long string of transactions relieved sellers and buyers on both sides of the Pacific, including some that might not be creditworthy, of the burden of tying up their capital in silk inventories. All parties received payment swiftly. In a similar manner, Japanese purchases of cotton and other U.S.

quoted commodities were financed by acceptances, with dollars flowing in the opposite direction. Acceptance financing was a necessity for Japanese firms purchasing raw cotton in the southern United States and advancing it through spinning and weaving in Japan, delivery of textiles to East Asia, and collection from customers there, a cycle about eight months long.

Even with smooth acceptance financing, however, the Yokohama Specie Bank's New York agency needed dollars to settle differences of inflows and outflows caused by shipping schedules, trade imbalances among countries, and the seasonality of spring silk crops and autumn cotton crops. When Japan abandoned the gold standard in December 1931 and linked the yen to the pound sterling, much of its trade financing returned temporarily to the London market. Japanese displeasure over Britain's prompting the League of Nations to denounce the takeover of Manchuria did not extend to shunning "The City." During the difficult Depression years London was more adept at handling transactions among third countries, whereas American bankers customarily handled trade directly involving a U.S. buyer or seller.

Japan's devisen resources were a mystery to U.S. analysts. One or two guessed that the Specie Bank and its branches needed $100 million of hard currency to facilitate Japanese international transactions. Yet of the bank's publicly reported holdings in mid-1937 of $135 million of *all* foreign exchange, three-fourths was apparently inconvertible Manchukuoan and puppet Chinese government money, implying only $35 million in dollars, sterling, and other hard currencies. Other large Japanese banks held $12 million. The official composite figures of all Japanese banks were similarly awkward; foreign exchange assets in the vicinity of $200 million suggested $50 million of hard currency. Reported New York deposits fluctuated between $1 and $10 million, implying that London was indeed the focal point of Japanese trade finance, an impression heightened by a swap into sterling of proceeds of some gold sales in the United States in 1937.

Upon the start of the war in China, Japan shifted back to dollar trade credit. It was a practical decision. Japanese gold was regularly sold to the U.S. Treasury, war-related commodities were available mainly in the United States, and British bankers were quick to tighten credit terms as the British and European empires husbanded war materials and clamped down on currency exchanges. By the end of 1937 Japan's sterling balances, equivalent to $10 to $20 million, were below its global trade needs, whereas excess sales of gold lifted New York balances to $50 million, 70 percent of it in the Specie Bank's agency. The flight from London concluded in late 1939. Just before declaring war on Germany, Great Britain let the pound decline and imposed controls that effectively rendered sterling inconvertible into dollars, the currency Japan coveted. In November 1939 Japan severed the yen's link to sterling and devalued the yen in parallel with sterling's devaluation of August 1939 to a new yen-dollar cross rate of 23.4 cents. Wisely acting before British exchange control solidified, Japan repatriated its remaining funds, perhaps as much as $20 million, from London to New York.[62]

Officials in the U.S. Treasury and Federal Reserve had made little sense of Japan's fluctuating dollar positions. In 1940, however, they felt they could better track Japan's devisen because the New York branch of the Specie Bank had become, de facto, the overseas marshaling yard of Japan's liquid assets. It was required, like all banking entities operating in the United States, to report to the Bank Examinations Department of its district Federal Reserve Bank the accounts and balances it held for non-U.S. individuals, firms, and government agencies, some of the information weekly, some monthly, and some semiannually. The reports were not as informative as might be desired. The most complete one, a semiannual report due several months after the period ended, lumped together the accounts of "All Asia." Japan was the largest constituent, but the Specie Bank agency also held assets of the governments of Manchukuo and the puppet Chinese Nanking regime. The Federal Reserve classified these, and the Bank of Japan's accounts, as "official" but deemed the deposits of the Specie Bank's own home office and its sister branches as "private" because the Specie Bank system was legally, though not in reality, a commercial bank enterprise.

From 1938 to 1940 Japan's dollar bank balances fluctuated beyond the range American analysts expected from observing trade figures and gold sales. Balances generally seemed to shrink in line with a Treasury belief that U.S. banks were tightening credit to a country of suspect worthiness and demanding shorter usance (maturity) of drafts they still accepted. In June 1938 the Commerce Department advised U.S. exporters to obtain a confirmed irrevocable letter of credit, a form of bank pledge to ensure payment of bills, before filling Japanese orders, further constraining short-term trade financing. Longer-dated credit for machinery exports had practically dried up. The Specie Bank's New York balances had, therefore, peaked at the end of 1937 at $50 to $55 million, reflecting Japan's large gold sales late that year, then bottomed counterseasonally at $20 million early the next year. In 1938 the Specie Bank agency raised $72 million by borrowing against Treasury securities it had bought with the Bank of Japan's excess gold proceeds, but the securities and the loan were liquidated later in the year to take care of seasonal trade swings. New York balances ended the year at $43 million, a normal figure. U.S. analysts saw no reason to worry that Japan was building a war chest of dollars. They were wrong.

No Freeze Contemplated

Between the "quarantine" and *Panay* episodes of late 1937 and early 1941, nobody in Washington again suggested a policy so drastic as freezing Japan's money by invoking the Trading with the Enemy Act. The financial bureaucrats in Washington and New York expected that Japan would run short of dollars and, of necessity, halt the attack on China. U.S. leaders from time to time inquired, rather naïvely, whether the United States ought to try to hinder Japan's aggression by refusing to purchase its gold. The experts always answered that it would be futile and would harm the United States more than Japan. In October 1937 White and Haas explained to Morgenthau that Japan could dispose of gold on the London market at a slight extra cost and swap the proceeds into dollars. Even if Britain cooperated with the United States, other countries would gladly trade gold for a small spread. In August 1939 Roosevelt himself inquired if the United States could restrict its gold purchasing to friendly nations. "What is your slant on this?" he asked. Treasury officials and lawyers replied that the origins of gold bars were easy to conceal and their movements difficult to trace. Japan could sell to other countries at a trivial discount, and the United States could not feasibly refuse gold from those countries. Any notion of cutting the official global price in order to harm Japan was even more absurd. A fixed price and free movement were bedrock principles for the United States, holder of most of the world's monetary gold.[63] Any restriction at all, White wrote, "cannot help but have some adverse psychological influence on the usefulness and sacredness of gold as a medium of international payments." It would unnerve holders and destroy gold's prestige. Even though the outbreak of war in September 1939 shut down European and British gold markets so that Japan could sell only to the United States, it was far better policy, Morgenthau's staff believed, to pressure Japan by commodity embargoes—the strategy the United States had, in fact, already begun to pursue.[64]

Discovery of the Fraud

On 3 August 1940 a New York Federal Reserve official, Walter Rozell, noticed a transaction in a report filed by the New York agency of the Yokohama Specie Bank that triggered an alarm in his mind.[65] Thus began the unmasking of a devious Japanese scheme to hide a war chest of more than $100 million in New York under the noses of U.S. watchdogs. In the next few months, as facts came to light, officials' reactions ranged from anger at banking laws violated to embarrassment over foolish predictions of imminent Japanese bankruptcy and, finally, a resolve to block Japan from spending its secret American hoard, and any future dollars it might acquire, for war preparations. Experts peering through direct windows overlooking Japan's gold sales and dollar movements had glibly predicted its financial exhaustion. In fact, Japan had gulled them by secreting a cache large enough to fund a long war against China and to prepare for possible war against the United States. After its scheme was revealed, Japan realized the game was up. It scrambled to spend its dollar hoard, or remove it to safety, before the guillotine of a financial freeze descended (chapters 8 and 14). Belated knowledge of the secret reserve wrecked the confident predictions of the American financial officials. Their interest in potent financial controls soon revived. Meanwhile, an alternative bureaucracy was far advanced in imposing on Japan an alternative form of sanctions: the embargoing of exports of strategic raw materials.

Birth of an Embargo Strategy

THE ALTERNATIVE TO BANKRUPTING JAPAN

U ntil the summer of 1941 the United States declined to deploy its most powerful economic sanction against Japan, dollar freezing. In the meanwhile, beginning as early as 1935, it sought to regulate its position as the world's most important supplier of materials for war. The first steps, taken at a time when Japan was not yet an aggressor in China, were aimed at keeping the United States from being drawn into another foreign war. Later steps were taken by so-called voluntary means and by executive orders to ensure that the nation's exports did not support Japanese aggression in China.

The 1935 Neutrality Act

The United States' initial step was the Neutrality Act of 1935. Hitler was consolidating his power in Germany, Italy was about to attack Ethiopia, and a disarmament conference at Geneva had failed. Congressional isolationists proposed legislation to avoid a war trap by restricting exports of munitions to countries engaged in war. In response to their concern, Senator Key Pittman of Nevada sponsored the Neutrality Act, which was passed by joint resolution of Congress and signed by President Roosevelt on 31 August 1935. The act forbade export of "arms, ammunition or implements of war," directly or through third countries, to any nation at war. It banned U.S. ships from transporting arms to belligerents, prohibited Americans from sailing as passengers on their ships, and closed U.S. ports to their warships. Munitions-producing firms were obliged to register with the secretary of state and to list their products. A

National Munitions Control Board consisting of five cabinet secretaries and chaired by the secretary of state was charged with promulgating regulations and administration. Although *all* arms exports required licenses from the Department of State, the act did not target Japan because licenses were automatically granted for arms sales to neutrals for their own use, and Japan was not yet at war.

FDR, advised by the Munitions Control Board, defined six categories of exports subject to licensing, with a focus on air power that became a theme of U.S. policy in the next few years. Weapons were self-evident: rifles, machine guns, cannon, and ammunition; bombs, naval mines, and torpedoes; tanks and armored cars; warships of all kinds; poison gas; and aircraft designed to carry guns or bombs along with weapons mounts and racks. Category IV, however, extended the list to *all* aircraft, engines, propellers, and parts, whether or not adaptable for combat, reflecting a special sensitivity to the bombing of civilians. (Ships and vehicles convertible to combat were not limited.)

Roosevelt wished for flexibility to embargo munitions sales to aggressor states, perhaps in concert with League of Nations sanctions, while allowing sales to victimized countries. But congressional sponsors feared that doing business with one side only, as in 1914–17, was inherently dangerous. They insisted on evenhandedness in order to "take the profits out of war." FDR was busy with New Deal legislation and did not resist. He settled for an amendment limiting the term of the act to six months. The Neutrality Act also authorized the president to determine whether a conflict was actually a war. In October 1935 he proclaimed that a war existed between Italy and Ethiopia and imposed an evenhanded munitions embargo. Mussolini was the aggressor and little inconvenienced because ordinary commodities such as oil were not restricted, but landlocked Ethiopia could not acquire anything. The 1935 act was irrelevant to Japan, then at peace, but it signaled U.S. leanings toward avoiding dangers by refusing to help powers that went to war.[1]

The 1937 Neutrality Act

After a 1936 amendment (chapter 2), on 1 May 1937 Congress extended the Neutrality Act for two more years and further amended it. A cruel civil war had erupted in Spain, drawing in several European powers. The new act empowered Roosevelt to impose arms and shipping embargoes against those parties in a civil war that might "threaten or endanger the peace of the United States." Significantly for Japan, Congress instructed the president to identify products that could be used to manufacture armaments abroad, and to forbid sales of them to belligerents if exports would also impair the security or peace of the United States or threaten its citizens. The amendments also strengthened registration and licensing of munitions firms and, oddly, required licenses for *import* of munitions.

The 1937 act introduced a concept that indirectly allowed the president to favor one warring power over another. One professor of political science called it "qualified neutrality," but Hull called it a "neutrality disaster." The law prohibited U.S. ships from carrying munitions, or the materials for making them, to any country at war. Exports of other products to them could continue if embarked on foreign ships and if title and control passed before they cleared from a U.S. port, the famous "cash-and-carry" rule that barred U.S. financing and carriage to war zones. In principle the rules applied to all sides, aggressors and victims alike. In practice it was evident that Britain and France, having large merchant fleets, command of the sea, and reserves of dollars and gold would retain de facto access to U.S. products during a war against Germany or Italy while those Axis powers would not. Japan was not targeted by the May 1937 act—its attack on China lay two months in the future—but in case of war the same advantages of shipping, sea control, and money would ensure it of access to U.S. supplies while China would be denied. What Congress would not do explicitly, tolerate the favoring of one side in a war, it did indirectly. When in July Japan attacked China, American sympathy was entirely with the beleaguered Chinese. Given the perverse logic of an evenhanded munitions embargo and cash-and-carry, Roosevelt declined to label the conflict a war, because a mandatory arms embargo would have harmed China more than Japan. For the next four years Japan continued to import and stockpile war materials (although not armaments) from the United States.[2]

Moral Embargo on Aircraft

The first constraint on an export to Japan was extralegal and exceedingly narrow. The Department of State frequently condemned attacks on U.S. interests in China, including the bombing and sinking of the naval gunboat *Panay* in the Yangtze River on 12 December 1937. (Japan apologized and paid restitution.) Hull lectured Tokyo about air raids that slaughtered Chinese civilians; the world was not yet inured to aerial devastation of entire cities. Public opinion was especially outraged because U.S.-built planes and equipment were thought to be flown by Japanese pilots. Before the invasion of China the United States annually sold to Japan less than a dozen planes of all types, worth in total $1 or $2 million including spare parts. In 1938 exports jumped to sixty-six planes, fifty-six unmounted engines, and accessories, and totaling $11 million, or 5 percent of all U.S. exports to Japan. In May 1938 public indignation rose to a crescendo after gory air raids on Canton. Hull felt inspired to take some action, but State Department counsel opined that the government could not legally embargo airplane exports without either a presidential proclamation that Japan was at war or an act of Congress. Learning of Japan's large aircraft orders, Hull told the press that the United States would "frown upon" selling any planes suitable for bombing civilians. FDR agreed. On 1 July 1938 Charles W. Yost, chief of the department's Office of Arms and Munitions Control, notified the 148 U.S. aircraft manufacturers and exporters who had registered with his office that only with "great regret" would he issue export licenses for warplanes and their munitions, without naming Japan specifically. Civil aviation parts were exempted.

Within a month the Aeronautical Chamber of Commerce, an industry trade group, reported that the "moral embargo," as it came to be called, was 95 percent effective. In 1939 the United States sold only two airplanes to Japan, and none thereafter. Parts and accessories sales declined 90 percent by 1940 and virtually ended in 1941. The aviation industry, awash in orders for U.S. civil transportation, and after late 1939 from France and Britain for war planes, did not object. But the moral embargo scarcely troubled Japan. It had produced more than one thousand planes in 1936 and was expanding toward a goal of five thousand per year.[3]

Termination of the Commercial Treaty

By 1939 majorities in both U.S. political parties leaned toward a more tangible expression of irritation toward Japan. The administration reacted by terminating a treaty that governed commercial relations. In 1911 Secretary of State Philander C. Knox and Japan's representative in Washington, "being desirous to strengthen the relations of amity and good understanding that happily exist between the two nations," had negotiated the Treaty of Commerce and Navigation. It granted each others' citizens and companies the rights and privileges of domestic commerce, freedom of ships to come and go (except coastwise trade which was accorded most-favored-nation treatment), equal travelers' rights, and mutual rights to open consulates. Export duties were to reflect "perfect equality of treatment," a meaningless provision as the United States Constitution, Article 1, Section 9, prohibited duties on exports. Import duties were not to exceed those imposed on third countries under a most-favored-nation rule. The treaty, as renewed from time to time, could be abrogated by either party on six months' notice. If terminated, the United States could legally discriminate against Japanese commerce.

On 26 July 1939, at the start of the third year of fighting in China, Secretary of State Cordell Hull served notice on Ambassador Kensuke Horinouchi that the United States would withdraw from the treaty in six months, ostensibly to reconsider the protection of its commercial interests in Asia, a reference to war damage to U.S. business operations in China. State Department lawyers advised Hull that the U.S. Code levied an automatic 10 percent duty and other charges on cargoes arriving in vessels of treatyless states. However, the president could suspend the duty if Japan did not discriminate, and, confusingly, an 1872 proclamation by President Ulysses S. Grant exempting Japan was still in effect. Tokyo was taken by surprise. Aware of U.S. public indignation and worried that the United States might label the China incident a war and invoke Neutrality Act embargoes on strategic commodities, some Japanese officials proposed a new treaty or at least a temporary stopgap agreement, while others sulkily denied any war damage. Hull shunted the proposals to Ambassador Joseph Grew in Tokyo. Tokyo pledged to reopen the Yangtze River to U.S. shipping. At the last minute Grew announced that the United States would not impose penalties when the treaty expired on 26 January 1940. Japan gratefully announced an Imperial ordinance pledging no increase of duties and most-favored-nation treatment. The administration had fired a popgun across Japan's bow. It did not yet appreciate its powers of international control of money in a world at war.[4]

The 1939 Neutrality Act

In March 1939 Hitler's troops marched into partitioned Czechoslovakia in violation of the Munich Pact, signed in 1938. As war in Europe appeared imminent, FDR called for revision of the Neutrality Act in order to aid the democracies. On 1 May the cash-and-carry provisions of the act expired. In the summer the House of Representatives voted to restore the rule, but the initiative died by one vote in the Senate Foreign Relations Committee, deferring action until 1940. On 1 September Germany invaded Poland. On 3 September Britain and France declared war. Two days later Roosevelt declared U.S. neutrality.

The three-week German-Soviet conquest of Poland shocked Congress into action. Polls showed a sharp change of public sentiment in favor of the Allies. Roosevelt mused that the United States had always championed freedom of seaborne trade with two disastrous exceptions: Jefferson's embargo of 1807–9 and the 1935 Neutrality Act. Helping the democracies, he said, would protect U.S. security and speed development of U.S. defense industries. Furthermore, in modern war distinctions between munitions and other goods were artificial—aluminum sheets became airplane wings and brass plumbing tubes became artillery shells. The president favored controlling exports of eleven strategic raw materials and restriction of iron and steel exports, but he had no legal authority to do so. The State Department opposed export controls on any commodities that clearly targeted Japan as the largest buyer.

On 21 September 1939 Roosevelt assembled Congress in special session to unblock munitions exports while retaining the cash-and-carry rule. The Allies controlled the sea and had ample money (or so it seemed at the time), whereas Germany, blockaded and cash poor, could neither buy nor carry U.S. products. Congress reacted favorably. On 4 November 1939, by large majorities, it amended the neutrality acts as requested. The United States returned to the business of selling arms to belligerent states as it had in 1914–18, but only to those who could pay cash and carry them away in their own or other foreign ships.[5]

Moral Embargoes of Metals, December 1939

The November 1939 neutrality amendment did no harm to Japan, deemed to be still at peace. Japan had dollars and ships for purchase and transport of war-related materials. Administration officials fumed over civilian suffering as the Soviets bombed Finland and Japanese air attacks in China continued unabated. The executive branch and some legislators pondered embargo laws against Japan, but the president, keeping his options open, preferred informal steps to halt materials and services explicitly for Japanese bombers. The moral embargo on aircraft had been of little consequence because Japan was self-sufficient in warplane design and production. It relied, however, in varying degrees, on U.S. metals and know-how. On 15 December 1939 the administration asked U.S. producers of three strategic metals—aluminum, magnesium, and molybdenum—voluntarily to halt exports to Japan. The United States could not imply that is was conserving for national defense as it had ample supplies of those metals.[6]

Aluminum, a metal one-third the weight of steel, constituted 80 percent of airframe weight. Before 1934 Japan had imported five thousand to ten thousand tons annually. Thereafter Tokyo launched a plan to refine aluminum at home from foreign raw materials. Imported materials, primarily bauxite ore, comprised only 12 percent of the cost of aluminum sheet. Electricity was by far the largest input, but Japan was self-sufficient, 55 percent from hydroelectric dams and the rest from domestic coal. Aluminum smelters consumed electricity voraciously, ultimately taking 25 percent of Japanese power production. As early as 1933 U.S. Army G-2 Intelligence had recommended dropping aluminum metal from lists of materials Japan would lack in a war. By 1936, two years after its first electrolytic smelter came on line, Japan was 40 percent self-sufficient in aluminum. In 1938 subsidized new plants raised output to twenty-one thousand tons. In 1939 the government took over production.

For its pre–Pacific War program of five thousand planes per year before Pearl Harbor, Japan needed about 20,000 to 30,000 tons of aluminum, depending on plane types. As Japan concentrated on bombers, planners anticipated 4.5 tons of aluminum per airplane, but inefficiencies due to wastage in cutting complex shapes from sheets and tubes raised the requirement to 6.5 to 7 tons per plane. The mobilized economy also needed aluminum for machinery, ground transportation, and especially lightweight cables to wheel electricity from mountain dams an average of three hundred miles to metal and chemical plants on the coast. (In-plant scrap was too low in quality for recycling into aircraft.) In 1937–39, therefore, Japan resumed large-scale importation of aluminum ingots and slabs, initially from Europe and Canada until war restricted those sources. In 1939, despite Japanese Empire production of almost 30,000 tons, imports rose to a peak of 36,701 metric tons.

The United States had been a negligible supplier of aluminum to Japan until it provided about 20 percent of the 1939 buying surge. Foreclosure by the moral embargo of December 1939 caused no injury to Japan's goals, nor its civilian economy, which had never consumed much aluminum and could use aircraft factory scrap for curtailed production of household goods such as pots and pans. Japan's ultimate aluminum achievements were astonishing. Production rose to 80,000 tons in 1941 and a 1944 peak of 151,000 tons, including 37,000 tons in Korea, Formosa, and Manchukuo. A deliberate U.S. and Allied attempt to slow Japanese aircraft production did not occur until the embargo of aluminum raw materials in 1941. Although the United States itself relied on foreign bauxite, Japan depended on it for two other minerals essential for aluminum smelting: fluorspar and petroleum coke (see chapter 10).[7]

Duralumin, the hard aluminum alloy preferred for airplanes, contained 1 percent magnesium along with some copper and manganese. Japan had unlimited sources of magnesium oxide from Manchukuoan deposits and from seawater. It began electrolytic refining of magnesium simultaneously with aluminum, building plants in the home islands and Korea. At the time of the moral embargo it was thought to have sufficient magnesium. Output rose to 2,559 tons in 1940. But in Europe the Germans, and soon the British, adopted alloys primarily of magnesium, 35 percent lighter than aluminum, for ailerons, turrets, castings, and landing gear. Japan lacked the magnesium capacity to emulate them, so the moral embargo of magnesium probably retarded aircraft quality. Civilian uses were negligible.[8]

Nature endowed the United States generously with molybdenum. The Climax Mine in the Colorado Rocky Mountains produced 66 percent of the world's output, and U.S. copper mines recovered a further 28 percent as a byproduct. Dissolving as little as one-quarter of 1 percent ferromolybdenum or molybdenum oxide in a steel melt, along with other alloying elements, imparted toughness and resistance to abrasion and corrosion. Tool steels for machining hard metals contained 8 to 9.5 percent molybdenum. In the late 1930s molybdenum demand from Europe and Japan flourished for guns, armor, aircraft engines, and the machine tools to manufacture them. The United States exported two-thirds of its molybdenum production. The Japanese Empire mined only tiny amounts in Korea. In 1939 Japan imported from the United States 9.4 million pounds of molybdenum concentrates worth $3.7 million, about 15 percent of U.S. output. An embargo of molybdenum was a pet project of Secretary of the Treasury Morgenthau, a friend of Harold Hochschild, whose family controlled Climax and who had lived in China. The moral embargo of molybdenum, however, was not a serious impediment. Japan had accumulated a stockpile. It could substitute other alloying elements, especially tungsten, which was mined abundantly in China. At British request, the International Nickel Company of Canada, the dominant world supplier, also stopped selling nickel to Japan, an important metal for stainless and alloy steels.[9]

Aviation Gasoline Know-How

In a follow-up moral embargo notice of 20 December 1939 the U.S. government requested American firms to make "no future delivery to certain countries," including Japan, "of plans, plants, manufacturing rights, or technical information" for aviation gasoline. Airplane engines were evolving toward higher compression ratios, that is, squeezing more gasoline and air into tighter volumes so that explosion in the cylinder exerted maximum thrust. But hotter high-compression mixtures ignited prematurely, causing "knocking" vibrations that sapped power and threatened a pilot's control. Aviation gasolines were rated by octane number, the relative content of iso-octane chemicals that retarded premature ignition. Older airplanes performed well on 72-octane fuel, but modern engines required at least 87 octane. To upgrade, refineries added to the fuel tiny amounts of tetraethyl lead, an antiknock chemical, or blended it with benzol or alcohol. The most promising solution pointed to catalytic cracking, a refinery process that exposed oil feedstock to a platinum-coated catalyst that accelerated reactions and minimized coking (clogging). In 1938 a consortium of major U.S. oil companies developed a moving-bed "platforming" process that solved the problem of mass production of high-octane gasoline.[10]

The Japan Gasoline Company, a cartel, since 1928 had been purchasing technology rights from Universal Oil Company of Illinois, a firm employing six hundred fuel specialists. Japan was eager to produce iso-octane chemicals and feedstocks to refine high-octane gasoline from California crude oil. On 31 October 1938 Japan Gasoline contracted for the rights to use Universal's refinery processes through 1946. In 1939 Universal, which designed iso-octane units for Mitsubishi Oil and Nippon Oil, sent over blueprints and American engineers. By the time Universal terminated the contract in deference to the moral embargo, the Japanese had the know-how and a stockpile of catalysts. Japan ultimately built five catalytic cracking plants with a total capacity of fifteen thousand barrels per day of high-octane gasoline. The moral embargo came too late.[11]

Futile Export Sanctions, 1935–1939

From 1935 to 1939 the United States deployed legal and extralegal export restraints, at first to shield itself from war risks but increasingly in hopes of reining in aggressors. The first actions, aimed primarily at the European Axis, impacted Japan very little. Because Roosevelt refused to label the Sino-Japanese conflict a war lest support of China also be proscribed, the neutrality laws did not much inconvenience Japan, nor did the cash-and-carry policy pose a barrier to its purchases of strategic materials. Moral embargoes did halt sales to Japan of warplanes in July 1938, and of three nonferrous metals and fuel know-how for aviation in December 1939, but they took effect after Japanese stockpiling surges, too late to do much harm to Japan's preparations for war. Abrogation of the 1911 Commercial Treaty in January 1940 was a meaningless gesture because the United States did not invoke any trade penalties. As to Japan's civilian economy, the U.S. embargo actions prior to the middle of 1940 scarcely impacted it because they inhibited only items of direct military use.

Export Controls, 1940 to Mid-1941

Until mid-1940 Washington paid little attention to trade controls as an element of national security, other than restraining munitions exports. The cabinet-level Council of National Defense, authorized in 1916, had lain neglected. Since World War I officers at the Army Industrial College had studied future raw material needs and pondered the limiting of exports of strategic commodities in an unknown emergency. In the late 1930s foreign countries bought such commodities from the United States in large quantities. Not until January 1940 did the Army-Navy Munitions Board, which was founded in 1922 to "coordinate plans for the acquisition of munitions and supplies necessary for the proper prosecution of the Army and Navy war programs," list fourteen "strategic" materials not produced in the United States and fifteen "critical" materials produced in less-than-essential amounts.

Regulating exports of strategic materials emerged first as an adjunct to domestic mobilization, not as a weapon of economic warfare to deter potential enemies. In the spring of 1940 the "phoney war" in Europe came to an end as Nazi troops conquered Norway, the Low Countries, and France. The surrender of France on 22 June shocked the U.S. government into a vigorous effort to build up neglected national defenses. Overnight, officials became obsessed with the production of ships, planes, and guns and with erecting the factories and shipyards to make them. The need to acquire, conserve, and stockpile vital resources was obvious.

In May 1940 Roosevelt set in motion two agencies to guide economic mobilization. He activated the Office of Emergency Management (OEM), which had lain dormant since he established it by an executive order in

September 1939, to serve as his "eyes and ears" for liaison with future defense agencies. He reestablished the National Defense Advisory Commission (NDAC), created by Congress in World War I. The NDAC was a purely advisory committee of industrial leaders recruited from the private sector, legally without a chairman to avoid the appearance of an omnipotent "defense czar" who might irritate isolationists, while keeping control of economic defense in FDR's hands. The president appointed to the committee six men and one woman, including two chief executive officers, who worked without salary. Edward S. Stettinius Jr. of United States Steel Corporation headed the Industrial Materials Division of the NDAC, staffed with industry recruits. It advised on raw materials and semifabricated metals and surveyed the availability of resources, plant capacities, foreign purchases, and stockpiling, but only incidentally addressed export control. William S. Knudsen of General Motors Corporation headed the Production Division, which took responsibility "at the point at which materials were cut up." As the NDAC geared up, the need of materials for defense proved to be far larger and more varied than the Army-Navy Munitions Board had expected. Waging economic war by denying resources to future enemies was not on the NDAC's agenda.[1]

Export Control Act of July 1940

On 2 July 1940, ten days after France surrendered, an alarmed Congress passed "An Act to Expedite the Strengthening of the National Defense." Four sections of the act dealt with upgrading Army posts and equipment. Section 5 authorized the president to spend up to $66 million over the next two years to procure strategic and critical materials. Of profound significance to Japan, Section 6 declared:

> Whenever the President determines that it is necessary in the interest of
> national defense to prohibit or curtail the exportation of any military equipment
> or munitions, or component parts thereof, or machinery, tools, or material, or
> supplies necessary for the manufacture, servicing or operation thereof, he may
> by proclamation prohibit or curtail such exportation, except under such rules
> and regulations as he shall proscribe.

The president's new powers were comprehensive in regard to controlling defense-related products but did not apply to most U.S. exports, and not at all to imports. They were thus far less potent than the unlimited control over foreign trade available to him had he chosen to invoke the international payments controls of the Trading with the Enemy Act instead.[2]

Complexities

Control of strategic exports evolved in uncoordinated lurches. Cordell Hull recognized that the program would trump his efforts to liberalize international trade. He settled for a sliver of authority in a new administrative hierarchy while maneuvering to restrain more adventurous agencies, in particular Morgenthau's Treasury Department, which were eager to bend export controls into a form of economic warfare against Japan. But the emergency control system had no place for financial hardliners. The United States had chosen direct control of exports, not a financial freeze.

The State Department's Office of Arms and Export Controls had been registering munitions producers under the 1935 Neutrality Act. Joseph C. Green, a fifty-three-year-old Princeton University professor who had joined the department's Western European Division in 1931, headed the office and served as secretary of the Munitions Control Board, which consisted of five cabinet members with Hull as chairman. Green gained a reputation for firmness by advising Senator Gerald Nye's Special Committee on Investigation of the Munitions Industry in its probe of arms exports. He bemoaned the absence of laws to track U.S. munitions that supplied both sides in a Cuban revolution and in the Chaco War between Bolivia and Paraguay. Du Pont sold explosives-making machinery to Japan. After Green's statement that the Versailles Treaty prohibited Germany from importing arms, the State Department informed U.S. arms dealers that it frowned on exports to the Nazi regime. However, Green had little experience in control of commodities as he was forbidden to deny export licenses. (As late as January 1940 only helium and tin scrap were generally denied licenses, no inconvenience to Japan.) In his new assignment Green took a firmer stance against Japan than most of his colleagues in the State Department by advocating more rigorous licensing, wider definitions of restricted materials, and new commodities to be banned. His assistant, Charles W. Yost, twenty years younger, had followed a similar career track as his boss—the Hotchkiss School, Princeton, and diplomatic assignments in Egypt and Poland—but he had no relevant experience.[3]

As the United States geared up for economic defense, bureaucratic turf battles flared among old-line cabinet departments and upstart emergency agencies and committees—some sixty-five were eventually identified by the Bureau of the Budget—that exercised overlapping and even contradictory powers. Roosevelt finessed the squabbling bureaucracies away from the export control function by adopting a suggestion of his confidant, Harry Hopkins. The president himself would designate commodities subject to export licensing by issuing executive orders from time to time. The actual approval or disapproval of strategic exports, he decided, was a quasi-military function that would report directly to the White House, ensuring his control.[4]

Roosevelt appointed Lt. Col. (soon Brig. Gen.) Russell Lamont Maxwell of the Army Staff Corps as administrator of export control (confusingly also known as the Export Control Administration, or ECA). Maxwell, a West Pointer, class of 1912, was a prominent expert on artillery and ammunition. After World War I he supervised an ordnance depot in occupied Germany. In 1925 he graduated from the Army Industrial College, which had been founded a year earlier to "train Army officers in the useful knowledge pertaining to the supervision of procurement of all military supplies in time of war and to the assurance of adequate provision for the mobilization of materiel and industrial organizations essential to war-time needs." Maxwell later served as ordnance officer of the Army Air Corps and ultimately as chief of the army's Planning and Equipment Bureau (G-4) with a focus on procurement of automotive and aviation materiel. In his new mission of conserving raw materials, he concentrated on recruiting a large staff to process the flood of license applications that poured in rather than grasping for authority to wage economic and financial war against Japan—at least for the first few months.[5]

In practice, Stettinius's advisory staff of the NDAC, in consultation with the Army-Navy Munitions Board, recommended to Roosevelt the commodities to be licensed by executive orders. The NDAC assigned as liaisons to the ECA W. Averell Harriman of the Industrial Materials Division and H. S. Vance of the Production Division. Recommendations on strategic materials mainly fell on the shoulders of A. I. Henderson, Harriman's assistant, who helped draft license procedures and sat on the Export Control Advisory Committee, which acted on applications from exporters. To confirm specific actions, Maxwell's team had to consult Green's tiny staff in the State Department, but Green was instructed to issue or deny licenses "in accordance with" ECA directives. Although the State Department legally retained the final say on specific licenses, in reality its role was reduced to assessing the impact of export controls on foreign relations. The Treasury Department sat on the sidelines with no say in the system.[6]

Licensed Commodities, July 1940

Maxwell's ECA swung into action, promptly issuing procedural rules for export licenses. A would-be seller of a commodity subject to licensing was required to submit a typewritten two-page application naming the product, destination, ultimate user, and specific end-use, the latter an often difficult question for the merchant to answer. The seller then mailed two copies to Green's Division

of Controls for forwarding to the ECA. If approved by the ECA and counter-
signed and impressed with the seal of the Department of State, it became a
nontransferable export license. The merchant sent the license to the Collector
of Customs at the appropriate port prior to a cargo's sailing. A customs officer
filled in the shipping details, stamped the license "Completed," and returned it
to the State Department for filing.[7]

On 5 July 1940 the president announced a long list of commodities that
would be subject to licensing, and he named more on 26 July. The lists
included most of the strategic and critical commodities already identified by
the army and the NDAC, including munitions regulated under the various
neutrality acts and items already denied to Japan by moral embargoes, namely,
aircraft, munitions, aluminum, molybdenum, aviation gasoline and lubricating
oil, plus tetraethyl lead (and in December bromine chemicals used to make
TEL). The orders added other bombardment-related articles: bulletproof glass,
optically clear plastic, steel armor plate, toluol and nitrate chemical feedstocks
for TNT explosives, fire control instruments, and quartz crystals for radios.
Also brought under licensing control were reexports of commodities that the
United States itself had to buy abroad, including tin and tin-plated steel
scrap, tungsten, manganese, most other steel alloying metals, rubber, silk,
wool, cattle hides, long-fiber asbestos, and quinine. Later, coconut oil, cork,
paintbrush bristles, and jute for burlap sacks were added. In a departure from
a pure national defense rationale, a few chemicals of broad civilian application
came under license, including ammonia, ammonium fertilizers, and sulfuric
and nitric acids, even though acids were not in short supply and were economically impossible to ship long distances. The products most vital to
Japan—steel scrap, nonferrous metals, machine tools, and petroleum—were
also subjected to licensing, but Japanese applications were freely approved, at
least initially.[8]

Japan's Attitude in 1940

The first designations of commodities caused little consternation in Tokyo.
Japan did not buy from the United States most of the controlled products, nor
was it singled out for special scrutiny of its license requests. The executive
order of 26 July, however, halted the granting of licenses for exports of aviation
gasoline (avgas) of 87 octane and higher, tetraethyl lead used to raise octane,
and aviation lubricating oils, except to U.S.-owned companies and to Western
Hemisphere countries, where U.S. airlines operated. The Japanese embassy in
Washington complained that Japan, as a buyer of "immense volumes" of avgas,

was a victim of unfair bias. The State Department retorted that the protest was unwarranted as the fuel was needed for U.S. defense. Japan was not seriously inconvenienced, however. It purchased, in ever-growing volumes, gasoline just below 87 octane and high-grade California crude oil that Japanese refineries could upgrade to fuel suitable for Japanese planes. In September 1940 further proclamations required licenses for sales to any country of plans and equipment for avgas refineries and for technical information of any kind concerning the design and construction of aircraft and engines, the latter supplanting the moral embargo in the case of Japan.[9]

Japan's Steel Problem

Steel was the most fundamental material for industrial and military might. For Japan in the autumn of 1940 the probability of an embargo of scrap iron and steel exports became a troubling issue because it depended heavily on U.S. scrap for its steel-making furnaces.

Old Japan had smelted iron for swords and small wares. The first modern steel plant was erected in 1901 at Yawata, on Kyushu, but Japanese production did not exceed one million tons per year before the 1920s. The islands lacked deposits of ferrous sulfide or oxide, the natural ores of iron. Japanese corporations developed low-grade ore deposits in Manchukuo and invested in high-grade mines, first in British Malaya and in the 1930s in the Philippines and Australia. Japan also bought from India pig iron, an intermediate product of almost pure iron produced in blast furnaces. The iron ore of the upper Great Lakes, which fed American blast furnaces, could not feasibly be shipped to faraway Japan. The United States exported to Japan only small tonnages of pig iron and finished steel shapes.

By 1936, despite strenuous efforts, Japan had raised steel output to only 3 million tons, insignificant compared with U.S. capacity of over 50 million tons and a similar capacity in Europe. (Japan reported in metric tons of 2,204.6 pounds.) In 1938 Tokyo adopted a five-year plan to expand empire capacity in 1942 to 16.9 million tons, including 12.7 million tons in Japan proper. But the dream was hobbled by the expense of building the necessary huge coke ovens and blast furnaces, which devoured 4 to 5 tons of iron ore, coal, and limestone flux for every ton of pig iron. And iron and ore were not the only deficiencies. Japan mined only low-grade "steam coal" for ordinary fuel; it had to import special coal for manufacturing coke, the hard carbon residue that remains after heating coal in ovens to drive off volatile gases. Good coking coal had complex chemical ingredients that glued the carbon into strong lumps that did not crush under the weight of iron ore stacked in tall blast furnaces, allowing air to be blown through the charge to smelt the ore.

Japanese Need for Scrap

Most worrisome was the supply of ferrous scrap for charging the steel furnaces. Japan produced most of its steel by the basic (alkaline) open hearth process, the method used for 90 percent of U.S. and world steel. Open hearths of superior efficiency and quality of output, which had displaced Bessemer converters since the late 1800s,[10] required a charge of about 50 percent pig iron and 50 percent scrap, in some cases 60 percent scrap. Furthermore, electric furnaces operating on charges of 100 percent scrap had risen from 5 percent of Japan's steel produced in 1935 to almost 20 percent, including the crucial alloy steels needed for munitions and machinery. Steel works obtained about half their scrap needs, that is, 25 to 30 percent of the total charge, from home scrap ("mill run-around"), the residues in ladles and ingot molds after molten steel cooled and the edges and clippings from rolling ingots into plates, sheets, and rails. Manufacturers also returned small tonnages of "prompt" scrap, the wastage from shaping end-products of steel. To complete the charge, steel mills had to purchase "old scrap" on the open market, which posed a dilemma. As a recent industrializer, Japan had not used enough steel for enough years to generate a large base of scrap. In the late 1930s Japan recovered domestically only 40 percent of the old scrap it required. Given its ambitious plans to expand steel production, it had to import increasing tonnages of scrap, and the United States was the only substantial source.[11]

U.S. Scrap

In the United States two-thirds of all iron and steel eventually found its way back to the melting furnaces. (The rest disappeared as rust and unrecoverable small pieces.) Since the middle of the nineteenth century the country had consumed great quantities of iron and steel. The "above-ground mine" of scrap was thought to be as high as one billion tons due to peaks in railroad expansion about 1910 and in auto production in the 1920s. Heavy railroad and trolley equipment such as rails, plates, locomotives, and cars wore out and were scrapped, on average, after twenty-five years. Automobiles were junked on average after eight years. (Building and bridge girders, which lasted fifty to one hundred years, were relatively minor sources because they had not been widely used in construction before 1880.) Around the country two hundred thousand independent "rag picker" peddlers, typically with one truck or horse wagon, collected waste materials and sold to fifteen thousand junk yards that sorted, baled, and delivered twenty million tons of old scrap annually to the steel industry. In the 1930s the yards were full of scrap due to Depression-induced demolitions of railroads, machinery, and cars, while mill demand slumped 50 percent in the worst years. Unsold accumulations were huge in nonindustrial states such as California, Texas, and Florida because of the high cost of railroad hauls to the furnaces situated around Pittsburgh and the Great Lakes. Scrap in those coastal states could be more easily and cheaply shipped to the furnaces on the deep-water shores of Japanese harbors.

Scrap Imports and 1937 Embargo Ideas

Japan first imported scrap in quantity in 1931. From 1934 to 1936 it bought an average of 1 million tons. In 1937 it bought 2.4 million tons, including 1.9 million from the United States despite a price spike from ten or twelve dollars per ton to twenty dollars, reflecting temporary U.S. economic recovery and demand from Italy and Britain. Japan's scrap imports were somewhat understated because it also purchased old ships and steamed or towed them home for breaking up. Postwar Japanese data indicated eleven to twenty-four ships per year in the late 1930s except for an astonishing seventy-one imported in 1938. A salvaged ship that yielded, say, 5,000 tons of scrap was equivalent, however, to only twenty-five miles of torn-up railroad track.[12]

Japanese buying of U.S. scrap was a matter of early interest to the U.S. government. Between 1935 and 1940 purchases amounted to $131 million, 9.4 percent of all U.S. exports to Japan.[13] In the spring of 1937 a few congressmen, cheered on by hardliners Morgenthau at the Treasury Department and Stanley Hornbeck, adviser on political relations at the State Department, proposed resolutions authorizing the president to block scrap exports. However, a committee chaired by Assistant Secretary of State Francis B. Sayre found such action unjustified, even on grounds of national defense, because of the overhang of surplus scrap.[14] Hull seconded that view, despite Roosevelt's quarantine speech and the outrage of the "China lobby" over bombs raining on China said to be made of chunks of the demolished Third Avenue elevated railway in New York City. The Institute of Scrap Iron and Steel, a dealers' group, scoffed. Exports were a mere 0.5 percent of the national "reserve" of scrap, which was growing by 10 million tons each year because new scrappage exceeded steel mill requirements. Steel industry leaders felt that if an embargo became necessary it should restrict only the most desirable No. 1 heavy melting scrap, that is, tracks, plates, chains, heavy springs, and the like. There was no shortage of No. 2 bales—thin sheet metal from autos, rail cars, storage tanks, and farm equipment—which was less uniform, painted, and prone to wastage in melting. When the United States entered a recession in 1937–38 and scrap prices fell again, pro-embargo sentiment faded. Nevertheless, Japanese buying in 1938 declined to 1.4 million tons as Tokyo sought to conserve foreign exchange. Japan also bought odds and ends of junk from India and the Netherlands East Indies, but Europe, where the scrappage rate was lower and steel output less depressed than in the United States, had none to spare from its own armaments race.

Scrap Embargo

In 1939, as a European war loomed, Japan hastened to purchase another two million tons of U.S. scrap at a cost of $32.5 million. In the first half of 1940, although U.S. steel output at last surpassed 1929 levels and American mills demanded more, scrap was still abundant because exports to continental Europe had ceased and to Japan had slowed. Steel executives anticipated no overall shortage although some worried about exports pushing up prices and leading to price controls on steel. The Army-Navy Munitions Board did not rank scrap as important for defense.[15]

With conservation adopted as a defense policy in July 1940, Morgenthau grew concerned that heavy scrap would grow scarce. He recruited allies in other agencies, including Secretary of the Interior Harold Ickes and Leon Henderson of the National Defense Advisory Commission, and convinced Stettinius of the NDAC to recommend conservation.[16] On 26 July Roosevelt designated scrap subject to export licensing regulations. No. 1 scrap, believed to comprise 15 to 20 percent of Japanese purchases, was considered most likely to come under restrictions. (Separate data for No. 1 and No. 2 were not collected.) But the State Department wished to keep Japan friendly by selling "normal" levels of commodities, so Maxwell's control staff licensed generous shipments of 563,000 metric tons of No. 1 scrap in the following three months. Ninety-nine percent of Japanese license applications for scrap were approved. Lower grades were unrestricted. Exports to Japan rose in the third quarter of 1940 to an annual rate of 1.6 million tons, double the rate of the previous six months, a quantity too large for available shipping.[17]

In September 1940 Washington's attitude hardened as Japan occupied northern French Indochina and prepared to join the German-Italian Axis. With steel orders from Great Britain and for U.S. defense surging, the industry turned in favor of a full embargo of scrap exports. Hawkish administration officials outmaneuvered the reluctant State Department and ignored Ambassador Grew's objections. On 26 September the White House announced that all scrap export licenses would be revoked effective 15 October and new ones issued only for Great Britain and Western Hemisphere destinations. Japanese diplomats indignantly accused the United States of favoritism and an intent to pressure Japan that mocked the supposed rationale of defense necessity. The discrimination, they warned, caused "high feelings" in Japan and forebodings of ruptured economic relations, with ominously unpredictable political results. Hull brushed off their notes, denied discrimination, told them U.S. defense policy was none of their business, and delivered his customary lecture against aggression.

On 27 September 1940 Japan signed the Axis Tripartite Treaty.[18] Nevertheless, No. 2 scrap remained unlicensed and flowed to Japan until 10 December 1940 when the president incorporated into the embargo system iron and steel of every variety, from ores and scrap to semifinished ingots to finished plates, sheets, tubes, rails, and forgings, and ferroalloys as well. Japan grumbled that the intention was obviously discriminatory as she was the principal buyer of steel raw materials, but the State Department merely repeated its previous stance. Thereafter no scrap went to Japan. The United States justified the "unfriendly act" because ferrous scrap had become essential for U.S. and British defense and because it had not singled out Japan for harsh treatment. Studies indicated Japan had access to enough steel-making raw materials to provide for its economy if the government stopped channeling so much into war. U.S. officials did not believe the deprivation would paralyze Japanese economic life. (It was not, in fact, the first time the United States had attempted to use withdrawal of steel to pressure Japan politically.)[19]

The U.S. assessments were correct. The scrap embargo pinched but did not retard Japan's aggressive policies. As early as 1936 Tokyo had ordered steel plants to accumulate raw materials. In 1937 it began allocating steel output to end users. In 1940 the army and navy received 35 percent and shipbuilding another 7 percent, offset by drastic cuts for utilities, transportation, railroads, and factories, leaving very little for consumer goods. Japan stepped up imports of iron ore from Malaya and the Philippines as well as efforts to make steel in Manchukuo from low-grade local ores. Above all, Japan had stockpiled scrap, as U.S. analysts were aware. From 1937 to 1939 Japanese mills consumed an average of 4.4 million tons of scrap, of which 2.1 million was mill run-around and 1 million was from domestic salvage, implying consumption of 1.3 million tons of imported scrap. Because imports averaged 2.1 million tons, Japan had accumulated 0.8 million tons of scrap annually, almost all from the United States. In 1940 the stockpile stood at 5.7 million tons from all sources, equal to fifteen months' total scrap needs or an astonishing three years of imports from the United States. In 1941 Japan began to live off its hoard, drawing down 22 percent of the scrap stockpile to maintain steel production.[20]

Machine Tools

Machine tools exports emerged as another delicate problem in U.S.-Japan relations. Regulations accompanying the licensing act of 2 July 1940 did not apply to fabricated articles ready for consumption, even those manufactured from restricted materials, except machinery "necessary for the manufacture" of military equipment or munitions. The United States exported about thirty varieties of machinery and machine tools (according to Department of Commerce categories) in an infinite variety of models and specifications, in both metric and U.S. standards. Intended uses by customers, whether martial or peaceful, could be surmised by manufacturers and government analysts more readily than batches of raw materials. Machinery deemed critical for armaments was brought under license in 1940, notably tools and related equipment for melting, casting, pressing, cutting, grinding, and welding of metals. Exports of machinery for innocent activities such as woodworking and mining remained unrestricted. In November Japan protested that machines it purchased had been denied export licenses on grounds of U.S. defense needs even though they had been built to Japanese specifications. No U.S. company wanted to buy them when frustrated Japanese customers tried to unload. U.S. machine tool firms were even refusing orders from Japan for ordinary equipment not subject to licensing. U.S. authorities retorted that the orphaned machines might some day prove useful to American defense, and that rejection of non-metalworking tools freed up plant capacity for urgently needed machines. The noose gradually tightened. The ECA extended license denials to plastic molding machines, hydraulic pumps, any tools with industrial diamonds, and instruments for measuring and testing. Maxwell reported to Dean Acheson that in January and February 1941 fourteen of the eighteen Japanese tool and parts applications were disapproved; the others, approved after appeals, consisted of three micrometer or gage sets and a second-hand molding machine. In May 1941 U.S. agents arrested two Japanese men in San Francisco for conspiring to smuggle tool bits out of the country. They pleaded guilty. In July a Mitsubishi affiliate was apprehended shipping to Japan used oil drilling machinery from Mexico, which it plotted to replace with new U.S. equipment freely licensed for use in Mexico. In a rare moment of mercy that month, Maxwell okayed export of lathes and steel forgings worth $420,000 because they were already partially manufactured and resale to U.S. factories had proved "fruitless." Nevertheless, Green, the State Department gatekeeper, refused to license them and arranged for government requisition. Exports of machine tools lurched to a stop.[21]

More Export Controls, 1941

In the opening days of 1941 executive orders expanding the list of commodities under license poured out of the White House in rapid succession. On 10 January the most important nonferrous metals, whether in ores, shapes, or products of any kind, were added: copper and copper-based alloys of brass and bronze; zinc; nickel; and, on 4 March, lead. From February to mid-April came a flood of entries, including fifty-one on 27 March alone. The metals list swelled with mysterious specialties: titanium, radium, and uranium. Dozens of organic and inorganic chemicals appeared: coal tar petrochemicals, feed stocks for synthetic rubber, and pine oil for metal flotation in ore-grinding mills. Licensing was extended to "bottom of the barrel" refinery residues: petroleum coke, carbon and graphite electrodes for aluminum smelting and electric furnaces for steel, and carbon black for rubber tires, as well as equipment for oil drilling and refining. On 4 March the ECA added designs, plans, and photos relating to manufacturing of any articles needing licenses, well over a hundred by then. For the first time raw materials for consumer goods made an appearance on the control list: borax for household soaps and mixtures; flax and vegetable fibers that the United States did not export to Japan and high-grade wood pulp for rayon that it did; nylon; shoe leather; and belladonna drugs native to the United States. On the other hand, foodstuffs were scarcely mentioned; the United States did not export many to Japan. Only animal and vegetable cooking oils were listed for licensing because of shortages in the United States, a matter of little concern to Japan with its abundant soy and fish oil supplies. Finally, on 28 May 1941, the president with the approval of Congress extended licensing to exports to Japan from the Philippine Islands, although wide discretion was allowed to local authorities. By 25 July the only major commodities freely exportable to Japan were cotton (of which there was a worldwide glut), food, and non-aviation oil fuels, for which generous licenses continued to be granted as a matter of U.S. foreign policy (chapter 11).[22]

Stresses and Strains of Export Control

The hastily rigged export control system of 1940–41 suffered aches and creaks. Morgenthau described a complex example. Suppose an American firm tried to sell a product to a country that imposed its own exchange controls, as almost all countries did by 1941. The U.S. exporter had to win approval from the customer's country to get paid in dollars, gain clearance from a U.S. liaison committee to negotiate a sales contract, apply through the ECA for a license, and hope eventually to receive one after endorsement by the State Department. Morgenthau proposed to centralize everything in the Treasury but got nowhere against vociferous opposition from the other agencies. Another report described the awkward procedures of six agencies involved in the export process. A banker told Acheson that it took three weeks or longer to get a license for a simple sale of steel to Latin America, and the mills could neither schedule production nor commit to a firm price so far in advance. An appeals committee in the Export Control Administration spent two to four weeks to rule on challenged cases. To amend an application was impossible once it entered the bureaucratic maze. In desperation, exporters abused an informal ECA practice of automatically granting licenses for orders of less than five thousand dollars by splitting large orders into several applications. Suggestions to cut the red tape, such as exempting general merchandise for the Western Hemisphere, made no headway. Bureaucrats interfered at whim. For example, "so-called experts" in the State Department urged restriction of Sitka spruce lumber, useful for airplane construction but rarely sold to Japan, on obscure grounds of foreign policy. More seriously, the State Department often retarded shipments by demanding that applicants for every licensed commodity (other than for the British Empire) append statistics of the seller's previous exports to the destination country since 1936—for nonferrous metals since 1935—so U.S. authorities could troll for hints of evasion through third countries.[23]

From inception in July 1940 to 23 September 1941 the ECA granted ten thousand export licenses, yet at the latter date still struggled with a backlog of twenty thousand unprocessed applications.[24] The burdensome complexities of export licensing, and diplomatic stresses of refusing specific products for specific countries, proved to be an important factor in the turn to the simpler and more powerful device of freezing Japan's dollars to halt *all* exports and then—at least in concept—to release funds to pay for exports to Japan case by case.

Summary of Export Control Before the Freeze

By the spring of 1941 the United States had brought under restriction all commodities important for national defense that were, or threatened to be, in short supply. The percentage of U.S. global exports subject to license rose from 25 percent in December 1940 to 44–47 percent in April–May 1941. About 80 percent of metal and 50 percent of machinery exports (but only 5 percent of purely civilian goods) were subject to licensing. In April 1941 rejections amounted to 13 percent of applications, by value, rising to 23 percent in May.[25] Japan was supposedly not singled out for discrimination but in fact it had been, step by step. In 1939 air warfare materiel was barred "voluntarily;"

in the fall of 1940 steel scrap was halted; and in 1941 machinery and most metals were limited to "friendly" regions. By the second quarter of 1941 hardly any strategic goods were licensed for Japan, other than non-aviation oil products, as a deliberate U.S. policy. (Japanese stockpiles of most materials cushioned the blows.) The stated objective of export controls remained conservation for defense, and there was plenty of oil from the producing regions of the United States accessible to Japan. Severe deprivation of the Japanese economy had to await financial sanctions aimed precisely at Japan by invocation of the Trading with the Enemy Act.

8

The Japanese Financial Fraud in New York

hile the United States pursued a policy of gradually restricting exports to Japan, the alternative policy of financial pressure lay slumbering, out of mind in Washington. Only once, in December 1937 shortly after the invasion of China, had Morgenthau contemplated freezing Japan's dollar assets, an action the president could have authorized by declaring an emergency under the Trading with the Enemy Act, but Roosevelt had dropped the idea (chapter 2). From 1937 to 1940 analysts and officials of several U.S. government agencies confidently predicted that if Japan continued to wage war in China, it would "bankrupt" itself, that is, spend all its reserves of gold and hard currency to buy essential commodities. The inference of their many studies of Japan's finances was that the United States need not threaten financial sanctions to deter aggression. Instead, tentatively at first but with increasing intensity, the United States discontinued exporting to Japan most strategic commodities in lieu of deploying its most devastating financial weapon.

Confidence that Japan's international reserves were rapidly evaporating was due in large measure to precise knowledge of its continuous sales of gold to the U.S. Treasury. Analysts were certain that Japan was spending the dollar proceeds for raw materials because a buildup of dollar balances, whether from gold, liquidating investments, or any other sources, would have appeared on the books of banks domiciled in the United States.[1] All banks and banking agencies operating in the United States were obliged to file reports of funds they held for foreign entities and any changes in the balances. The Federal Reserve published aggregated statistics, country by country, without disclosing the data of individual banks and depositors. Japan's government and trading corporations centralized their hard-currency assets in branches of the Yokohama Specie Bank (YSB) in New York and London. The YSB, founded in

1880, was nominally a private bank, but it served as overseas agent for the Bank of Japan (BOJ), the nation's central bank analogous to the Federal Reserve. The Specie Bank's most important branch was its New York agency (YSBNY), also established in 1880.[2] The YSBNY was legally required to file weekly, monthly, and semiannual reports with the Federal Reserve Bank of New York, which compiled statistical data of foreign deposits and transactions in the Second Reserve District, including New York City. Until the summer of 1940 the YSBNY's reports showed no unusual hoard or movements of Japanese-owned dollars.

Discovery of the Fraud

On 3 August 1940 Walter H. Rozell, an official of the Foreign Department of the New York Fed, spotted an unexpected entry on Form B-2, submitted by the Specie Bank's New York agency. During the week ending 31 July overdrafts (loans) extended by the YSBNY to an unnamed Japanese bank had diminished by $12 million. Rozell was puzzled. If a bank in Japan was repaying money it had borrowed, previous reports ought to have shown a rise in that bank's deposits at the YSBNY when it first drew down the loan principal. But other reports, on Form B-1, hadn't disclosed that a Japanese bank had received or owned unusual dollar balances at any recent time.[3] Furthermore, a mysterious deposit of $10.9 million had just popped up on the agency's books. The YSBNY listed $28.6 million of balances of the puppet Manchukuoan and North Chinese governments, but these did not explain the mystery.[4]

Rozell, as a good bureaucrat, felt embarrassed. He would have to correct statistics already published. The next week's B-2 reported a further reduction of $38.7 million of unrecorded loans by the YSBNY to unknown banks in Japan, raising the total of curious debt repayments to $52 million. "Further investigation is called for," he urged Assistant Vice President J. W. McKeon.[5] Mr. Nakano, accountant of the YSBNY, proffered a bizarre explanation for the figures to McKeon. The "borrower" and "repayer" of dollars had been the Bank of Japan. Before 31 July the BOJ had indeed held cash in New York, he said, and perhaps some U.S. securities, altogether $50 million. But the holdings had been in a "custody account," therefore not recorded on the YSBNY's books as a deposit. As Nakano explained it, the agency had recently transferred dollars internally on its books from an undisclosed custody account into a deposit in favor of its head office in Yokohama, which apparently acted as an intermediary for the Bank of Japan. For unexplained reasons the dollars were no longer held "in custody."[6]

Fed officials were puzzled. A custody account was a safekeeping arrangement for the assets of customers. A custodian bank did not record such assets on its own books. Custody accounts were customarily established to hold stocks and bonds, usually physically segregated in the bank's vaults from its own security holdings. (Analogously, the Federal Reserve Bank of New York recorded no assets on its books in respect of the gold owned by foreign governments earmarked for safekeeping in its basement vaults.) A custody account sometimes included incidental cash temporarily awaiting investment, or to clear the buying and selling of securities, but an all-cash custody account was practically unheard of. Banks did not physically lock away millions in currency or coins for a customer. While not justifying the bizarre accounting classification and reclassification, Nakano made clear that no funds had recently left or entered the United States.[7]

During the rest of August L. Werner Knoke, the vice president in charge of international operations of the New York Fed, watched the weekly reports suspiciously. He admonished Nakano and Mr. Nishi, head agent of the YSBNY, that the Fed was required by executive order to report accurately all movements of international capital. Unexpectedly, Nishi confessed that the custody account had earlier amounted to $100 million in cash and U.S. Treasury securities. It had been built up over "a number of years" through gold sales by the Bank of Japan that exceeded the dollars needed to settle Japan's trade deficits. In a series of convoluted transactions the BOJ had regularly shipped gold to San Francisco for sale to the U.S. Treasury for dollars. The Treasury credited the proceeds to the Yokohama Specie Bank's San Francisco office, which transferred the funds by telegraph through Chase National Bank to the Specie Bank agency in New York. But instead of the normal accounting procedure of recording a dollar deposit in favor of the Bank of Japan, as required by U.S. regulations, the YSBNY had deemed the money to be held in custody, highly inappropriate accounting for cash. The Japanese bankers promised to investigate further.[8] During the autumn of 1940 they filed corrected reports for prior weeks. Fed analysts immediately noted that on 24 July 1940 the custody account had bulged with at least $61.6 million, perhaps more including securities. Joseph B. Knapp, a young banking officer on the staff of the Fed's Board of Governors, called for corrected statements reaching back to the creation of the exotic custody account.[9]

On 28 August Frank M. Tamagna of the FRBNY's Foreign Research Division reviewed Japan's dollar position for the Federal Reserve Board of Governors in Washington. U.S. officials had naïvely assumed that Japan financed its perennial trade deficit with the United States through short-term credit arranged by overseas branches of Japanese banks, and that such temporary loans were paid off a few weeks later when the Bank of Japan delivered gold to the United States and sold it for dollars. In other words, gold proceeds were supposed to flush through the banking system rapidly, leaving no residual accumulation of dollars. But Japan's financial behavior had changed on or about 24 October 1939, when it officially cut the yen's tie to the British pound and pegged its value to the dollar. Japanese funds fled from London, until then an important center for Japanese liquid assets.[10] The Department of Commerce had noted, for example, that in 1937 Japan sold $256 million of gold to the U.S. Treasury while its trade deficit with the United States was only $89 million, concluding that "Japan used the difference in these amounts largely to acquire sterling balances."[11]

Great Britain, just before and after the outbreak of war on 3 September 1939, had imposed exchange controls to conserve dollars for buying American supplies. Sterling owned by foreigners could not, without approval of the Bank of England, be swapped into dollars and transferred out. British pounds could be spent only within the sterling area, that is, Britain, its colonies and dominions (other than Canada, a dollar country), and a few small countries appended to the sterling area by treaties. All such countries and territories had legislated exchange controls to prevent funds escaping from the "fortified sterling area" without permission. During the relaxed "phoney war" period, however, the Chamberlain government had hoped to maintain London's stature in world finance by allowing a semblance of convertibility. Banks, companies, and persons who were not legal residents of the sterling area were allowed to sell pounds for dollars, which were provided by the British Treasury from its reserves, and remove them to the United States, which is no doubt what the Japanese banks did. Britain did not impose a truly hard freeze on foreign-owned sterling assets until the collapse of France in May–June 1940. John Maynard Keynes, adviser to the His Majesty's Treasury, calculated the leakage from Britain at $400 million since the war began, a "major scandal" that came close to paralyzing Britain's war effort before Lend-Lease rode to the rescue in March 1941.[12]

In 1939, even though Japan reaped a $35 million windfall due to a spike in raw silk prices, its $40.8 million of gold sales to the United States had again exceeded trade needs. One clue was that the Yokohama Specie Bank had swapped at least $5 million of British pounds into dollars in late 1939, but it and other Japanese banks apparently had converted and withdrawn a far greater sum of dollars converted from sterling through early 1940. As a result of flight from London, excess gold sales, and the usual favorable seasonal trade balance in the spring, the Bank of Japan accumulated $45 million in the YSBNY. The agency temporarily invested the funds through the New York money market in short-term trade bills, and later in U.S. Treasury securities. Its officers may have believed that the brief holding of securities justified the custody accounting travesty.

As excess gold sales continued in 1940 it was thought that the buildup of dollars in New York grew to at least $75 million. Rozell expected that revised data would show a cumulative surge of $100 million of Bank of Japan funds into the United States. Federal Reserve analysts wrote in an angry tone that "it has been a constant policy of the Bank of Japan since last October [1939] to keep a substantial part of the special fund for foreign exchange in dollar balances, rather than in gold as originally constituted." Japan's "actual secret war chest" had not been emptying as thought, but had been converted into dollars hidden under the noses of bank regulators in New York. The Fed's Foreign Research Division summed it up: "This intricate accounting procedure is undoubtedly made to conceal, rather than to clarify, the operations of the Bank of Japan special fund for foreign exchange," of which the stash in the New York Specie Bank agency was the most important item.[13]

Knapp also inquired of U.S. brokers why they had failed to report the securities trades of the Japanese as required for a foreign customer. The reason was that the YSBNY had again violated regulations by not telling the brokers that the trades were on behalf of, and settled from funds owned by, a foreign entity, that is, the Bank of Japan.[14] The YSBNY and its officers were subject, under a 1933 amendment to the TWEA, to fines of ten thousand dollars or imprisonment up to ten years or both, for willfully misrepresenting the facts. The Fed staff believed that was the case even though the Japanese could mount technical defenses. The Specie Bank agency promised to comply in the future but Charles H. Coe, a vice president of the New York Fed, wanted to pursue the infraction through his bank's general counsel, if only as a counter to possible abuse of U.S. businesses in Japan.[15]

Treasury Interest Stirs

Henry Morgenthau may have heard talk of the secret Japanese financial hoard in the fall of 1940 because he began to think anew, after a long lapse, about economic pressures against Japan. On 23 September 1940, Edward H. Foley Jr., general counsel of the Treasury, outlined to him several alternatives. President Roosevelt was empowered under the 1930 Tariff Act to impose retaliatory duties of up to 50 percent on imports if Japan was found to be discriminating against U.S. commerce in occupied China. Under a 1916 act he could restrict imports if Japanese laws restricted U.S. sales to Japan. He could prohibit landing of cargoes carried in Japanese vessels from anywhere in the world. He could stretch the July 1940 act that authorized licensing of exports of materials needed for defense to products as innocent as raw cotton. Foley asserted, however, that such trade pressures would lack the sweeping impact of a financial freeze.[16] But Morgenthau, at the moment, was more interested in neutering the dollar assets of Germany, Italy, and their Balkan allies. With annoyance, he wished the press would quit speculating about freezing Japan because the timing was awkward, presumably a reference to rocking the boat during the campaign for Roosevelt's reelection in November 1940.[17]

Other Financial Freezes

By 1941 the U.S. Treasury had gained considerable experience administering foreign asset freezes. Roosevelt, having stood by futilely without protecting the gold and U.S. assets of Austria, Czechoslovakia, Poland, and Albania, acted with alacrity on 10 April 1940 when the Nazis assaulted Denmark and Norway. His Executive Order No. 8389, promulgated under authority of Section 5(b) of the 1917 TWEA as amended, locked in place the U.S. assets of those luckless countries. His order was sweeping. Unless specifically authorized by the Treasury, blocked Danish and Norwegian funds could not be transferred to a foreign bank or even to another U.S. bank. Dealings in devisen, gold, silver, and securities, both foreign and domestic, required Treasury authorization. Evasive and sham transactions were prohibited. The order also established a system of reporting by all banking entities.

Whenever the dictators invaded another country, or were deemed to have seized control, Roosevelt stretched the protective wing of EO No. 8839: to Holland, Belgium, and Luxembourg on 10 May 1940; to France on 17 June; to three small Baltic states in July; to Rumania in October; and to the rest of the Balkans and Greece when Hitler attacked in March and April 1941. Most victimized nations had formed governments in exile with more valid claims to the funds than Nazi puppet regimes.[18] By the spring of 1941 the United States had blocked foreign assets amounting to $4 billion.[19] The Treasury Department had learned to administer controls and to grant or withhold licenses for transactions in blocked accounts. The United States, however, had yet to sterilize the funds of a potential enemy power.

Treasury Gets the News, October 1940

On 9 October 1940 the Federal Reserve formally reported its discovery of Japan's secret war chest to the Treasury Department, the agency responsible, along with the State Department, for foreign financial policy. V. Frank Coe, assistant director of the Treasury's Division of Monetary Research, demonstrated to Harry Dexter White, his superior and Morgenthau's right-hand man, that the deception had begun long before the war in Europe. It probably began in July 1938, when the Bank of Japan set aside $95 to $98 million in gold in its Special Foreign Exchange Fund, supposedly for smoothing out temporary fluctuations in foreign trade. Instead, the BOJ had begun converting the gold into dollar deposits. The New York Specie Bank's false reports had to be restated retroactively for two years.[20] Morgenthau himself heard about it first from Herbert Feis, economic adviser to the State Department. He was taken aback that State knew of the problem before him. "Did we miss by a hundred million?" he asked the day after Coe's report.[21]

On 31 October Andrew M. Kamarck, a Treasury economist recently transferred from the Fed, estimated that Japan held $102 million in dollar deposits including $10 million of Treasury securities. He advised that Japanese officials, alerted to discovery of the secret war chest, began that month to shrink the dollar funds in New York. It had started with a rush to buy scrap iron prior to the embargo two weeks earlier. But reduced spending after scrap was embargoed, and presumably steady gold output, placed Japan in "a not greatly dangerous position," he felt.[22] Frank Tamagna had guessed gold available to Japan for foreign use at $62 million, about one year's production, a far cry from his earlier guess of $10 million.[23] Kamarck guessed $85 million of free gold.[24] From Tokyo, George A. Nakison, first secretary of the embassy, wrote on 22 November (received in Washington on 8 January 1941) that Japan had plenty of dollars as a result of the United States curb of exports of metals and machine tools and Tokyo's harsh cuts in imports of foreign cotton and wood pulp. Japan was not going broke after all. Japanese liquid assets in the United States were sufficient for another year without further gold shipments, he emphasized, "*if these assets are not frozen or voluntarily reduced or withdrawn.*"[25]

Morgenthau Takes Aim at Germany

On 7 November 1940 Morgenthau prodded FDR to extend funds controls to potential enemies—but not against Japan. J. Edgar Hoover, director of the Federal Bureau of Investigation, reported that German, Italian, or Vichy French funds were subsidizing propaganda and sabotage in the Western Hemisphere. For example, the FBI had traced serial numbers of currency passed from the German consulate for propaganda work and watched Italian funds moving to Latin America. But there were thirty-seven hundred suspect bank accounts in New York City alone, far beyond the FBI's capacity to scrutinize.[26] Morgenthau instructed his staff attorney Wiley to draft a memo to persuade FDR and the recalcitrant State Department to support foreign funds controls on the European Axis immediately. As Wiley wrote, "A situation in which we are not masters in our own house is unenviable," yet the U.S. government was powerless to regulate or even investigate foreign transactions. Germany and Italy hid investment income behind Swiss and Swedish intermediaries. Washington needed to know the amount and location of Axis and looted assets, the purpose of any money transfers, and who was behind them. A census of all foreign-owned assets was essential. Besides, Congress was thinking of investigating on its own.[27]

Morgenthau proposed to FDR invoking Section 5(b) of the Trading with the Enemy Act to impose financial controls on Germany and Italy, enforced by penalties. Those countries could not protest because they had already taken control of U.S. assets throughout Europe. With his customary enthusiasm he volunteered the Treasury to mastermind a flexible program, one that would minimize interference with legitimate trade by granting blanket licenses for whole regions of the world.[28] Early in December, Jacob Viner, Morgenthau's distinguished academic adviser, condensed the rambling memo to emphasize countersubversion, a line that would play well with Congress and the public.[29] Morgenthau got his moment of opportunity on 28 December 1940. The president had returned the proposal with orders to haggle it out with the ever-cautious State Department, which opposed it. According to Herbert Feis, Morgenthau mistook Cordell Hull's silent reaction for agreement, but it was only another chapter of the bureaucratic struggle. Hull and Undersecretary of State Sumner Welles were not about to acquiesce in granting Morgenthau "decisive influence" in foreign policy. Their adamant opposition, Feis later wrote, dissuaded Roosevelt from authorizing financial warfare against any Axis power on the debatable rationale of clandestine activity.[30] A freeze of the financial assets of Germany, Italy, and the European neutrals had to wait another six months.

And what of Japan? There was little evidence of a Japanese fifth column observed by the FBI or Army G-2. Brig. Gen. Sherman Miles, chief of military intelligence, learned that the German chargé d'affaires was warning the Japanese embassy that Washington was toying with a freeze.[31] But the Wiley-Viner-Morgenthau proposal promised soothingly that if financial controls were imposed on Japan under an "elastic" system, they would not be a casus belli or even a real provocation. Japan needed trade with the United States, so it would seek commercial licenses rather than a rupture of relations. Ambassador Grew advised against financial sanctions until a deal was struck to liquidate at fair value U.S. business assets frozen in Japan.[32] (U.S. firms held $47 million of industrial and marketing assets and $41 million of banking funds in Japan in 1936–37, the last available figures.[33]) Much as Treasury hard-liners wished to clamp down on Japan, it was "a question of very high politics," in the words of John Pehle, who ran the department's Foreign Funds Control Office.[34] Cooler heads of the administration knew the timing was not yet ripe politically during the push to legislate Lend-Lease to aid Britain. The financial weapon was slipped back in its sheath.

Evaluation of the War Chest Completed

On 6 December 1940 the Fed delivered to Harry Dexter White its final statistical revisions of the clandestine Japanese cache back to 27 July 1938. H. E. Hesse of the Treasury staff calculated that the hidden custody account at the YSBNY had peaked on 10 April 1940 at $110.6 million, in addition to a further $3.4 million held for the Reserve Bank of North China. It was an eye-popping sum, equivalent to twelve months of U.S. silk imports or twenty-two months of the gold mining output of the Japanese Empire. From November 1938 to December 1939 the YSBNY had invested some of the money in short-term securities.[35] Treasury staff estimates of the current balance ranged widely. H. Merle Cochran, technical assistant to Morgenthau, reckoned $70 million worth of government bonds "in that strong box."[36] In U.S. eyes, Japan was now wildly imagined to be preserving the war chest by collecting payments for its exports in cash while financing imports on credit. But a look at the three West Coast branches of the Yokohama Specie Bank disclosed insignificant foreign balances and no suspicious concealment. The Bank of America, the largest bank in California, said it extended "liberal credit" only for diplomatic mission costs.[37] Frank Coe felt other foreign bank branches ought to be investigated for concealments.[38] Harry White later presented an exaggerated estimate of $140 million of secret Japanese funds, sent a man to New York to get details, and considered turning the matter over to administration lawyers, but Morgenthau did not react.[39]

Upon full knowledge of Japan's financial fraud at the end of 1940, the anticipated certainty of imminent bankruptcy evaporated. Rozell on 23 January 1941 opined that Japan could subsist on newly mined gold without depleting its gold and dollar hoards and "therefore could go on almost indefinitely at this rate."[40] On 7 February 1941 Wayne C. Taylor, an assistant secretary of the Treasury and former banker, put forth an exceedingly pessimistic conclusion. Even at the spending rate of 1940, which was much higher than spending expected in 1941 because many commodities had recently been embargoed, Japan's assets in the United States could finance its needs for up to eighteen months. Japan's *total* exchange resources could enable it to conduct the war against China for three more years—until 1944![41]

White's Warnings, Early 1941

Harry Dexter White, director of the Treasury's Division of Monetary Research, was Morgenthau's most influential adviser on foreign financial affairs.[42] On 25 February 1941 he wrote to the secretary that Japan faced "increasing difficulties . . . that will multiply in 1941," so that "Japan is particularly vulnerable to the freezing of her assets in the United States." He warned, "If this is contemplated and is to be effective it must be done at once." Japan was racing to draw down its war chest.

White's tabulations of Japan's dollar position were faulty. He assumed arbitrarily that Japan needed to maintain $100 million of hard-currency working balances overseas. Exaggerating an analysis prepared for him by Assistant Secretary Taylor, White added up $212 million of gold and dollars that he reckoned Tokyo had on hand, plus $78 million of gold to be mined in 1941, less spending of $222 million if continued at the 1940 rate. Thus the $68 million remaining at the end of 1941 would fall short of the need he assumed.[43] But White and Taylor had failed to acknowledge that U.S. exports of strategic commodities had been sharply circumscribed by formal and informal embargoes, especially since late 1940. Japan could comfortably shrivel its dollar reserve below the supposedly irreducible $100 million of working balances. Nevertheless, White concluded that "drastic reductions" of Japan's freely spendable dollars and gold regardless of amount—by a freeze?—would "tend to place Japan's national economic structure in immediate jeopardy," a rare acknowledgment by a senior official of the dire impact of a financial squeeze on Japan's economic life, not just its foreign and military policy.[44]

On 21 March 1941 Taylor incorporated revised information into a more reasonable review. Japan had stopped selling gold. The Treasury had bought only $6.1 million worth in January and none thereafter, compared with first-quarter purchases of $48.4 million in 1940 and $54.6 million in 1939. In the first week of March Japanese bank balances in the United States stood at $103 million, down 35 percent from the average of $160 million in January–March 1940. (No figures were available for 1939.) White told Morgenthau that the drawdown was a deliberate Japanese policy. Japan was continuing to buy U.S. products, notably oil. Its bank balances were declining because it no longer replenished them by gold sales, a policy Taylor attributed to Japan's anxiety over "the threat . . . that the United States may freeze Japanese funds. If this is the reason we may expect that Japan's dollar balances will be allowed to fall even more noticeably in the future."[45] On 3 April White told Morgenthau that dollar removal was a deliberate Japanese policy.[46] Harry Dexter White's urgings to freeze Japan's assets early in 1941 were not among the postwar charges against him for disloyalty or worse.

An Aborted Financial Freeze, Early 1941

The first months of 1941 marked a turning point in the will of the United States to advance from a patchwork of export restrictions to full-blooded financial warfare against Japan. A spurt of work from January through March established the nature of the financial punishment it would mete out when the time came. Above all, that the levers of control would be manipulated not by learned economists and banking technicians, nor by moderate diplomats seeking bargaining leverage, but by truculent lawyers determined to show Japan no mercy.

Dean Acheson

The vigorous thrust for freezing Japan's dollars emerged abruptly from a new corner of the soft-line State Department. On 31 January 1941 Roosevelt appointed Dean Acheson, a forty-eight-year-old attorney and Democratic party activist, as an assistant secretary of state.[1] Acheson, son of an Episcopal minister and a well-to-do mother, had graduated from Harvard Law School, been mentored by Supreme Court Justices Felix Frankfurter and Louis Brandeis, and worked his way up in a prominent Washington law firm. In 1933 Roosevelt appointed him undersecretary of the Treasury. However, he earned the displeasure of FDR, and of Morgenthau (then heading the Farm Credit Administration), by objecting to the president's anti-Depression plan to buy gold in order to inflate the currency and raise farm prices. He resigned after six months on the job and returned to private practice. Roosevelt then named Morgenthau to head the Treasury in place of the ailing secretary, William Woodin.

Dean Acheson, emotionally and philosophically a Europhile, was known in Washington circles as ardently anti-Axis and a friend of Britain. In 1940 he rendered legal services to the administration on a deal to exchange overage U.S. destroyers for naval base sites in British Western Hemisphere colonies. Although in 1934 Acheson had coveted the post Morgenthau now held, they respected each other and held the same views on foreign friends and enemies. Morgenthau borrowed him to work with Edward H. Foley Jr., the Treasury's general counsel, on drafting the Lend-Lease bill to aid Britain. Acheson's appointment to the State Department was ostensibly a reward from FDR.

Acheson typified the consummate opportunist, a midlevel policy official stretching out to create and control the nation's most potent weapon of foreign policy save for actual war, but he found that State Department headquarters operated with a relaxed prewar mindset. His job, "coordination of commercial and economic questions with questions of major policy," was a hodgepodge of settling minor treaties and other trivia. ("Coordination of financial questions" was the duty of another assistant secretary, Adolf A. Berle Jr.) But Acheson's domain included one plum: supervision of the State Department's Division of Controls, the division under Joseph C. Green that was established by the Neutrality Act of 1935. From July 1940 onward it had approved or rejected export licenses in cooperation with the ECA. "Everyone in Washington 'wanted in' on economic warfare," Acheson wrote in his memoirs. He soon allied himself with hardliners in other agencies, especially Morgenthau and Harold Ickes, the secretary of the interior.[2]

Dean Acheson understood that the president had been maneuvering around the State Department's resistance to economic coercion of Japan. Roosevelt had personally designated by executive orders the commodities subject to export control. He had assigned the ECA as a "military matter" to Colonel Maxwell, who reported directly to the White House, and he later appointed his personal aide, Harry Hopkins, as administrator of Lend-Lease. Roosevelt undoubtedly wanted an energetic anti-Axis presence in the Department of State. As a former Treasury official, furthermore, Acheson bore unique credentials for launching *financial* warfare.

Agency Firefight, February 1941

Acheson had hardly reported to work on 1 February, in the drafty Old Executive Office Building next to the White House, when he took up the notion of freezing the assets of Germany and Italy and possibly Japan. On the sixth he attended a meeting in Maxwell's office to learn from the U.S. military attaché, recently returned from London, about the techniques of Britain's

Ministry of Economic Warfare. Thomas Hewes of the ECA briefed Acheson on his Planning Division's goals.[3]

Morgenthau had rebounded from Roosevelt's silent rejection at the end of 1940 of his plea for a freeze to fight Axis subversion in Latin America. He took heart that Berle and Herbert Feis disagreed with Hull's intransigence, and probably from Acheson's appearance on the scene. On 9 February he tested the issue with Roosevelt again and hinted to reporters that some kind of freeze was imminent. In retaliation, Hull, although conceding the logic of curbing espionage and subversion, told a private press gathering on the thirteenth that freezing was a terrible idea, because Germany and Japan would take revenge against the much larger U.S. investments in their countries. Acheson, and probably others in the State Department, then consulted Francis M. (Frank) Shea, assistant attorney general, about a compromise that might be acceptable to the bickering parties. By 14 February their work emerged as a three-point memo that Hull sent to Roosevelt in advance of a cabinet meeting later in the day. Hull conceded that foreign entities should register their U.S. assets with the government and report regularly any transactions. But, Hull grumbled, a general freezing of Axis assets would invite retaliation and complicate relations with the neutral Swiss and Russians. He proposed instead a "mobility" plan, a selective freezing of assets of subversive companies and persons the attorney general would identify. The Treasury would administer the selective freezing orders.

Morgenthau called a staff meeting with White, Foley, and others. Registration, reporting, and a freeze administered by the Treasury were, of course, acceptable as he had recommended them all along, as was freezing of entire countries or regions, but not Hull's "ad hoc" freezings of certain companies. The suspects would immediately spirit away their money—Axis funds were already fleeing to South America—or switch them to other owners, so their reports would become obsolete overnight. Legal probes would unjustly embarrass some companies. Foley ridiculed the FBI as "[having] the G-man put on his derby and black coat and walk in and say, 'Any subversive activities today, boys?'" Morgenthau felt dismayed that Acheson backed such a plan without consulting the Treasury. Perhaps, his aides suggested, Acheson was inexperienced, or didn't understand it, or had been taken in by his State Department colleagues.

Morgenthau phoned Attorney General Robert H. Jackson, who knew nothing about the matter. Frank Shea hadn't told his boss; his scheming exemplified the culture of opportunism, a grasping for power over economic war, that was blossoming all over Washington. Jackson mused, "Well, you can tell these fellows a hundred times that you don't want the jurisdiction of your department extended but they will try to do it." He wanted no part of playing detective in a "witch hunt," putting a knife into Hull's ad hoc scheme. But Shea, overreaching even further, had also conjured up an extravagant executive order to meld together every aspect of economic defense, domestic and foreign, under a so-called Civilian Economic Defense Committee. This gambit also went nowhere.[4]

Morgenthau grew anxious as to who might administer the ECA if a reorganization occurred. Shea had shown Bernard Bernstein, an assistant general counsel of the Treasury, two draft executive orders. His own version awarded the Treasury an overlordship of export control—subject to State Department veto. Another, by Dean Acheson, awarded the State Department jurisdiction over the ECA (or at least its budget, spending and employment). It was a transparent ploy by which Acheson, the supervisor of State's Division of Controls, would almost certainly take command of the ECA. Acheson's first foray into economic and financial warfare was a clumsy power grab. General Maxwell continued to report directly to President Roosevelt.[5]

After that day's confusion the ball was in Acheson's court. He phoned the next day to arrange a Treasury-State conference in his office. On 17 February the team of Foley, White, Bernstein, and John W. Pehle, a special assistant to Morgenthau, arrived to educate Acheson on the realities of asset control. First, they apologized for a misunderstanding: "freezing" meant control and licensing of money transactions, not an absolute lock-up of funds. They disparaged Hull's "Gestapo" nightmare of hobbling and prosecuting individuals and companies. Only freezing of whole countries was viable. Berle ventured that State was amenable to freezing Europe but not Japan. Acheson, who said he was impressed by the "very worthwhile and helpful" discussion, had learned that the road to power ran through financial warfare, not pumping up his thin role in export controls. Afterward Foley and Pehle consulted Norman Davis, a distinguished diplomat whom Hull respected. Davis felt happy that Acheson was now a key player, telling Hull that Acheson would work out a friendly arrangement with the Treasury.[6]

Roosevelt's Request for a Freezing Committee

Roosevelt, feeling ready for a plan to freeze Axis assets at the right moment, hunted for a way to solve the impasse in his cabinet. On 26 February 1941 he sent a memorandum to Hull, Morgenthau, and Jackson stressing the urgent need to control foreign assets:

> I am sure that this is a matter that needs to be prosecuted at once, and, after considering the various proposals, it seems to me the most satisfactory one is to have a Committee composed of the Secretary of State, the Secretary of the

Treasury, and the Attorney General to approve of any actions that are to be taken by the Treasury. It is clear to me that all three Departments are vitally involved, and I should like, therefore, to have the approval of all the Departments prior to any recommendation for action whenever a specific proposal is submitted for approval. Inasmuch as the Treasury is responsible for the actual issuance of the orders, I believe it would be advisable to have the Secretary of the Committee chosen from the Treasury staff.

The chronicler of the Morgenthau diaries remarked, "The solution was typically Rooseveltian. The structure of the committee gave special weight to Treasury influence, but the State Department retained a full veto."

Treasury Preoccupied

Morgenthau did not react, other than to reaffirm his disinterest in nonfinancial options such as tighter export licensing of Japan. "I wouldn't touch anything other than the freezing thing," he said.[7] In March 1941 he and his aides were distracted from Pacific matters by the urgent task of spearheading aid to Great Britain. After reelection to a third term, Roosevelt disclosed his plans for a Lend-Lease Act, to be drafted by the Treasury. Morgenthau, Foley, and other lawyers drafted it and testified before House and Senate committees. Congress passed and FDR signed the act, HR 1776, on 11 March. The secretary and his senior staff next prepared and lobbied for a $7 billion Lend-Lease appropriation. In those weeks and afterward Morgenthau conferred frequently with British officials, and in May he met with John Maynard Keynes representing His Majesty's Treasury.[8] The lobbying for financial sanctions against Japan ceased temporarily despite indignation over the secret war chest and evidence that it was fleeing day by day. The distraction left the initiative for financial warfare in the hands of the traditionally peaceable State Department.

One diplomat, Ambassador Joseph Grew, was trying to stir up anger in Washington about problems of American businesses in Japan. Executives of the few remaining U.S. investors operating there, including General Motors, Ford Motor, Otis Elevator, and oil companies, beseeched him for help against Japanese officials who were conducting intrusive inspections and forbidding remittances of money to the United States, harbingers of a coming takeover if not outright expropriation. On 10 March Grew repeated an earlier appeal to prohibit Japan from withdrawing dollars from the United States unless it granted U.S. firms a quid pro quo. Herbert Feis, the department's adviser on international economic affairs, thought that conditional financial blocking to force reciprocity "would be a good prelude to hermetic isolation" of Japan.

Other department officials, however, admonished Grew that U.S. policy shunned both general exchange controls and financial discrimination against nations, even Axis countries and others that blocked U.S. assets. Any freezing or blocking actions would originate from the Treasury and would likely be semitolerant, for example, allowing Japan to repatriate dollar revenues earned after a freezing order.[9] The State Department did not care to neuter Japan's dollars just because of the pains of a few U.S. corporate branches.

Draft Executive Order, March 1941

In March 1941 the cautious State Department designed the definitive financial weapon for future action. Carlton Savage, a veteran department attorney, drafted an executive order to impose severe freezing and exchange control exclusively on Japan. Savage was a counsel in the Office of the Historical Adviser (reorganized in 1938 as the Office of the Editor of Treaties), which advised the secretary on historical and constitutional questions. He had achieved prominence through coauthoring best-selling volumes of the diplomatic papers of the Woodrow Wilson administration concerning U.S. entry into World War I titled *Policy of the United States Toward Maritime Commerce in War* and had prepared testimony for Congress on the neutrality acts.[10] As a historian and lawyer, Savage was certainly familiar with the Trading with the Enemy Act as applied in World War I, in Roosevelt's banking and gold actions at the beginning of the New Deal and, more recently, in freezing assets of occupied countries. He was, moreover, a trusted aide to Hull.

On 24 March 1941 Savage delivered the draft order, nominally addressed to Sumner Welles. It presumed an invocation of Section 5(b) of the TWEA because of a continuing period of national emergency to be declared by the president. A presidential order would bar Japan from unauthorized foreign exchange dealings, export or withdrawal of gold, silver, currency, securities, or other documents of ownership, and transactions intended to evade the order. It defined Japanese assets as those which Japanese governments, companies or individuals held an interest, then or *at any time previously*.[11] Implementation was to be vested in the secretary of the treasury, who in accordance with the 1917 act would issue regulations, rulings, and licenses.

In a highly significant departure from all invocations of the TWEA, detailed administration of the freeze was to lie in the hands of a cabinet-level policy-making Foreign Exchange and Foreign Owned Property Committee consisting of the secretaries of the State and Treasury Departments and the attorney general. The committee could prohibit all Japanese transactions, even those wholly *within* the United States, and thereby nail Japan's money and assets precisely in place. It could demand reports, even from non-Japanese entities that did business with Japan. But the decisions of Morgenthau were to be automatically deemed committee policy, and he could appoint and supervise a committee staff, if any were needed. This scheme of a freewheeling committee to control the reins, despite the powers reserved to the secretary of the Treasury, was to have fateful consequences for Japan, the United States and the world. It was odd that an attorney of the reluctant Department of State prepared the order for actions that were quintessentially a function of the Treasury Department. Acheson, seven weeks on the job, was almost certainly the motivator; no other officer of the State Department had shown any taste for financial warfare, nor were any as qualified in finance as Acheson. Although the committee structure ensured a management seat at the table for Hull, his position was to be distinctly junior.[12]

But no action followed. Savage's draft slumbered on the shelf while Acheson and the Treasury staff were busy lawyering for Lend-Lease. In April Acheson prodded Morgenthau to lobby the president again to launch the "powerful weapon" of freezing, but Morgenthau was reluctant to try once more.[13] Yet Acheson, a senior officer of the State Department, had advocated all-out financial war against Japan and had set forth who would control the campaign—a team, most likely including himself as Hull's alter ego and the reigning financial expert on the three-man committee.

ECA Clamors for Financial Warfare

If nature abhors a vacuum, so do bureaucracies. Into the planning vacuum resulting from the tug-of-war in the cabinet slipped another group of opportunists at General Maxwell's Export Control Administration. Not content with studies that urged embargoes of trade with Japan (chapters 10 through 13), even of nonstrategic U.S. exports and of imports from Japan, the ECA delved into the more potent strategy of financial attack. As early as 10 January 1941 Chandler Morse of the ECA Projects Section, always an advocate of energetic action, recommended to Thomas Hewes, his chief, educating Maxwell by conducting studies of financial sanctions. These included refusal to buy gold, restriction of financial assets, and other steps to "disorganize the financial system" of enemies.[14] Another colleague, Eugene Staley, advocated tracking of foreign transactions and licensing controls of unfriendly countries' funds balances and movements, citing the shopworn rationale of thwarting spies and saboteurs. But another study for the section by Hal Lary of Japan's vulnerability to financial pressure was labeled unsatisfactory and returned to him for reworking.[15]

On 31 March, during a meeting with Noel Hall, the British Minister of Economic Warfare who was visiting Washington, Hewes complained that the

U.S. arsenal lacked financial weapons. His Projects Section had formed a Financial Committee to look into sequestering enemy property, and he hoped to spawn subcommittees to investigate financial actions against various regions and countries to educate General Maxwell. He had solicited the Commerce Department for expertise on direct investments, and the Federal Reserve was cooperating with him. But as dollar controls were the Treasury's domain, Hewes tried to enlist Bernard Bernstein, Morgenthau's assistant general counsel, into the embryonic committee. Hewes stressed that a Treasury expert could take charge of all the financial investigations.[16] A reply from Bernstein has not been located but it is clear that he spurned the invitation. Morgenthau was certainly not going to subordinate his department's prerogatives to a novice bureaucracy.

Hewes, undeterred, pressed to advance the ECA's role from proposing commodity embargoes into conducting studies of more virile strains of economic warfare. On 8 April, echoing the interagency approach of the "vulnerability" teams studying strategic commodities, he proposed to launch four analytical task forces covering all foreign nations of interest. The first, the vulnerability teams, were already finishing their work on Japan. The second team, just getting organized, would address international loans and insurance, matters largely inapplicable to Japan, and management of alien property. A third team, not yet assigned, would consider financial help for friendly powers and the freezing of funds. The fourth, when all else was completed, would investigate foreign dollar holdings. In the mindset of a bureau charged with limiting exports, the ultimate power of trapping enemy dollars ranked as the final step. As presciently but prematurely remarked by Warren S. Hunsberger, a junior ECA staff member and later the State Department's chief of research on the Far East, "The United States is now using its financial power in the international political and economic struggle. Whether or not one calls the use of financial weapons in international competition warfare, these weapons are powerful, and this country has begun their use."[17]

However, the ECA's dream of sallying into financial combat was soon to be doomed. The State Department was the agency properly charged with conducting foreign affairs, and the Treasury Department was the agency with the knowledge and authority to control funds under the Trading with the Enemy Act if and when the president invoked it.

Japan's Vulnerability in Strategic Resources

U.S. international economic policy early in 1941 remained focused on conserving defense materials through the export licensing system, in some cases selling strategic exports only to the Western Hemisphere and the British Empire, a policy not specifically targeted at depriving Japan. Commodities that were plentiful were rarely restricted. Petroleum, other than aviation grades, for example, remained generously licensed for Japan.

During the summer of 1940 the newly established Economic Control Administration had rushed to develop and administer the export licensing program for conservation, too busy to consider applying economic power against potential enemies, which in any case was a task beyond its authority. But the impulse to scale up to offensive economic warfare was not long in coming. In September the administrator, Gen. Russell L. Maxwell, submitted planning issues to the Army Industrial College in Washington, D.C. The college operated an Economic Warfare Section to teach courses and "lay the groundwork" for economic warfare, and its commandant had anticipated Maxwell's need. On 23 September he offered his staff as a nucleus of a national organization for economic war. Maxwell agreed that he needed such a staff, if only to collect economic information. Secretary of War Stimson, in concurrence, ordered transfer of the college's Economic Warfare Section to the ECA effective 15 December.[1] Once aboard, the college staff metamorphosed into the Planning Division, subdivided into three sections. Two dealt respectively with administration and with statistical information on commodities. The third, and most important for economic warfare, was the Projects Section to investigate foreign production, trade, and shipping and make "comprehensive plans for the coordination of economic power as an effective instrument of national policy."[2]

A second push toward economic warfare emanated from the Advisory Commission of the Council of National Defense. On 27 November 1940 the civilian commission urged President Roosevelt to designate an agency that would stretch beyond conservation. It would deny resources to potential enemies by targeted controls on exports and shipping and preclusive buying of commodities from neutral countries. Germany and Japan, it was believed, were circumventing the British blockade by obtaining U.S. supplies via other countries. The Advisory Commission pointed out abnormally high Japanese purchases of fourteen commodities since licensing began in July, including oil products, ferrous and nonferrous metals and scrap, and phosphate fertilizer.[3]

The head of Maxwell's Projects Section, Thomas Hewes, was a rather odd choice. A bright, fifty-three-year-old, Yale-educated attorney-politician, he had been active in Democratic party affairs since 1912 and on Connecticut state commissions. Although he had served brief stints as assistants to both the secretaries of State and the Treasury early in the New Deal, he had no obvious experience in trade control as an instrument of foreign policy. Given to writing flamboyant, courtlike proposals, he typified the "culture of opportunism" that was sweeping through Washington bureaucracies.[4] Such men, newly appointed to new functions, strove to inflate the roles their agencies played into exciting new adventures. Hewes's key aides were Harvard-educated analysts in their thirties, recruited from traditional agencies, each having a background suited to a niche in trade studies. Chandler Morse, an economist and former professor at Dartmouth College, had served twelve years with the Federal Reserve System in New York and Washington. His interests did include international trade (ultimately focusing on Africa), but his experience was in financial matters.[5] Richard H. Sanger, an economic analyst with an interest in the Middle East, held a degree in business administration, a rare specialty in the bureaucracy of those days. He had floated between the Commerce Department's foreign service and the staff of the Republican National Committee and had tried his hand at writing and reporting.[6] Louis Serge Ballif, an accountant, had served six years with the Federal Trade Commission and, more recently, the Tariff Commission, where he studied production costs of European businesses. While cost accounting was a relevant skill, his main value to the Projects Section lay in his understanding of the need to bring together experts with knowledge of specific commodities.[7] Hewes's aides eagerly supported his grasping at opportunities to aggrandize the ECA's role by moving from materials conservation into economic war of the broadest type. Neither they nor Hewes had any knowledge of Japan per se.

On 17 December 1940 Hewes drafted for General Maxwell a letter to Roosevelt recommending a policy of economic warfare. Because the U.S. and

British navies controlled the seas and the United States was an essential market for most neutrals, he pointed out, America could bring to bear pressures amounting to "strangulation" of the Axis. Economic victory, he believed, was preferable to armed combat. Early in 1941 Hewes's aide Chandler Morse advocated stern measures to "attack the enemy on a broad economic front" by export restrictions and interference with purchases anywhere in the world, enforced by an independent agency of "transcendent potency" to operate in parallel with the Army and Navy.[8]

British Encouragement

The advocates of economic war took heart from Britain's experience. In February 1941, during a visit home, Brig. Gen. Raymond E. Lee, the U.S. military attaché and head of U.S. Army intelligence in London, met with Maxwell's senior staff and Dean Acheson. British leaders deemed economic warfare a military function, according to Lee. They believed the war's outcome depended on it. The British had established a highest-level Ministry of Economic Warfare; not organizing it prewar had been a costly mistake, they believed. The U.S. "reward and punishment" idea for prodding neutral suppliers seemed pale in contrast. In late March, Noel Hall, joint head of the British Ministry who was visiting Washington, described his policies and procedures to the Projects Section and other officers of the ECA. As further elaborated by U.S. attachés' reports, the British distinguished between "economic aspects of war" and "economic warfare." Hall's so-called Fourth Service was an offensive agency—more warfare and less economics. It was charged with damaging and destroying enemy economies by denial of shipping and preemption of foreign supplies. In fact, it used every means short of combat, but it coordinated with the armed forces, going so far as choosing economic targets for air attack and naval blockade.[9] The muscular British precedent suited Maxwell, a professional soldier, and his eager team of neophytes.

Multi-Agency Task Forces

The staff of the Projects Section was keen to prepare for economic war by investigating trade conditions of foreign countries, including Japan specifically, but lacked information and experience. General Maxwell had to ask the Tariff Commission for data on U.S. imports, a subject alien to his export controllers. A staff report, "The International Use of Economic Pressure as an Instrument of National Policy," apparently added little despite an evocative title. Three later reports by the ECA's Far Eastern Division addressing the effects of trade restriction on both Japan and the United States were of no significance to judge from later derogatory remarks about them.[10]

Back in November 1940 the Projects Section had come up with a grandiose idea: to educate itself on overseas production and trade by assembling commodity experts from other government agencies into teams to launch investigations in depth. In December Louis Ballif pointed out to Hewes that troves of data were available in the files and libraries of the Departments of Commerce and Agriculture, the Maritime Commission, and other bureaus. Ballif's recent employer, the Tariff Commission, in particular employed personnel qualified for field investigations of international commodity trade. Ballif advocated assembling ad hoc committees of such experts to study and report. He envisioned hierarchies of country task forces, for example, a committee on Japan with subcommittees on its economy, trade, and finance. The president could authorize such activity under the Trade Agreements Act.[11]

Maxwell blessed Ballif's idea. On 24 February 1941 Chandler Morse set in motion a series of interagency task forces by convening a steering committee of six midranking officers of the Departments of Commerce and Agriculture, the Bureau of Mines, the Tariff Commission, and the Export Control Administration itself. Later, the Forest Service and Federal Reserve were added to the group. The Projects Section also opted to exclude specialists from the private sector to "keep it as quiet as possible." The proposed task forces would evaluate the impact on Japan of embargoing U.S. materials and denying it alternative sources of industrial, farm, and mineral products respectively. The Tariff Commission would assess the effects on American business, consumers, and labor of curtailing trade, including *imports* from Japan, a leap beyond the limitation of exports toward a possible termination of all trade. Morse assigned his deputy, Richard H. Sanger, to coordinate the work but decided he would personally select the commodities to be studied. Army Industrial College reports were available for some. Each team was granted flexibility to decide the details of its work, other than petty rules on statistical formatting and the color of report covers. Speed was paramount. Preliminary reports, sketchy if necessary, were to be submitted by the end of March.[12]

The ECA's drive toward trade warfare received a boost from the Army and Navy—with qualifications. At the end of January 1941 U.S. and British military planning staffs met in Washington to confer on war plans. Their effort culminated in May with adoption of Plan Rainbow Five, the blueprint for Allied grand strategy over the next four years, famous for the "Germany first" doctrine of defeating the most powerful enemy while consigning a war against Japan to second priority. Adm. Harold R. Stark, the chief of naval operations, and Gen. George C. Marshall, army chief of staff, told Maxwell on 4 April that the combined U.S.-British strategy included economic pressure by "control of commodities at their source by diplomatic and financial measure" as well as actual attacks. The military conferees expected to exchange liaison officers to coordinate the work of the ECA with the British Ministry of Economic Warfare, aiming toward cooperative economic warfare plans against all the Axis powers. Maxwell had already proposed to form a U.S. Economic Warfare Committee on Far Eastern Trade consisting of experts he was recruiting from civilian agencies. On 17 March, Marshall and Stark agreed to assign representatives to his committee while sternly cautioning that economic warfare endeavors must flow from needs of their Joint Basic War Plans. Extreme secrecy must be maintained, they warned, especially because of inferences that the civilian study committees might wander into selecting actual targets of attack.[13]

The Vulnerability Studies Under Way

The scope of the commodity task forces broadened rapidly from objective analytical surveys to recommendations for economic warfare policies to proposals for punitive actions against Japan. On 11 March 1941 Morse recommended to C. K. Moser, chairman of the ECA's Far East Research Unit, that he focus on bottlenecks in Japanese industry that could be exploited to apply significant economic pressure. (He added, far beyond his authority, that the information might prove useful for targeting air attacks.) On the fifteenth he directed that the team studies were to be uniformly titled "The Economic Vulnerability of Japan in [name of a commodity]." The reports, ultimately on about fifty commodities, came to be known as the Vulnerability Studies.[14] Four days later the teams were instructed to quantify the injuries to Japan if the United States preclusively bought up raw materials from neutral countries to keep them from Japan's grasp—not just for U.S. defense needs—and to comment on the impacts on those neutrals and on world prices and production. They were also to suggest other means of isolating Japan and to assess the difficulties it would face in obtaining needed materials in 1941, an indication that early sanctions against Japan were anticipated by the ECA planners. Since the Lend-Lease Act and combined military planning had committed the United States to global cooperation with Britain, the studies were further broadened to include parallel embargoes, shipping denials, and preclusive purchasing by the British Empire. The goal of the ECA was no longer merely conserving for national defense. It was intent on denying commodities to Japan and even penalizing its economy by cutting U.S. imports of its products. On 3 April, Hewes, the leader of the program, reported to Maxwell that the Projects Section's highest priorities were the team investigations for "economic warfare," as they were bluntly called.[15]

Hewes's section assembled sixty government analysts into thirteen committees to study groups of commodities, about half minerals and half vegetable and animal products.[16] A committee typically had four to six members drawn from three or four agencies. The largest number, including seven committee chairmen, were former colleagues of Louis Ballif at the U.S. Tariff Commission, an unusual entity for leadership because it mainly kept an eye on U.S. *imports*, whereas most teams were investigating *exports*. The United States imported few strategic commodities and those it did, such as tin and rubber, entered duty-free and were of no concern to the Tariff Commission; however, the commission's staff had studied foreign industries for resetting tariff rates from time to time, for example, to adjust for dumping. The second largest number of analysts, and three team chairmen, came from the Commerce Department, the agency that collected statistics on both exports and imports and posted commercial attachés in a few countries, including Japan, to report on business conditions. The vulnerability teams, to judge from their reports, consulted published aggregated data, not confidential information submitted to Commerce by individual American companies. The Department of Agriculture and the Bureau of Mines contributed experts to a few panels. Only one ECA employee served, and one from the Federal Reserve, both on iron and steel. Having no experts from industry, several teams advanced naïve conclusions about Japan. The State and Treasury Departments did not participate at all. Either the ECA wished to plot an independent course, or those departments responsible for foreign economic and financial policy wished to avoid participation with the ad hoc effort of an untested emergency agency. In any case, nearly all the vulnerability analysts were seized by that culture of opportunism affecting other bureaucracies in 1940–41. They enthusiastically strived to influence policy by recommending economic war against Japan by means of embargoes.

By late March 1941 preliminary studies began flowing in, some just a few pages long, some a hundred or more. Because of broad interest, mimeographed copies were widely distributed throughout the government. (In a comical misunderstanding Lt. Col. J. S. Bates of the Planning Section locked reports in his desk because they were marked "confidential," so the crucial studies of steel, oil, and chemicals did not reach Maxwell for two to four weeks.) Quality and value were far from uniform; the Commerce Department offered to reorganize and conform the statistical data more professionally. Since most committees recommended halting export licenses for Japan immediately, for the sake of urgency Hewes forwarded their reports without a personal review. By 11 April nearly all were ready for delivery to military and civilian agencies.[17]

The Coordinated Plan

The end point of the vulnerability studies and related efforts of the ECA's Projects Section was a two-volume report titled "A Coordinated Plan of Economic Action in Relation to Japan," rushed to completion on 1 May 1941. It included the vulnerability studies, other recent investigations of Japanese vulnerabilities in food, shipping, and machinery, and generalized studies of the Japanese government and economy by the ECA's Far Eastern Committee. Maxwell delivered the report to Stark and Marshall, their intelligence chiefs, most cabinet secretaries, and in mid-May to Vice President Henry Wallace, albeit with a disclaimer that he had not thoroughly reviewed it nor granted final approval.[18] Hewes enthused that he had submitted a coordinated, integrated, written plan of action that "first exposes the economic vulnerabilities of Japan and then lays out in one, two, three order the exact steps by which to carry through an aggressive American effort to isolate and strangle her" in order "to endeavor to wrench Japan from the Axis" by an "enduring an all-out campaign to isolate her economically" if diplomacy failed. The U.S. government must deploy *"all* our economic potency" against Japan," he argued, "driving straight at the heart of the enemy's internal living and his fighting power." To accomplish the grand objective the United States must immediately adopt an economic warfare policy under a single administrator charged with preparing detailed plans of action. Maxwell, Hewes, and their minions obviously expected the mantle to fall on their shoulders.[19]

The Vulnerability Studies

The vulnerability studies of April 1941constituted the most detailed effort the United States government ever undertook to evaluate the impact on Japan of a near-total curtailment of trade. The chosen commodities, nominated by a midlevel official, included most of the major articles of trade between the two countries, several minor ones of military value, some that the United States did not export or even produce, and the principal articles that it imported from Japan. For most of the commodities the interagency teams recommended complete embargos. For only a few did they propose no action, or omit recommendations altogether. They also commented on the burdens facing the U.S. economy from eliminating trade in each commodity, which they believed to be minor in all cases. What emerged was a show of determination of the export control bureaucracy to deny Japan almost all commerce with the United States and with the British Empire and other powers friendly to the Allies, a program nowhere authorized by the laws and orders that empowered the ECA.

Despite his staff's enthusiasm Maxwell did not commission a grand summary report of the impact of commercial isolation on the entire Japanese economy. Nevertheless, the vulnerability studies merit serious historical consideration. They are the main contemporary evidence of U.S. government judgments of the *specific* difficulties Japan would face, commodity by commodity, if and when trade ended. (For a reconstruction of what U.S. authorities might have concluded had they undertaken a *comprehensive* study in 1941, see chapter 18.)

Although the vulnerability studies were not presented in a particular order, they are summarized here in four groupings:

1. Commodities of strategic importance that Japan bought from the United States or its allies, or from U.S. companies operating in Latin America, described in the remainder of this chapter. Embargoes would primarily harm the Japanese army and navy. Of course, metals, oil, and some others were also important for Japan's civilian economy but they are fairly labeled as strategic because Japan most desired them for war.
2. Commodities primarily for civilian needs of food, clothing, shelter, and other amenities of life that Japan obtained largely from the United States and its allies (chapter 4). Embargoes would punish the population, an extreme manifestation of total economic warfare.
3. Commodities that America imported from Japan (chapters 3, 4, and 11). A few were desirable for the U.S. economy although not crucial. None were deemed vital for U.S. military needs. Import embargoes were recommended for silk and several other articles, to deny Japan foreign exchange and in a few cases to disrupt internal Japanese economic life.
4. Crude and refined petroleum, by far the most sensitive and critical of commodities (chapter 13) (charts 10, 11, and 12).

Iron and Steel

Japan's vulnerability in ferrous raw materials had not changed since the U.S. embargo decision of late 1940 (chapter 7). Exports to Japan had previously averaged $45 million per year. Analysts surmised that the complete halt of

CHART 10 **U.S. Exports to Japan, 1939 (in Millions of Dollars)**

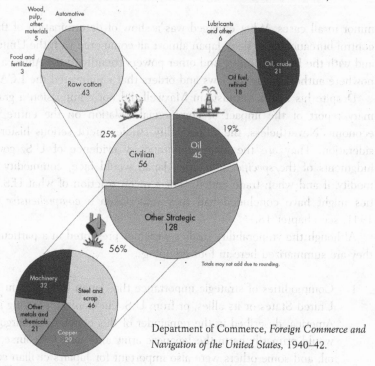

Department of Commerce, *Foreign Commerce and Navigation of the United States*, 1940–42.

CHART 11 **U.S. Exports to Japan, 1940 (in Millions of Dollars)**

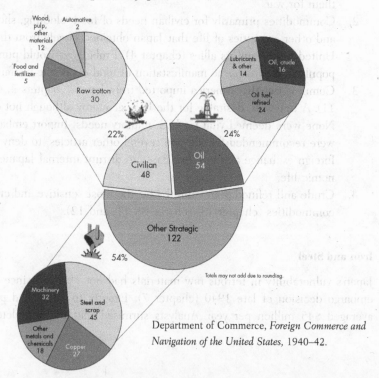

Department of Commerce, *Foreign Commerce and Navigation of the United States*, 1940–42.

CHART 12 **U.S. Exports to Japan, 1941 (in Millions of Dollars)**

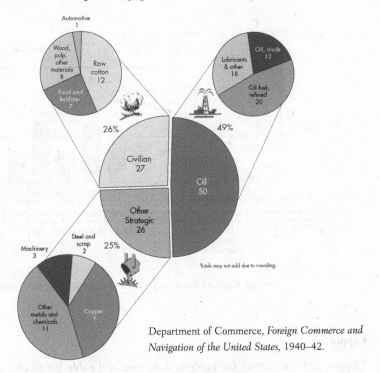

Department of Commerce, *Foreign Commerce and Navigation of the United States,* 1940–42.

U.S. scrap metal sales, and to a lesser extent restriction of pig iron from India to one-third of 1938 levels, posed serious problems for Japanese open hearth and electric furnace steel production (chart 13). They believed that in 1941 the steel mills were drawing down "fairly large" stockpiles of scrap previously imported. Yen-bloc iron ores were considered low grade and uneconomic, but high-grade iron ore still flowed in from Japanese-owned mines in British Malaya and new U.S.-owned mines in the Philippines, Japan being their only customer. Japan lacked blast furnace capacity to process more ore, however, and could not complete new capacity for two or three years. The study team felt it was desirable to cut off the ores from U.S. and Allied colonies to impede steel output. But how? The United States and Britain could not buy the huge ore tonnages mined in the Far East due to lack of shipping. Storage at the mines was impractical. Shutting them would harm the colonial economies. With an air of resignation, the analysts recommended pressuring the Philippine and Malayan authorities to halt production, cushioned by grants of money to compensate labor and non-Japanese owners. They glumly hoped that Japanese ore stocks were "not so great as to render futile efforts to restrict further shipments of such materials to Japan."[20]

CHART 13 **Japan's Scrap Iron and Steel Imports and Stockpile, 1931–1942**

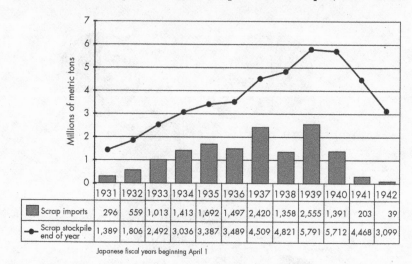

	1931	1932	1933	1934	1935	1936	1937	1938	1939	1940	1941	1942
Scrap imports	296	559	1,013	1,413	1,692	1,497	2,420	1,358	2,555	1,391	203	39
Scrap stockpile end of year	1,389	1,806	2,492	3,036	3,387	3,489	4,509	4,821	5,791	5,712	4,468	3,099

Japanese fiscal years beginning April 1

USSBS, *Coal and Metals in Japan's War Economy,* appendix Table 8.

Copper

Copper was a necessity for modern war: wire and cable for electrical circuitry of ships and planes, cartridges and artillery shells of brass alloys, and nonrusting bronze and brass fittings for navies and air forces. Japan's civil economy also required copper for electrical transmission, and steam and water tubes for factories and transportation. Before the First World War Japan had mined copper enough for itself while exporting 60 percent of its production. In 1917 production accelerated to 122,000 metric tons, making it briefly the world's second largest producer (after the United States). With a postwar price collapse and return of competition, exports dwindled. As Japan pursued an ambitious electrification program, by 1926 it was a net importer. It bought Latin American semirefined copper, concentrated ore from the Philippine Islands, and U.S. scrap. By 1937 Japan had to import half its requirements. Despite a large smelter capacity estimated at 130,000 tons of metal, in 1939 U.S. shipments of refined copper ingots and shapes soared to 125,000 tons (and another 116,000 tons in 1940 in spite of licensing requirements), plus some scrap and finished goods. Next came a scramble in January 1941 before an announced termination of exports, effective 3 February, due to shortages in the United States. Altogether Japan obtained about 80 percent of its copper from the United States. Copper constituted 12 percent of Japan's U.S. purchases in those years, at a cost of $25 to $28 million per year (ranking third behind oil and iron). It bought lesser quantities from U.S.-controlled companies in Chile and Peru; a plan to buy concentrated ore from several other countries did not work out, except for small quantities from the Philippines. By 1941 the United States was invoking contractual rights to demand cancellation of exports from Chile and diversion to the United States, and was buying up Peruvian output.

The vulnerability analysts had no information on the split of consumption, military versus civilian. Japan's shift from importing wire and cable to buying crude and scrap inferred a trend toward war uses, as well as conserving foreign exchange by refining at home. The copper team recommended continuing the ban on export licenses, persuading South American countries to halt all sales to Japan, and possibly buying up Philippine ores. (Britain absorbed the output of Canada, Australia, and southern Africa.) Meanwhile, since war operations in China did not seem to consume much copper for artillery shells or replacing lost ships and planes, the analysts were certain that Japan had been stockpiling imported copper in fear of U.S. controls. In fact, the stockpile and yen-bloc production proved adequate well into World War II.[21]

Minor "Bottleneck" Commodities

Vulnerability analysts examined exports of several industrial commodities of small dollar value viewed as potential bottlenecks for Japanese war industries. All were abundant in the United States and its possessions, and in some cases exported, so the embargoes they recommended would constitute a direct form of economic war rather than conservation:

- *Abrasives*. Japanese industry consumed silicon carbide and other synthetic abrasives for metal grinding by machine tools. In the 1930s its factories migrated from inferior natural emery to artificial abrasives produced in electric furnaces, but capacity limits required importing from the United States and Europe. In 1940 America supplied $1.5 million worth, five times the 1938 amount, indicating Japanese stockpiling. Although production in the United States and Canada was plentiful, the analysts recommended embargoes by both countries.[22]

- *Carbon black*. The United States was practically the only international supplier of carbon black, a high-grade sootlike residue of oil refining, for compounding with rubber in the manufacture of long-lived vehicle tires resistant to abrasion. Japan had few private automobiles but it manufactured tires for bicycles and, more importantly, for military trucks and planes and mobile industrial equipment. In the late 1930s Japan imported an average of thirty-seven million pounds of American carbon black annually, 2 percent of U.S. output. Although worth only half a million dollars, the analysts believed Japan had no other source and recommended an embargo to "seriously handicap" tire production.[23]

- *Abaca*. Manila hemp, stronger and more durable than other fibers, was the preferred cordage material for ropes and nets of naval, merchant, and fishing vessels. Philippines farmers were virtually the only growers. Japan bought fifty thousand tons of abaca per year, 60 percent of its cordage needs, from the islands. In April 1941 the Philippines came under the U.S. export licensing system. A vulnerability study recommended an embargo, albeit at serious cost to growers because preclusive buying was impractical. Nations harvesting other tropical cordage fibers were to be coaxed to follow suit. Japan would suffer "marked inconvenience."[24]

- *Fluorspar*. Aluminum exports to Japan had been halted by the U.S. moral embargo at the end of 1939, an ineffective sanction because Japan had expanded metal production several fold (chapters 5 and 10). The vulnerability analysts were impressed, however, by the "very great significance" of fluorspar, a calcium fluoride mineral utilized in smelting aluminum and a potential bottleneck for Japan. In the Bayer process, the only practical refining method, alumina (aluminum oxide refined from bauxite ore) was dissolved in a bath of cryolite (sodium aluminum fluoride) in large electrolytic cells. Molten aluminum was precipitated by passing electric current through the cells. The world supply of natural cryolite came from a single mine in the Danish colony of Greenland. Japan normally imported 1,300 tons of cryolite per year but in 1939 bought a precautionary 6,147 tons, still inadequate for its soaring aluminum industry in the analysts' opinion. In 1940 the Nazi occupation of Denmark cut off the source. Japan switched to synthetic cryolite manufactured from high-grade fluorspar. Therein lay an opportunity to hobble its aluminum output. Japan controlled only low-grade ores, in Korea and Manchuria. (Low-grade fluorspar was added as a flux in steel furnaces; although empire supplies were thought to be sufficient for Japan's 15,000-ton demand, the study did not comment on a possible steel bottleneck.) The United States mined 30 percent of the world's fluorspar of cryolite grade, and Germany mined about the same. When the war isolated Germany, Japan snapped up the small outputs of South Africa and Mexico. The vulnerability analysts enthused that a U.S. embargo, in conjunction with friendly countries, presented "a real opportunity to cripple the Japanese aluminum industry." The clever notion failed, however. After fluorspar exports ended, Japan's aluminum expansion continued unhindered by the imagined fluorspar bottle-neck.[25]

- *Organic solvents.* After four years of war Japan was known to be a large producer of explosives. The vulnerability analysts reviewed U.S. exports of explosives raw materials that were derived from petroleum refining. Methanol was a feedstock for TNT (trinitrotoluene), and acetone for cordite (and, along with butanol, both were widely used for lacquers, resins, and cellulose plastics). The United States produced nearly two billion pounds of these organic chemicals annually, and exported globally. Japan's small petrochemical industry was believed to lack adequate capacity. Japan purchased from the United States annually more than thirty million pounds of organic alcohols and solvents, and prior to 1939 it imported methanol from Germany. The vulnerability analysts recommended embargo of all three, including butanol in order to divert Japanese refineries' capacity away from the explosives feedstocks.[26]

- *Petroleum coke.* Petroleum coke was a solid "bottom of the barrel" residue of oil refining. The purest grades were pressed into carbon elec-trodes for aluminum refinery cells and for steel electric furnaces. Low grades were burned as cheap fuel. From 1938 to 1940 Japan imported about $1 million of high-value U.S. "pet coke" annually. Nevertheless, because Japan's refineries could produce it as long as they got crude oil, the vulnerability analysts opined that cutting Japan off would be "hardly worth while" unless part of a total petroleum embargo.[27]

Articles Japan Imported from Non-U.S. Sources

The vulnerability studies recommended severing Japan from strategic commodi-ties that the United States did *not* export by urging the British Commonwealth and other Allies to embargo them and by joint preclusive buying of neutral production.

- *Bauxite.* American hardliners had been frustrated by their inability to deprive Japan of aluminum. The U.S. moral embargo and the unavail-ability of European metal meant little to Japan; with ample power from hydroelectric dams and thermal coal plants, local production surged ahead. The self-sufficiency in smelting was so evident that the ECA did not bother to commission a vulnerability study of aluminum metal. Japan, however, imported 100 percent of its bauxite, the common commercial ore that contained about 25 percent aluminum. When Japan began to produce aluminum in the mid-1930s it purchased 10,000 to 15,000 tons of bauxite annually from India, Malaya, and Greece because the Netherlands East Indies, the largest regional producer, sold its output to Germany. Mines on three Japanese mandated islands in the Pacific yielded some bauxite, of which little was known, but experiments in Manchuria to process low-grade aluminous shales were correctly suspected as technological dead ends. In 1939, with Germany isolated, Japan stepped in to purchase an astonishing 168,000 tons from the Indies. This indicated to the vulnerability analysts that it was procuring "a large accumulation (possibly a two years' supply) of bauxite over and above the requirements." The studies reckoned that preclusive buying of East Asian bauxite was impossible because of lack of shipping for the bulky ore. (The United States itself relied on imported ore from British and Dutch Guiana.) Japan would be "seriously crippled in her efforts to make aluminum for airplanes" only if the bauxite of British Asian colonies and especially the Dutch Indies were cut off, and then only after two years, the analysts gloomily concluded.[28]

• *Ferroalloys.* Manganese was the most essential ferroalloy for common grades of steel. Adding 14 pounds of it contained in ferromanganese, an iron-manganese alloy, to a ton of molten steel scavenged sulfur impurities to yield stronger steel amenable to heat treatment. The analysts estimated Japan needed 90,000 to120,000 tons of high-grade manganese ore per year for steel making and even larger tonnages for chemicals and furnace refractories. Empire production, 66,000 tons in 1936, was increasing. Nevertheless, from 1935 to 1939 Japan imported an average of 210,000 tons of ore, largely from India supplemented by mines of British Malaya and from 1939 the Philippines. The purchasing was far in excess of needs, indicating massive stockpiling. The United States depended totally on imports of manganese, and feared that its main supplier, the Soviet Union, might soon be cut off. It was trying, along with Britain, to contract for the ores of all accessible countries. The vulnerability analysts inferred that Allied buying was pinching Japan because it accepted ores of less than the 50 percent manganese content demanded by American steel companies. They recommended pressure by the United States and Britain and their Asiatic dominions and colonies to sell all to them and none to Japan. In their rather extreme opinion, the Allies "would be justified in using any available measures to prevent manganese ore being exported to Japan from any source of supply, even if these two countries themselves did not need all the ore which is obtainable anywhere."

Chromium was the key ingredient of the stainless steels essential for navies. Japan appeared to be self-sufficient in manufacture of ferrochrome. Its mines fulfilled its demand for thirty-nine thousand tons of chromite (chromium ore), except in 1939, when it imported some from the Philippines. Yet vulnerability studies were prepared on the hypothetical grounds that the United States and Britain needed Pacific basin ores that Japan *might* buy. The analysts worried that Japan might seek to control the outputs of the Philippines and of New Caledonia, a French island colony governed by De Gaulle's Free French. Both sources were of rising importance to the United States, which had no chromite deposits. The country ought to acquire all their production, the analysts advised.

Tungsten was a critical ingredient of extraordinarily tough tool steels. Unusually, the yen bloc produced a surplus. Japan consumed two thousand tons per year of 60 percent–grade tungsten oxide concentrated ore from Korea and another two thousand tons procured "in one way or another" from unoccupied China, the largest world producer, despite a U.S. government contract to buy all the output of Nationalist China. Not much could be done to inconvenience Japan, except to continue the embargo of pure U.S. tungsten metal and preclusively buying British Burma's mine output.[29]

The United States was the world's dominant supplier of molybdenum for alloying tough steels. Exports to Japan had ceased under the moral embargo of December 1939 (chapter 6). The studies recommended formalizing it by executive order.[30]

Nickel was an indispensable strategic metal for armor, for stainless and alloy steels, and for plating ordinary steel. Oddly, it was not a subject of a vulnerability study, even though the Japanese Empire had no internal sources. Japan relied largely on Canadian nickel and, in part, on ore from French New Caledonia. The key world supplier, International Nickel Company of Canada (Inco) in which U.S. investors held a large stake, was booked up with deliveries to the United States and England. Presumably nickel was omitted from the vulnerability agenda because Inco was not supplying Japan.

- *Asbestos*. Asbestos fiber more than three-eighths of an inch long was a strategic material used to line brakes and clutches and to insulate and fireproof ships and buildings. (Short fibers, not strategic, were mixed into cement.) Neither the United States nor Japan mined any asbestos. Canada, the top producer, along with South Africa and the Soviet Union, supplied the world. There was no shortage in 1941. Japan had stopped buying U.S.-manufactured asbestos sheet, which was soon embargoed in any case. Since the late 1930s, however, its imports of long-fiber asbestos from Canada had risen sharply, an indicator of stockpiling. The "quite easy" solution for economic war was to induce Canada to embargo sales.[31]

- *Exotic strategic specialties*. War industries consumed certain articles of high value, measured in pounds, not tons, and found in only a few locations. Preemptive buying of most was feasible, and recommended by the analysts in most cases, along with diversions of British Empire output. Brazil was the indispensable source of three such commodities. Perfect quartz crystals, "highly strategic" for their piezo-electric qualities in radios and instrumentation, were still reaching Germany, and Japanese buying had soared. The studies urged that a U.S. agency in Rio buy the crystals direct from the mines, avoiding shady middlemen.[32] Sheet mica, a rare transparent variety of a common mineral, was used in radio condensers and tubes, gauge glasses, and other technical equipment. India, the larger of the two producers, had halted sales to Japan, but in Brazil Japanese traders were buying recklessly at any price. The proposed solution was preemptive U.S. buying.[33] Industrial diamonds were essential for metalworking drills, saws and dies for defense work, and rock drilling. Output was tightly controlled in British Africa, and the Belgian Congo under British supervision, which together mined 95 percent of the world's diamonds. None were reaching Japan for its need of forty thousand carats per year for war production. But Brazil, the only neutral source, was infested with smugglers. Again, the answer was preclusive buying.[34] Natural graphite flakes and lumps were fashioned into crucibles and retorts for defense plants. Japan had no deposits. The British had halted sales from Ceylon in January 1941 at U.S. request and were blockading Vichy French Madagascar, actions sufficient to pinch Japan.[35]

The vulnerability analysts, rather unusually, advised against embargoes of two other minor commodities. Germany had been the main supplier of high-grade optical glass for periscopes, gun sights, camera lenses, and the like, but as trade with Germany was already reduced, no action was proposed. Nor was an embargo of kapok from the Dutch East Indies, for flotation life preservers, necessary because substitutes were easily available.[36]

Other Items Not Studied

Surprisingly, a few other important strategic commodities already under U.S. licensing did not merit ECA studies. Japanese deficiencies in such materials were briefly considered in a State Department report of 27 May 1941. Zinc was vital for galvanized steel, brass, and complex castings, and lead for ammunition and gasoline refining. The yen bloc was 60 percent self-sufficient in zinc but only 20 percent in lead. Japan imported both metals from dollar-area countries—Canada, Mexico, and Peru—and some from Australia, at a cost of $5 million annually. As for tin, a $10 million requirement for solder, brass, and canning sheet, the yen bloc was one-third self-sufficient. Sources friendly to the United States, namely, Malaya, the Dutch Indies, and Bolivia, were logical candidates for preclusive buying.[37]

Conclusion

From a policy point of view the embargoes of strategic resources advocated by the vulnerability study teams were of two broad categories. First, the materials needed for U.S. rearmament and in short supply in the United States, whether actual or threatened, had been restricted from sale to Japan by the spring of 1941. The recommended embargoes, therefore, did not really amount to waging economic war. On the other hand, the embargoes advocated for materials in ample supply, even if military in their end-uses, amounted to a limited economic war—limited because the intention was to hamper military aggression, not to penalize the Japanese economy and people. But the vulnerability project went far beyond advocating embargoes of strategic materials. They also pressed to embargo goods essential for maintaining the life, health, and standard of living of the Japanese people, the ultimate U.S. move to a full economic war.

The Vulnerability of the Japanese
Economy and People

I n the spring of 1941 the ECA interagency teams looked beyond Japan's vulnerability in war materials. The Project Section's zeal for economic warfare prompted investigations of Japan's imports of food, clothing, and shelter materials on the premise that in total war, even of the economic variety, no moral distinction need be drawn between soldiers and civilians. Identifying targets for embargo proved a challenge, however. The Japanese civilian economy did not widely depend on U.S. resources—oil, a special case, is dealt with in chapter 13—but the United States did supply some commodities of importance to Japanese agriculture and consumer life. If embargoed, the people would suffer a decline in standard of living, with the unspoken supposition that they might dissuade their leaders from aggressive foreign policies.

Land, Population, and Food

Japan's problem of feeding its own citizens was widely known.[1] In Tokugawa times, before Japan opened to trade in the mid-nineteenth century, rice culture was productive enough to feed a stable population of about thirty million.[2] After 1860, birth rates rose and death rates fell. Population grew steadily at 1 percent per year, despite emigration. In 1937, 30.8 births and 17.0 deaths per thousand contrasted with U.S. figures of 17.1 and 11.3, a natural accretion rate *four times* as great as in the United States during the Depression. By 1941 the population had grown to seventy-three million, 143 percent higher than at the time of Commodore Perry's visit.

However, land under cultivation had barely expanded, from 12 percent of Japan's area in the 1880s to 16 percent in 1921, including the valleys of Hokkaido, suited only to crops of low nutritional value. At that point virtually all the arable land had been planted. The rest of the terrain was too mountainous for farming. Yet Japanese food production rose 1.3 percent per year, 75 percent between 1880 and 1920, even as farm workers migrated to the cities. The Meiji government encouraged rice culture with subsidies, tariffs, and low taxes. In 1918 soaring rice prices provoked riots, a traumatic event that impelled the government to seek food self-sufficiency within the empire. Subsidized rice culture in Korea and Formosa paid off handsomely. By 1941, when Japan imported 20 percent of its food, the yen bloc as a whole was self-sufficient in rice in most years.[3] In Japan proper, each cultivated square mile of the home islands fed 3,596 people, about twenty times the ratio of the United States (U.S. 1950 figures).[4] The gain in productivity resulted in part from superior strains of rice and better irrigation, and farm families may have worked longer and more efficiently, but such factors had topped out by the 1930s. The key factor of productivity had been extravagant applications of fertilizers, more intensively than in any other nation of the world.

The Japanese diet was spartan. In 1934–38 the average intake of 2,180 calories per capita ranked well below the 2,800 to 3,100 of Western Europe and the 3,150 calories of the United States (although it was 200 calories higher than India).[5] The Japanese people consumed five-sixths of their calories as grains and starches, over half from rice alone. The diet was low in protein, fruits, and vegetables. Prewar Japanese were short in stature—one source cites five feet three and a half inches for males and four feet ten and a half inches for females—so that relative to body mass the Japanese people were not generally undernourished.[6]

In 1940 and 1941, due to crop failures in Korea, Japan imported non-empire rice. It bought largely from French Indochina, which by then was virtually absorbed into the yen bloc, and from Thailand, which was independent but susceptible to political pressure. Only small amounts came from British Burma. Some American vulnerability analysts mistakenly suggested that Japan could not afford to buy more rice from elsewhere.[7] The most perceptive correctly understood that coping with vulnerability in food required ever greater productivity. A slight setback might lead to significant undernourishment. (The "starvation blockade" of Germany was well understood as a decisive factor of World War I.) Probing for weaknesses, the analysts identified two of the three essential fertilizer minerals as viable targets for sanctions. The yen bloc was self-sufficient in nitrogen, but Japan had to spend hard currency for most of its phosphorus and nearly all its potassium needs. (Plant food values are expressed as percentages of elemental nitrogen [N], phosphoric oxide or phosphate [P_2O_5], and potash or potassium oxide [K_2O] contained in fertilizers.) In late 1939 the European war disrupted normal supply channels, leaving the United States as the main accessible source of phosphate and potash. Therein lay an opportunity to pressure Japan by embargo, although necessarily of gradual effect because those minerals leached out of farming soils gradually over two or three growing seasons. Embargoes would not precipitate an immediate food crisis but would eventually undermine the health and nutrition of the Japanese people.

Organic Fertilizers

Since earliest times Japanese farmers had applied to crops the "green manure" plant and animal wastes of farms and human "night soil" collected in the villages. But green manures, containing about 1 percent plant nutrients, required much labor for limited gain. Supply could not increase much. At the turn of the century Japanese agriculture turned more to off-farm organics containing 10 to 15 percent nutrients: sardines and fish processing wastes, "oil cake" residue from pressing Manchurian soybeans, and ashes from burning wood and charcoal.[8] The organics, however, could not keep up with six hundred thousand new mouths to feed every year. In the twentieth century Japan's future depended on industrial fertilizers (chart 14).[9]

Nitrogen

Farmers grew rice, the staple food of Japan, in flooded paddy fields where soil chemicals and bacteria fixed nitrogen from the air into compounds that plant roots could absorb. Wet rice culture tamed the vagaries of climate and typhoons, maximized nutrient release, and suppressed weeds, but water migration limited the efficiency of the natural process. Japan needed nitrogen fertilizer, which stimulated growth of large, dark leaves, forcing rapid maturity and allowing the planting of two crops per year. Ammonium sulfate crystals containing 20 percent N, drilled a few inches into wet soils with acidity neutralized by limestone, were highly efficient for rice because the ammonia remained in solution through the growth cycle. Rice yields could be increased markedly, for example, from twenty-four hundred pounds to better than four thousand pounds per acre by application of one hundred pounds of chemical nitrogen.[10] In the 1930s Japan successfully expanded ammonia production. Output in Japan and Korea rose fivefold, to a peak in 1941 of 524,260 tons of contained nitrogen. Japan alone ranked third in world production.[11] Byproduct

CHART 14 Japan Proper: Fertilizer Mineral Sources, 1924–1936

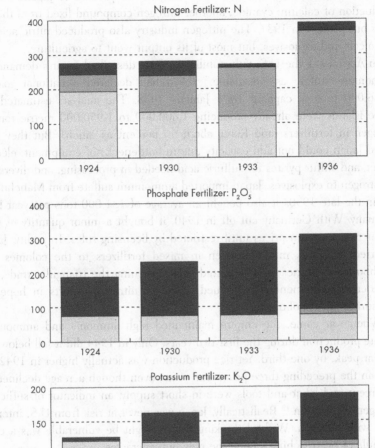

Nitrogen Fertilizer: N

Phosphate Fertilizer: P_2O_5

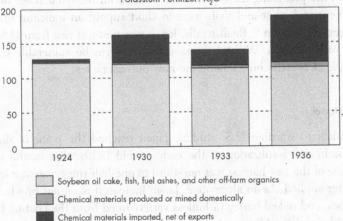

Potassium Fertilizer: K_2O

☐ Soybean oil cake, fish, fuel ashes, and other off-farm organics

☐ Chemical materials produced or mined domestically

■ Chemical materials imported, net of exports

OCL, "Place of Foreign Trade in the Japanese Economy," vol. 1, pt. 2, tables II-7 to II-11.

ammonia, from converting coal to "town gas" for illumination, and imports, both formerly important, dwindled to less than 10 percent of Japan's supply. Production of calcium cyanide, another nitrogen compound fixed from the air, grew but peaked in 1937. The nitrogen industry also produced nitric acid for chemicals and explosives, but most of its output went to agriculture.

In April 1941 the U.S. vulnerability analysts described Japan's demand for ammonium sulfate as "insatiable." Tokyo had declared a national goal of 2,266,000 tons of capacity by 1 January 1938. The analysts estimated the home islands were already producing 1,600,000 to 1,950,000 metric tons of nitrogen in fertilizers (and Korea about 50 percent as much). But they supposed Japan could not add capacity due to bottlenecks of equipment, electric power, and sulfur pyrites for sulfuric acid needed in processing, and diversions of nitrogen to explosives. Japan imported ammonium sulfate from Manchukuo, but in the late 1930s it also bought an average of 131,000 tons per year from Germany. With Germany cut off in 1940, it bought a minor quantity of U.S. product at premium prices until restricted by licensing rules. In reality, Japan exported nearly as much nitrogen in mixed fertilizers to the colonies and neighboring countries as it imported. Misconstruing the triangular trade, the Americans recommended continued denial of nitrogen exports in hopes of pressuring Japan politically.[12]

When war came, the empire maintained high ammonia and ammonium sulfate production during the first two years. Only in 1944 did it fall below the prewar peak, by one-third. Yet rice production was actually higher in 1942–44 than in the preceding three peacetime years, even though acreage declined by 3 percent and labor and tools were in short supply, an indicator of sufficient nitrogen application.[13] Realistically, Japan was never at risk from U.S. interference with nitrogen. Wishful thinking that it might be vulnerable was a clear example of overreaching among the new bureaucracies.

Phosphates

According to wartime U.S. studies, Japan reached the point of diminishing returns in rice fertilization in the early or mid-1930s, that is, the *percentage* increase of the rice harvest was one-third to one-half the *percentage* increase in fertilizer applied. As an alternative, Japan increased plantings of wheat, barley, potatoes, and naked barley (a hulless variety freed from the coating by threshing). Phosphate addition was essential for dry farming of these grains and starches in northern valleys and cool uplands. Phosphate enhanced rapid growth, developed better roots, and accelerated tillering (sprouting) and faster ripening, enabling multiseason cropping. It also retarded plant diseases and provided insurance by underwriting yields in bad climate seasons. The dry grains responded to phosphate applications with yield increases up to an extraordinary 50 percent. By 1941 they furnished 20 percent of Japan's calories with the help of imported phosphate minerals.[14] Potatoes and sweet potatoes, 7 percent of the national diet, responded to phosphate with 7 to 29 percent higher yields. In comparison, phosphate increased rice yields only 5 percent or so because paddy water converted enough soil phosphorous to soluble compounds.

World agriculture relied on shallow beds of phosphate rock pebbles mined in Florida, in North Africa, and on Pacific islands. Insoluble phosphate rock contained up to 77 percent BPL, "bone phosphate of lime," a commercial measure of phosphate content. A ton of rock reacted with sulfuric acid yielded 1.5 tons of superphosphate, a chemical containing 20 percent P_2O_5. In the 1920s Japan developed a large superphosphate industry. By 1941 forty-six plants located near deposits of sulfur pyrites produced 1.5 million metric tons of superphosphate from 1 million tons of imported rock, all of Japan's needs and a surplus for the colonies, plus phosphorous chemicals.[15]

Japan imported phosphate rock from four regions. Prospecting in the 1920s had turned up deposits on its Pacific Mandated Islands. Production on Angaur, in the Palau group, reached 143,000 tons in 1939. Smaller productions commenced in the 1930s on Peleliu in the Palaus, Fais in the Caroline Islands, Saipan in the Marianas, and, nearer home, Daitojima near Okinawa. The empire's production of 375,000 tons of rock provided 32 percent of Japan's rising needs in 1939. North Africa, primarily Egypt and to a lesser extent Morocco, was a steady supplier. "Land pebble" rock from central Florida, shipped through the port of Tampa, was another reliable source. The closest non-yen sources—freight costs mattered for a commodity worth only three dollars a ton—were four tiny Pacific islands controlled by British, British-Australian, or French enterprises. Mines on Christmas Island, south of Java, and Makatea, a French island in the Tuamoto group, shipped mainly to Japan, but their outputs were small. On the other hand Nauru and Ocean Islands, atolls mandated to Australia, had a combined capacity of 1,250,000 tons—the world's fifth largest producer—but they supplied Australia and New Zealand and only a residual bit to Japan. By 1940 the Pacific phosphate islands had neared practical limits of production.

The war in Europe curtailed two of Japan's foreign phosphate sources. Egypt was cut off after Mussolini entered the war in June 1940. In December 1940 two German raiding ships bombarded the loading docks and booms at Nauru and sank several special freighters, putting the operation out of commission. The other phosphate islands diverted sales from Japan to Australia and New Zealand. (Ironically, Japan had permitted the German ships to use its Caroline Islands bases.) Japan hurriedly developed small mines in China and French Indochina.[16] In the emergency, however, the United States offered the largest accessible source of phosphate rock. Florida's mines supplied almost all U.S. agricultural needs, and exported 1.1 million tons until loss of markets in Europe due to the war. Phosphate reserves were so enormous, and production so expandable by simple dredging and washing in shallow pits, that the mineral was not critical nor even "strategic," according to a congressional committee report in 1938 in response to Roosevelt's inquiry.[17]

Nevertheless, Japan did not spend its dollars for American phosphate. The vulnerability specialists assumed, wrongly, that Tokyo was focused on production of rice, the crop least responsive to phosphates, because labor shifting to industry inhibited expansion of dry grain farming. They also calculated that it had been importing excessively and had built a one-year stockpile of rock and superphosphates. Thus they concluded that a phosphate embargo would have "minor if any effect" unless all sources, presumably including the empire island sources, were cut off. They did not evaluate any crop loss Japan might suffer.[18]

In fact, Japan's stockpile was inadequate. Superphosphate manufacture declined rapidly from a 1940 peak of 1,846,000 tons, by 50 percent within two years and nearly 100 percent after mid-1944 as U.S. submarines isolated the Japanese-controlled islands. (Nauru and Ocean were occupied by Japan but bypassed by the U.S. offensive, surrendering at the end of the war along with Angaur.) The prompt phosphate shortage had dire consequences. Whereas Japan maintained its prewar rice production until the last year of the war, the harvest of wheat, its second most important foodstuff, dropped precipitously after 1940 despite acreage expansion. Barley declined soon after. It was a rare instance of U.S. analysts, perhaps lulled by Washington's "nonstrategic" attitude toward phosphate, underestimating the deprivation a shortage would inflict on the Japanese people.[19]

Potash

Potassium improved the health and vigor of grains, benefits important in cloudy weather with low sunshine.[20] In traditional Japanese agriculture wood ashes, and seaweed in some places, had provided potassium. Until 1914, mines in Germany supplied the world with potassium sulfate, a mineral containing 50 percent K_2O. The World War I blockade of Germany drove prices above $100 per ton, raising havoc with global agriculture, especially in the United States, where corn, cotton, and tobacco were heavy potassium consumers. After the war France and Spain entered the export trade, and the U.S. government subsidized prospecting, successfully, at a cost of $2 million, a lordly sum for the times. In the 1930s U.S. firms commenced production from deep-lying beds of potassium chloride containing 60 percent K_2O in New Mexico, and from brines of Searles Lake, California. Because of freight economics, however, the United States continued to import half or more of its needs from across the Atlantic while exporting to Japan. The Spanish Civil War and the general European war forced the United States back on its own production, which proved so readily expandable that by 1941 it was self-sufficient.

The case for vulnerability of Japan in potash was persuasive. Potassium from organic sources and some local low-grade salts fell short of needs in the 1920s. Japan turned to foreign potash minerals. In the late 1930s imports from Germany and the United States averaged 180,000 tons per year, a small tonnage compared to 1 million tons of phosphate rock; however, high-grade U.S. potash sold for forty dollars per ton versus three or four dollars for rock, and freight was more expensive due to the train haul to the West Coast and special handling to keep the soluble salts dry. Thus Japan's import bill for each mineral was similar, $3 or $4 million per year. The European war limited its potash imports to 75,000 tons, some from the United States where some fertilizer plants resold for a quick profit despite voluntary rationing by the mining companies (which extracted largely from federal lands) to reassure American farmers. The vulnerability analysts wondered if the lower imports were due to Japan's lack of hard currency, which was hardly a problem for such minor payouts.

The vulnerability studies concluded that potash was Japan's Achilles heel and that an embargo would be the strongest possible pressure the United States could inflict on the Japanese people, albeit one that would pinch gradually:

> The results of a failure to apply potash to the soil, in quantities necessary for maximum crop yields, will be manifest in Japan in the first year of sparse application following cessation of imports. The depletion of potash stocks and the exhaustion of the soil should cause a critical situation to develop in the second year. . . . It would be impossible to produce potash in Japan in appreciable quantities from uneconomical sources without large investment in research, plant equipment, and a delay of years.

The analysts predicted that an embargo of commercial grade potash, along with British closure of a Dead Sea brine plant in Palestine, interference with

Spanish shipments, and preclusive buying of Chilean salts, would totally deprive Japan. A presidential order of 10 January 1941 placed potash salts exceeding 27 percent K_2O under export control, leaving available only "manure salts" of very low grade. For such grades Japan would have to spend more dollars for potassium than for oil, hypothetically because shipping was unavailable. Nevertheless, because Japan might out of "dire need" buy 27 percent grade manure salts, the analysts recommended embargoing them.[21]

The decline of potash available to Japan was sudden and extreme, a drop of two-thirds in 1941 and almost 100 percent thereafter. It was far more drastic than the 40 percent decline of phosphate supply and the insignificant drop of nitrogen in the same period. During the war a marked decline of dry crop harvests reflected shortages of imported fertilizer minerals. The U.S. analysts may have exaggerated the impact of an absolute cut-off of potash compared with the partial cut-off of phosphates as the benefits of the latter were greater. Taken together, an implied crop deficit from lack of mineral imports of, say, 30 percent of dry grain harvests and a few percent of the rice crop, might equate to a loss of 7 percent of Japan's grain and 5 percent of its overall calories. Meanwhile population was growing 1 percent annually. The U.S. experts' supposition that a fertilizer blockade would, in time, cause a disastrous food shortage was fundamentally correct. It constituted one of the harshest threats of economic war against the Japanese population.[22]

Other Foodstuffs

The yen bloc was self-sufficient in nonstarch foodstuffs, which provided one-sixth of Japan's nutrition. The vulnerability studies recognized the importance of protein for health and vigor but they estimated that the Japanese diet contained only 3 percent protein, 65 calories per capita per day, nearly all in three ounces of fish. (Lacking grazing land, Japan was thought to rank lowest in per capita meat consumption of any major country, about 15 percent that of western countries, less even than India where cattle slaughter was taboo in places.) The analysts had trouble calculating the fish supply. The catch of edible fish was about 2.2 million metric tons, but another 1 to 1.5 million tons of sardines were thought to be pressed for cooking oils and fertilizer residue. They reported that potential U.S. interference would have to be indirect, through embargoes of oil fuel, hemp for nets, and steel and lumber for vessels. During World War II shortages of fuel and materials, requisitions of vessels, and sinkings indeed reduced the catch drastically.[23]

It is surprising that the Japanese did not consume more soybeans, a high protein food. The available supply was large, 75 percent imported from Manchukuo and 25 percent home grown. Mills extracted cooking oil and sold the residue mostly as fertilizer. Soybeans were eaten mainly in miso paste and shoya sauce, condiments of low caloric value. Other than oil, soybean consumption was a minuscule 8 grams per day in 1941, less than 1 percent of caloric intake. Therefore no vulnerability team investigated soybeans. Yet as the war progressed the Japanese of necessity consumed more and more, shipped via Korea. The consumption of soybeans as food rose to 13 grams per capita in 1945. But more than sixty years after the war the average Japanese person consumes about 40 grams of soybeans per day in tofu, enriched flour, and other foods, along with much more protein in fish and meat.[24]

Edible oils for food and cooking provided an estimated 2 percent of the Japanese diet, forty calories per day. Japan produced 800 million pounds annually from sardines and soybeans, and exported 350 million pounds. Japan did not usually buy animal fats, although, mysteriously, imports of lard worth $1.8 million amounted to 3 percent of all Japanese purchases from the United States in 1941. Perhaps Japan was hastening to spend its dollars for an available product. The analysts saw no opportunity for harming Japan other than cutting off copra (dried coconut) from the Philippines and Allied colonies.[25]

The Japanese people had a taste for sweets. Sugar intake of 140 calories per day provided 6.5 percent of their calories. Imports of about a million tons per year came mostly from Formosan sugar cane and smaller amounts raised on Okinawa and Saipan. Sugar beets were grown on Hokkaido. Fertilizer needs were not great. No opportunity for U.S. pressure was apparent. The vulnerability project ignored sugar as well as the remainder of the Japanese diet, a miscellany of fruits, vegetables, eggs, and dairy products raised within the yen bloc.[26]

Rayon

The vulnerability teams rendered split opinions about the two most common clothing fibers. They recommended embargoes of wood pulp and salt, the basic ingredients for rayon manufacture, while shying away from an embargo of raw cotton because of the plight of American farmers.

In the 1930s Japan greatly expanded production of long-filament rayon, a yarn extruded from bleached sulfite pulp chemically digested in caustic soda. For durable textiles it imported pure alpha-cellulose "dissolving pulp" from the spruce and hemlock forests of Scandinavia and North America that contained long-chain molecules relatively free from lignin. In 1935 Japan (along with Germany and Italy) decided to conserve foreign exchange by substituting low grade pulp from the inferior softwoods of northern Japan, Korea, and Sakhalin. Processing of local pulp yielded short rayon fibers that were spun together into rayon staple yarn, far less durable than cotton or long-filament rayon. After the Sino-Japanese War began industrial laws mandated a switch from cotton, the most important textile, to rayon staple cloth. In 1938 rayon clothing surpassed cotton. But, unless blended with sturdier fibers, staple cloth lost 50 percent of its strength when wet and was liable to fall apart in Japan's humid weather. The rayon mills had no standards for pulp and poor quality control. A Tokyo Women's Federation petitioned for sturdier goods. The fabric broke at the first washing, the women said, looked wrinkled, and "lasts not more than one day."

Japan's five-year plan anticipated self-sufficiency in rayon pulp by 1942, but in 1940 supply fell short of need by 200,000 tons. It imported 123,000 tons, 96,000 tons of which came from the United States, a jump of U.S. sales from $1.8 million in 1939 to $6.3 million in 1940. With Scandinavia inaccessible due to war the U.S. vulnerability analysts saw an opportunity. They recommended embargoing rayon pulp exports, in cooperation with Canada. They expected that Japan would maintain a reduced output of staple fiber from local pulp, but fabric quality would decline further, another blow to the quality of Japanese life.

A second necessity for rayon production was caustic soda (sodium hydroxide, NaOH, also known as lye), an alkali derived from common salt that dissolved the wood pulp and also was used for manufacturing dyes and soaps. Japan consumed 2.5 million tons of salt, including large tonnages for food processing, but was only one-third self-sufficient because rainy weather interfered with evaporation from seawater ponds. It imported salt from East Africa, a shipping burden for a bulky mineral worth $2 per ton, and from China. The five-year plan targeted 1 million tons from China by 1943, although typhoons upset production there from time to time. The United States supplied a minor 100,000 tons. The vulnerability analysts reasoned that caustic soda was essential to the Japanese economy and that a shortfall would have disastrous economic effects. They recommended an embargo along with a British halting of East African salt. After the war it was learned that rayon fabric production had already slipped from 1.086 billion square yards in 1939 to 633 million in 1941.[27]

Raw Cotton

Raw cotton was the only major commodity for which U.S. economic needs overrode the impulse to punish Japan. Unlike most commodities, there was a glut of cotton due to war. The textile mills of Britain and Europe had cut back drastically, and cotton-raising countries were buried in surpluses. An embargo was a hopeless prospect.

In normal times the Japanese cotton textile industry provided 70 percent of the country's clothing fabric and a large surplus for export to the yen bloc, East

Asia, and the Americas. Japan grew no cotton; before the China Incident its factories processed 1.6 to 1.9 million bales (of 473 pounds each) of foreign raw cotton. After 1936, to conserve foreign exchange, Tokyo enacted laws to eliminate cotton from most domestic clothing in favor of rayon, because pulp comprised only 10 percent of that fabric's cost whereas raw cotton comprised 50 percent of cotton fabric cost. A "link system" allowed mills to import raw cotton only for exports, further limited in 1938 to exports only to non-yen countries. Cotton was channeled to military uniforms, work clothes, and to some blending with rayon. Domestic consumption shriveled to 617,000 bales in 1939. Imports of wool, primarily Australian and South African and used for the military, were also sharply curtailed. Silk of course, was plentiful after the financial freeze but the quantity was too small to matter.

Japan historically imported half its raw cotton needs as long-staple U.S. cotton, half as short-staple from India and minor amounts from China and elsewhere. In the crop year August 1940 to July 1941 Japan slashed its already low purchases, largely at the expense of the United States, from which it bought only 200,000 bales, switching to long staples from Brazil and Peru. U.S. analysts expected further cutbacks due to large inventories of cotton and textiles. It appeared that China could provide most of the 500,000 bales minimum need, although Chinese short staple was of such weak quality that it ordinarily was used for nonwoven applications such as padding. But quality was improving, and Japanese-owned mills in occupied cities might serve Japan by depriving Chinese consumers.

It would have been absurd for the Department of Agriculture vulnerability analysts to propose an embargo. "Surpluses of cotton throughout the world are abundant to the point of being burdensome. . . . Cotton [growers] will face impoverishment or even disaster," they wrote. Preclusive buying was inconceivable because surplus inventories of 14.5 million bales in the United States alone were about one and a half years' needs and were mostly financed by loans from the U.S. Reconstruction Finance Corporation. To buy up 8.5 million surplus bales in the rest of the world would cost $300–350 million. Faced with political clamor from the depressed southern cotton belt, the analysts used the occasion to appeal for international agreements to curtail production everywhere, not to embargo America's largest foreign customer.[28]

Other Clothing Materials

Japan's rather small leather industry depended 100 percent on imported cattle hides, primarily from China, but 20 percent from the United States and some from Argentina and Australia. Leather footwear was a luxury for civilians; wooden "geta" clogs were a necessary substitute. U.S. hide exports had been subject to license since 1940. The vulnerability analysts recommended an embargo, which would be meaningful only if Argentina and Australia collaborated, and even then not very damaging. U.S. sheepskins, 14 percent of the Japanese supply, offered even less opportunity because Manchukuo and China were the major sources. They also advised embargoes of vegetable-based chemicals for tanning leather, but substitutes from China and from synthetic chemicals would suffice for Japan.[29]

Rubber was the only tonnage industrial commodity more readily available to Japan than the United States. In addition to tires for military vehicles and planes Japan manufactured car and bicycle tires and tubes, industrial belting, boots, and shoes with rubber lowers and canvas uppers. It exported 20 to 30 percent of such manufactures, largely to the yen bloc. Most of the world's natural rubber trees grew on Southeast Asian plantations. (Synthetic rubber was not produced in quantity in 1941.) British Malaya was the largest supplier, especially to the United States. French Indochina and Thailand, drawn "into the economic if not the political orbit of Japan" in 1941, exported 115,000 tons, well in excess of Japan's calculated demand of 65,000 tons. Japanese control there edged out U.S. buyers and was an affront to U.S. international influence, said the analysts indignantly. Yet they did not suggest a Malayan embargo. The only remaining option, beyond the 1940 embargo of reclaimed scrap rubber, was an unlikely interference with Thai and Indochinese shipments to Japan by force.[30]

Lumber

Japan relied on lumber for construction more than any other country. Houses damaged by fires and earthquakes needed replacement routinely. During the economic expansion of the 1930s, as villagers migrated to urban jobs, construction of dwellings soared in crowded cities. The forests covering more than half of Japan yielded ordinary dimension lumber sufficient for local use, and for the yen bloc where skimpy forests were suitable only for pulp. Yet Japan lacked the large trees for logs up to twenty-four inches in diameter and twenty to sixty feet long needed by its important plywood industry. Douglas fir was the best plywood core material, which Japan imported as logs and "Jap square" hewn logs from the U.S. Pacific Northwest and Canada. Other woods sufficed for plywood veneers. After 1937 Japan severely restricted lumber imports in order, in the opinion of U.S. analysts, to save foreign exchange. It substituted lauan, a cheap hardwood from the Philippines and Southeast Asia, for plywood cores. By 1939–41 U.S. exports had dwindled to $1.5 million or less per year, down 70 to 90 percent from earlier peaks. A vulnerability team recommended embargoing all logs from North America, the Philippines, and British and Dutch Asia to "seriously affect" the plywood industry. In addition, an embargo of "airplane grade" Sitka spruce, though small in value, would impair construction of training aircraft. Even cedar for pencils ought to be embargoed.[31]

Miscellaneous Consumer Commodities

A vulnerability team rummaged in odd corners of trade data to find U.S. commodities enjoyed by Japanese consumers that might be blocked. They saw little real opportunity. The Japanese were avid readers, but the yen bloc was self-sufficient in the pulp used to make paper. Gum rosin, a turpentine chemical for soap, paper, and paints, was not an essential product, and an embargo would hurt American producers. Borax from California, a chemical for household products, was already embargoed and Japan was thought to have stockpiled enough a few years earlier.[32] The United States formerly sold ten thousand passenger automobiles per year, assembled or crated for assembly in Japan, and auto engines and parts. By 1940 Japan's imports of three cars per week may have been for foreign diplomats and businessmen.[33] No study was necessary.

Summary

The interdepartmental vulnerability teams of 1941 identified civilian commodities that if embargoed by the United States would lower the standard of living in Japan, by outright food shortages in the case of fertilizer minerals and oil and by debasing the quality of clothing and construction. They made no attempt, however, to quantify the impact of halting exports on the standard of living or the economy as a whole, nor did any American agency do so before the war. Toward the end of this book a plausible scenario of economic squalor, based on post-1941 studies, presents such an evaluation (chapter 18).

The Vulnerability of Japanese Exports
to the United States

In the spring of 1941 Gen. Russell L. Maxwell's vulnerability project over-stretched the mission of his agency. The Export Control Administration, as its founding purpose, was charged with conservation by limiting exports of materials the president deemed vital for national defense. Most of the designated commodities were in short supply in the United States, or threatened to be, especially after passage of the Lend-Lease bill. The vulnerability teams, by recommending embargoes of Japan specifically, moved a step toward setting foreign policy. They traveled even further in that direction by urging termination of exports to Japan of commodities that were abundantly available, such as phosphates, oil, and some other minerals and chemicals. Ultimately, seeking to burst the bonds of their assignment, they investigated the products the United States *imported* from Japan, recommending embargoes of most. To cut off the United States from a source of useful products was a far cry from conserving for national defense. To the contrary, it would impose burdens by cramping production of some industries or depriving U.S. consumers of products they desired. The rationale for such a move was harsh: to directly injure Japan by denying it dollars to spend in the United States or other dollar countries, for strategic or other materials, and, in the extreme, to disrupt the Japanese economy and distress the Japanese people. The vulnerability analysts were indulging in the culture of opportunism blooming in Washington as bureaucracies sought to seize control of and direct economic foreign policy against Japan.

Nylon Day

The foremost imported commodity under study was raw silk, which comprised two-thirds of the value of Japan's exports to the United States and virtually 100 percent of the U.S. supply. Sales amounted to $107 million in 1939 and $105 million in 1940, 95 percent of it destined for women's hosiery. Raw silk, in fact, comprised 25 percent of *all* Japanese exports outside the yen bloc, but the benefit to Japan was far greater. Most other exports contained foreign raw materials, whereas silk was entirely of domestic origin. Raw silk yielded about 57 percent of all U.S. dollars Japan earned from exporting to North and South America at a time when dollars were essential to purchase war materials. The great bilateral silk trade had survived many a shock over seven decades, but a year before the vulnerability project it encountered an appalling, and ultimately catastrophic, shock on "Nylon Day."

The fifteenth of May 1939 was Nylon Day at the New York Worlds Fair, a day of lavish promotion of a new kind of full-fashioned hosiery. The stockings were an instant hit. Women across the country thronged the counters of department stores to buy stockings of gossamer nylon, sheerer than the finest Japanese silks, that clung smoothly to their legs in unblemished beauty. E. I. du Pont de Nemours and Company, whose motto was "Better things for better living through chemistry," had recruited Dr. Wallace Hume Carothers from Harvard University to research the creation of a perfect artificial silk. In 1934 he triumphed by creating a long-chain polymer from coal, air, and water, the first true synthetic fiber, not derived from wood or vegetation. Du Pont called it nylon. The extruded yarns were strong, light, stretchy, and absolutely uniform. Test-knit stockings fulfilled the company's fondest hopes. It erected a plant in Seaford, Delaware, that, in December 1939 began to produce four million pounds annually, reserving nearly all the output for hosiery mills. In 1940 nylon took 7 percent of the hosiery market, and its share was growing rapidly as Du Pont lowered yarn prices.[1]

For the ECA vulnerability project, Ruth E. K. Peterson—the reigning expert of the U.S. Tariff Commission, the only one-person "team," and perhaps the only woman in the project—reported on the outlook for hosiery on 15 April 1941. Du Pont was doubling the capacity of its Seaford nylon plant to eight million pounds and building another plant for hosiery, except 10 or 15 percent for nylon bristles to replace Chinese hog bristles in paint brushes and for other uses. Peterson stated:

> Another Du Pont nylon plant is under construction at Martinsville, Va., which is to have a capacity of 8 million pounds . . . to be in full production in the spring

of 1942. The hosiery industry probably consumes about nine-tenths of the total nylon yarn production, and can manufacture approximately 20 pairs of hose from each pound of nylon [vs. 12 from a pound of raw silk due in part to wastage in throwing]. On this basis [Du Pont] . . . would provide within the year sufficient nylon to manufacture between 140 and 150 million pairs, equivalent to about 30% of the total output. . . . Should the industry consume 85% of the 16 million pounds of nylon which are expected to be available in 1942 it would be able to make 272 million pairs of nylon hose or 54% of the present annual rate of production of full-fashioned hosiery. If it is true, as many consumers claim, that nylon hose outlasts silk, then any given output of nylon would actually displace more than the corresponding number of pairs of silk hose.

Raw silk stocks on hand in the United States were only one and a half months' worth of normal demand. Peterson shrugged off the immediate unemployment of 133,000 U.S. workers that would result from an embargo of raw silk because stocking mills would switch to other fibers. Only the 18,000 engaged in throwing silk were in jeopardy because nylon and rayon did not require throwing.[2]

Sanctions?

Peterson's assumption that Japanese silk would retain nearly half the future hosiery market was challenged by Wirth Ferger, an analyst of the Far Eastern Committee of the ECA, on 27 April 1941. He accepted Du Pont's claim that nylons lasted up to twice as long as silks if properly washed, and that customers would accept other fibers in feet and welts. Nylon stockings, he calculated, would capture 100 percent of the full-fashioned hosiery market by the end of 1942. Silk stockings would disappear, and there would be no other outlet for Japanese raw silk.

Peterson had refrained from recommending sanctions against Japanese silk, unlike most of her colleagues on vulnerability teams. The outspoken Ferger advocated step-by-step actions to hinder Japan's war effort: promoting and subsidizing nylon, tariffs and licensing restrictions on raw silk, and finally a funds freeze and total embargo. "Through the indirect effect of curtailing her supply of exchange available in this country for purchase of supplies she needs," he said, Japan would feel a "real pinch disrupting her internal economy," even though silk workers could migrate to other jobs. U.S. export controls would be "the first and primary measure" in "a general offensive plan." Interestingly, Ferger assumed a program lasting two years during a period of general emergency, a rare explicit assumption of duration that was scarcely mentioned by other analysts' studies in the spring of 1941 and not at all in July, when the financial freeze was imposed.[3]

In September 1941, after the freeze of trade, Ruth Peterson came to the same conclusion about the market. Women demanded sheers and ultra sheers (four to five thread and two to three thread, respectively) for 89 percent of their purchases of full-fashioned hosiery but accepted other fibers for feet and welts. Even though considering nylon's run resistance unproven, she forecast a shortage of high-quality hosiery in 1942 if raw silk were embargoed. Women would then have no choice but to wear bulky, unsightly rayon and cotton stockings, six-thread or more, if production of such yarns were stepped up, otherwise heavy sport hose or ankle sox. She expressed no sympathy for women's loss of a treasured fashion accessory.[4]

Silk for Defense

U.S analysts also delved into Army and Navy needs of silk parachutes—the cry of aviators bailing out was "Hit the silk!"—and for flares and pyrotechnical signals. A man-carrying 'chute required 11.7 pounds for canopy and shrouds. Given Roosevelt's goal of fifty thousand airplanes and assuming an average four parachutes each, the 2.34 million pound requirement of raw silk was a mere four weeks of imports from Japan. The ECA estimated parachute demand at only 1 to 2 million pounds of raw silk, which easily could be supplied by commandeering industry stocks, said to be 11 million pounds, or by using nylon, a promising substitute.[5]

The analysts were more concerned about Asian waste silk, the short fibers from broken cocoons and filature clippings, that U.S. plants drew and spun into low-strength filling yarns. Demand for spun silk velvet clothing had flowered in the 1920s, but by 1939 only 1.1 million pounds were woven into pile fabrics. But very coarse spun silk, 425 to 620 deniers, was needed for cartridge cloth, igniter cloth, and laces for large-caliber naval and coast defense artillery. It burned quickly, leaving no smoldering residue in the gun breech. There were no substitutes. (Cotton and other fibers sufficed for field artillery.) U.S. hosiery mill waste and old silk clothing were unsuitable due to hard twisting of yarn, while chopped-up raw silk lacked the necessary bulk and cost ten times as much. Silk waste imports of 2.5 million pounds in 1940, enough for 2.8 million square yards of naval cartridge cloth and costing about $1 million, came from China via Japanese merchants. (Japan was thought to be conserving its waste silk for its navy.) During World War I, 28.5 million pounds of cartridge cloth had been produced, even though most of the battle fleet was idle, but the U.S. military now held only a 6 million pound reserve of waste silk. Ruth

Peterson urged accumulation of 3 million pounds of waste for stockpile. Wirth Ferger clamored to import 8 million pounds. Eventually commercial inventories sufficed for the artillery problem.[6]

Measuring Japan's Silk Disaster

During the four years from the start of war in China to the U.S. financial freeze, Japan earned $394 million from silk exports (chart 15), nearly all for U.S. women's stockings. It was a source of dollars second only to gold sales of $711 million, which came largely from Bank of Japan reserves. Each year dollars from silk exports were almost twice the value of new gold production (chapter 6). The impending demise of the once-lucrative silk trade may have contributed to a sense of isolation felt by Japanese leaders even before the financial freeze that shut it down, although documentation is not available.

Did nylon contribute to Japan's choice for war? If it had accepted U.S. demands to withdraw from conquered territories in exchange for reopened trade, could Japan have earned enough dollars to buy materials it needed, especially to support its army and navy? Japan's trade deficit with the dollar area, partly offset by newly mined gold available to sell to the U.S. Treasury, had averaged $120 million per year before 1941. In 1941 Japan had at most around $250 million of gold and dollar reserves, enough, along with future gold production, to cover two years of dollar trade shortfalls.[7] But if nylon entirely displaced $100 million in annual revenue from raw silk, the dollar deficit would expand, reducing the financial cushion to one year (chart 16). Cabinet records in Tokyo do not mention silk, yet the looming trade disaster could not have encouraged any leaders who preferred survival by renewal of trade rather than by war. In any case, during World War II Japan virtually shut down sericulture and uprooted the mulberry trees, permanently sealing the fate of its once-great silk industry.[8]

Vulnerability of Japan's Other Exports to the United States

Several vulnerability teams investigated some of the articles that made up the rest of U.S. imports from Japan, none large in value. They sensibly recommended against embargoes for a small number of commodities the United States needed while proposing to embargo many nonessential items for the purpose of denying bits of dollar exchange to Japan:

- *Fish.* The members of a vulnerability committee on fisheries cavalierly dismissed sea foods from Japan as unimportant to the United States. The embargo they recommended "would not work the slightest hard-

CHART 15 **U.S. Imports of Raw Silk from Japan, 1935–1941**

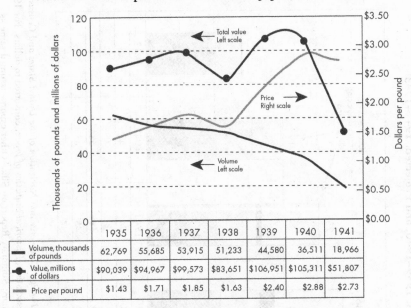

	1935	1936	1937	1938	1939	1940	1941
Volume, thousands of pounds	62,769	55,685	53,915	51,233	44,580	36,511	18,966
Value, millions of dollars	$90,039	$94,967	$99,573	$83,651	$106,951	$105,311	$51,807
Price per pound	$1.43	$1.71	$1.85	$1.63	$2.40	$2.88	$2.73

Department of Commerce, *Foreign Commerce and Navigation of the United States*, 1936–42.

ship" on U.S. consumers because domestic and Canadian fleets could fill the gap if and when prices rose while Japan would suffer "serious economic injury." Sensibly recognizing the importance of fish livers for health and nutrition, and the lack of alternatives, they proposed no embargo of Japanese sources (and ignored the seed oysters essential for U.S. shellfish farming).[9]

- *Hat materials.* A committee reasonably opposed an embargo of hat materials unless the United States launched "all-out economic warfare" on Japan. No substitutes could be had, perhaps for years until production started in the Bahamas or South America or synthetics were developed. An embargo would needlessly injure workers and firms in both countries.[10]

- *Ceramics.* A committee opined that the "loss of the United States market alone might seriously disrupt the Japanese pottery industry and would result in an appreciable loss of foreign exchange." Although halting imports would deny a popular product to the American middle class, dishes were not essential, they declared, recommending an embargo in conjunction with the Allies.[11]

CHART 16   Japan: Sources of Dollars, Actual, 1939–1940, and Projected, 1941–1943

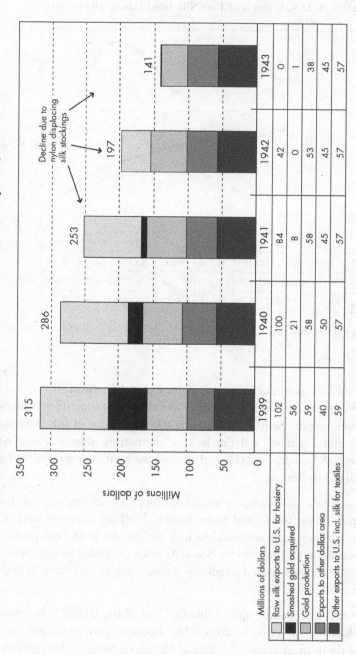

Millions of dollars

Decline due to nylon displacing silk stockings

141   197   253   286   315

Millions of dollars	1939	1940	1941	1942	1943
Raw silk exports to U.S. for hosiery	102	100	84	42	0
Smashed gold acquired	56	21	8	0	1
Gold production	59	58	58	53	38
Exports to other dollar area	40	50	45	45	45
Other exports to U.S. incl. silk for textiles	59	57	57	57	57

For 1939 and 1940: Exports to U.S. and silk uses: Department of Commerce, *Foreign Commerce and Navigation of the United States* and *Census of Manufactures* (various goods). Exports to other dollar area: Japan Statistical Association, *Historical Statistics of Japan*, converted to dollars. For 1941 to 1943: Raw silk exports for hosiery calculated by author from AEC, "Preliminary, Summary Report on Silk." Other exports assumed same as 1940–41. All years, gold production, actual: SCAP, *Gold and Silver in Japan*. Smashed gold, actual: Survey of the Gold Fund Special Account, c. August 1945, OASIA.

- *Miscellaneous wares.* A vulnerability committee glanced at dozens of Japanese "miscellaneous products." The knick-knackery of Japanese toys, beads, shells, buttons, brushes, umbrellas, lacquerware, combs, and the like netted $1 to $2 million for Japan. The committee concluded sensibly, "[It] is too heterogeneous a grouping to make economic warfare feasible."[12]

The Vulnerability of Japan's Exports

In April 1941 the U.S. vulnerability committees, having recommended an embargo of the $105 million of raw silk imports, considered other Japanese imports, worth $52 million in 1940. In many instances the United States was the main or only market. A few advocated embargoing of $9 million of products they condescendingly called "luxuries" Americans could do without: crabmeat, tuna fish, and chinaware (but for some reason not pearls and mink pelts) to deny Japan bits of foreign exchange, to cause minor disruptions of its economy, and implicitly to hinder the war in China. It was irrelevant to the experts that women and children especially would be deprived of popular goods unavailable elsewhere. Others committees showed common sense in advising against embargoes of $18 million of essential imports: silk waste for artillery, drying oils and paintbrush bristles, and fish livers for health, which were in short supply; irreplaceable hat materials that would hurt U.S. manufacturers; a myriad of inexpensive household articles and playthings deemed too insignificant to study. Nor were cotton textiles to be embargoed, probably because of political sensitivity of U.S. farmers and ginners who normally sold Japan raw cotton four or five times the value of cotton textiles entering from Japan. Other Japanese products ranging from tea and canned fruits to bamboo wares, silk fabrics, light bulbs, and zippers were simply not important enough to study. Most committees paid little attention to the impacts of embargoes on U.S. employment or on the Japanese economy other than its dollar earnings.

Before 26 July 1941 U.S. trade warfare against Japan consisted of curtailing exports of strategic commodities needed for U.S. defense in accordance with the licensing act of July 1940. There was no legal mechanism to halt imports, except a potential executive order to freeze Japanese assets under authority of the 1917 Trading with the Enemy Act. The commodity analysts recruited from various civilian agencies by the Export Control Administration had reached opportunistically far beyond that agency's authority in urging embargoes of imports from Japan.

13

The Vulnerability of Japan in Petroleum

In no resource was Japan more vulnerable than petroleum, for its economic life and especially for its army and navy. The U.S. government was well aware that supplies from the United States were irreplaceable. Shutting off the oil tap would tectonically shift Japan's foreign policy, perhaps toward a diplomatic settlement of tensions, or perhaps toward war before its storage reserves ran out and the Imperial Army and Navy could no longer wage war.

U.S. Views of Oil, 1930s to Early 1941

Japan's era of self-sufficiency had been brief. In the Meiji period Japanese prospecting companies discovered and developed minor deposits of petroleum in the home islands. Production in Japan rose to a peak of 2,965,000 barrels in 1915.[1] As late as 1928 the country's own production met, on balance, its minuscule consumption of 2,055,800 barrels of petroleum products, but in the following five years the expansion of transportation and industries tripled demand to 6 million barrels. The national modernization program demanded every grade of refined product. The government promoted construction of refineries to produce light fuel oil for factories and engines, diesel oil and gasoline for fishing boats, trucks, buses and taxis—private autos were relatively few—and heavy fuel oil for the merchant marine and navy. But Japan had been thoroughly prospected. Despite drilling subsidies, crude oil production sank to 1.4 million barrels trickling from seventy-two fields of "stripper" wells that lifted about one barrel per day, one-tenth of the average U.S. well. Exploration in Taiwan and Manchuria yielded only disappointments. Concessions operated by Japanese companies in the Soviet Union's northern half of Sakhalin Island did yield about 10 percent of national needs, but output could not be expanded. By the late 1930s Japan was importing over 80 percent of its oil needs from foreign operations thousand of miles away.

Washington grew curious about Japan's oil problem a few years before the Sino-Japanese War. In 1934 the U.S. Department of Commerce recognized the empire's serious deficiency in a study, "Fuel and Power in Japan." That year Tokyo enacted a law directing refineries to install large scale equipment and ordering refining and marketing companies to accumulate liquid fuel stocks equal to sixth months of imports, a financial burden unnecessary for commercial reasons as world petroleum was abundant and cheap during the Depression. The law signaled anxiety about strategic dependence on foreign supplies. By 1938, with the war in China adding to demand, U.S. analysts reckoned that the burning of liquid fuels had surged to 46 million barrels, a twenty-two-fold increase in a decade. The empire self-supplied only 15 percent of demand, of which 2.5 million barrels of crude, 3.3 million barrels of substitute coal and alcohol liquids, and barely 1.1 million barrels from costly experimental plants in Manchukuo that processed oil shale (an oil-bearing rock). Japan imported the remaining 85 percent, consisting of 33.5 million barrels from the United States, 4.7 million from the Dutch and British East Indies, and minor volumes from Sakhalin and elsewhere. The United States delivered primarily crude oil, along with 5 million barrels of light fuel, 3 million barrels of heavy fuel, and an insignificant 1 million barrels of gasoline annually. In 1939, due to civilian rationing and reduced combat operations in China, Japan cut back on U.S. oil. Total imports dwindled by 7 percent to 43 million barrels, and in 1940 by a further 10 percent to 38.7 million barrels. Nevertheless, U.S. analysts believed that the reduced imports were sufficient to increase stockpile reserves every year.[2]

In the twenty-first century it is hard to imagine how overwhelmingly the United States dominated the global petroleum industry. In 1940 it lifted 1.35 *billion* barrels of crude oil, 63 percent of world output. It consumed about the same percentage of global supply. U.S. refineries, built on tidewater, poured out every liquid product at competitive prices. California, the producing state nearest to Asia, ranked second to Texas in crude liftings. Japanese refineries bought all grades of California crudes, rich in either light or heavy fractions as needed. Other dollar countries—Venezuela, Mexico, and lesser producers in the Caribbean and South America—lifted 14 percent of the world's crude oil, nearly all for export. Rumania and Russia together pumped 12 percent of world supply but did not export to the Far East. The Persian Gulf was sparsely developed. British companies produced 6 percent of the world's petroleum in Iran and Iraq, but U.S. operations in Saudi Arabia had barely started, accounting for 0.25 percent.[3]

Far Eastern countries other than Japan drew from the wells and refineries of Sumatra and Borneo in the Netherlands East Indies. The Anglo-Dutch syndicate Royal Dutch–Shell and Stanvac, a fifty-fifty American joint venture of Standard Oil of New Jersey (Esso, later Exxon) and Standard Oil of New York (Socony-Vacuum), which had pooled their regional investments in production and marketing operated there. The Dutch Indies produced only 3 percent of world supply, but its 61 million barrels were equivalent to almost twice Japan's import needs, according to U.S. analyses. (The British colonies of Sarawak and North Borneo also exported oil, but only one-tenth the Dutch islands' volume.) Indies oil was well situated for Japan. Tanker round-trip time of twenty-eight to thirty-one days compared favorably with forty-four days to California, sixty-two days to the Persian Gulf, or seventy-three to eighty-three days to the Caribbean or the U.S. Gulf Coast. However, the two corporate giants operating in the Indies had traditionally sold little to Japan. Their markets lay in Australia, New Zealand, continental Asian countries and colonies, and the storage tanks on Singapore and nearby Dutch islands that bunkered ships of all nations plying that busy region. Japan purchased only 4 million barrels in a typical year, 5 to 7 percent of Indies output, until late 1940, when it pressured the orphaned Dutch colony to allocate a larger share.[4]

U.S. Focus on Avgas, 1940–1941

Although Japan's oil dependency was well understood by U.S. observers, and hardliners had mused now and again about limiting exports, before 1941 the administration devoted little thought to constraints except for aviation gasoline. The export licensing act of July 1940 halted exports of avgas of 87 octane or higher (see chapter 7). Japan shifted to buying 86-octane gasoline and rich crudes that could be upgraded in Japan. The ECA controllers were not authorized to curtail exports of non-aviation fuels. Crude and other refined products were amply available in the Western Hemisphere. U.S. and Latin American producers had lost their European markets due to war. Britain conserved dollars by importing Persian Gulf oil invoiced in sterling, and from Dutch refineries on Aruba processing Venezuelan crude that accepted payment partly in sterling.

In January 1941 Japanese oil purchasing began to attract concern in Washington. Stanley Hornbeck, the State Department's adviser on political relations, assessed the situation for Hull, who was meeting with an oil company executive. Since the summer of 1940, he reported, Japan had purchased "extraordinary amounts" of U.S. gasoline just under the 87-octane limit, shipped in metal drums, enabling it to stockpile six to nine months' worth of needs, "a regrettable situation." The United States had behaved "very circumspectly" because "there was for some time a very important political reason for not taking any new action regarding exports of petroleum products." Hornbeck was referring to Tokyo's demands on the Netherlands Indies authorities, backed by hints of military coercion, to sign a five-year contract to supply 3,150,000 tons (about 22 million barrels) annually, enough to cover two-thirds of Japan's import needs, according to U.S. estimates. The State Department had been nervous about reducing shipments from the Americas lest Japan intensify pressure on the Dutch. The Indies' governors and companies, however, had resisted staunchly, grudgingly agreeing to sell to Japan only 1,800,000 tons at an annual rate (about 12.5 million barrels) renewable on a six-to-twelve-month revolving basis. In Hornbeck's view the deal encouraged U.S. oil companies, at home and abroad, to exercise "self-restraint and discreet self-denial" in meeting Japanese demands, especially for gasoline. He suggested curtailing exports only of metal drums and storage tanks. American foreign policy remained skittish on reducing even "excessive" oil sales to Japan.[5]

Slowing the Gasoline Pump

U.S. export controllers still focused narrowly on avgas exports. Reports circulated in early 1941 of evasive Japanese ploys such as mixing avgas with ordinary fuels for separation in Japan. The State Department had denied Mitsubishi a license for half a million barrels of gasoline mixed into California crude oil. Army intelligence reported Japanese purchasing in Texas of avgas blended with kerosene. In April customs inspectors running strict new tests discovered that some gasoline exports might have exceeded the 86-octane limit. Thereafter, vigilance sharply diminished exports of fuel mixtures.[6]

Japanese companies continued to purchase gasoline of permissible lower grades in fifty-five-gallon steel drums. The drums were classified as manufactured products, hence immune from ECA control of "commodities" like steel sheet. In December 1940 Mitsubishi obtained an export license for 100,000 drums filled with about 130,000 barrels of "high-grade" gasoline, a three-month supply for Japan at the 1940 rate of export. Six weeks later the State Department's Division of Controls reversed the permission and barred "excessive" shipment of drums, although not of gasoline. Japan also scoured the United States for second-hand steel tanks for reassembly in Japan. Regulators did not object because the dismantled tanks were neither proscribed steel sheet nor scrap, until April 1941, when they reversed and denied licenses.[7]

In the six months through January 1941, the period since the ban on 87-octane avgas, according to a summary for Harry Dexter White the monthly average sales to Japan had risen to 3.4 million barrels of "other" gasoline, mostly near-avgas grade, five *times* the 1939 rate. Fuel oil and crude exports had declined, however, so total volume of petroleum sales remained virtually unchanged. In the first five months of 1941 matters reversed. Gasoline exports dropped 45 percent to 1.2 million barrels (of which only 0.4 million barrels "high grade") and crude also declined, but fuel oils rose. Altogether, liquid fuels shipped to Japan fell 30 percent by volume. Japan switched to buying premium-value lubricating oils in drums at a cost of $11 to $12 per barrel f.o.b. vessel; in comparison, average bulk export prices in 1941 were gasoline $3.05, light fuel oil $1.14, heavy residual oil $.87, and crude $1.30 per barrel (chart 17).[8] (Crude cost more than fuel oils because of its gasoline content.)

The switch suggested a rush to spend dollars for an expensive strategic product transportable on dry freighters, but Japan's buying mix more likely resulted from tighter export rules by informal actions. Joseph C. Green, head of the State Department's Division of Controls noted, "Theoretically, licenses are issued freely" for non-aviation gasoline and lube oils, and for crude oil from the Kettleman Hills and Special San Joaquin fields of California, which yielded 3 percent or more of aviation gasoline or lubes. "In fact, however," Green reported on 6 March 1941, "by agreement with the Administrator [of Export Control] and without any pubic announcement, the Division of Controls, in accordance with instructions has been holding without action" Japanese applications for such "high-grade" liquids. His action blocked shipment of $12.9 million of fuels already licensed to Japan, including 3.6 million barrels of near-86-octane gasoline, 1.4 million barrels of rich crude, and 123,000 barrels of lubes. The denials were equivalent, at recent delivery rates, to seven months of high-grade gasoline, three months of rich crude, and one month of lubricating oil. Licensing of petroleum coke was also suspended.[9] The unpublicized policy of restricting selective grades would have been even more draconian if stringent testing by customs officers ordered on 30 July had been applied earlier because, as Sumner Welles remarked, almost all crudes could yield through ordinary refining more than the forbidden 3 percent of aviation fractions.[10]

The Vulnerability and ONI Studies

In March and April 1941 U.S. defense agencies got around to serious study of Japan's overall petroleum problem. On 12 March Lt. Cdr. Arthur H. McCollum of the Office of Naval Intelligence submitted a detailed analysis. The following month the Export Control Administration submitted a brief vulnerability study of oil, prepared by a committee chaired by E. Dana Durand of the Tariff Commission assisted by technical experts from the Commerce

CHART 17 **U.S. Exports of Petroleum Liquids to Japan, 1935–1941**

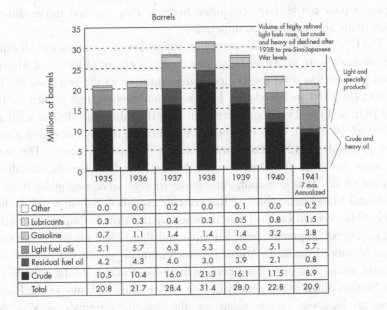

Barrels

Volume of highly refined light fuels rose, but crude and heavy oil declined after 1938 to pre-Sino-Japanese War levels

Light and specialty products

Crude and heavy oil

Millions of barrels

	1935	1936	1937	1938	1939	1940	1941 7 mos. Annualized
☐ Other	0.0	0.0	0.2	0.0	0.1	0.0	0.2
▨ Lubricants	0.3	0.3	0.4	0.3	0.5	0.8	1.5
▨ Gasoline	0.7	1.1	1.4	1.4	1.4	3.2	3.8
▨ Light fuel oils	5.1	5.7	6.3	5.3	6.0	5.1	5.7
▨ Residual fuel oil	4.2	4.3	4.0	3.0	3.9	2.1	0.8
■ Crude	10.5	10.4	16.0	21.3	16.1	11.5	8.9
Total	20.8	21.7	28.4	31.4	28.0	22.8	20.9

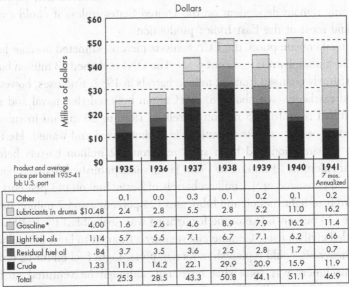

Dollars

Millions of dollars

Product and average price per barrel 1935-41 fob U.S. port		1935	1936	1937	1938	1939	1940	1941 7 mos. Annualized
☐ Other		0.1	0.0	0.3	0.1	0.2	0.1	0.2
▨ Lubricants in drums	$10.48	2.4	2.8	5.5	2.8	5.2	11.0	16.2
▨ Gasoline*	4.00	1.6	2.6	4.6	8.9	7.9	16.2	11.4
▨ Light fuel oils	1.14	5.7	5.5	7.1	6.7	7.1	6.2	6.6
▨ Residual fuel oil	.84	3.7	3.5	3.6	2.5	2.8	1.7	0.7
■ Crude	1.33	11.8	14.2	22.1	29.9	20.9	15.9	11.9
Total		25.3	28.5	43.3	50.8	44.1	51.1	46.9

*Including avgas in barrels $7.75

Department of Commerce, *Foreign Commerce and Navigation of the United States*, 1936–42.

Department, Bureau of Mines, and the ECA itself. The authors of the two papers appear not to have consulted because they reached rather different conclusions about Japan's oil difficulties.[11]

The ONI and ECA readily agreed on supply because statistics of all exporting countries were available. Japan imported 90 percent of its oil, of which 75 to 80 percent was from the United States and most of the rest from the East Indies. The ONI reckoned that Japan's oil procurement had peaked in 1937 and 1938 at 44 to 45 million barrels per year, then diminished to 37 million in 1939 and 34 million in 1940. The ECA committee merely calculated a rough average supply of 42 million barrels "during the last few years." The recent Japanese deal with the Dutch would deliver 12 million barrels annually, 20 percent of the Indies' output. Alternative sources were negligible: domestic crude and Manchurian shale oil had scarcely expanded, Sakhalin had declined since 1936, Persian Gulf oil was absorbed by the British Empire's war effort, and occasional shipments from Rumania and Russia had ceased. Japan might buy a bit more from Latin America—which normally provided 1 percent of its imports, although it provided 3 percent in 1940—through Pacific ports of Peru and Mexico, albeit at the penalty of long tanker hauls. (Closure of the Panama Canal to Japanese vessels ruled out the Atlantic terminals of Venezuela, Mexico, and the U.S. Gulf Coast.) Both studies concurred that Japan would necessarily remain dependent on the United States unless it could coercively command most of the East Indies' production.

As to oil consumption, the ECA analysts merely estimated average Japanese use of 38 million barrels in recent years. The ONI reckoned 33 million barrels in 1940, scarcely changed from 32 million barrels in 1937. End uses, however, had changed markedly (see chart 18). McCollum believed that naval and military demand had risen from 5 million barrels in 1936 to 20 million in subsequent years, more or less, as war operations in China waxed and waned. He thought civilian consumption had been squeezed from 22 million barrels before the China Incident to 13 million in 1940. Japan's last published demand figures, in 1936, had consisted of 9.1 million barrels of heavy fuel oil (43 percent), 5 million barrels of light fuel oil and lubricants (24 percent), and 7 million barrels of gasoline (33 percent). (Kerosene for lighting was negligible.) By 1940 rationing had stifled civilian uses. Commercial steamers, thought to burn 5.5 million barrels of heavy oil, could replenish in foreign ports. Light fuel oil for factories and other machinery was somewhat restricted, although he ventured no figures. Gasoline use had declined precipitously. Fishermen were encouraged to blend alcohol into gasoline or diesel. Smaller vessels were forced to revert to sails. Motor vehicles were scarce in Japan, only 160,859 trucks, buses, cars, and motorcycles in 1937 (less than half of 1 percent of the U.S. number), yet in May 1938 the government slashed gasoline for vehicles by 40 to 60 percent. The daily

CHART 18   **Japan's Oil Fuel Consumption, 1939–1941**

Barrels	Apr.1931- Mar.1932	Apr.1932- Mar.1933	Apr.1933- Mar.1934	Apr.1934- Mar.1935	Apr.1935- Mar.1936	Apr.1936- Mar.1937	Apr.1937- Mar.1938	Apr.1938- Mar.1939	Apr.1939- Mar.1940	Apr.1940- Mar.1941	Apr.1941- Mar.1942
☐ Civilian	12,288	14,681	15,352	18,109	23,552	22,148	23,638	20,861	17,405	19,336	10,497
■ Military	2,642	3,595	4,268	4,556	5,040	5,551	6,289	7,090	7,856	9,222	12,151

USSBS, *Oil in Japan's War*, Table 35.

ration in the Tokyo area, three gallons a day on average, was halved again in 1940. The allowance was 2.5 gallons for buses, less for taxis, and one *quart* for private cars. Road consumption slumped 70 percent to an estimated 2 million barrels. Charcoal-burning steam vehicles, smoky and unreliable, became familiar sights in city streets. Civil aviation demand was minor; Japan had a commercial fleet of 147 planes in 1937, as opposed to several thousand military planes by the late 1930s.

The ONI's analysis concluded that, by strangling civilian consumption, Japan had added to inventories 9 to 15 million barrels annually in the early years of the China Incident, tapering off to 5 to 7 million barrels in 1939 and 1940 when it scaled back imports from the United States. McCollum reckoned stocks at 75,495,000 barrels of liquids in early 1941, 90 percent higher than in 1936 despite three and a half years of war (table 1). Known storage capacity of 40 million barrels, plus 20 million inferred from quota laws and imagined secret installations (which may have included salvaged oil tanks from the United States) was assumed to be adequate. Contemplating his inventory calculation, McCollum concluded that Japan's key oil stratagem had been stockpiling, more important even than threatening the Indies government. He imagined, wishfully, that stockpiling had provided Japanese leaders hope of withstanding a possible U.S. embargo without plunging into the Indies and provoking war.

The ONI was far off the mark in its estimate of 75.5 million barrels in reserves. On 31 March 1941 the actual stockpile was only 42.7 million barrels

TABLE 1 ONI Summary of Japan's Petroleum Supply and Demand, 1936–1940

(in Thousands of Barrels of Petroleum and Petroleum Products)

	1936	1937	1938	1939	1940
DOMESTIC PRODUCTION					
Japan (1)	2,494	2,485	2,616		
Manchuria	1,100	1,043	1,042		
Total domestic production	3,594	3,528	3,658	3,600	3,600
IMPORTS					
United States		29,707	35,012	27,430	25,442
Mexico, Ecuador, Peru		192	342	303	1,342
Russia and North Sakhalin		2,137	1,102	910	-
Rumania		-	209	96	-
Bahrain		1,706	403	-	456
Netherlands East Indies (2)		5,768	4,347	3,478	4,864
British Borneo and Malaya		4,131	3,508	2,081	-
Other and unknown discrepancy		221	(215)	2,942	1,896
Total imports	30,333	43,862	44,708	37,240	34,000
Total supply	33,927	47,390	48,366	40,840	37,600
Import dependence	89%	93%	92%	91%	90%
CONSUMPTION: (3)					
Civilian	22,000	22,000	18,000	18,000	13,000
Military	5,000	10,000	21,000	16,000	20,000
Total consumption	27,000	32,000	39,000	34,000	33,000
Difference, added to stockpile	6,927	15,390	9,366	6,840	4,760
Stockpile, end of year	39,200	54,589	63,955	70,795	74,495
Months of consumption in stockpile	17	20	20	25	27

(1) Includes minor production of Formosa.
(2) Includes Port Bintan, island station for transshipment near Singapore.
(3) Chiefly gasoline and residual oil.
(4) Includes consumption of Manchuria, approximately 5% to 6% of total.

*Figures approximated due to rounding decimals.

Navy Department, ONI "Report on Petroleum Situation of Japan," 12 March 1941.

TABLE 2 **Japanese Oil Tanker Facilities, March 1941**

	Vessels	Average Tonnage	Gross Tonnage	Normal Speed (knots)	Total Capacity (barrels)	Round Trips per Year, Japan to California	Annual Capacity, Japan to California
Navy tankers	10	8,000	80,000	12	560,000	7	3,920,000
Fast merchant tankers	23	9,743	224,095	18	2,187,000	10	21,870,000
Slow merchant tankers	16	7,209	115,349	12	1,200,000	7	8,400,000
Whalers (potential tankers)	6	16,793	100,755	12	736,710	7	5,500,000
Totals	**55**		**520,199**		**4,683,710**		**39,690,000**

Navy Department, ONI "Report on Petroleum Situation of Japan," 12 March 1941

of petroleum and products (plus 3 million of nonpetroleum liquid fuels). The ECA's simplistic guess, that Japan had inventoried 4 million barrels per year on average, yielded a lower and thus more accurate estimate. Postwar studies by the U.S. Strategic Bombing Survey revealed that Japanese oil consumption in the twelve months ended 31 March 1941 was about 29 million barrels, almost the same level as before the China War, albeit 3.7 million more barrels were allocated to the military and 3 million less for civilian use, the latter slashed far less severely than the ONI imagined.

Tankers

Both the U.S. Navy and ECA analyses agreed that ocean transportation had become a crucial bottleneck for Japan. In 1941 almost all foreign tankers had withdrawn from Pacific routes. According to the FBI, Japanese ships had loaded 2 million barrels in San Francisco from February to April, a surprisingly small volume. The ONI calculated the transpacific capacity of Japanese-owned tankers—including whaling ships reassigned—as 10 to 20 percent greater than the 30 to 33 million barrels of annual imports (see table 2).

But diversion of whalers was uneconomic and unlikely, while some navy tankers were engaged in China and in fleet training. The ECA vulnerability team again assumed a starker problem. It assumed longer tanker voyage times, citing industry norms of six days in port at each end for loading and unloading, in-port transfer, and minor repairs. Although East Indies round trips of 29.5 to

31.0 days in lieu of 43.8 days on the San Francisco run could enhance a ship's annual capacity by 30 percent, the tightfisted Dutch contract offered little opportunity for shifting. Anyway, some very long hauls from Latin America partly offset any advantage. Dry cargo ships could haul some products in drums, an extraordinarily expensive improvisation suitable only for highest priority airplane lubricants and gasoline, but drum exports had been embargoed. Whatever the numbers, the U.S. analysts agreed that shipping severely hampered Japan's race to stockpile oil.

Oil Study Conclusions

The twin studies of March to April 1941 reached different conclusions from different assumptions. The ONI believed that unless Japan could coerce much more oil from the Dutch it could not expand inventories, even if it throttled back civilian use another 3 million barrels, to 10 million per year. A global embargo of Japan, therefore, would force it to rely, in case of war, almost entirely on inventoried oil unless it seized the Indies. ONI's inflated inventory guess equated to two years of war against the United States and allies, at a 31,350,0000 barrels annual rate of burning. The ECA deemed its less exuberant stockpile estimate sufficient for at least six months of extended warfare.

The vulnerability analysts tread warily in offering embargo recommendations because they had been warned that trade was a matter of broad national policy. They considered the ban of near-avgas grade gasoline and aviation lubricants meaningless because Japan could upgrade ordinary gasoline to 87 octane by adding three cubic centimeters of tetraethyl lead (TEL) per gallon, or extract it from rich crudes without additives. Even an embargo of *all* refined fuels would be futile because Japan's refineries already processed half its product needs and could swiftly expand. Similarly, embargoes of $2 million U.S. sales of lubricating grease, petroleum coke for electrodes, and petroleum jelly for machine lubrication and medical purposes would hardly be worthwhile except as part of a total embargo of petroleum. Policies other than embargo looked futile. Preclusive buying of surplus foreign oil was utterly impracticable because of the huge quantities involved, nor was it feasible to entice Latin American producers to cut output because the United States and its allies would have to compensate them extravagantly for lost revenues and unemployment. As to transportation, Japan could get by with its own vessels, many of them large and fast, as long as access to California and the East Indies remained open, although tightness had arisen from withdrawal of the last few foreign bottoms and barring of the Panama Canal.

If "drastic steps" were decided upon, only an embargo of all fuels, refined and crude alike, would be effective. A 100 percent world embargo would be necessary, requiring Dutch and British cooperation and discouragement of other producing countries, perhaps by threatening them with closure of U.S. markets for their goods. In summary, the ECA vulnerability study of April 1941 sounded a trumpet for total embargo, at odds with the alternative notions of many higher U.S. authorities of a partial embargo when the time came, which would allow "normal" exports to dissuade Japan from seizing the East Indies and leave it hope of relief by diplomatic bargaining.

Momentum for the Financial Freeze, May–July 1941

S ince discovery of Japan's secret cache of dollars in the summer of 1940, word had percolated through Washington that Japan was whisking money out of its New York bank accounts. As early as 15 November 1940 the U.S. commercial attaché in Tokyo had "reliably" warned of "near future heavy withdrawals of Japanese funds from American banks." His information was plausible, but the supposed reason, dollar payments to Germany, was not. Japan and Germany were bickering over trade settlements, the Germans refusing sterling and demanding dollar payment from Japan's U.S. balances, said to be $125 million, through German firms in South America or Swedish or Russian firms in the United States.[1]

Japan's Money Flees

Japan, in fact, was trying to reposition its dollar accounts in anticipation of a U.S. freeze. Agents of the Yokohama Specie Bank in Rio de Janeiro, the bank's only South American branch—it had other account relationships in Chile and possibly Peru—negotiated a transfer deal that took effect at year's end. The YSBNY opened a dollar account at the Banco do Brazil and in the last eleven days of January 1941 transferred $5 million into it. Once again, the Specie Bank agency did not disclose the transfers as required by law, so U.S. authorities could not readily track the funds. Not until May did the Federal Reserve realize that another $10 million had fled to Brazil in April.[2] The Treasury heard a rumor that the Specie Bank planned to forward all its dollars to the Banque

Nationale of Haiti![3] In reality, Japan was hastening to spend dollars in Latin America for copper, oil, animal hides, and other commodities difficult or impossible to obtain from the United States.[4]

U.S. officials were also puzzled by a shuffle involving De Javische Bank, the central bank of the Netherlands East Indies. Since the fall of Holland the Indies had been controlled by the Dutch government in exile in London. It held $60 million on deposit in Guaranty Trust Company of New York for a purchasing commission that bought U.S. aircraft and munitions to defend against Japan. In March 1941 the YSBNY began moving dollars to an account of the De Javische Bank at the Guaranty Trust. That bank, naïvely or otherwise, considered the Netherlands Purchasing Commission a domestic entity, exempt from reporting regulations because of its registered New York address, but told the Fed sub rosa that about $16 million of Japanese funds had migrated to it. This was strange. The Dutch Indies and Japan traded actively through a settlement deal whereby each maintained accounts in the other's currency, yen and guilders, for routine trade. They settled net difference from time to time in U.S. dollars. The Indies, cut off from the mother country, usually bought more from Japan than it sold. Even though an oil contract with Japan had been negotiated in November 1940, oil deliveries had probably totaled no more than $5 million since then, not enough to reverse the trade balance. Dollars should have been flowing from the Dutch *into* Japan's dollar accounts, not vice versa. Stranger still, De Javische Bank transferred $15.2 million back to the Specie Bank in New York in mid-June, at the very time when Japan was anxiously yanking dollars from its American accounts. U.S. officials wondered if the Java bank was receiving gold from Japan and holding dollars secretly for it in New York, or if there were some other quirk in the deal.[5]

Meanwhile, State Department officials nipped at the heels of Japanese firms trying to repatriate dollars. Insurance company branches, some of which had operated in the United States for decades, could be readily liquidated. In September 1940 the U.S. branches of the Tokio Marine Insurance and Meiji Fire Insurance Companies had stopped writing all but marine policies, reinsured their liabilities with other firms, and freed up $5.5 million of excess reserves over several months for remittance to their parent companies. The New York state insurance commissioner consulted Sumner Welles for political guidance, but as no law had been violated, Welles offered no comment. Then, on 17 May 1941, the Aetna Insurance Company sounded out State's attitude about purchasing the local subsidiaries of Tokio Marine for about $7 million. The Japanese, worried about freezing, wanted to close the deal within a week. Maxwell Hamilton, chief of State's Division of Far Eastern Affairs, hated to see liquid dollars escape in view of Grew's indignation over maltreatment of U.S. businesses in Japan. Since there was no "immediate prospect" of freezing, however, and as Acheson reported that Japan had more than $90 million in U.S. banks, Hull expressed no objection, grumpily because of getting last-minute notice. In June, Herbert Feis offered extralegal advice about a $1 million partial remittance from the 1940 insurance company liquidations; he advocated limiting capital transfers, but his superiors still opposed discriminatory actions against Japan. The New York insurance authorities, though lacking a good faith reason, delayed approval anyway. On 9 July Feis connived with Welles and Hornbeck to ask them to defer approval for "several weeks," thus delaying the escape of dollars until the rumored freeze took effect.[6]

American businessmen got in the habit of approaching State for guidance. On 20 June Bankers Trust Company of New York sought Acheson's advice on its routine financing of Baker and Company, a U.S. firm that bought $10 to $15 million per year of silver from, or through, Japan for resale to manufacturers and to the Treasury. The Japanese had allowed Baker fifteen days of grace to pay but now demanded instant payment at U.S. dockside. Acheson, without legal authority, responded that U.S. policy opposed even such ephemeral credits.[7]

On 1 July Japan ordered all dollar transactions by Japanese subjects to be conducted through a "concentration account" at the Yokohama Specie Bank in New York acting on behalf of the Bank of Japan. To calm the foreign exchange markets, Tokyo fixed a tiny rise in the official value of the yen, from 23-7/16 cents to 23-9/16 cents, the first change since October 1940. A similar sterling concentration account had been established on 31 May in London, where Japanese market interventions protected the quotation of the yen. Japan was mobilizing foreign exchange in anticipation of a freeze.[8]

Indignation over Oil Exports, May–June 1941

Despite the evidence of lower Japanese fuel oil purchases, to a range of 1.2 to 1.6 million barrels monthly versus about 2 million previously, alarms sounded in Washington about a renewed buying surge. On 21 May J. Edgar Hoover told Maxwell that, barred from the Panama Canal, the Japanese would hugely accelerate tanker dispatches to the West Coast to thirty-five or forty vessels per month, implying that nearly every Japanese liquid carrier, naval and civilian, would be steaming full draft toward California.[9] Yet some vessels were surely serving elsewhere. A more sane Treasury review cited eight tankers loading West Coast crude in May, inferring, as crude takings were about half of all loadings, sixteen Japanese ships embarking all fuels. This was approximately correct. Japan raised the loading rate to 1.9 million barrels of liquids in May and continued at that rate through June and most of July.[10] The takings in the last months before the freeze were much less than the export licenses in hand, probably due to tanker limitations.

A Rising Tempo

During May and June 1941 a rush of events accelerated Washington's impulse toward freezing Japanese assets. U.S. and British purchasing agents were already preempting strategic resource exports of neutral nations. British liaison representatives declared their country's willingness to join economic sanctions against Japan.[11] On 27 May, Roosevelt told the American pubic in a radio "fireside chat" that the United States had entered a condition of unlimited national emergency.[12] The declaration strengthened his moral authority to control foreign assets under Section 5(b) of the Trading with the Enemy Act by updating the outmoded link to the 1934 gold emergency, which had underlain his prior European freezing orders.

On 14 June FDR extended the sweep of his executive order, which since April 1940 had frozen the assets of conquered nations, by adding to the list the remainder of Europe, that is, Germany, Italy, the Soviet Union, Sweden, Switzerland, Spain, and Portugal. His true intention, of targeting only the Axis, emerged in follow-up orders granting easy general licenses for ordinary dollar transactions to the four neutrals as well as to the Soviet Union a few days after Germany invaded it on 22 June. Global general licenses permitted deposits by most countries *into* blocked accounts to facilitate payments for authorized exports and services. Broad relaxations were soon granted to Sweden and Switzerland on condition that their governments certify every transaction as bona fide for their needs and not for helping Germany. Controls were also eased for routine U.S. trade with the American republics, British Commonwealth, Soviet Union, and the unconquered colonies of the Netherlands, Belgium, and Denmark. On 17 July another presidential order empowered an interagency committee to draw up a blacklist of U.S. and foreign individuals and firms suspected of plotting to supply munitions to Germany or Italy. It also prevented machine tool exports that would cause unusual hardship for U.S. firms, thus closing a gap left partly open because the ECA's statutory powers usually extended to licensing of raw materials exports.[13]

No diplomatic repercussions ensued. German trade with the dollar and sterling areas was moribund due to the British blockade. Edward H. Foley Jr., general counsel of the Treasury Department, later pointed to the European freezes as signaling a significant change of attitude in Washington on financial warfare: "This step [of 14 June] changed the emphasis of freezing control from a defensive weapon primarily intended to protect the property of invaded countries, to a frankly aggressive weapon against the Axis."[14] Morgenthau had won his desired blow against Germany and Italy.

Census of Foreign Assets

The U.S. Treasury sprang to life at last. Morgenthau's aides realized they lacked information about U.S. assets controlled by foreign interests, friendly and not, other than the gold and dollars of foreign governments held on earmark deposited in the Federal Reserve Bank of New York. (Reports of commercial banks and brokers to the Federal Reserve disclosed the nationality, but not necessarily the identities, of asset owners.) On 14 June the Treasury ordered disclosures, in a census of foreign-owned assets, of holdings as of that date and on 30 June 1940 in order to measure changes during the prior year. Forms TFR-300 were printed, to be completed and returned to district Federal Reserve Banks on the impossibly early date of 14 July—instructions were not circulated until 16 August—a deadline extended to 30 September and finally to 31 October. The regional Federal Reserve Banks eventually collected 565,000 reports of assets from 23,000 corporations, 4,000 banks, and 132,000 individuals. Some banks filed hundreds of forms on behalf of their clients. The secret data, not fully published until 1945, revealed that $12.7 billion of U.S. assets were owned by foreigners, largely by Western European and Canadian entities. Only 4 percent were Axis owned, 1.3 percent Japanese owned. On 14 June 1941 the reported assets of 3,214 Japanese entities and aliens amounted to $160.5 million, consisting mainly of $104 million in bank deposits and $12 million of portfolio securities (mostly U.S. government paper) held principally by U.S. branches of Japanese banks. Other Japanese firms had invested $35 million in nonbank businesses, mainly in trading and finance, but almost nothing in real estate, manufacturing, or other operations. The Treasury found the census returns to be "significant aids to the economic warfare program."[15]

On 22 June 1941 Hitler launched Operation Barbarossa, the invasion of the Soviet Union. The attack terminated Japanese trade with Germany and the rest of Europe via the Trans-Siberian Railway. High-value goods, such as rubber and quinine from Asia and machine tools from Germany, had moved over that expensive route. As an alternative, a few German ships ran the blockade to Japan.[16] Now almost entirely isolated from Europe, and with sterling assets tightly restricted, Japan's only medium of international exchange was the U.S. dollar. If and when the United States decided to declare financial war, Japan would be at its mercy.

In June and July U.S. officials began seriously to consider denying shipments of ordinary fuels without waiting for a dollar freeze. Japanese firms held approved licenses on 1 June for 7.1 million barrels of gasoline, 21.9 million barrels of crude oil, and 33,000 barrels of lubricants, altogether worth about $50 million (of which 3 percent was destined for Manchukuo and occupied China). Japan could thus legally acquire from the United States, if embarked at the January–May 1941 rate, gasoline for another nine months and ordinary crude oil for an astonishing thirty-two months—enough to supply it until the end of 1943! Japan had ample dollars and gold to pay for it. On 19 June, upon instruction of Acting Secretary of State Sumner Welles, Green's control division drafted legal orders for a possible announcement that *new* applications for export of any grade of oil product to Japan would be delayed until 15 August. Green expected August relicensings to be cut to a maximum level of half the average exports of 1935–36, to be allocated pro rata to firms that applied. On 30 June Maxwell proposed that Green's division send all license applications filed for Japan, occupied China, and Thailand, both current and future, to his controllers, there to lie dormant until the administration decided its foreign policy. The general withdrew his extraordinary request after conferring with Dean Acheson, who awaited a financial solution, not a jiggering of the export licensing system.[17]

Indochina Occupation Provokes the Freeze Decision

After Japan allied itself with Germany and Italy in the Tripartite Pact of 27 September 1940, negotiations between Cordell Hull and Ambassador Kichisaburo Nomura to settle tensions had begun in Washington. Hull aimed to persuade Japan to pull back from conquests in Asia. He made little progress. Operation Barbarossa freed Tokyo from fears of a Soviet attack on Manchukuo. The Japanese government focused on a "southern option," the seizure of foreign colonies in Southeast Asia. The most immediately vulnerable territory was southern French Indochina. In July 1940 Japan had coerced the Vichy French administration to permit it to occupy the northern half under the plausible rationale of severing a railway from the port of Hanoi that was free China's only rail link to the outside world. But in 1940 the United States was unready for a confrontation; it merely protested. Southern Indochina, which had no transportation links to China, posed a more serious risk to the Western powers. Japan could place bombers within range of the British naval base at Singapore and threaten the Netherlands Indies (although "outflanking" the U.S.-defended Philippines was less significant because the islands were surrounded on three sides by Japanese bases). In addition, Indochina had supplied vital tin and rubber for U.S. industries. Occupation of Thailand would pressure that country into Japan's orbit. Nomura countered that Japan needed Indochina's rice and industrial commodities in view of Western trade restrictions.[18] Relations with the United States grew more tense.

At the beginning of July 1941, Japanese military planners decided to occupy southern Indochina. Between 12 and 15 July U.S. authorities became aware of the plan through British intelligence and by code breaking Japanese diplomatic messages. Roosevelt decided to express extreme displeasure by imposing, as Welles described it to the British ambassador, "various embargoes, both economic and financial, which measures had been under consideration for some time past and which had been held in abeyance."[19] In the following days British and U.S. officials discussed probable sanctions. The high-principled Cordell Hull, foremost opponent of economic and financial war, caved in on the seventeenth. Resting at a resort from overwork, Hull telephoned the State Department that he would go along with strong sanctions.[20]

Staff officials at the Treasury and State Departments suggested that trade sanctions ought to allow a modicum of business, say, swaps of silk for cotton and limited amounts of oil.[21] Rear Adm. Richmond Kelley Turner, chief of the Naval War Plans Division, had predicted that, if the United States barred *all* petroleum exports, Japan would attack British Borneo, Malaya, and the Dutch Indies, seize the oil fields, and draw the United States into war. Turner concluded, "Recommendation: That trade with Japan not be embargoed at this time." The secretary of war and the army chief of staff, however, raised no objections to a financial freeze. On 23 July the British agreed to join any U.S. freeze and to convince their dominions to do the same.[22]

FDR had not yet fixed on a precise course. Welles and Acheson were not sure the president understood that an asset freeze might be tantamount to an absolute trade embargo. As Feis told it, "The Navy favored prudence; the Treasury wanted freezing; the State Department did not object to freezing, but was not clear as to what would follow; the British government seemed ready for anything; and the secretary of state, from White Sulphur Springs, was telephoning that he thought it best to leave the decision to those on the ground."[23]

Oil Quota

The president instructed Sumner Welles to draft an order regulating the freeze. Welles was an unusual choice because financial sanctions under TWEA were the province of the Treasury Department. Perhaps Roosevelt thought an official of the softer State Department would carry out his policy of a partial freeze more reliably than the pugnacious Morgenthau. Welles prepared a simple freezing order the next day and assigned the drafting of administrative rules to Dean Acheson, commanding him not to launch a total oil embargo.[24] He also told Stanley Hornbeck to prepare by the twenty-first orders that would restrict the amounts and grades of oil exports to Japan, suspend silk imports, and, most significantly, impose a freeze of Japan's financial assets.

Two days earlier Welles had requested a staff paper recommending an oil export quota based on "a period in which the exports were not abnormally large."[25] Joseph Green, head of State's Division of Controls, which reported to Acheson, suggested a base period of 1935–36, the last peaceful years in the Far East. Acheson, in draft regulations of 21 July, duly proposed a ceiling on shipments at the average export rate of 1935–36. The precise number of barrels would be determined by the ECA when it issued licenses. (He also suggested lowering the definition of aviation gasoline to 80 octane, a proposal not adopted.) Welles went along with the proposed quota.[26] Acheson may not have been aware that Japan had purchased large volumes of U.S. petroleum liquids, 20.8 million barrels in 1935 and 21.7 million in 1936, an average of 21.3 million barrels, because the 1934 stockpiling law required oil companies to build storage reserves equaling six months of imports. Thereafter exports to Japan rose to an average of 29 million barrels in 1937–39, but had dipped back to 22.8 million barrels in 1940 and an annual rate of 20.9 million barrels in January–July 1941, the latter slightly below the base years.[27] A quota of 100 percent of 1935–36 would actually have allowed Japan *more* oil than its recent rate of purchases.

Green, aware of historical statistics, had actually suggested a limit of *half* the 1935–36 average, that is, 10.3 million barrels per year.[28] The quota proposal was corrected accordingly. The record is unclear as to why U.S. officials thought that figure was a proper volume to chastise Japan yet keep it calm. Japan had stockpiled 4 million barrels in 1936, according to the ONI (1935 was not stated.) Perhaps Green compensated for that, and for Japan's higher recent receipts from the Dutch Indies of 12.5 million annual barrels under the contract of November 1940 versus 4 or 5 million in the base years. Recalibrating for those events, 10.3 million U.S. barrels annually would have ensured Japan of fuels equal to its actual pre-China war consumption. Or 50 percent may have been arbitrary for negotiating simplicity.[29] In any case, the corrected figure was adopted on 1 August, and Grew and the U.S. Allies were notified.[30]

The oil quota, however, was to be applied product by product, rendering it far more severe than it appeared. In the mid-1930s Japan had mainly bought cheap crude and residual oil. In 1941 it bought expensive gasoline, light fuel oil, and lubricants. Purchases in the first seven months cost $47 million at an

annual rate versus $21 million in 1935–36. This reflected the richer mix and a
25 percent higher price of refined fuels, including products shipped in drums,
whereas crude and residual oil prices had not changed much. If a product-by-
product quota had been in effect in January–July 1941, permissible takings of
all U.S. liquids would have declined by 63 percent to a 7.8 million barrel
annual rate, and sales of gasoline and lubricating oils would have plummeted
90 percent (chart 19).[31]

Programming the Freeze

Acheson reported back Monday morning, 21 July. As agreed, the United States
would not grant Japan a broad general license of the kind awarded to friendly
neutrals. Every transaction using frozen funds would require specific Treasury
licenses, as Roosevelt wished. Acheson, however, scheduled a pause of a few
weeks during which no release of blocked money would be allowed, ostensibly
to allow the Treasury time to develop a licensing system for trade, including
raw silk, and to coordinate with the Allies' freezes.[32] Welles accepted the proposed oil quota, the precise number of barrels to be determined by the ECA
when it issued export licenses. However, for submission to the cabinet meeting of 24 July, he struck out the temporary trade halt and eliminated a barter-
like assumption that when trade resumed, Japan, in order to obtain oil, would
have to deliver goods needed in the United States.[33]

The Freeze Decision and the Rules

On 24 July 1941 Japanese transports disembarked troops at Camranh Bay in
southern Indochina. Roosevelt summoned the cabinet. He wished to react by
imposing a dollar freeze that would subject all transactions with Japan to
licensing. The United States could decide later, if it wished, how much trade
to allow, one shipment at a time, and how Japan would be allowed to pay dollars. It was the sort of flexible policy Roosevelt cherished. A last-minute conference to warn Nomura proved ineffective. The president left for a weekend
at his home in Hyde Park, New York.[34]

The next day Acheson and Treasury officials agreed that export licenses for
oil would continue to be "automatically granted" by the ECA and State
Department but that payment would have to come from blocked Japanese
accounts rather than from dollars earned by future exports to the United
States. A Foreign Funds Control Committee (FFCC) of State and Treasury
officers would release funds for licensed exports. In a compromise with
Acheson's push for a few weeks' hiatus before releasing funds, Welles subsequently suggested that the FFCC should temporarily delay acting on export
applications Japan had already submitted and consider releasing blocked funds

CHART 19   U.S. Oil Exports to Japan, 1935–1941, and Possible Annual Quotas after 26 July 1941

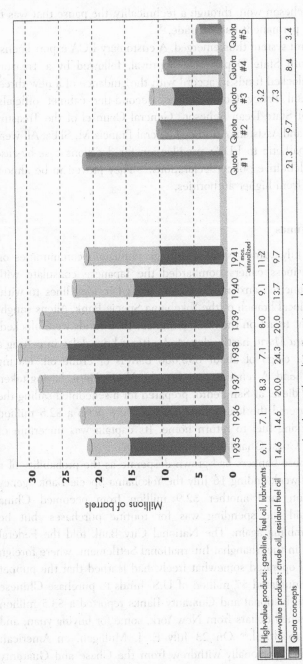

Millions of barrels

	1935	1936	1937	1938	1939	1940	1941 7 mos. annualized	Quota #1	Quota #2	Quota #3	Quota #4	Quota #5
High-value products: gasoline, fuel oil, lubricants	6.1	7.1	8.3	7.1	8.0	9.1	11.2			3.2		
Low-value products: crude oil, residual fuel oil	14.6	14.6	20.0	24.3	20.0	13.7	9.7	21.3	9.7	7.3	8.4	3.4

Quota concepts

Quota concept 1: Total barrels same as 1935-36 actual purchases without distinction as to products.

Quota concept 2: Separate quota for each product equal to 1935-36 actual, but no increase of any product above 1941 actual rate.

Quota concept 3: Joseph C. Green's quota proposed 19 July 1941: 50% of actual 1935-36 average calculated for each product separately.

Quota concept 4: Same as Concept 3 less increase available from Dutch East Indies. (Indies' product mix resembled 1935-36 U.S. shipments.)

Quota concept 5: Same as Concept 3 less increased volume available from Dutch East Indies reduced to and offset Japanese stockpiling in 1935-36.

For 1935–41: Department of Commerce, *Foreign Commerce and Navigation of the United States*, 1940–42. Quotas calculated by author: No. 3, Joseph C. Green, Division of Controls to A-A, 19 June 1941, File 811.20 Regulations, microfilm series LM-68, Records of the Department of State, RG 59, NA; Nos. 4 and 5 same but adjusted for Indies and stockpiling estimates in Navy Department, "Report on Petroleum Situation of Japan."

only for new ones. Acheson won, through a technicality, the pause that was to evolve quickly into a permanent halt of trade.[35]

A dual-track control system thus emerged. A customary ECA export license would be granted with State Department approval, followed by a Treasury license to pay from blocked funds in accord with the guidance of a new three-man Interdepartmental Policy Committee of second-tier cabinet officials: Assistant Secretary of State Dean Acheson, General Counsel of the Treasury Edward H. Foley Jr., and Assistant Attorney General Francis M. Shea. All were "adroit lawyers" sympathetic to FDR's predilection for decisions case-by-case and his aversion to definitive policy declarations.[36] They proved to be almost immune to direction from higher authorities.

Desperate Flight of Funds

That day, Friday, 25 July, rumors swirled through immigrant communities on the West Coast. Business callers bombarded the Japanese consulate with questions. In San Francisco anxious depositors waited in long lines to withdraw funds from the local branch of the Yokohama Specie Bank. Aliens sought out naturalized citizens to act on their behalf in case their funds were blocked. A big tanker, the *Ogura Maru*, hastily departed, after a brief delay in getting a sailing permit, with a cargo of about 650,000 barrels of crude oil, leaving behind an assurance bond. A remaining tanker, the *Nissin Maru*, having taken on 120,000 barrels of diesel at San Pedro, prepared for a scheduled sailing the next day. Offshore hovered the luxury liner *Tatsuta Maru*, with a $2.5 million cargo of raw silk, lacking fuel to return home. Its captain was uncertain of what to do. The U.S. Coast Guard awaited instructions.[37]

In New York Japanese bankers had grown desperate as the probability of a freeze loomed. In the week ending 16 July the Yokohama Specie Bank agency disbursed $7.4 million, and another $2.9 million from occupied China accounts. Nakano said the spending was for routine purchases, but he appeared to be dissembling again. The National City Bank told the Federal Reserve that its office in the Shanghai International Settlement, where foreign banks and traders still operated somewhat freely, had learned that the puppet China Central Bank liquidated $7 million of U.S. funds to purchase Chinese yuan there. The Chase National and Guaranty Banks reported a $3.5 million outflow of Japanese-owned dollars from New York, some for buying yuan, and a further $2 million to Brazil.[38] On 23 July E. J. Mulligan, an American employee of the YSBNY, personally withdrew from the Chase and Guaranty banks $400,000 in $50 and $100 bills.[39] The next day the Specie Bank agency deposited a $5 million check drawn on another bank into the French American

Bank's New York branch office for credit to the Bank of Indochina, an institution that Japan influenced if not controlled. The French American bankers were bewildered because transactions of French and colonial accounts in the United States were subject to license by the Treasury. The check was drawn against uncollected funds, however, and was returned without deposit.[40] On 26 July, the day of the freeze, the FBI suspected that Specie Bank agents in San Francisco were smuggling $5 million of Japanese government bonds from the basement of their office onto a ship. Japanese bank officials claimed they were worthless cancelled securities. After Pearl Harbor U.S. bank liquidators found $3.85 million of Japanese government bonds of a 1924 issue, payable in dollars, in the bank's San Francisco branch.[41]

How Much Money Escaped?

Japan succeeded in withdrawing most of its dollars before the freeze order of 26 July 1941. The amount became clear after 7 December when Treasury agents seized control of enemy bank branches and subsequently passed control to the office of the Alien Property custodian on 11 March 1942. The APC staff calculated that between 14 June and December 1941 the Japanese government withdrew $27 million from its account at the Yokohama Specie Bank in New York, nearly half that agency's assets. Most of the drawdown occurred before 26 July. By the time of Pearl Harbor only $29 million was left. All Japanese-owned assets in the United States then totaled $61.2 million, of which $39.1 million was in cash and $11.1 million in accounts receivable. The Japanese holdings had a net worth after liabilities of about $53 million.[42] (Confusingly, the APC sometimes reported gross assets and sometimes assets net of liabilities.)

How much money escaped the freeze? Japan's secret war chest at the YSBNY had peaked at about $160 million in early 1940. It stood at $90 million as late as May 1941, and, as noted, the YSBNY held only $29 million on 7 December.[43] Thus as much as $131 million may have escaped, almost all before the freeze. The course of withdrawals can only be guessed. Half or more was probably expended to settle Japan's $69 million trade deficit with the United States in the first seven months of 1941, of which only $6 million was funded by final gold sales in January 1941. Much of the rest was likely expended on a buying spree in Latin America. Trade with the American republics normally resulted in a $2 to $4 million annual deficit for Japan. In 1940 the deficit rose to $13 million, and in 1941 it surged to $65 million. However, Japan's gold sales to the region, as learned after the war, amounted to only $3.2 million in the twelve months beginning 1 April 1941 (with no

sales before or after that period). A $10 million trade deficit with the
Philippines in 1941 was probably also funded.[44] The aggregate flight of dollars
estimated here was large indeed, equivalent to fifteen months of silk exports to
the United States or more than two years of Japanese Empire gold production.[45] Harry Dexter White had been correct when he told Morgenthau in
February 1941 that for a freeze "to be effective it must be done at once."[46]

Secretary of the Treasury Henry Morgenthau Jr. was the first to urge Roosevelt to launch financial warfare against Japan. (Library of Congress)

Japanese farmers bred cocoons by feeding mulberry leaves to silkworms on bamboo trays in their houses. (Library of Congress)

Japanese filatures employed girls and young women for the exacting task of unreeling silk cocoons and matching away the natural flaws. (Library of Congress)

Loading raw silk bales in Yokohama. Silk was Japan's steady source
of dollars until the ravages of the Depression and substitution of
rayon and nylon. (Library of Congress)

Transpacific liner *Kashima Maru*. Large, luxurious passenger ships carried
gold and silk to U.S. ports. (Library of Congress)

A GOLFLEX FROCK

Of Exclusive Calvio Crêpe

The sort of exquisitely simple Frock which the smart world selects for all day wear—one piece, the skirt pleated at front and cleverly accented with visible stitching. Its forest green, Patou red, and winter leaf tan colorings make it an adorable accompaniment to the new black coats. You may choose it in a lovely navy, too! Calvio—the lustrous silk crêpe which tailors so beautifully—is to be had only in Golflex Frocks.

Wilkin & Adler, Inc., 500 Seventh Avenue, N.Y.C.

Short skirts in the 1920s and 1930s made sheer silk hosiery a fashion necessity regardless of price.

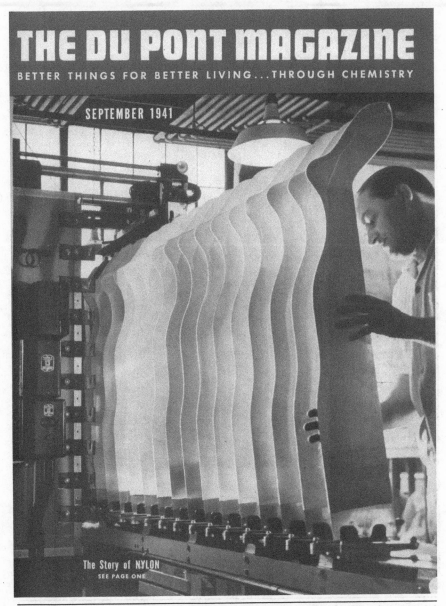

THE DU PONT MAGAZINE
BETTER THINGS FOR BETTER LIVING...THROUGH CHEMISTRY

SEPTEMBER 1941

The Story of NYLON
SEE PAGE ONE

"Boarding" nylon stockings in a hosiery factory. Du Pont's synthetic fiber for perfect sheer stockings was driving Japanese silk from its last market after 1939. (Courtesy of the Hagley Museum and Library)

A junk yard in Washington, D.C. with the Capitol Building in the background. The Japanese steel industry depended on U.S. iron and steel scrap, but exports were embargoed in late 1940. (Library of Congress)

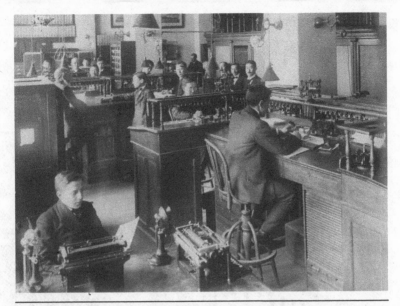

An Asian branch of the Yokohama Specie Bank. The bank's New York agency, the mobilization "safebox" for Japan's dollars, perpetrated a fraud to mislead U.S. investigators. (Library of Congress)

The Bank of Japan's gold, acquired during World War I and from mining, was Japan's vital reserve for acquiring dollars. (Library of Congress)

The Federal Reserve Building, Washington, D.C. Fed experts tracked Japan's
international dealings and uncovered the fraudulent dollar cache in the
summer of 1940. (Library of Congress)

Oil production in California was in surplus after shipments to Japan were halted. Lack of pipelines and tankers precluded alleviating a so-called shortage on the East Coast. (Library of Congress)

The Department of the Treasury building adjacent to the White House, Washington D.C. The Treasury had administered dollar freezes since 1917 but ceded authority to a hard-line committee dominated by Assistant Secretary of State Dean Acheson in 1941. (Library of Congress)

Ambassador Kichisaburo Nomura feted at a banquet in the Waldorf-Astoria Hotel, New York City, June 1941. (Library of Congress)

Sadao Iguchi, counselor of the Japanese embassy, and family at Pennsylvania Station, New York City, 1941. Japanese financial agents struggled vainly to obtain relief from the freeze. (Library of Congress)

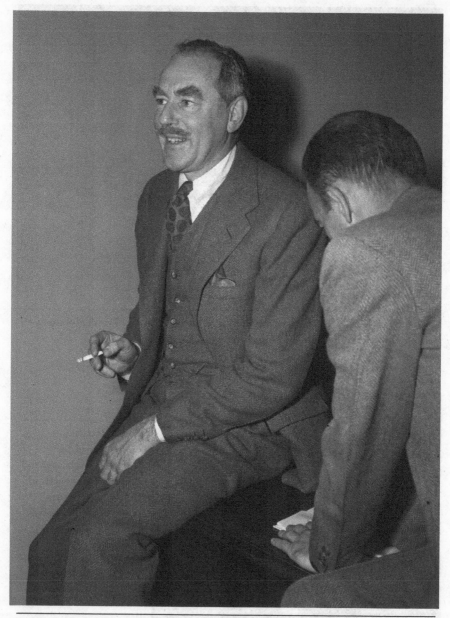

Dean Acheson. His harsh direction of the freeze trumped Roosevelt's intention to "bring Japan to its senses, not its knees." (Corbis photo)

15

The Fictitious U.S. Oil Shortage

A s his aides readied financial sanction orders, Roosevelt needed a further political justification for cutting off oil from Japan, even partially. Oil was a unique commodity. It was, of course, the lifeblood of Japanese naval and air forces, and it was vital to segments of the Japanese economy. Japan could only obtain it in adequate quantities from the United States, and if cut off, its reserve in storage tanks would not last very long. Unlike the strategic resources that the United States conserved for rearmament and its Allies, or that were vital to its own economy, there was no domestic shortage of oil or refined products. Nevertheless, to help justify an embargo the president offered a false rationale promoted by his petroleum coordinator for national defense, Harold L. Ickes, that Japanese buying caused a shortage in the United States. In fact, Japanese buying did not at any time pinch American oil users, but the facts were complex. There was both a predicted shortage on the Atlantic Coast and a glut of oil on the Pacific Coast. Roosevelt linked the two circumstances in his policy even though neither coast could solve the other's imbalance.

Oil in California

In the spring of 1941, California, the only producing state capable of exporting petroleum to Japan, which had limited tanker capacity, pumped 15 percent of U.S. crude production (about the same percentage as today). It drew largely from three regions close to the Pacific Ocean: the San Joaquin Valley, the Coastal District near Santa Barbara, and the Los Angeles basin. The state's huge reserves had been widely developed by drilling, including most of the world's wells deeper than thirteen thousand feet. Its theoretical lifting capacity of 3,755,000 barrels per day was almost as large as the actual production of the entire United States. A more realistic measure of its potential, however, was its refining capacity of 810,700 barrels per day, 18 percent of U.S. processing capacity. Pipelines gathered and delivered crude from the oil fields to nearby refineries or to tanker piers for shipment to refineries clustered around Los Angeles. Due to lack of demand, however, a proration committee established during the Depression restricted refinery runs to 613,000 barrels per day. Thus California was home to half the excess refining capacity of the United States. Thirty small plants were idle.

American leaders well knew that California was awash in surplus oil. Despite demand from factories, railroads, and workers as defense orders rose and as avgas refining expanded, supplies were so ample that inventories increased during the first half of 1941. Prices were low: crude averaged ninety-seven cents per barrel in 1941, 17 percent below the price in Texas and 12 percent below California's own anemic pricing during a 1935–37 economic slump. Although the industry claimed to be losing money, the proration committee further curtailed crude liftings. In May, J. K. Galbraith of the Office of Price Administration rolled back a price increase. No rationale of shortage or defense needs compelled a reduction of exports to Japan from California.

The California oil industry served the Pacific Rim almost exclusively. Refined fuels moved through pipelines as far north as San Francisco (fig. 1). A fleet of about fifty tankers carried products to Washington, Oregon, Vancouver, Alaska, and Hawaii. Until 1941 three tankers had hauled gasoline equivalent to oil production of fifteen to twenty thousand barrels per day, 3 percent of California's output of all products, to U.S. Atlantic ports via the Panama Canal. A similar volume of products to other Atlantic ports virtually ceased after foreign tankers abandoned Pacific routes. Exports to the Philippines and the Asian continent were minor because the region was more efficiently served from the East Indies. Japan was California's number one foreign customer, a buyer of fifty-five thousand barrels per day of liquids in the spring of 1941, or 9 percent of the state's petroleum products. Japan benefited from the arrangement. California's light crudes yielded high fractions of gasoline and fuel oil. Its heavy crudes yielded residual oil for ships (a major reason the U.S. Fleet relocated from the Atlantic to southern California in 1919). California offered low prices and the shortest haul from any Western Hemisphere producing region, which maximized Japanese tanker capacity and minimized shipping costs. A final advantage, which Japanese diplomats and strategists appeared not to notice, was that California's oil could not practicably be diverted to Lend-Lease aid for Great Britain.

FIGURE 1   **U.S. Oil Pipelines and Tanker vs. Tank Car Capacities, 1941**

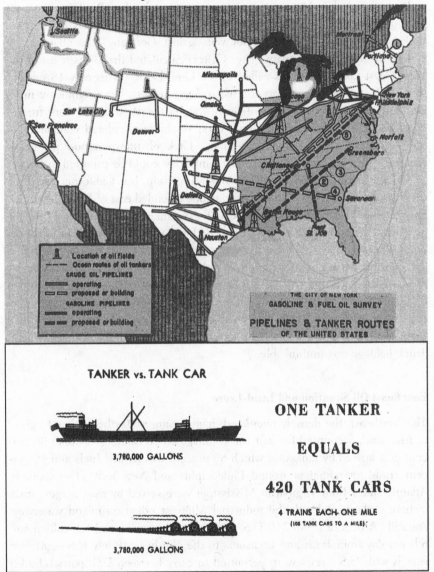

Congress, Senate, Special Committee to Investigate Gasoline, Hearings, 497, chart 1.

In May 1941 distribution bottlenecks began to hamper the marketing of California's oil. The U.S. government requisitioned a few Pacific tankers for Atlantic service to Britain and, in June, four or five more to carry Lend-Lease fuels to Vladivostok for the Soviet war against Germany. The chairman of California-Texas Oil Company (later Caltex) calculated that 38 percent of the West Coast tanker fleet was called up for Lend-Lease versus only 18 percent of the Atlantic fleet; there was confusion over numbers, but a significant number were conscripted. Because deliveries along the West Coast were further constrained by lack of railroad tank cars, Washington ordered companies to pool transport and terminal operations. Lack of transportation perversely increased the surpluses in port storage tanks that could be exported to Japan.[1]

On the Atlantic Coast fuel demand was strong, but California was then totally isolated from that market. No pipeline extended east of Bakersfield, seventy miles inland from the Pacific Coast. No tankers could be spared for the long haul through the Panama Canal. Railroad tank car movement was economically inconceivable, even had the cars been available. For comparison, a car shuttling between Texas and New York could deliver twelve barrels per day on a twenty-day round trip costing $2.37 freight per barrel, an extreme burden on liquids worth $1.00 to $3.00 per barrel versus tanker rates of 56 cents. Rail rates for a six-thousand-mile round trip between California and New York, had they existed, would have been ruinously prohibitive and absurdly inefficient. Truck haulage was unthinkable.

East Coast Oil Situation and Lend-Lease

The Northeast, the densely populated, high-income states from New England to Maryland, accounted for half the country's oil consumption. Some 96 percent of it arrived by tanker, of which 60 percent was refined fuels and 40 percent crude for refineries around Philadelphia and New York. (The southern Atlantic states from Virginia to Mississippi were served by river barges, small inshore tankers, and rail; the industrial Midwest relied on inland waterways and rail.) A fleet of about 250 U.S. seagoing tankers delivered 1.1 million barrels per day from Texas and Louisiana to the Northeast. (Only U.S.-registered vessels with U.S. crews were permitted to carry between U.S. ports.) Tanker capacity was usually so ample that many ships laid up seasonally. Another two hundred thousand daily barrels arrived in the Northeast aboard tankers from Venezuela and Caribbean refineries. The last 4 percent arrived in the western fringes of the northeastern states from midcontinent Kansas-Oklahoma oil fields via river and lake barges or by rail from a small pipeline that ended in Indiana.[2]

Tankers for the British

In 1941 Great Britain's oil situation was growing desperate. The sterling area (Britain and its colonies and dominions except Canada) was desperately short of dollars to buy Western Hemisphere fuels. The United Kingdom had liquidated most of its gold and had commandeered for sale the U.S. securities owned by British investors. Early in the war it had received oil from British-controlled companies in Iraq and Iran that accepted inconvertible pounds sterling, until Italy's declaration of war in June 1940 closed the Mediterranean route. The alternative ninety-day round trip around the Cape of Good Hope sharply reduced tanker efficiency and was vulnerable to U-boat attacks. East Indies oil, although available at least in part for sterling, was even more distant and in any case was committed to Australia, India, other British domains in Asia, and, since late 1940, Japan (20 percent).

The Lend-Lease Act signed by FDR on 11 March 1941 solved Britain's dollar problem for the rest of the war. The act authorized shipments of oil without compensation. The British government asked to borrow U.S. tankers to help replenish stocks that had fallen dangerously low despite civilian rationing. German U-boats had been sinking ships faster than the yards could replace them, while delays inherent in convoying imposed a 20 to 30 percent penalty on shipping efficiency. Reckoning 378 tankers needed for the UK, in April 1941 Prime Minister Winston Churchill appealed to the United States, which was "willing, and able, to respond." Sir Arthur Salter, joint parliamentary secretary to the Ministry of Shipping, came to Washington to confer with Harry Hopkins, FDR's confidant and director of Lend-Lease. Britain must borrow 75 tankers during the remainder of 1941, he said, assigned at the rate of 20 per month, even if there were no further net ship losses. In June he upped the request to 91 ships. Under the Neutrality Act, U.S. ships could not sail into the war zone, however, and the administration rejected the subterfuge of reflagging them. Negotiations resulted in the famous "shuttle." U.S. tankers would haul oil and refined products from the Gulf Coast to New York, and sometimes to Baltimore and Philadelphia, for transfer to tankers owned or leased by Britain, cutting its transatlantic haul distance by half and, not incidentally, saving money.[3]

Enter Ickes

On 2 May 1941 Roosevelt called on U.S. ship owners and oil companies to release twenty-five tankers for Lend-Lease, twenty of which were from the Texas–East Coast route. Shortly thereafter he raised the call to fifty vessels, about half a million deadweight tons (DWT) of shipping.[4] (An average tanker displaced 10,000 DWT, that is, capacity for cargo, fuel, and stores expressed in long tons of 2,240 pounds. One DWT volumetrically ranged from six barrels of heavy oils or crude to eight barrels of gasoline. The approximate average of seven barrels per ton equated to 10,000 tons of fuels per one "tanker equivalent" vessel).[5] On 27 May the president's proclamation of an unlimited national emergency politically reinforced the call (chapter 14).

Roosevelt established the office of petroleum coordinator for national defense headed by Secretary of the Interior Harold L. Ickes, a prickly and opinionated man who called himself the Old Curmudgeon. He was given to angry outbursts, even against Roosevelt, and often threatened resignation. A lawyer steeped in Chicago politics, Ickes had organized progressive Republicans in 1932 to vote for Roosevelt, who rewarded him with the cabinet post, saying, "I liked the cut of his jib." Ickes, who championed the civil rights of American Indians, minorities, and the oppressed Jews of Germany, joined other cabinet hard-liners in antipathy to aggression. He advocated aid to China in 1938 and an oil embargo of Japan in 1940. Ickes had genuine credentials in energy policy, including management of petroleum reserves on federal lands and of hydroelectric projects, but none in foreign policy. Nevertheless, he searched opportunistically for a role in economic warfare. As petroleum coordinator he gathered data on supply and demand, consulted with the industry, and advised defense agencies how to coordinate actions and fix problems. He recruited as his coequal deputy coordinator, Ralph K. Davies, a vice president of Standard Oil Company of California who had impressed him during a failed push to conserve oil in California. The assignment emboldened Ickes to press vigorously for an oil embargo of Japan, ostensibly to conserve U.S. resources.[6]

The first shuttle tanker sailed on 21 May 1941. Ship transfers were gradual at first. The U.S. Maritime Commission reported that on 30 June, 243 tankers were still on the Gulf–East Coast service, versus 244 a year earlier.[7] But Ickes and Davies calculated that the expected diversion of 20 percent of the Atlantic tanker fleet would inevitably cause shortages on the East Coast. They reckoned that the brunt of the shortage would occur in gasoline, the largest volume product yet the one most easily sacrificed because "pleasure driving" was thought to be widespread (although no studies backed the presumption). Assuming no reduction of fuel oil for factories, trains, and home heating, they predicted an imminent shortage of 33 percent of gasoline supply on the East Coast.[8]

As to the Pacific, since late 1939 Ickes had warned FDR that oil conservation would some day be necessary in California and that public sentiment there was adverse to supplying Japan. On 8 June 1941 he wrote in his diary, "I went into action about Japan." He demanded from General Maxwell the roster of Japanese licenses approved by the ECA and insisted that no new ones be issued until he received it, apparently unaware of the recent stalling actions by the export controllers. He singled out a cargo of lubricating oil loading in Philadelphia for Japan as a test case for restrictions. Davies sent a telegram to all shippers to cease exporting, without approval, oil products from the Atlantic Coast except to Western Hemisphere countries, Britain, and British forces in Egypt. The State Department bridled that oil export was a matter of extreme importance to its foreign policy. FDR sided with Hull. In a "peremptory and ungracious" letter he warned the Old Curmudgeon to desist. Ickes grumbled that loading-point control was his prerogative as domestic oil czar and that Japan could load up on the Gulf or West Coasts, where no shortages loomed. After he threatened to resign, he won his point. Shipments to Japan from the East Coast ended. Shipments from California, however, continued without hindrance. The president specifically declined to revoke a Japanese license for 5.3 million gallons (about 650,000 barrels) of gasoline in drums. Ickes, growling that Americans should not deprive themselves "to appease Japan," was delighted when Dean Acheson applauded his agitations.[9]

Industry Debunks Shortage

By the middle of July 1941 forty-three U.S. tankers were shuttling oil on behalf of Britain, yet industry executives expected no gasoline shortage on the East Coast. Crude oil and refining capacities were ample for all needs; transportation was the only bottleneck. Throughout the spring and summer they publicized their views in the authoritative *Oil and Gas Journal*, as early as 15 May listing compensating efficiencies their firms could implement. Gulf Coast refineries, for example, were installing pumps to double loading flow to eight thousand barrels per hour, which cut idle tanker time by fifteen hours and round-trip time by 5 percent. On 10 July the journal listed possible actions that could make up for as many as one hundred "standard tanker equivalents."

Forty-nine ships by increasing voyage capacities:

- Twelve ships by deep loading to natural safety lines rather than an overly conservative international treaty line. On 10 July Congress authorized it.
- Eleven ships by eliminating hauls to the East Coast from the Caribbean and California, cross-hauls, and multiple-destination voyages.
- Eighteen ships by commandeering neutral and Axis tankers sheltering in Western Hemisphere ports. (The industry was poorly informed. A later investigation found that of twenty-two such vessels, ten were

damaged and nine neutrals were already carrying Mexican oil to the
United States.)

- Eight ships by advancing the shuttles of Venezuelan oil to Halifax,
  Nova Scotia, instead of New York, shortening the British haul and
  releasing borrowed U.S. tankers. (This proved unacceptable because
  under the Neutrality Act Canada was a belligerent.)

Up to forty ships by substituting other transportation:

- Nine ships by increasing throughput of small pipelines from midcontinent to inland cities of the Northeast.
- Four to six ships by increasing barge movement and substituting
  barges for tankers on rivers, lakes, and canals.
- Twenty-five ships by railroad tank car movement. (Highway tank
  trucks were unsuitable for long hauls.)[10] The Railroad Association,
  then lobbying against allocation of steel for long distance pipelines,
  claimed to know of 20,000 idle cars. Petroleum experts were dubious
  because some cars were in seasonal reserve or in disrepair, and loco-
  motive and platform bottlenecks were common. A later survey by
  Ickes' OPC turned up only 5,192 idle cars.

The industry's wish list of substitutes for about one hundred tanker equivalents was overly optimistic, but compensating for fifty seemed feasible in the
short run. In the longer term sixty new civilian tankers were scheduled for
completion in 1941–42, the Navy had ordered another seventy-seven. Oil
companies hoped to construct, at their own expense, pipelines from Texas to
the East Coast (sixty-five tanker equivalents) and local distribution pipelines in
the Northeast (fifteen tankers). Conservation offered further solutions. The
American Automobile Association later estimated a possible 20 percent gasoline savings by carburetor adjustments, avoidance of jackrabbit starts, and
lower speed limits. Morgenthau suggested taxing both cars and gasoline. The
Oil Burner Institute said furnace tune-ups could save 20 to 30 percent of
heating oil.[11] In spite of the industry's confidence, and the complaints of eastern congressmen and businesses about possible rationing, Ickes and Davies
kept up a drumbeat of warnings. On 24 July 1941, two days before the freeze
of Japanese assets, Ickes publicly demanded an immediate one-third reduction
of gasoline use in sixteen eastern states as a "patriotic duty."[12]

Roosevelt Sets the Stage

In the run-up to the dollar freeze order of 26 July 1941, other domestic rationales for denying oil to Japan had been debated in the administration. On 22 July Maxwell M. Hamilton, chief of the State Department's Division of Far Eastern Affairs, suggested "proceeding with some finesse" in any press statement about oil by blaming it on "the defense needs of the United States." But Roosevelt understood the regional oil economics and that there was plenty for defense. He paid no attention to Hamilton then or when Welles repeated the suggestion after the freeze.[13] On 24 July, the same day as Ickes's outburst, he personally told Nomura that public opinion strongly favored an oil embargo, that he had thus far persuaded the public against it in order to maintain peaceable relations. But due to Japan's aggressions "he had now lost the basis of this argument" and hinted at an embargo. He instructed Admiral Stark, the chief of naval operations who was going to lunch with the Japanese ambassador, to tell Nomura "that it is rather difficult to make our people understand why we cut oil and gas at home and then let Japan have all she wants." The president added, "Of course, we understand this, because Japan carries the oil in her own bottoms—and our shortage in the East is due not to lack of oil and gas at the refineries, but to our inability to transport it from the oil fields to points where needed."[14] Roosevelt was soon to ignore publicly his own astute observation.

That day, when FDR summoned the cabinet for the decision to freeze Japanese assets, he took the extraordinary step of telling the American public that there was an odious link between the predicted East Coast gasoline shortage and oil sales to Japan. While addressing a volunteer group for civil defense headed by Mayor Fiorello LaGuardia of New York—the city bearing the largest volume of risk for rationing of gasoline—FDR told the press,

> You have been reading that the Secretary of the Interior, as Oil Administrator, is faced with the problem of not having enough gasoline to go around in the east coast, and how he is asking everybody to curtail their consumption of gasoline. All right. Now, I am—I might be called an American citizen living in Hyde Park, N.Y. And I say, "That's a funny thing. Why am I asked to curtail my consumption of gasoline when I read in the papers that thousands of tons of gasoline are going out from Los Angeles—west coast—to Japan; and we are helping Japan in what looks like an act of aggression."[15]

Roosevelt's linking of Atlantic and Pacific supplies was a brazen political canard to guide public opinion and perhaps soothe Japanese anger. There was no conceivable possibility of satisfying East Coast needs with West Coast oil. Nevertheless, in the weeks following 26 July, as a relentless oil embargo by means of the dollar freeze descended on Japan, Ickes continued to insist, against the advice of government and private experts, against all remedies offered by the industry, against the findings of a senatorial investigating committee, and even against evidence that Britain did not need U.S. tankers, that an East Coast gasoline crisis was inevitable. The specious rationale of a shortage continued almost to the eve of Pearl Harbor: the United States could not spare California oil for Japan because it was scarce in New York (appendix 1).

16

Freeze

On Friday, 25 July 1941, after the close of the financial markets in New York and on the West Coast, President Roosevelt announced Executive Order No. 8832 from his home in Hyde Park through his traveling office at Poughkeepsie, New York. The order subjected to license all movements of Japanese assets in the United States, substantially in accordance with Carlton Savage's draft of four months earlier. The White House press release stated,

> In view of the unlimited national emergency declared by the President he has today issued an executive order freezing Japanese assets in the United States. . . . This measure in effect brings all financial and import and export trade transactions in which Japanese interests are involved under the control of the Government and imposes criminal penalties for violation of the order. This executive order . . . is designed among other things to prevent the use of the financial facilities of the United States and trade between Japan and the United States in ways harmful to national defense and American interests, to prevent the liquidation in the United States of assets obtained by duress or conquest and to curb subversive activities in the United States.[1]

That evening Acheson and Foley hosted a press conference. They offered little clarification to reporters about preventing the use of funds "in ways harmful to the national defense and American interests." Foley said the announcement referred to cargoes but not ship movements, otherwise it spoke for itself. Acheson "protested vigorously" that it was not "an embargo."[2]

EO No. 8832 was officially issued in Washington on Saturday, 26 July. The order was nothing more than a few words added to EO No. 8389 of 10 April 1940, which first froze the dollars of European victim countries: "Foreign country designated in this Order means . . . China, and Japan." It extended the freeze automatically to assets of Japanese colonies and occupied Manchukuo and China because EO No. 8389 had defined "foreign country" to include territories over which a country had "de jure or de facto sovereignty." It froze Nationalist China's assets, at its request, to conserve them from Japanese poaching and to prevent Japan from acquiring Chinese currency to swap into unblocked dollars. General licenses to unfetter dealings were issued to Nationalist China (but not Hong Kong) and the Philippines. Within a few days Great Britain announced a nearly identical freeze on behalf of the British Empire, followed by the Netherlands Indies authorities.

Regulations issued under EO No. 8832 were stringent in every regard. They froze all assets owned 25 percent or more by Japanese persons, businesses, or government. They required specific licenses for transfers of Japanese funds between any banks, whether U.S. or foreign, for dealings in foreign exchange and securities both domestic and foreign, for export of gold, silver, or currency, and for transactions that sought to evade the rules. Violators were subject to fines of ten thousand dollars and ten years in prison.[3]

The president, as he waited for developments to unfold, felt confident that Japan would not react violently. The drafting of recommendations for administering the freeze was assigned to the Foreign Funds Control Committee (FFCC), now consisting of Assistant Secretary of State Dean Acheson, General Counsel Edward H. Foley Jr. of the Treasury Department, and Assistant Attorney General Francis M. Shea. As Herbert Feis described the scene of enthusiastic bureaucrats grasping the opportunity for power and authority,

> During the last days of July concerned men rushed from office to office trying to teach each other reason and strategy; the diligent young lawyers who surrounded Acheson, the assertive young advocates who came from the Treasury, the financial and trade specialists from the office of the economic Adviser [Feis' office], and the diplomats of the Far Eastern Division. They were excited, for they perceived that the schedule and geography of war might be in their keeping. Acheson managed to get this platoon of talent to agree, more or less.[4]

Initial Response to the Freeze

At the opening of business on Wall Street on Monday, 28 July, the moribund foreign exchange market for yen vanished altogether. Japanese dollar bonds, already severely depressed, crashed by seven to thirty points on negligible trading volume to as low as 70 or 80 percent below par value; the Japanese Minister of Finance soon announced that debt service of the bonds would continue. On Tuesday the Yokohama Specie Bank New York Agency, the paying agent for Japanese bonds, applied to the Federal Reserve to unfreeze enough dollars to pay interest and sinking funds on government and corporate issues due on 1 August. Bond prices rallied a bit. The Tokio Marine and Fire Insurance Company office stopped writing marine policies but hoped frozen dollars would be released to settle customers' claims. In Japan the National City Bank, the last U.S. bank still active, suspended business in Tokyo and closed its Osaka branch. The Yokohama Silk Exchange shut its doors, but no panic ensued as market control had been assumed by the government-owned Japan Raw Silk Control Company. The New York Commodity Exchange suspended dealings in silk futures, ignoring the optimism of a prominent silk trader, Paolino Gerli, that imports would soon resume, perhaps on a barter basis. Share prices of rayon companies rose and the cotton market remained unruffled. The Japanese Tourist Agency on Fifth Avenue remained hopefully open.[5]

By this date U.S. regulators had gained fifteen months of experience in processing license applications for $7 billion of blocked funds of thirty-three foreign countries and colonies. The Treasury's Foreign Funds Control Section under John Pehle employed 650 men and women who specialized variously in securities, trade, remittances, and blacklisted firms, assisted as needed by Federal Reserve bank examiners.[6] On Monday morning, 28 July, the Treasury and Fed ordered banks in the United States to suspend unlicensed dealings with Japanese individuals and companies. The regulations permitted normal operations with American clients of the branches of the Yokohama Specie Bank and of Sumitomo Bank branches in Honolulu, San Francisco, Los Angeles, and Seattle, which were banks of deposit. Japanese-owned businesses on the West Coast were authorized to withdraw frozen funds to meet payrolls and operating costs, as were those in Hawaii and the Philippines, provided they did not "substantially diminish or imperil" their assets.[7] The Office of the Comptroller of the Currency, a Treasury agency, installed examiners in Japanese banks who ordered correspondence to be conducted in English and posted guards at vaults during night hours. Japanese bankers, claiming they were making "utmost efforts" to comply with regulations, said they appreciated the examiners' prompt advice on the legality of transactions.[8]

Denial of Dollars for Shipments

On Tuesday, 29 July, applications for the release of blocked dollars began flowing into the regional Federal Reserve banks acting as agents of the Treasury. License applications, one-page form letters in use since 1940, listed the parties' names and addresses and the amount requested for release; an attachment explained the transaction, and a notarized affidavit attested to truthfulness (see back end-sheet).[9] Fed officials ruled on them, usually in a few days. They followed a rule of reason on pre-freeze trade: If an export license had been issued and payment guaranteed by a bank letter of credit before Roosevelt's announcement, the shipment could proceed, with payment allowed from a blocked account (except for oil, for which export licenses had been revoked). For example, a regional Fed office licensed payment of $67,000 of blocked funds to honor drafts drawn on Mitsubishi for Douglas fir lumber that had departed from Oregon and Washington on Japanese ships because they sailed before 4:15 pm local time on 25 July, forty-five minutes before announcement of the freezing order. However, the released dollars went into a Mitsubishi blocked account and could not be spent or transferred to anybody without a Treasury license. Conversely, the Fed refused to license a Specie Bank advance to a flour mill for an export order or allow payments by Mitsubishi of a $494,5000 advance for Canadian wheat destined for Japan and occupied China that was scheduled for loading at U.S. ports. The applications became moot when the designated ship, the *Heian Maru*, abruptly departed on 1 August. By the end of August no further dollar licenses to settle pre-freeze orders from blocked funds were approved, with one exception: an 1 October license to pay a Cincinnati company for machinery it had shipped to Japan a year earlier.[10]

Stranded Goods

The freeze seized up the import payments system as well. Since foreign shiplines had abandoned Pacific routes, Japan was serving as an entrepot for U.S. trade with the rest of the Far East. Products of the Philippines, Hong Kong, Southeast Asia, Manchukuo, and free China moved aboard costal freighters to Kobe and other ports for transshipment on oceangoing Japanese vessels, the only ones crossing the Pacific. The goods were neither of Japanese origin nor controlled by Japanese firms, so payments logically should not have been blocked. In any case, Japan halted cargoes destined for the United States, leaving $2 to $3 million of goods on wharves and in warehouses there.

In normal practice, an Asian seller received an order, forwarded merchandise on a vessel, wrote a draft for the sum due, and mailed it along with the ship's bill of lading to the United States, entitling him to receive dollars promptly upon presentation and acceptance of the draft. The middleman banks then received reimbursement from the U.S. importers. Some orders were backed by irrevocable letters of credit issued by U.S. banks. Hardest hit were several dozen furriers in New York, many of them small and shaky firms. Banks had extended credit to them secured by title to the furs as they passed from ship to train to U.S. warehouse. But the new situation was unique and not covered by insurance. Drafts were arriving in New York, but the goods remained in Japan. A trade association obtained a court injunction to delay payments, then appealed to the Treasury to impose a moratorium on payments or to reimburse the furriers, presumably from blocked Japanese funds. The problem landed, predictably, on the desk of Dean Acheson. Predictably, he showed little sympathy. He suggested that Japan forward the cargoes as a gesture of good will but offered no act of reciprocity. On 20 September, Japan, eager to make a gesture to thaw the freeze, however unlikely, decided to deliver them on a ship that was to repatriate Americans from the Far East.[11]

Acheson's Timetable

Immediately after the freezing order Acheson set to work on a timetable. He coached George F. Luthringer, an aide in the State Department's Office of Advisor on International Economic Affairs, to draft a freeze schedule that would unfold over three successive time periods. Luthringer presented a memo "to embody the suggestions which you [Acheson] made following the meeting of the Interdepartmental Policy Committee yesterday evening," the next day. It proposed that during the first two weeks all applications to release Japanese blocked funds would be held in abeyance while the United States coordinated with its allies. The Policy Committee would approve dollar licenses only for emergencies, such as buying bunker oil necessary for Japanese ships to return home. The next two months were to constitute a trial period. Limited trade would be allowed, of roughly equal values in both directions, with licenses granted for raw silk imports and cotton exports, and oil exports (except high-grade gasoline and lubes) at the quota level. Japanese officials would have to explain each transaction in detail. Finally, if continuing trade seemed desirable after about mid-October, some sort of clearing arrangement would be established to match import and export payments. No general policy was to be announced, however, during any of the three periods. It was the sort of modus operandi Roosevelt cherished, keeping his options open and his adversary off balance by revealing his intentions gradually through decisions on specific transactions.[12]

The Policy Committee blessed the key elements of Acheson's proposal as drafted by Luthringer. Hull was out of town for six weeks recovering from illness and exhaustion. Sumner Welles, as acting secretary, was effectively in charge of the State Department. Welles approved most of the committee's recommendations but changed a few of them in a memo he wrote that was delivered to the president on 31 July. He agreed with facilitating exports of cotton, and of oil subject to the quota, but he decided against licensing payments for raw silk imports because the U.S. military reported it didn't need any; payments for other Japanese products could be licensed if actually needed by the United States. Welles retained in principle the concept of balanced future trade, although the amount would certainly shrivel if raw silk, two-thirds of the value of U.S. imports from Japan, were banned. Finally, Welles acceded to the export controllers' call to extend the list of products prohibited to Japan to include all metals, manufactures, machinery, rubber products, wood pulp, and chemicals (other than a few pharmaceuticals).

The acting secretary of state had stiffened the president's anti-Japanese order but kept alive Roosevelt's intention to resume some trade in the near future, especially in oil, as the government's de facto if unannounced policy. Roosevelt initialed Sumner Welles's memorandum "SW OK FDR." His laconic approval turned out to be the president's final written instruction about the intensity of financial and economic war to be waged against Japan.[13]

Free Dollars for Oil Purchases?

The program Roosevelt blessed on 31 July 1941 not only sterilized Japan's assets in the United States but effectively barred it from spending any gold or dollars held outside the United States. Gold, Japan's largest potential source of dollars—between $80 million and $231 million at the Bank of Japan, according to Treasury guesses, which depended on whether gold backing the yen was included—could no longer be sold to the U.S. Treasury (chapter 5). U.S. banks and dealers were already forbidden to buy gold under the 1934 invocation of the Trading with the Enemy Act, which banned private gold ownership. No other significant gold market functioned anywhere in the world. Permission to resume gold deliveries and sales was so unlikely that it was never suggested by a U.S. official after 26 July. The Japanese made one feeble attempt in September, when the embassy in Washington proposed to send some gold bars aboard a Japanese passenger vessel that was repatriating Americans in hopes of spending the proceeds for U.S. goods. The Foreign Funds Control Section of the Treasury squelched that proposal, alleging that it required the okay of the Policy Committee, which rarely met.[14] With its large gold hoard immobilized, Japan concocted schemes, both daring and foolish, to find unfrozen dollars for American products.

American officials suspected that Japan had parked some dollars beyond the reach of the freeze regulations but had only sketchy ideas of how much and where. On 11 August, Henry Gass, a Treasury analyst, submitted to Harry White a best guess of $14 million, equivalent to eleven weeks of U.S. exports to Japan at recent rates, although he imagined the figure might be as much as three times higher. In comparison, about $75 million had "escaped" since December 1940, he said, when the Japanese government halted gold sales and adopted "a deliberate policy of running down their assets in the United States, in anticipation of freezing." He calculated that by 16 July Japan had reduced liquid assets in the United States from a peak of $124.8 million to $76.3 million, and funds of the puppet Chinese regime of Nanking had dropped from $38 million to $11.9 million. The rundown largely reflected legitimate payments to U.S. and South American exporters, but there had also been opportunities to conceal dollars. Since the end of 1940 Japan had centralized South American transactions through the Banco do Brasil, depositing dollars it earned by exporting to the continent but likely disbursing them for local goods. Suspiciously, in the most recent six months the New York branch of the Yokohama Specie Bank had dispatched to Brazil thirteen transfers aggregating $12 million (net of some reverse flows). It had also forwarded $1 million to Peru and Argentina for unidentified payments. U.S. diplomatic agents in Rio de Janeiro had reported on 24 July that Japanese balances there stood at $8 million, a bit higher than Gass's estimate of $6 million. Nervous of U.S. influence in Rio, the Japanese sought approval of Brazilian exchange control to remove $4.9 million. The Brazilian authorities refused, allowing only payments to local exporters, locking some dollars into a "special account" and converting the rest to milreis (local currency) for future Brazilian goods. The action emasculated Japan's modest cache in Latin America, but U.S. suspicions were not allayed.[15]

Gass also reported that Japan sought to acquire unblocked dollars in China by swapping yen for yuan (also called the fapi), the national currency of the Chiang Kai-shek regime. The yuan was convertible to dollars at a stable exchange rate because of a U.S. support loan. In the international settlement of Shanghai, a free market of sorts traded in military yen, an occupation currency that actually stood at a higher value than ordinary commercial yen and provided the only free market indicator of the yen's value. The commercial yen traded in Shanghai via the dollar-linked yuan at wildly fluctuating discounts below its pegged rate of U.S. 23.6 cents. American and British officials in Shanghai believed that Japanese firms and subservient Chinese banks bought yuan in July, estimated by Gass at $6 million equivalent. Japan could try to evade the freeze in two ways. It could order U.S. products for delivery to Chinese-controlled fronts and pay yuan as permitted by the general license granted to Nationalist China. Or, it could swap yuan for U.S. paper currency believed to be circulating in Shanghai. The State Department also knew that

U.S. bank branches in Shanghai facilitated black market dealings but the amounts were minor.[16]

Japan's dollar holdings in China and Brazil were small, but they provided U.S. regulators with the ammunition to accuse it of dissembling during discussions in Washington as Japan probed the payments barrier. Dickering reached seriocomic proportions over accusations that Japan also had hidden $1 million in "free" currency in the United States. Gass elaborated on pre–26 July stories that the YSBNY had withdrawn that sum from other banks in large-denomination bills during the three days prior to the freeze. He believed the currency had been turned over to an agent of the Japanese navy, and some of it carried by hand on a passenger flight to an embassy safe in Washington thought to hold $500,000. Trusted U.S. employees had taken smaller withdrawals, some in $1,000 dollar bills, but probably for bank operating costs.[17]

Oil Shipment Test Cases

Sumner Welles' memo that Roosevelt okayed on 31 July called for revocation of oil export licenses (except to the Western Hemisphere and British areas) and a moratorium on processing pending Japanese applications. On 1 August Welles telegraphed the collectors of customs at U.S. ports to revoke Japanese oil export licenses.[18] At that date the U.S. government still intended to allow some oil shipments to Japan in a few weeks, subject to the 1935–36 quota and, of course, awarding of licenses to pay from blocked accounts. By 11 August, however, U.S. officials undermined this accommodative intention by erecting barriers that prevented Japan from paying dollars out of any source whatsoever.

Earlier in August Japan had asked the Export Control Administration to approve new licenses to export $2,111,412 of crude and diesel oil (about seven weeks of pre-freeze deliveries of those products) and some lubricants. The State Department, which had the final say over export licenses, approved only 8 percent of the request, $178,650, largely for Mitsui and Mitsubishi. It rejected $729,910 because the grades were too rich and deferred action on $1,202,852, which it never approved. The licensed quantity, about twenty thousand barrels, was approximately the capacity of two commercial tankers awaiting cargoes in California, variously named in the applications. (To avoid embarrassment Japan had recalled a third vessel, the naval tanker *Shiriya*, seeking a cargo of crude.)[19] In all likelihood the ECA and State Department granted the export permits as test cases to demonstrate to Japan the nation's intentions of processing dollar licenses case by case, rather than by an orderly policy, just as Roosevelt wished. Sure enough, on 11 August the State

The financial freeze of 26 July 1941 choked off most of Japan's vital supply of oil. (Library of Congress)

Department again telegraphed the customs houses to prohibit the loading of newly ECA-licensed oil unless Japanese buyers presented Treasury licenses permitting them to pay dollars, which of course were not forthcoming and never would be.[20]

Over the next three months charades stage-managed in Washington signaled to Japan the awful news that the freeze was airtight and permanent. U.S. government files bulge with sorry accounts of appeals to release Japanese-owned dollars to buy the $178,650 of export-licensed oil, a mere two-day supply for Japan. Pleading Japan's case were Sadao Iguchi, minister counselor of the embassy, who Acheson called "indefatigable" in pursuit of loopholes, and Tsutomo Nishiyama, the commercial attaché. Parrying for the United States were the three subcabinet officers of the FFCC, most prominently Dean Acheson and, as the committee had no staff of its own, financial and techni- cal experts of assorted cabinet departments and agencies.

On 15 August Iguchi paid one of his many unhappy calls on Acheson. The cash withdrawn before the freeze, he explained, had been handed to agents of the Imperial Navy, which was not subject to civilian control and would not relinquish it. Acheson scoffed at the alibi. Iguchi offered three counterpropos- als: sale of silk to earn unblocked funds; acquiring dollars in Shanghai with yuan; or helping to prod the Dutch to release some dollars they had frozen. Acheson rejected all three. He counter-counter-proposed repatriating dollars parked in Latin America; a leisurely week later the Treasury said it would con- sider allowing such funds for oil payments. Four days later State and Treasury officers told Iguchi they would not unfreeze money in U.S. banking offices until Japan complied with Acheson's demand to disgorge the suspected hoards of "free" dollars. Returning the currency spirited out of New York banks just before the freeze would improve diplomatic relations and "public opinion," they said. On 4 September Iguchi conferred with Charles Yost of the State Department's Division of Controls. If Japan repatriated dollars from Latin America, Iguchi asked, could it spend them for export-licensed goods without fail? Yost backtracked, demanding the currency said to be hidden in U.S. vaults. The next day, with Acheson pulling the strings, Yost phoned Iguchi that relief was impossible unless Japan fully disclosed to the Treasury the sources and locations of all funds in South America. Iguchi's suggestion needed further study even though it complied with Acheson's demand, he said. Besides, he was told, many State Department high officials were absent in those hot sum- mer days.[21]

Why Was Policy Set by Secondary Officials?

How were Dean Acheson, the quintessential opportunist of U.S. foreign policy in 1941, and the committee he dominated able to impose a bulletproof freeze of Japanese funds? The evidence is circumstantial, and the answers may be posed as four questions.

Why was an interagency committee formed to regulate the freeze of Japanese assets? It was an extraordinary departure from previous freezes under the Trading with the Enemy Act. In 1917–18, by presidential order, the Treasury had admin- istered financial controls, and again since April 1940.[22] The interagency commit- tee idea grew out of the battle over freezing Axis assets between State and

Treasury, the departments with overlapping responsibilities in foreign economic relations. In late 1940, Morgenthau, determined to freeze Germany and Italy and perhaps Japan, urged the idea on Roosevelt. He was helped by the Federal Bureau of Investigation, which reported that Axis funds were spent for subversion and propaganda in North and South America. Roosevelt sided with Hull against a freeze, but the attorney general was now involved, as the FBI was a semiautonomous arm of the Department of Justice. In February 1941 Acheson, newly appointed to the State Department, renewed the demand. He cooperated with Assistant Attorney General Shea in a proposal to freeze selectively the suspicious accounts, a fiasco killed as unworkable. Treasury staffers then worked patiently with Acheson and Shea on a suitable three-agency cooperation. The result was Roosevelt's memo of 26 February 1941 stating, "It is clear to me that all three Departments are vitally involved" and demanding the approval of State and Justice to join a committee "to approve any actions that are to be taken by the Treasury." Perhaps FDR added Attorney General Jackson because of the subversion threat, but he may also have wanted a neutral member who could mediate between Hull and Morgenthau. Carlton Savage's draft freezing order of 24 March 1941, therefore, called for a "Foreign Exchange and Foreign Owned Property Committee" of the three cabinet secretaries, subsequently renamed the FFCC in the regulations drafted before and after the 26 July freezing order (see chapters 9 and 14).

Why was committee membership passed down to subcabinet officers? In the draft regulations of 25 July the members of the FFCC appointed by presidential authority were named as Assistant Secretary of State Dean Acheson, General Counsel (of the Treasury) Edward H. Foley Jr., and Assistant Attorney General Francis M. Shea. The record is not clear on why membership was downgraded. Hull, elderly and in frail health, was personally negotiating with the Japanese ambassador and swamped with other issues of the world crisis, including the threat of war in the Atlantic, as well as running a bureaucracy of worldwide embassies. Morgenthau might well have enjoyed serving despite his many important responsibilities, such as federal debt and taxation, but it seems doubtful that Hull would have agreed lest he dominate the proceedings by virtue of rank. Jackson had shied away from the morass of investigating foreign companies and must have been happy to pass down the assignment. Each cabinet secretary seemed satisfied to nominate a subordinate ranking immediately below him.

Why were Acheson, Foley, and Shea specifically chosen? With choices limited to assistant secretaries or equivalent grade the possible nominees were few. Of the four assistant secretaries of state—Welles, the sole undersecretary had his hands full as acting secretary during Hull's absences—Acheson was the best qualified. His one important function was directing State's trade licensing function; he had experience in finance, having once been a Treasury undersecretary; and he had drafted the freeze rules, directly or indirectly. Why Morgenthau nominated Ed Foley, not even an assistant secretary, is a bit of a mystery. One would have expected a stronger appointee from the department historically responsible for freeze management under the TWEA, and which FDR had confirmed as "responsible for the actual issuance of the orders" and for providing a committee secretary from its staff. Foley's background was in municipal bonds and taxes, not international affairs. A stronger candidate might have been Harry Dexter White, a brilliant and assertive economist with deep knowledge of foreign financial flows and unburdened with operating duties. Among other possibilities were John W. Pehle, a special assistant to the secretary who directed the large staff coping with billions worth of frozen assets, and H. Merle Cochran, a financial market–oriented technical assistant to the secretary. Morgenthau may have considered them too junior. Foley's main credentials were probably enthusiasm, shared with Morgenthau, for freezing Japanese assets and the excellent working relationship he had developed with Acheson. Or perhaps Morgenthau trusted Acheson to be firm while knowing that Treasury staff could still influence the detailed operations of the freeze. In the Justice Department, the choice was more obvious. Only Shea had shown an interest in financial sanctions (other than the FBI's narrow criminal focus) and had worked on the orders freezing Japan. The seven other assistant attorneys general held portfolios unrelated to foreign affairs. In any case, the cabinet chiefs all delegated attorneys whose lawyerly minds devised legal or quasi-legal arguments for denying Japan use of its dollars rather than judging license applications in the context of foreign policy, economics, or banking.

Why did Acheson dominate the committee? While nominally equal in rank, Acheson stood head and shoulders above the others in prestige. He was senior in age (forty-eight vs. thirty-five and thirty-six) and experience. His training at Harvard Law School, as a protégé of two supreme court justices, and in a private practice with international experience outshone Foley's Fordham University degree and specialization in taxes, bonds, and litigation of government claims. Shea compared well in education, with a Harvard degree and service as dean of a law school, but in government he worked mainly as a litigator against corporations. Acheson had relevant financial experience as a former Treasury undersecretary involved in gold policy, and in 1941 experience in regulating trade as supervisor of the State Department's Division of Controls. Foley's less relevant practice had been in municipal bonds, and in previous government jobs in the domestic Public Works Administration (under Harold Ickes) until joining the Treasury as a tax specialist. Shea came to Washington in 1939 to head the Justice Department's claims division, where he litigated fifty cases before appellate courts. Neither Foley nor Shea had much exposure to foreign affairs, whereas Acheson, an officer of the diplomatic branch, usually negotiated with Japanese agents on freeze matters after 26 July 1941. Future careers further demonstrate that Acheson was the most ambitious and accomplished member. As a dedicated antifascist and Europhile, Dean Acheson was devoted to flexing U.S. power. There is no evidence that the two younger members resisted his leadership. Finally, Acheson was a favorite of Roosevelt's close confidant Justice Felix Frankfurter, and to a degree of Roosevelt himself. FDR had long since forgiven his 1934 resignation from the Treasury. He had personally solicited Acheson to join the State Department in 1941 with the implied mission of shaking up its sluggish ways and pushing it aboard the anti-Axis steamroller. Acheson poured his prodigious willpower and energies into the task.[23]

End-Running Hull and Roosevelt

Roosevelt and Hull were apparently unaware of the FFCC's ironclad financial freeze, which violated the plan of flexibility and limited trade resumption that FDR had approved. In the words of historian Jonathan Utley, "The freeze was designed to bring Japan to its senses, not its knees."[24] Hull returned from his rest cure on 4 August, but apparently his aides did not bring the actual situation to his attention. He first learned on 4 September, from Nomura, that no financial licenses had been awarded, not even for ECA-licensed oil. Confronted with a de facto situation, he was reluctant to change because of the negative effect on Chinese morale, among other reasons. Historians have also made much of the fact that Roosevelt was preoccupied with meeting Winston Churchill at Argentia, Newfoundland, a voyage that took him (and Welles) secretly away from Washington between 3 and 16 August. When he returned the president did not countermand the FFCC's absolute freeze. Recent writers have proposed that FDR was influenced by opinion polls showing the freeze was popular with the public. Roosevelt felt wary about seeming to appease Japan. In the background was Ickes' tub-thumping about a gasoline shortage. As another historian put it, "When it gradually became apparent what had happened, Hull and Roosevelt elected to leave the situation as it was, and in effect ratified the unplanned embargo."[25]

Another scenario is possible: Roosevelt wanted all along to prod Japan more forcefully than his diplomatic and naval advisers wished, and Acheson was carrying out the unwritten and possibly unspoken wishes of the commander in chief. Roosevelt knew from Acheson's walking out of his first administration that he had an iron will, and he knew Acheson's anti-Axis credentials. Morgenthau supported Acheson's hard line, but the State Department's Far Eastern Division sulked about his authority and favored licensing some oil payments. Some have said Acheson was not familiar with Asian affairs or with the decoded intercepts that revealed Japanese turmoil over sanctions.[26] His memoirs confirm his hardline proclivities but do not admit he usurped power.[27] The president left few written papers about his decisions. The views of his aides are sparsely recorded, sometimes known best from reports of British and Canadian diplomats they briefed. An absence of evidence prevents an undisputed conclusion as to whether Roosevelt accepted the unconditional freeze of Japan's dollars because it was thrust upon him or because it was the policy he desired.

17

Barter and Bankruptcy

During the summer of 1941 the U.S. government reorganized its creaky, conflicted "economic defense" agencies by injecting a guiding authority, the Economic Defense Board (EDB), chaired by Vice President Henry A. Wallace. President Roosevelt established the board by executive order on 30 July, charging it with the oversight and coordination of all economic defense functions. He named as its members the secretaries of the State, Treasury, War, Navy, Agriculture, Commerce, and Justice Departments. Presumably FDR thought only the vice president had the independent stature to force cooperation among the fractious departments. In the international sphere (only a part of the EDB's responsibilities) economic defense included trade, allocation of imported materials, preclusive buying, and shipping, with tasks including estimates of materials to support friendly neutrals and serving as "a central clearing service" for trade regulation. Another committee chaired by Wallace recommended consolidating the work of the ECA (renamed the Office of Export Control) with the State Department's Division of Controls, and placing the function under EDB guidance, which Roosevelt ordered on 15 September.[1] The ECA, established in July 1940 as a military function, was now a civilian institution; General Maxwell, cut off from his pipeline to the White House, was transferred to other duties.[2] Acheson lost his perch supervising the Division of Controls yet retained a far more potent role. As de facto chief of the FFCC he held Japan's international purse strings enabling him to undermine resumption of trade with Japan should the EDB decide to advocate any.

Wallace felt that the "international crisis requires a determined intensification of our policy of preventing shipments to Axis-dominated countries."[3] Nevertheless, he showed interest in easing a bit the standstill of trade with

Japan at a meeting on 19 August with Col. Charles McKnight, new head of the ever-hopeful ECA Projects Section (Thomas Hewes having departed) and his assertive deputy Chandler Morse. In their briefing titled "The Economic Orientation of the Far-Eastern Crisis, July–August 1941" they seemed unaware of the severity of the financial freeze, which had already halted all trade. In a rehash of the ECA's Coordinated Plan of May 1941 they recommended stepwise acceleration of sanctions and pressures on Japan: specifically, a formal embargo of all trade, including oil (a step already accomplished de facto by the FFCC's denial of funds) but with some relief if Japan offered tin, manganese, rubber, and silk, perhaps in exchange for oil within the 1935–36 quota. Wallace concurred in general provided the ideas were not likely to provoke a war.[4]

The Economic Defense Board was also charged with oversight of financial warfare activities, including controls of foreign exchange, investments, loans, and foreign-controlled assets including frozen funds. This made the board an operating as well as planning agency.[5] The authority of Acheson's FFCC was thus rendered subject to challenge if the EDB cared to recommend a moderation of the freeze. By coincidence, Japan at that time presented to the vice president a remarkable plan to override the iron-bound dollar freeze.

Japan's Desperate Gambit

The Japanese government concocted an audacious plan to obtain oil and other resources by end-running the financial freeze. Stranded with unredeemable gold and dollars, denied release of funds for petty oil cargoes, barred from earning spendable dollars by exporting, and prodded by U.S. sleuths to surrender vestigial hidden sums, Japan contrived a plan to exchange over $100 million of commodities by the oldest of human exchange devices: barter.

In mid-August 1941, as it became clear that the freeze was unbreakable, Minister Counselor Sadao Iguchi suggested that Japan would happily resume some exports if it could buy U.S. commodities with the proceeds, in essence via a semibarter system. On the fifteenth Acheson squelched the idea, at least temporarily, by telling Iguchi that raw silk, Japan's only significant export to the United States, was of no importance. The United States wanted only vital defense materials. When Iguchi asked for examples Acheson changed the subject.[6] Six days later Japan launched a mission to appeal to higher authorities, over Acheson's head, on the wishful presumption that barter trade was immune from the money freeze.

The Japanese chose a curious spokesman for their last-ditch effort: Raoul E. Desvernine, a New York corporate and banking attorney, president of the Crucible Steel Company of America, and disgraced Democratic party activist.

Desvernine had earned Japan's gratitude in the late 1930s by his efforts to help the Manchuria Industrial Development Corporation, "Mangyo," a Japanese-owned business syndicate. Yoshisuke Ayukawa, the president of Mangyo, was promoting a five-year plan of industrial development in Manchukuo but had been hobbled by Tokyo's refusal to allocate dollars to buy steel and machine tools. Hoping that U.S. firms would supply him on credit, Ayukawa approached Crucible, the Bethlehem Steel Corporation, and the United States Steel Corporation through a middleman to buy $15 million of steel, to be financed with five-year loans from National City Bank and three other New York banks. Desvernine expressed "strong interest" in the project, but the State Department, at that time terminating the 1911 commercial treaty with Japan, frowned on investment in Manchukuo. Nothing came of the deal.[7]

In August 1941 the Japanese engaged Desvernine to propose an extraordinary swap of raw silk for oil and other U.S. commodities. On 21 August he paid a visit to Cordell Hull, accompanied by Jouett Shouse, a Washington legal associate. The next day the two attorneys "talked the matter over" with Vice President Henry A. Wallace in his capacity as chairman of the EDB. Joining them was Charles B. Henderson, chairman of the Reconstruction Finance Corporation, which had jurisdiction over the Defense Supplies Corporation, an agency that supervised stockpiling of strategic materials. Wallace asked for "the exact proposal" in writing.[8] Desvernine thereupon resigned from his post at Crucible Steel and set to work for the next two weeks drafting a proposal, assisted by Tsutomu Nishiyama, the Japanese embassy's experienced commercial attaché (and in the 1950s Japan's ambassador to India), and stayed in touch with Tokyo about the project.

Japan's selection of Raoul Desvernine as emissary was a bizarre if not suicidal choice, suggesting a political tone-deafness. Early in the New Deal, Desvernine had been vehemently anti-Roosevelt. In 1934 he cofounded the American Liberty League, a right-wing propaganda association, to mobilize businessmen and lawyers to defeat FDR's second-term reelection bid in 1936. Desvernine's book, *Democratic Despotism* (still offered in some college curricula), accused the administration of unconstitutionally engorging its power and forcing the country down the roads to fascism, nazism, and communism. He likened a New Deal logo to the swastika and the hammer and sickle. The book vented special vitriol on Henry Wallace, then secretary of agriculture, as a "mystic prophet" who regarded capitalists as an "enemy class [that] is being, as Stalin would vulgarly express it, 'liquidated.'" Although the Liberty League closed up shop after Roosevelt's landslide reelection, and in 1941 Desvernine supported defense preparations, it is hard to imagine him as persona grata to Wallace, a left-leaning architect of the New Deal, or to Cordell Hull, who fumed with moral outrage over Japanese aggression.[9]

Barter and Clearing Accounts

American policy makers had toyed with notions of barter trade while designing the freeze rules against Japan in late July. Dean Acheson may have been briefed on British practices by Noel Hall of the Ministry of Economic Warfare. The 30 July memorandum from the Interdepartmental Policy Committee to Welles on freeze procedures had included a suggestion that, after a few months, exports and imports of certain products might proceed under a barter-like arrangement. U.S. importers might be licensed to pay, most likely for raw silk, into a special bank account in favor of Japan. Japanese importing firms would be licensed to spend the dollars for U.S. goods that might be licensed for export, perhaps cotton. The barter idea survived, less specifically, in Welles's memo, which FDR okayed the next day.[10]

Bilateral barter trade was a viable mechanism when two countries desired each others' products, the normal case for the United States and Japan. In modern barter, the dates and values of cargoes never precisely matched, so bank clearing accounts were necessary. During the Depression many countries had enacted laws to channel trade payments through clearing accounts, usable only for reciprocal purchases, most famously the system installed by Hjalmar Schacht, president of the German central bank before and during the Nazi era. Germany was the premier market for Eastern Europe's agricultural products, but its finances were too weak to sustain a freely convertible reichsmark. Under Schacht's scheme, German importers of grain from Hungary, for example, paid reichsmarks into a special clearing account. The exporter could buy German goods or, more likely, sell the money only to another Hungarian firm for buying, say, German machinery. Schacht stimulated or discouraged trade, country by country, through manipulating the levels of clearing balances and the web of exchange rates applicable to the various accounts. He forced Germany's neighbors to accept disadvantageous terms if they wanted Germany as a customer. In 1939 Great Britain and its dominions and colonies established clearing accounts with neutral countries to control sterling movements and exchange rates during the war. In 1940 Japan and the Dutch Indies authorities adopted a modified clearing system whereby trade was settled through reciprocal yen and guilder clearing accounts with periodic settlements in dollars of relatively small net differences.[11]

On 12 August Hall informed Acheson of Britain's intention to establish a clearing account at the Bank of England for trade with Japan. If Japan offered goods "of essential importance," Britain would buy them, paying sterling into a special account. Japan could withdraw the sterling, but only to pay for non-essential goods the British might choose to license or for other approved pur-

poses, such as paying interest on prewar loans. The Japanese agreed to coop-
erate, even though the system denied them the automatic right to transfer
funds among countries of the sterling area as permitted to other neutral trade
partners. India and Burma expected to set up similar accounts with Japan.
However, almost no Japanese-owned sterling movements took place after the
freeze, except payments for Indian raw cotton ordered previously.[12]

Japan's Barter Offer

On 5 September 1941 Desvernine returned to the State Department to present to Hull his far-reaching proposal (table 3). Japanese agencies offered to
ship thirty-seven thousand bales (4.9 million pounds) of high-quality raw silk,
78 to 83 percent seriplane, white and yellow, "of grade utilizable for national
defense." The bales were owned by the Imperial Silk Company, a quasi-
government agency, and ready for prompt shipment by its agent, Mitsui and
Company. The delivered value would be approximately $14,970,008 at $3.04
per pound, the U.S. government's average buying prices for raw silk, which it
commandeered from domestic warehouses and factories. Japan wished to
receive in exchange twenty commodities worth $14,970,000 at current market
prices. All the commodities were available on the West Coast. All cargoes,
inbound and outbound, would sail in Japanese bottoms.

Japan's shopping list paralleled its actual purchases in the first seven
months of 1941, other than metals, machine tools, and high-grade gasoline,
which had been effectively embargoed prior to the freeze.[13] First and foremost, Japan wanted 913,000 tons (about 6.4 million barrels) of petroleum and
refined products worth $10,620,000, of which $3,804,000 was to be crude oil
from the San Joaquin Valley fields and $6,816,000 refined fuels, primarily
ordinary gasoline and diesel oil, plus small volumes of light oil and kerosene.
The total volume, roughly one hundred tanker loads, was equal to four
months of pre-freeze oil-product purchases. Second, Japan wanted $3.5 mil-
lion of California cotton, the long-staple variety for weaving superior fabrics
and for strengthening ordinary cloth by blending with Indian short-staple cotton. It was an unusual request, perhaps for uniforms, because Japan's textile
exports had virtually ceased while cloth for the civilian market was severely
restricted in quality and quantity. Finally, Japan requested fourteen innocuous
items worth a total of $819,000, three of which exceeded $100,000: scrap
rubber, butyl acetate, and manure salts (low-grade potash). A miscellany of
clays, pitch coke, wood pulp, minor chemicals, Vaseline, printing ink, paper
rolls for office adding machines, and hops for beer rounded out the shopping
list. The scattered list of nonpetroleum articles suggests a Japanese effort to

TABLE 3 **Japanese Barter Proposal to United States, 5 September 1941**

SILK
Utilizable for national defense
(On hand in Japan ready for shipment)

Grade	Quantity	Price per Pound*	Price per Bale	Total
20/22 WHITE				
83%	7,050 bales	$3.07	$410	$2,890,500
81%	7,760 bales	$3.04	$406	$3,150,560
78%	5,730 bales	$3.02	$404	$2,314,920
Total	**20,540 bales**			**$8,355,980**
20/22 YELLOW				
83%	3,650 bales	$3.02	$404	$1,474,600
81%	7,360 bales	$2.99	$400	$2,944,000
78%	5,550 bales	$2.97	$397	$2,203,350
Total	**16,560 bales**			**$6,621,950**

Grand total 37,100 bales $14,977,930

or approximately   14,978,000

*Note: United States government price.

American commodities proposed to be taken in exchange and payment for silk

Commodity	Quantity	Approximate Value
CRUDE OIL		
1. Kettleman Hills crude oil	240,000 tons	$2,808,000
Pogo Creek crude oil	120,000 tons	$996,000
2. Gasoline (motor fuel)	100,000 tons	$2,516,000
3. Kerosene	45,000 tons	$826,000
4. Light diesel	47,000 tons	$522,000
5. Diesel oil	360,000 tons	$2,952,000
Total items 1 to 5 (oils)	**913,000 tons**	**$10,620,000**
6. California cotton	47,080 bales	$3,531,000
7. Scrap rubber	3,000 tons	$150,000
8. Pitch coke	3,000 tons	$66,000
9. Vasoline	50 tons	$7,000
10. Fusel oil	150 tons	$57,000
11. Asbestos (long fiber)	600 tons	$27,000
12. Butyl acetate	300 tons	$126,000
13. Manure salts	6,000 tons	$156,000

Table 3 (continued)

Commodity	Quantity	Approximate Value
14. Hops	100 tons	$78,000
15. Gilsonite	300 tons	$11,000
16. Ethyline dichloride	50 tons	$9,000
17. Ethyl acetocetate	60 tons	$10,000
18. Unbleached sulphate pulp	600 tons	$49,000
19. Printing ink	600 tons	$56,000
20. Paper cards for Powers automatic adding machines	60 tons	$17,000
Total items 6 to 20 (non-oils)		**$4,350,000**
Total oil items 1 to 5		**$10,620,000**
Total items 6 to 20		**$4,350,000**
Grand Total		**$14,970,000**

curry political favor with depressed cotton growers and to lend a peaceable coloration to the deal.

The two-way exchange of about $30 million of products was Japan's "initial" offer for discussion, Desvernine said, limited only by the bales of highest grade silk on hand from the spring crop. Within three or four months Japan would offer from the next crop another 10,000 to 15,000 bales of high-grade silk worth $6 million. It also had on hand 100,000 to 120,000 bales of ordinary commercial grade silk, of unstated value but at current prices worth up to $40 million.[14] The total value of all the bales on offer, $60 million, exceeded the $52 million worth of raw silk exports to the United States in the first seven months of 1941 and was equivalent to one year's gold production of the Japanese Empire. Tokyo was inviting, in the aggregate, a two-way swap of $120 million of commodities. The offer did not specify the counterpart U.S. commodities for the second and third lots of silk, but if Japan were again to ask for two-thirds of its recompense in oil, it would acquire altogether twenty-five million barrels, equal to almost one year of pre-freeze oil imports from the United States.[15]

Barter Declined

Hull forwarded the proposal to Dean Acheson, his aide most likely to reject it. Acheson inquired through the Office of Production Management whether U.S. military forces needed any silk. On 13 September he reported back to

Hull that the Army and Navy had silk "more than sufficient" for two years for parachutes and other needs and did not want more. Nor was silk for hosiery a necessity, he said, because the OPM was rationing it and directing supplies of substitute fibers. Acheson rendered a peculiar legal opinion, that Roosevelt's freeze directions prohibited Treasury licenses because silk had been Japan's main source of dollars to buy oil. It was a wildly improbable interpretation because, in the usual case of trade under freeze rules, a payment to a Japanese seller from blocked funds would languish in his frozen account unless Acheson's own committee awarded further licenses to spend it. Furthermore, he warned Hull, "private" negotiations like this deal involving Mitsui were harmful to U.S. policy. According to Shanghai sources, the barter scheme was a ploy to incite hosiery manufacturers to lobby for raw silk. Japan had tried similar approaches to other parties, he declared.[16]

Acheson's arguments convinced the secretary. Hull orally informed Desvernine's colleague Shouse three days later that the United States found it impossible to discuss barter with Japan. This was the moment for Henry Wallace, if he wished, to advocate that his EDB intervene and to suggest at least a possibility of barter with Japan. He did not. According to Hull, Wallace scolded Desvernine, telling him that U.S. policy was against the "appeasement" of Japan. Likening the barter ploy to Hitler's reviled Munich Pact was the kiss of death. At Acheson's urging, supported by Hull, the vice president dropped the matter altogether, without the courtesy of a written reply. Acheson was never again to be directly challenged about alleviating the freeze of Japanese funds.[17]

The death of the barter fiasco occurred five days afterward. On 18 September 1941 Nishiyama approached Acheson and Edward G. Miller Jr., the Treasury's liaison man with State, to ascertain the State Department's reaction. Nishiyama, believing that applications to deliver raw silk and receive unblocked dollars might be held up because of banking problems, submitted a dense memo by an American silk industry expert purporting to show that Japanese trading firms effectively financed U.S. silk dealers and manufacturers. The inquiry, of course, ended up in Acheson's hands. He retorted that the State Department could not consider "isolated requests" for commercial deals while Hull and Nomura were engaged in broad policy discussions. "He [Nishiyama] did not press the matter further," Acheson reported laconically.[18]

The prodigious barter scheme, sponsored by the government in Tokyo, was certainly not an isolated commercial offer. Nevertheless, Japan's last hope died that day, no doubt adding to Nishiyama's frustrated outburst in October. Nomura immediately cabled Tokyo that according to "Desburnin" the prospects of negotiations were now much poorer than when the effort began and that "for the present no consideration would be given to the question of bartering silk for oil."[19] It was the moment when the leaders in Tokyo understood that no trade was possible on any terms at any foreseeable time unless it offered far-reaching concessions in the negotiations dealing with peace in East Asia. On 5 December Cordell Hull groused to Nomura that he had been "severely criticized" for permitting oil exports to Japan in the period before it took southern Indochina. In a classic understatement on that late date the secretary observed "that it was very difficult to resume the supply of oil to Japan under the present circumstances."[20]

A postscript to the sorry barter episode unfolded over the next few years. After Pearl Harbor, Desvernine broadcast *Wake Up America* harangues on the NBC radio network to defend wartime profits and complain of controls on business. Perhaps in retaliation, Attorney General Francis Biddle opened an investigation of his prewar representation of an arm of the Japanese government. Nishiyama had boasted of official authorship of the barter proposal, which was not actually made by Mitsui. Desvernine had also tried to help reopen cotton sales to Japan. Among documents the FBI seized from Japanese files in the United States after Pearl Harbor was a letter from Desvernine to Kazuo Nishi, manager of the Specie Bank's New York agency, dated 6 December 1941, thanking Nishi for honoring him at a cocktail party. In September 1943 a Justice Department investigator, Jesse Climenko, contacted Acheson. Because in 1941 Hull had telephoned the substance of Acheson's rejection yet Desvernine "had continued to act as though he was unaware" of it, he might be prosecuted under the Logan Act of 1799. (The act, stemming from a rivalry between John Adams and Thomas Jefferson, prohibited private citizens from interfering in official relations with foreign governments. Nobody has ever been convicted under it.) Nothing came of it. In December 1945, the gossip columnist Drew Pearson broke a story that Bernard Baruch, a confidante of FDR, had intervened to squelch Desvernine's prosecution. Desvernine and Baruch, it was said, had worked all along with Postmaster General Frank Walker "to get information from the Japanese in order to know what they were up to."[21]

Oil Denouement

After collapse of the barter scheme Nishiyama pecked away at other appeals to the Treasury Department. The twentieth of September witnessed him confronting Miller, Fox and Pehle, the department's Foreign Funds Control staff, with an offer to deliver gold or dollar notes from "Japan and/or China" aboard a ship that would also carry the Asian merchandise stored in Japan to U.S.

buyers. The Treasury team brushed him off, telling him that gold and currency were such unusual mediums as to require action by the Interdepartmental Policy Committee—Acheson and friends—which wouldn't meet for a
week. Privately, they thought that greenbacks might be acceptable if rounded
up in Japan, but not in China, closing off any serious prospect of that
solution.[22]

The desultory minuet moved to higher levels. On 3 October 1941 Ambassador Nomura appealed personally to Cordell Hull to release payments for the
two tankerfuls of oil licensed for export since August. Two uneasy weeks had
elapsed without response to Nishiyama's proffer of gold or currency. Therefore,
Nomura said, "despite serious difficulties" Japan had decided to remit dollars
from Brazil as proposed earlier by the United States.[23] Japan did transfer
$170,000 to the United States, Welles learned on 17 October, on the under-
standing it would be released to the Japanese embassy to pay for the oil cargoes. But the Treasury refused to unfreeze that money from Brazil or any other
funds. Another week passed. Then came the denouement. Nishiyama met
again with Treasury and State staffers Fox and Miller, who clucked solicitously
over his "anxiety for a decision." He learned, however, that the Interdepartmental Policy Committee could not decide because a new problem had
arisen: the insolvency of the Yokohama Specie Bank's New York agency, the
bank that held almost all of Japan's frozen dollars. Acheson disingenuously
accused the Japanese of fomenting a banking crisis by secreting in Brazil more
money that ought to be returned to the YSBNY. This was untrue. The solvency
crisis arose from U.S. government interference with transfers of money owed
to the bank for settlements of silk delivered before the freeze. The surprised
and "very disturbed" Nishiyama, shedding his diplomatic sangfroid, complained that the two tankers had been idling in California ever since the
freeze. He "wondered whether the question would ever be resolved." Had the
committee rejected the offer of funds from Brazil? Perhaps not, he was told, if
Japan produced detailed reports of movements of funds in South America. He
would try to respond, he said, but money was fungible and almost impossible
to trace specifically. Anyway, what was the connection between minor payments for oil and the solvency of Japan's largest overseas bank? Would "any
method of payment ever be satisfactory?" Smoothly the Americans replied,
"This government is always willing to consider any suggestions the Japanese
may advance for effecting such payment." The Japanese diplomat morosely
observed, with polite Japanese understatement, that a favorable decision "wasn't
promising."[24] His colleague Iguchi briefed Nomura about the sour news prior
to the ambassador's next meeting with Sumner Welles. Afterward, Welles and
Acheson agreed to continue stalling by giving "thorough consideration" to

Japan's proposal.[25] Japan's best course would be to send the tankers home, which is what Tokyo ordered. Acheson, in his memoirs, mused that the last remaining vessel, the *Tatsuta Maru*, "like the USS *Maine* and Jenkins' ear, became the instrument of great events." It departed in late October with a ballast cargo of asphalt.[26]

The Oil Shortage that Never Was

While regulators in Washington stonewalled Japanese pleas to license a few dollars for test shipments of oil, others continued the charade that parts of the United States were running dry of petroleum products, by inference justifying the continued stoppage of oil exports to Japan. Roosevelt, at the urging of Harold Ickes, his petroleum coordinator, had told the nation a parable that curtailing Japan's oil was appropriate policy because of an impending fuel shortage on the East Coast (chapter 15). The shortage was supposedly due to the British borrowing fifty U.S. tankers to carry Lend-Lease oil across the Atlantic, one-fifth of the fleet that supplied the northeastern states from Maine to Virginia. Ignoring evidence to the contrary, Ickes doggedly persisted in spreading alarms that gasoline consumption would have to be curtailed by 33 percent in the Northeast to leave shipping space for winter fuel oil. The story is told in detail in Appendix 1.

In September a special Senate Committee under Senator Francis Maloney held hearings and concluded that there was no shortage of oil products, nor a shortage of transportation because of efficiencies in shipping as the industry had predicted, and more efficient driving. The railroad companies testified that they could readily make up for any remaining deficiencies by bringing into service twenty thousand idle tank cars. Ickes, outraged, returned to testify in October. He still insisted he was correct and that the railroads were exaggerating. Meanwhile, California had so much surplus capacity after the freeze ended exports to Japan that it was curtailing production and running short of storage tanks. In any case, because of fewer losses to submarines than expected and more tankers leased from the fleets of Norway and Holland, the British began returning tankers and completed the returns in November.

Meanwhile, California crude, fuel oil, and gasoline could not be carried to the East Coast for lack of transportation, which called into question Roosevelt's pronouncement of 24 July that oil ought not to go to Japan while Americans suffered. Upon imposing the freeze two days later, the White House had declared it designed "to prevent the use of the financial facilities of the United States and trade between Japan and the United States in ways harmful to the national defense and American interests." Whatever the virtues of the freeze of Japanese assets, the rationale of a U.S. fuel shortage was a political contrivance.[27]

The Final Days

In the last weeks before Pearl Harbor financial dealings between Japan and the United States dwindled to sniping over trivial sums. A Japanese ship stranded in California without funds for fuel and dock charges was granted money from blocked accounts and discharged after a flurry of high-level correspondence.[28] A Japanese-owned cotton exporting firm in Texas, its accounts frozen and with nothing to sell, asked permission to switch to domestic dealings. The Treasury refused, for no obvious reason since the company's funds would have remained frozen due to its ownership.[29] In California odd lots of Japanese goods ordered before the freeze had been offloaded from the vessel *Heian Maru* and released from customs control, but authorization to honor drafts payable by the U.S. buyers had to be negotiated one by one. Permissions trickled out grudgingly during October and November for a few hundred dollars each of window glass, fishing nets, hog bristles, Christmas ornaments, Kikkoman soy sauce, $80.00 of crabmeat, $31.00 of fishing tackle, and $11.32 of ceramic squirrels. The money was deposited into frozen accounts in Japanese bank branches.[30]

Japanese diplomats, businessmen, and resident aliens were cut off from drawing on their bank accounts, as were Americans caught by freezing orders in Japan. Tokyo and Washington agreed to allow them to withdraw for subsistence—five hundred dollars and five hundred yen per person per month, respectively, two thousand dollars for Ambassador Nomura—but not dollars to pay Japanese officials in South America.[31] Japanese seeking passage home on the repatriation ship needed special dispensation to buy tickets.[32] Japanese immigrants traditionally remitted money to wives and children at home, typically twenty-five or fifty dollars at a time. The Federal Reserve Bank of San Francisco refused to grant a general license, although it allowed the Seattle branch of the Specie Bank to honor 754 "benevolent remittances" under extremely tight supervision.[33] As late as 3 December payments for trade journals mailed to Japan was debated at senior levels. The foreign ministries of two great powers had been reduced to quibbling over one hundred dollars in magazine subscriptions.[34]

Yokohama Specie Bank Insolvency

Within a month of the freeze it became apparent that the U.S. operations of the Yokohama Specie Bank faced a terminal predicament. On 20 August Attaché Nishiyama furnished the Treasury a report showing that the New York agency's obligations during the rest of 1941 totaled $11.5 million, $8.5 million of which was for interest and redemption of dollar bonds of Japanese governments and companies payable to owners outside Japan, and $3 million was for operating expenses of the YSB's U.S. branches. He hoped to have licenses issued to pay from blocked funds.[35] According to Herbert Feis, the State Department's adviser on international economic affairs, dollar bonds issued by or guaranteed by the Japanese government, mostly in the 1920s, totaled $238 million (excluding $27 million of private company issues). He estimated 40 percent were held by Americans, the rest having been resold to Japanese owners. Some $105 million bore interest coupons payable in 1941.[36] The Specie Bank agency in New York, the paying agent, had available only $6 million to meet such obligations that, in happier times, it could easily have serviced. But the bank was in trouble because a special freezing order barred it from collecting $16 million it had advanced on imports of raw silk, and $3.5 million for other Japanese goods. The bank held warehouse receipts evidencing its ownership of the silk bales, which had arrived in America before the freeze. Like all Japanese-controlled assets, transfer of the bales to customers required Treasury licenses. The bank had pleaded for permission to release the silk to local Japanese importing houses for onward delivery to U.S. factories and to collect the money it was owed.[37] Edward G. Miller Jr. demurred. The Treasury could not, he said, agree to obligate itself to issue licenses for a series of transactions over a long period of time. It would only deal with specific licenses on the facts of each transaction.[38] The State Department regarded the bank's dilemma as genuine. Feis had recommended to Acheson on 19 September that the U.S. government license the silk settlements and allow payments to bondholders; funds flowing into the bank agency in excess of bond service would remain blocked by the freeze while the silk would remain in the country subject to government order.[39]

In October bank examiners of the office of Comptroller of the Currency determined that, without an inflow of money, the YSBNY could not survive for long. Nevertheless, it objected to releasing the bank's valuable security (the bales of silk) to unknown and possibly insolvent buyers, or even to a first-class buyer such as Mitsui, ostensibly because the customers had not applied for licenses to take ownership and pay the Specie Bank. It was a charade of circular reasoning. The U.S. Defense Supplies Corporation had commandeered all silk inventories in the United States to be held for its purchase. If the USDSC had paid promptly there would have been no problem. It had insisted, however, on leisurely retesting to confirm quality, even though raw silk was subjected to rigorous commercial testing in both Japan and America. With its banking license coming up for renewal on 15 November, the YSBNY faced a crisis. The San Francisco branch was also in trouble.[40] On 28 November the five Japanese New York banking agencies announced plans for suspending activities if necessary. As the *New York Times* observed, in the event of war, their affairs would be taken over by the Alien Property Custodian.[41] That is exactly what happened.

On 7 December 1941 officers of the New York State Banking Department worked through the night in preparation for seizure of the Japanese banks. The following morning they took control of the offices, which ceased operations except as directed by the U.S. government. The Japanese staff was interned and eventually repatriated along with Japanese diplomats on neutral ships. Control of the banks passed in March 1942 to the Office of the Alien Property Custodian, which presided over liquidation of their assets.[42] During and after World War II, U.S. owners of Japanese bonds and other claimants filed for recompense from the blocked accounts. Some were paid, including Standard-Vacuum for oil it had delivered to Japan from the East Indies, but a $17 million claim by the Bank of Japan was disallowed after the war. Justice was long delayed to one group: citizens and residents of Japanese descent who were forcibly relocated during the war and who had deposited in small sums $10 million in Japanese bank branches in California, primarily at the Specie Bank. The Office of Alien Property Custodian offered compensation, but because the branches kept their books in yen, it ruled that the money represented funds in Japan and should be returned at the postwar yen exchange rate of 360 to the dollar versus the prewar rate of 4.3, that is, about 1 percent of the original value of the deposits. A few accepted. Others sued the United States. Their case was argued up to the Supreme Court, which accepted it for trial despite the U.S. government's arguing that the statute of limitations had run out. On 10 April 1967 the court ruled eight to zero that seventy-five hundred depositors were entitled to full compensation of $10 million. It reasoned that Congress had intended that procedures under the Trading with the Enemy Act were akin to bankruptcy proceedings in which belated claims were allowable; it did not concede that the government had acted "unconscionably."[43]

In 1947 U.S. occupation authorities ordered the Yokohama Specie Bank dissolved. It reemerged later as the Bank of Tokyo with a much enlarged worldwide network of branches.[44]

Acheson's Boast of the Potency of the Freeze

Was the financial freeze a more potent form of economic warfare than commodity embargoes? Dean Acheson thought so. The assistant secretary of state, an officer of the department traditionally charged with peaceful solution of tensions through diplomacy, looked back with satisfaction on 22 November

1941. In a report to Hull on the "Present Effect of the Freezing Control," which may have gone higher in the administration, Acheson listed achievements that could not have been accomplished as well, or at all, by regulation of trade. With evident relish he reported:

- The freeze had slashed U.S. exports to Japan from $10 million per month to nil. Although export licensing control had been extended to petroleum and most other strategic goods, Japan might still have purchased lumber, raw cotton, foodstuffs, and other articles commonly available to neutral countries under general licenses. Acheson especially noted that foods for Japan and occupied China (other than edible fats and oils) were barred only by the financial freeze.
- Dollar freezing impeded or stopped Japanese commerce with South America and the rest of the dollar bloc. It helped end trade with the Netherlands Indies that was conducted partly in dollars, stiffening the Indies' own embargo.
- The freeze was "our machinery for controlling imports" from Japan, a policy not addressed by any other executive order. Japan would "undoubtedly" have sold silk despite the few U.S. goods still available to buy in return, in order to defend market share against conversion of the hosiery industry and consumer preference for nylon.
- Japanese assets in the United States, had they not been immobilized, would have been withdrawn because the United States did not have other legal exchange controls.
- The freeze of Chinese assets stabilized the yuan and blocked Japanese evasions through the Shanghai exchanges.[45]

While Acheson's boast acknowledged that tighter export licensing might have achieved some of the same results, it remained a robust tribute to the potency of dollar warfare. In 1941 the relentless dollar freeze threatened to pauperize Japan. Japan's response was not long in coming. On 22 November, the day of Acheson's self-congratulatory survey, the last of six Japanese aircraft carriers arrived at Hitokappu Bay in the Kurile Islands, from where they would sail four days later for Pearl Harbor.

18

Calamity

THE ECONOMY UNDER SIEGE

Extraordinary as it may seem, no agency of the U.S. government analyzed how the financial freeze would affect the Japanese economy and people in their entirety. Neither before nor after 26 July 1941 did the administration attempt to forecast Japan's national product, national income, employment, standard of living, or health and nutrition under freeze conditions. The oversight is astonishing. U.S. civilian and military officials had studied Japan's dependence on foreign trade for more than four years. They understood that a nation heavily dependent on overseas commerce, especially with the United States, would suffer grievously when its international financial resources were immobilized. It is hard to imagine a similar oversight in later times. During the Cold War, from 1945 to 1989, the United States alone or with its allies imposed economic sanctions against several dozen nations on seventy-five occasions.[1] In the computer era Washington must surely conduct thorough-going analyses of expected results. Such was not the case in the less sophisticated era before World War II.

After the freeze of 26 July 1941 U.S. civilian and military agencies did comment, here and there, on Japan's economic difficulties. They lacked current information other than the insights of the embassy staff members in Japan who relied on their contacts among Japanese and foreign businessmen and whatever they could glean from the local press. Most prominently, Francis S. Williams, the U.S. commercial attaché in Tokyo since 1934, sent commentaries to Washington based on "unofficial reports and personal studies over several years." Grew endorsed his findings.[2] Williams and a few observers in

Washington addressed limited aspects of Japanese economic life under a peacetime freeze. They did not evaluate the economic impact of a Pacific war on Japan, except for estimates of oil and shipping supply and demand. Their commentaries fell into three categories: exhaustion of stockpiles, declines of specific industries, and platitudes—often lurid—describing Japan's dire prospects.

Neither, it seems, did Japanese military or civilian agencies undertake a comprehensive analysis of their economy under the freeze between 26 July and 7 December 1941. Like their U.S. counterparts they evaluated the effects of the freeze in three aspects: stockpile exhaustion, travails of a few key industries, and dramatic outcries about the pauperization of Japan. They did not forecast the macroeconomic effects of the freeze on the total economy; they regarded civilian needs as a residual problem after military needs were provided for. Unlike the Americans, however, Japanese analysts turned immediately to considering the *wartime* economics of their country. Within a few weeks after the freeze began it was clear that it was absolute. Opinions in Tokyo moved toward assuming that negotiations would fail and war would erupt before the end of the year. Japanese planning staffs primarily contemplated their nation's economic ability to fight a three-year war—similar to the time frame of the U.S. War Plan Orange—by evaluating oil, steel, and shipping, economic activities that could be appraised with some validity for at least the first year of war.

Assessments of Stockpile Depletion

U.S. observers tried to guess at the adequacy of commodity stockpiles in Japan, usually expressed as the number of months on hand at pre-freeze rates of consumption. They understood that the Imperial navy and army held oil inventories directly, and that the stores for the general economy were controlled by other government agencies. U.S. estimates about civilian oil stocks, if no war occurred, ranged from six months cited in press articles to Harry Dexter White's guess of one year.[3] Williams believed nonnaval stockpiles plus local production were sufficient for ten to twelve months at reduced usage rates. "The bottom of the barrel is plainly in sight," he wrote in November, but Ambassador Grew had pointed out that rigorous conservation would extend stockpile lives.[4] Little was known about other commodities. A report to the chief of naval operations in October merely guessed that Japan would exhaust essential stocks other than oil in six months.[5]

In Tokyo, after Germany attacked the Soviet Union, the Cabinet Planning Board accelerated work on a plan to mobilize materiel. It reported to the cabinet on 29 July 1941 that civilian stocks of nine petroleum products and five other commodities would be exhausted very soon if consumption continued at the 1940–41 rate and if no imports arrived, except the minimal amounts from the "self-defense zone" (the yen bloc) and the "first supply zone" (Indochina and Thailand). Military storage tanks held most of the refined products: heavy fuel oil for the navy, motor gasoline for the army, and aviation gasoline for both. Oil products for the civilian economy were desperately short: ordinary gasoline at 2.5 months' supply and diesel oil at only 0.3 months' supply, until crude oil stocks of 4 to 6 months could be processed to provide some relief. Other commodities were disappearing. Manila hemp for fishing, for example, would be gone in one month. The planning board concluded that "the Empire will shortly become impoverished and unable to hold its own." The cabinet ratified the findings on 22 August.[6] On 6 September, Teiichi Suzuki, president of the board, reviewed the recent history of stockpiling. From late 1940 through February 1941 Japan had rushed to purchase about $154 million of "special imports," yet inventories remained far below needs. A final review of stockpiles, completed on 23 November 1941, predicted that if consumption of eleven critical commodities continued according to plans, eight would have fallen more than 50 percent by 1942. Caches of copper, zinc, and carbon black would be almost gone. Only wool would remain adequate, presumably due to yen bloc supplies and rationing.[7]

Assessments of Industries

The principal attempt by the United States to evaluate the dependence of Japanese industries on foreign trade had been conducted in April–May 1941 in the vulnerability studies prepared by interagency committees of experts for the Export Control Administration. The committees analyzed the effects of current and future sanctions on trade in specific commodities that Japan bought from or sold to the United States and its Allies (see chapters 10 through 13). None of the project teams quantified Japan's aggregate economic troubles under an expected dollar freeze, and only a few extrapolated their findings into evaluations of broad economic effects, notably those reporting on Japan's dependency on foreign mineral fertilizer. None measured quantitatively the effects of commercial isolation on Japan's ability to support its population. The vulnerability project was far too fragmentary for evaluating Japan undergoing a long-term crisis. In any case, the dominant initiative for economic war passed from the ECA's export squeeze to the Treasury's financial freeze in the summer of 1941.

After the freeze a few fragmentary comments on Japanese industries circulated in Washington. On 1 October, Harry White, responding to Morgenthau's inquiry about an article in the journal *China Today* predicting a rapid collapse of Japan, reviewed a few industries. He thought the steel mills could scrape by for a year by consuming more ore and pig iron and less scrap. Cotton textile production would drop to 50 percent of normal by the spring of 1942 (less than a 75 percent drop the article predicted), limited to processing raw cotton from the yen bloc and possibly South America. The Japan Federation of Cotton Spinning Companies had already restricted yarn operations to 50 percent of capacity. As to raw silk, White thought that demand would drop by half to two-thirds, a disaster to rural Japan, but he thought the slack could be taken up by domestic consumers. He naïvely misunderstood the impracticability of substituting the small volume of expensive silk for the vastly larger yardage of cotton piece goods that normally clothed the people. Attaché Williams understood that not much silk could be consumed in Japan, rendering the economic blow "particularly staggering." Grew reported great discouragement among Japanese businessmen. He and U.S. Army intelligence noted farm scarcities due to severe controls and rationing, compounded by flood damage to crops and transportation problems. No U.S. analyst, however, opined that Japan faced starvation in the near term. Naval intelligence flatly stated that food was not a problem.[8]

Among Japanese planners, oil and shipping were the industries of greatest concern. In July 1941 Japan halted the expansion of steel plants, ironically for lack of steel. Suzuki later reckoned that in the fiscal year ended 31 March 1941, 26 percent of the available 4.82 million tons of steel (12 percent below a planned 5.5 million goal) had gone to the military, whereas in the current fiscal year the army and navy took 45 percent despite a 10 percent lower availability. Yet the Imperial Navy in October demanded more steel for warships and merchant vessels. The Japanese army relinquished a tonnage from its allocation, temporarily sparing the economy. Nevertheless, the steel bottleneck loomed large as a reason other economic outputs were projected to drop an average of 15 percent.

The Japanese staffs studied oil most intensively. National reserves of crude and products stood at 42.7 million barrels in March 1941. Hope for synthetic oil from Manchurian shale was revealed as a pipedream; lacking high-pressure reaction cylinders from Germany, only 4 percent of the hoped-for production of gasoline, and no avgas, had been achieved. On 5 November the Cabinet Planning Board demonstrated that the fantasized self-sufficiency goal of about 40 million barrels of products per year from oil shale would absorb 380,000 miners, steel equal to half the navy's long-term ship program, consume 30 million tons of coal every year, and require nearly a billion dollars invested over seven years. On 14 November army leaders declared a national need for U.S. and Dutch oil of 56 million barrels per year, which Prime Minister Tojo reduced to 42 million barrels.

Shipping, a crucial variable for Japanese prospects in a Pacific war, was subjected to detailed studies that evaluated naval operations, sinkings, and new construction projected over three years of war. Suzuki's board reviewed the achievements of the 6.5 million tons of merchant shipping available in April–September 1941, of which 3 million tons had delivered 5 million tons of cargo per month for the civilian economy. Concerned about further requisitions for combat, Suzuki warned that 3 million tons of shipping was the necessary minimum to sustain economic production in wartime. Although neither the Japanese nor Americans evaluated shipping under a continuing peacetime freeze, with transpacific trade ended and Japanese vessels restricted to coastal routes no further than Thailand, the problem would have appeared manageable.

Tokyo devoted little attention to the general economy, and apparently none to the suffering of the Japanese people under a long-term freeze. An army estimate in September 1941 indicated that civilian material use was down 45 percent from already depressed levels. Studies alluded to severe fuel shortages for land transportation, fishing and factories but suggested no solution other than conquests of oil fields by war.[9]

Platitudes

Officials on both sides of the Pacific offered up platitudes about Japan's financial and economic predicament under the freeze. Grew expected that Japan's industrial, economic, and financial structure would be "very substantially weakened." White agreed that Japan faced a state of disintegration, although not as rapidly as some believed. All U.S. observers thought the economy was declining steadily. Williams opined that "Japan's economic structure cannot withstand the present strain very much longer"; without industrial materials, he declared, it could neither feed its people nor shore up wobbly transportation and utilities. While scoffing at Japanese pretensions of relief through trade with the yen bloc, Williams conceded only that "given a period of another ten years some measure of success might be achieved." Meanwhile, if Japan elected to slash production, conserve, and drift it would become a "weakling" economically and militarily within twelve months, unable to resist U.S. political demands or to wage an efficient war for more than a few months. On 5 December 1941 U.S. Army G-2 Intelligence concluded that "the economic situation in Japan is slowly but surely becoming worse." It lacked materials to support industry and the war in China let alone a major war. "In short," G-2 concluded, "economically Japan is in perilous plight."

U.S. officials tended toward an optimistic belief that, unless it chose war, Japan must soon cave in to U.S. diplomatic pressure. Maj. Gen. Sherman

Miles, the head of G-2, wrote, for example, that "through the advantage the United States has gained through the embargo, Japan finds herself in a very poor bargaining position." But Grew was a notable exception. The ambassador doubted "the theory put forward by many of our leading economists" that exhaustion of economic and financial resources would in short order bring about Japan's military collapse. They were assuming continuation of a market economy. Japan, however, had "dramatically prosecuted" converting into a state-directed economy. That a war in the Far East could best be averted by sanctions or even a blockade, the ambassador warned, was not supported by facts he observed.[10]

Japanese leaders also spouted platitudes by adopting the terms "pauperization" and "impoverishment" in reference to the freeze impact. In July the Cabinet Planning Board declared that the empire "will shortly become impoverished" and must quickly decide on a course for self-preservation. The prevalent attitude held that long-term commercial and financial strangulation would result in "gradual pauperization." Japan would die a beggar's death. Ambassador Nomura saw no alternative to war, except, as one historian phrased it, "to endure great hardship and privation, utterly and completely." The few moderates who warned of the price of war picked up the analogy. At a fateful conference of 26 November that committed Japan to the attack on Pearl Harbor, former prime minister Mitsumasa Yonai advised "that you be careful not to plunge into sudden pauperization in attempting to avoid gradual pauperization."[11]

Why No Comprehensive Study Was Done

Why didn't the United States government undertake a macroeconomic analysis of an isolated Japan in 1941? Lacking documentary evidence, one can only speculate. A possible inhibition was uncertainty about Japan's economic condition just before the freeze. Tokyo ceased publishing most economic statistics after 1936. National budgets were vague as to expenditures, especially for the military, that were incurred in foreign exchange rather than yen. On the other hand, abundant pre-1937 data were on hand from published sources such as the *Japan Year Book* and reports of Japanese banks and trading houses as well as up-to-date import-export data from non-empire countries with which it traded. Japan's industrial progress had been widely reported. Its published five-year plans had stated economic goals through the early 1940s. Thus ample information was available in the United States in 1941 to speculate rationally about the larger effects of a freeze, had anyone cared to do so.

Another possible inhibition might have been the unknown duration of the freezing policy. A short-term economic forecast of, say, a few months would have been of little utility because in the near term Japan could muddle through by dipping into stockpiles, skimping on maintenance, and deferring construction. Policies drafted in Washington at the time of the freezing order assumed partial resumption of trade after about two months, but the administration's refusal to release frozen dollars or to engage in barter killed that prospect. Deadlocked diplomatic negotiations indicated the freeze might well continue beyond 1941.

A hypothetical American economist would also have had to guess at world political alignments after 1941. Presumably he would have assumed Japan would still be at war in China. Would the United States be fighting Germany, as widely anticipated? If so, would the United States and its allies continue the freeze or try to pacify Japan by easing it, perhaps even seeking to buy Japanese ships and other goods? The United States fighting in Europe could not have offered Japan strategic resources, especially not metals, but cotton and foodstuffs were plentiful. California petroleum was unavailable for an Atlantic war due to a lack of tankers, at least until new ship construction weighed in. In any case, Japan would certainly attempt to adjust to the freeze by extending its austerity programs, substituting local and empire materials wherever possible and shifting workers from processing foreign materials to domestic-sourced industries, perhaps even back to agriculture.

The Wartime Study by the OSS and State Department

Whatever the reasons for inertia, there remains a tantalizing counterfactual question: What *might* a U.S. analyst have deduced about Japanese economic life if one had forged a comprehensive evaluation of a long-term freeze? Fortunately, a proxy can be found in the files of the National Archives, an elaborately detailed, secret 519-page study, "The Place of Foreign Trade in the Japanese Economy." It was prepared *during* World War II, entirely from prewar knowledge, by economists of the U.S. Office of Intelligence Coordination and Liaison (OCL), a joint office of the Department of State and the Office of Strategic Services (OSS) (fig. 2). The OSS, a wartime agency that organized and coordinated U.S. espionage and intelligence activities, headed by William J. Donovan, first launched the project in 1943. In 1943 and 1944 it assembled data on Japanese trade from both published and confidential sources and drew up preliminary analyses. The project was completed under the direction of Arthur B. Hersey, a thirty-five-year-old economist and statistician born in China but educated at Yale and Columbia Universities. Hersey, after postdoctoral work and a stint teaching mathematics, had joined the staff of the National Emergency Council, a New Deal agency that advised Roosevelt on

FIGURE 2 **Cover OSS/State Department's "The Place of Foreign Trade in the Japanese Economy"**

NOTE: This is Part I of Volume I of a
two-volume report. Volume II (Statistical
Summary: Tables and Charts) has been issued
in January 1946. Part II of Volume I will be
issued in September 1946.

THE PLACE OF FOREIGN TRADE IN THE JAPANESE ECONOMY

U. S. DEPARTMENT OF STATE. *Office of Intelligence Research*

INTELLIGENCE RESEARCH REPORT

OCL - 2815
Volume I, Part I

August 29, 1946

An analysis of the external trade of Japan proper
between 1930 and 1943, focusing on possible or
probable postwar developments. Volume I, Part I
deals with trade, production, and living standards
and presents projections of Japan's imports and
exports to "1950."

Distributed by

OFFICE OF INTELLIGENCE COORDINATION AND LIAISON

(OCL)
Monograph (incomplete)

labor and economic recovery issues. In 1935 he transferred to the Federal
Reserve Board of Governors as a staff economist in the Division of Research
and Statistics, performing quantitative studies of business expenditures and
other domestic subjects. In 1943 the OSS recruited him into its Research and
Analysis Branch for the study of Japanese foreign trade. In 1945 he returned
to the Federal Reserve, which granted him time to direct completion of the
study. (Afterward, he served as a senior economist and adviser in the Fed's
Division of International Finance until his retirement in 1972.)[12] Although he
completed his study in 1946 using some secret data from the prewar years that
the Japanese provided U.S. occupation authorities, his analysis and conclusions about foreign trade were based on open sources for 1930 and 1936, and
to a degree for 1938. Such information was available in Washington in 1941.
The study, declassified in 1948–50, is a unique document that plausibly suggests how American economists might have quantified the deterioration of an
economically isolated Japan, if Japan had not resorted to war and if the freeze
had continued for a few years in the early 1940s.[13]

Most relevant are Hersey's scenarios of Japanese standards of living in a
hypothetical year "1950"—always enclosed in quotation marks—which envisioned a defeated Japan almost recovered from physical war damage but
stripped of its colonies and conquests. (In 1943–44 he could not have fore-
seen the devastating firebombing attacks of 1945.) Japan in "1950" would not
be able to pay for vital imports due to a weak economy, feeble exporting
power, adverse "terms of trade" (relative international prices), and, possibly,
harsh restrictions of a peace settlement. Although Hersey addressed a theoretical postwar date and a far different world political situation than that of the
1940s, he projected conditions strikingly similar to those facing Japan in
1941, and worsening if it had to endure years of the freeze without resorting
to war.

Hersey expected the "1950" foreign trade of Japan to resemble that of the
difficult 1930s. In the 1940s economists widely assumed that Depression-like
conditions would reemerge in the world after a brief postwar boom. (U.S.
troops in the Pacific sang, "Golden Gate in '48, bread line in '49.") In both
hypothetical eras, postwar "1950" and the frozen early 1940s, Japan would
remain an overcrowded, resource-poor island nation that had to trade to maintain even a spartan standard of living, thus vulnerable to acute deprivation
when trade was hobbled for any reason. The adversities of the 1940s would be
due to isolation by potential enemies, and in "1950" to disadvantages in
reopened world markets, but the Japanese people would suffer similar deprivation in both situations. Other American economists studying the data available
in 1941 would in all likelihood have arrived at similar conclusions.

Hersey's methodology was complex and often arcane. (The technical details are summarized in Appendix 2 of this book.) His key economic variable was Japanese importation of foreign materials consumed by the domestic economy, comprising two-thirds of total imports, which he labeled "retained imports." (The other one-third was processed into finished goods that were reexported or, in some cases, offset by similar exports of different grades or stages of refinement.) Hersey grouped retained imports into eight categories, themselves aggregations of twenty detailed commodity groups. For simplification, retained imports are further condensed here into two broad categories: goods primarily consumed by households, and those primarily for industry, investment and military forces. Before 1941, 65 percent of retained imports had directly serviced the Japanese public's standard of living: food and fertilizer, 35–40 percent, and materials for clothing and shelter (cotton, wool, wood pulp for rayon and paper, and lumber), 25–30 percent. The 35 percent of retained imports not directly supporting the standard of living included metals, chemicals, and fuels (25 percent) and manufactures, mainly machinery (10 percent). (Japanese consumers rarely had access to foreign manufactured goods after 1937.) The two simplified categories are admittedly rough. Oil, for example, supported civilian transportation and fishing as well as industry and the navy, while lumber was needed for factories and railroads as well as housing. Errors of aggregation, however, tend to balance out.[14]

For this narrative two other adjustments have been made to Hersey's data: converting yen to dollars at the relevant exchange rates and recasting figures to a per capita basis to compensate for the effect of population growth, predicted at seven to eight million more people from 1941 to "1950." Hersey did not attempt to quantify the entire domestic Japanese economy. He noted, in fact, that retained imports of about $1 billion per year in 1938–39 were relatively small versus national income of $6 to $7 billion, but retained imports were crucial in maintaining Japanese life above a primitive level that domestic resources could sustain alone.[15]

Case A

The OSS–State Department analysis posed two scenarios for "1950," Case A and Case B (table 4). Case A assumed a standard of living forced back to the level of 1930, before Japan's decade of extraordinary industrial growth. Hersey considered Case A generous. He thought the bountiful terms of trade of 1930—high silk price versus cheap agricultural imports, for example—were unlikely to recur after the war, especially as nylon crowded out raw silk. Case A envisioned Japan affording to buy approximately the same value of imports

TABLE 4 **Japan Proper Retained Imports, Actual 1930s, and Projections to "1950"**[a]

	Actual			Projections, "1950"	
	1930	1936	1938	Case A	Case B
Population (millions)	64.4	70.3	72.0	73.7[b]	73.7
Food and fertilizer	290	362	338	383	112
Material for clothing and housing	229	248	230	233	108
Subtotal, for direct standard of living	**519**	**610**	**568**	**616**	**220**
Industrial raw materials and fuels	126	218	306	138	81
Manufactured goods mainly for industry, military, government	241	298	401	183	104
Total Retained Imports	**760**	**908**	**969**	**799**	**324**

[a] Millions of dollars converted from 1930 yen at yen=$.50
[b] Implied estimate of 1942 population for Case A and Case B.
Figures approximated due to rounding decimals.
OCL, "Place of Foreign Trade in the Japanese Economy," vol. 1, pt. 1, tables I–19 to I–21.

as those of a typical 1930s year (measured at constant prices; see Appendix 2). During that decade greater retained imports more than offset population growth, so that retained imports per person had grown from $11.80 to $13.45 per year in constant dollars. However, due to expected further population growth, a Case A postwar Japan with stagnant retained imports could afford at best $10.85 per capita, a reduction of about 15 percent from the 1930s average.

Japan's ability to feed itself had topped out in the 1930s. Nutrition had been maintained by a greater volume of retained imports. In "1950" a further increase in foreign food, fertilizer, and oil for fishing would be necessary to maintain the average diet at 1930 levels, about 2,250 calories per person per day. With export earnings lagging, non–food-related imports would necessarily be tightly restricted, with national priorities favoring essential materials for clothing, shelter, and infrastructure. "Luxury" consumer goods, such as food varieties and manufactures, would rank last, if at all. Hersey allowed for a slight moderation of the pinch on consumers by supposing Japan would increase the portion of retained imports destined for households from 65 to 70 percent. With scarce foreign exchange earnings mostly allotted to basic living, imports per capita of industrial materials and fuels would plummet to half the average prewar level, and imports of machinery and other manufactures even further.

Case A envisioned Japan maintaining frugal standards of decency in life's essentials, its economy sluggish and lacking foreign resources for growth and renewed industrialization, with little prospect of improvement. The Japanese diet would be spartan: more wheat and coarse grains and starches (barley, potatoes, sweet potatoes, and oats), less of the beloved Japonica rice, and much less variety of fish, meat, sugar, fruits, and vegetables. Tobacco would be scarce and expensive. Men and women would wear inferior clothing, mostly spun staple rayon with perhaps some blending of cotton and wool. Leather shoes would be scarce. Housing for the rising population would necessitate imports of lumber and pulp, although local cement could substitute somewhat. Few if any private automobiles would be manufactured, and probably none imported. Output of traditional small housewares could be maintained, more or less, but not better goods, let alone modern appliances. Industries needing chemicals and fuels, and structural materials beyond maintenance needs would stagnate. In sum, Japan's decade of strenuous national effort after 1930 would be nullified.[16]

Case B

For a speculation on the extreme grief of a freeze-hobbled Japan in the early 1940s, Case A is too optimistic, a "best case" because retained imports would have shriveled under the freeze even more than in the postwar austerity cases. But Hersey's Case B posited a "1950" far more dismal than a frozen Japan in the 1940s (chart 20). Case B assumed export earnings so drastically collapsed that nourishment and health could no longer be sustained through importing, as it had been in prewar years. A horrendous collapse of commerce and extremely weak terms of trade based on the adverse price relationships of 1936 (see Appendix 2) would compress exports by 60 percent below the prewar average. A drastic shortage of foreign exchange would restrict retained imports per capita to one-third of an average 1930s year. Japanese life would be thrust back to nineteenth-century standards. Diet would shrivel to 1,800 calories per capita per day, 20 percent lower than in the 1930s, necessarily consisting of 83 percent cereals and starches. (In comparison, in the 1990s the daily per capita consumption in Japan was 2,898 calories, of which only 40 percent was from cereals and starches.[17]) Hersey imagined either "semi-starvation of the urban

CHART 20 Japan: Retained Imports per Capita, 1930s and "1950" Projections

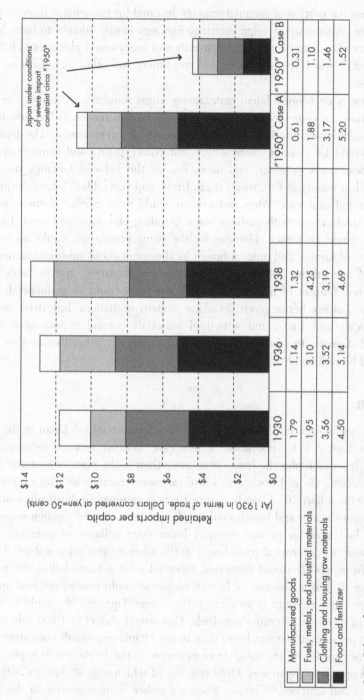

Japan under conditions of severe import constraint circa "1950"

	"1950" Case A	"1950" Case B	1938	1936	1930
Manufactured goods	0.61	0.31	1.32	1.14	1.79
Fuels, metals, and industrial materials	1.88	1.10	4.25	3.10	1.95
Clothing and housing raw materials	3.17	1.46	3.19	3.52	3.56
Food and fertilizer	5.20	1.52	4.69	5.14	4.50

Retained imports per capita
(At 1930 in terms of trade. Dollars converted at yen=50 cents)

OCL, "Place of Foreign Trade in the Japanese Economy," vol. 1, pt. 1, tables I-19 to I-21. Converted to dollars per capita by author.

population" or "chronic malnutrition for the whole population," depending on government food allocation policy.[18] Imports for other needs would have to be slashed even more drastically. The standard of living, broadly measured, would fall 25 to 33 percent below Case A, itself below prewar standards.

In Case B Japan's meager exports would earn barely enough to finance imports of essentials for human survival. The nation would subsist by exporting rural goods: raw silk to a fading market, fish, exotic farm specialties, cottage wares, and handicrafts, all lagging in price compared with its former advanced manufactures. Eighty years of advantages hard won in world markets by skilled labor and management would be nullified, leaving almost no surplus to buy materials for trade-oriented factories. The export-led growth that had buoyed Japan since Meiji times would shift into reverse.

Workers would suffer horrifically in Case B. Factories deprived of foreign materials would go dark. Steel from local ore and scrap would barely maintain railroads, utilities, and the most essential processing industries. Imports of machinery and manufactures would sink by 70 to 80 percent. Cities would suffer massive unemployment, and in a great migration to the countryside, possibly ten million Japanese would return to the already overcrowded land. Rural population might swell to forty million, the same 50 percent of total population as in 1920 but much larger in absolute numbers.[19] There they would find little relief. With overseas demand lost to synthetics, farm families dependent on raw silk for cash earnings would slide into poverty. No Japanese family would have found solace in Hersey's remark that its purchasing power would sink "not necessarily lower than that in other Asiatic countries," implying a standard of living at the level of China or India.[20]

A Probable Scenario, 1942–1943

Were Hersey's calculations a valid analog for the fate of Japan under a multi-year dollar freeze after 1941? Cases A and B probably bracketed the agonies facing a nonbelligerent, financially frozen Japan in the early 1940s. A more likely outcome was a middle scenario proposed here, an interpolation to adjust for differing circumstances of the two hypothetical eras.

A relatively more favorable circumstance for Japan in 1942–43 would have been its unimpaired trade with the yen bloc—the colonies of Korea and Taiwan, Manchukuo, the Mandated Islands, occupied parts of China, French Indochina, and probably Thailand. In contrast, in "1950," the former yen territories would be independent and its former members demanding hard currency for their goods. In the 1930s the yen bloc provided about 45 percent of all Japanese imports (29 percent from Korea and Formosa, 14 percent from

Manchukuo, Kwantung, and North China, and 1 or 2 percent from Indochina and Thailand). It supplied most of Japan's imported food, all of its rubber and tin, some iron ore and alloying metals, and some cotton, but only small quantities of fuels, ores, and metals and almost no manufactures. Yen bloc supplies were largely retained for consumption in Japan rather than processed for reexport. For example, the deliveries of Korea and Formosa typically consisted 70 percent of food and fertilizer. A frozen Japan in the 1940s would have continued its policy of paying them by delivering Japanese-produced articles such as cement, coal, nitrogen fertilizer, and machinery; by investing yen capital in pubic works and industries; and by transferring gold to Thailand and probably Indochina.

Hersey did not break out retained imports received from the yen bloc. If one assumes that Japan did not upgrade and reexport more than 10 percent of them in products such as refined flour and sugar or mixed fertilizers, Japan might reasonably have obtained 60 to 65 percent of its customary imports for consumers' needs from the bloc. Yen bloc rice and cereals, supplementing domestic agriculture, would have been adequate, or nearly so, to maintain nutrition of Japan's rising population at the 2,250 calories per person that prevailed in the late 1930s. (Hersey noted, however, that the climate had been unusually good in the last prewar years so that a regression to normal farm yields might squeeze food supplies.) On the other hand, the bloc could supply only 32 percent of the phosphate and almost none of the potash fertilizers normally imported by Japan. Sooner or later, perhaps after two years as U.S. vulnerability studies observed, slumping grain production in Japan would strain food supplies. Except for sugar from Formosa and the Marianas Islands the diet would be less varied than before the freeze and short of protein from a fishing fleet deprived of oil, especially for deep-sea fishing which was both the most productive and most fuel-dependent form of fishing.

The yen bloc could not have supplied Japan with other consumer needs. It had almost no wool for sale. China consumed its rather small cotton crop in its own textile mills. Except for scarce heavy-duty work clothes, the Japanese would wear rayon, not the durable long-strand variety from good foreign pulp, but short-staple spun rayon from local trees, woven into flimsy textiles well known to fall apart in Japan's wet climate. (Silk would be available for blending, but not in quantities to help much.) Leather for shoes and boots would be unavailable; rubber from Indochina would substitute, at least for the lowers. Luxuries would be scarce, perhaps a bit of sugar and tobacco. Gasoline and diesel motor vehicles would almost disappear from Japanese roads.

On the other hand, the standard of living of a 1940s freeze era could have been even worse than supposed for "1950" due to two other circumstances. First, the economic drain of the war in China had already caused dire shortages and rationing, made worse by the freeze. (Logically the China war and a freeze went together; if Japan ended the war the United States would have relaxed or ended the freeze.) Second, the freezing orders rendered Japan's gold production and gold reserves worthless internationally. Hersey assumed postwar gold and silver mining at only half the 1930s volume due to equipment shortages and loss of colonial mines, but after the war Japan could expect to freely sell its output for hard currency.

Hersey thought the "invisible" elements of Japan's balance of payments would be negligible in "1950," but the same would have been true in the frozen 1940s. The freeze halted hard-currency earnings from shipping; revenues could not have recovered much by "1950," so soon after a war in which 80 percent of Japan's merchant marine was sunk. The freeze also terminated earnings from Japan's overseas investments that were seized by its enemies, a result not much different from the "1950" scenarios because the investments were not returned after the war. Similarly, outgoing interest payments on Japanese foreign loans ceased at the end of 1941, when blocked dollars in New York ran out, and postwar Japan could not have afforded to resume payments until long after "1950." In neither era would Japan have had access to foreign loans, in the 1940s due to the freeze and afterward, Hersey thought, due to lack of creditworthiness. (He did not foresee postwar aid from the United States.) The Bank of Japan's gold reserves in its vaults were still large in 1941 but useless during the freeze. Hersey imagined they might still be unavailable in "1950" because they would be sequestered by the Allied authorities for restitution or occupation costs. A small exception, "compassionate remittances" from overseas Japanese settlers, halted by the freeze, would help a bit in "1950."[21]

The picture that emerges of the Japanese under a freeze, circa 1942–43, is of people with an adequate diet high in starches but deficient in other food groups, shabbily dressed as their wardrobes wore out, and suffering the effects of cold and damp. Transportation and utilities would be decaying. Depression-era unemployment would probably have returned to the cities, and extreme hard times to the villages. After a couple of years of embargo, Japan might have matched Case A in avoiding malnutrition, but with other aspects of life rolled back to primitive levels approaching those of Case B. While not as calamitous overall as Case B, a reduction of 35–40 percent of customary imports for consumption per person would have been a serious matter for Japan's trade-dependent society. It would equate to a rollback of the Japanese standard of living of about 15 to 20 percent in broad terms. An apt comparison might have been to the most poverty-stricken families in the most miserable regions of the United States in the worst depths of the Great Depression, surviving but enduring lives of grim deprivation with little hope of relief.

19

Futility

THE FINAL NEGOTIATIONS

J apan's de facto bankruptcy proved a crucial factor in the failure of negotiations for a peaceful settlement with the United States. The diplomatic maneuverings of 1940–41 have been exhaustively described in documents, memoirs, diaries, interviews, postwar investigations, and war crimes trials.[1] This chapter briefly summarizes the events, focusing on the significance of the dollar freeze.

U.S. resentment against Japanese aggressions began with the seizure of Manchuria in 1931 and accelerated when Japan assaulted China in 1937. The country initially reacted with diplomatic scoldings, aid to China, and embargoing exports of a few arms-related products. In 1940 tensions grew acute when Japan signed the Tripartite Pact with Germany and Italy whereby the three powers pledged to assist each other in wars, under certain circumstances. The United States, inching toward war in the Atlantic through pro-British policies, grew concerned that it might have to fight Japan as well.

Negotiations for a settlement of tensions began in earnest in April 1941. All discussions were conducted in Washington between Ambassador Kichisaburo Nomura (assisted after 15 November by special envoy Saburo Kurusu) and Secretary of State Cordell Hull. The Japanese diplomats also met directly with President Roosevelt, and occasionally with civilian and naval officials Nomura knew personally. Other U.S. officials played relatively minor roles.[2]

Positions in the Negotiations

Hull advanced four "principles" for Asia: respect for the territory and sovereignty of all nations, noninterference in their internal affairs, equal commercial
opportunity, and maintenance of the status quo in the Pacific—the principles
established by the Nine Power Treaty of 1922. For Japan the main stumbling
block was surrendering its decade of conquests by withdrawing from
Indochina and China, perhaps even from Manchuria. In Japanese eyes a
retreat would mean giving up any possibility of gain from a war that had cost
two hundred thousand dead soldiers, required huge outlays of national treasure, and caused economic hardships for its people. The United States further
demanded assurances that Japan would renounce the Tripartite Pact, or at
least refrain from fighting it as an ally of Hitler. To prod Japan, Washington
embarked on three programs: arms and financial aid to China, a buildup of
forces at Pearl Harbor and in the Philippines, and barring exports of commodities needed for its own defense.

The Japanese position was, simply, resistance to Hull's proposals: no U.S.
interference in China-Japan affairs, no military withdrawals from occupied territories, maintaining ties with Germany, and continuing trade with the United
States. In 1941 events in Europe emboldened Japanese leaders. Hitler's attack
on Russia on 22 June quelled the army's fears of a Soviet attack on the empire,
and it joined the navy in favoring a war to seize the resources of western
colonies in Asia. On 24 July, Japan, having coerced Vichy France, occupied
southern Indochina, triggering the U.S. freezing orders two days later and
those of the Allies soon after.

Role of the Freeze in Negotiations

After 26 July 1941 Japan's priority shifted to demanding an end of the dollar
freeze, or at least an easing so that deliveries of oil and perhaps other strategic
commodities might resume. At first Tokyo phrased the aim in generalities
while its representatives in the United States searched for loopholes. In
August banking and consular officials petitioned for financial licenses to pay
for two shiploads of oil and probed the possibilities of paying with dollars or
gold held outside the frozen accounts. They were rebuffed at every turn by the
Foreign Funds Control Committee dominated by Dean Acheson.

Early in August Prime Minister Prince Fumimaro Konoe launched an initiative to meet with President Roosevelt personally, perhaps in Hawaii or
Alaska, in what later generations would call a summit meeting. To placate the

generals and admirals, Foreign Minister Teijiro Toyoda drafted demands that the United States halt reinforcement of the Southwest Pacific, mediate a peace settlement in China (a euphemism for abandoning aid to Chiang Kai-Shek), and restore normal commercial relations (a euphemism for ending the freeze). In return Japan offered not to advance beyond Indochina and to with-draw troops from China when the war ended at some vague future date. FDR was intrigued but the State Department deemed the tradeoffs unacceptable, especially because Japan refused to start evacuating promptly. The United States declined the summit offer.

Japanese military and naval leaders moved forward with plans to launch a war before the year was out. On 6 September 1941 an imperial conference agreed to make a decision during the first ten days of October about war against the United States, Britain, and the Dutch Indies (a deadline gradually moved back to 29 November) unless Japan's demands were met.[3] On 18 September Acheson disclosed that the United States had rejected Japan's last-ditch barter scheme of oil for silk. Mobilizing for an attack began in earnest in Tokyo in the second half of the month. Nevertheless, Toyoda wished to test other avenues of negotiation. The deadlock between the war hawks on one hand and Konoe and Toyoda, who favored some troop withdrawals, on the other hand, led to the fall of Konoe and his replacement as prime minister by General Hideki Tojo on 17 October. Last-chance diplomacy passed to a new foreign minister, Shigenori Togo.

Japanese agents had continued to poke about desultorily for token financial licenses for oil or minor freeze-evading transactions, without success. On 24 October, however, Acheson told Counselor Tsutomo Nishiyama that the loom-ing insolvency of the Yokohama Specie Bank in New York, where Japan had mobilized its dollars—a bank failure engineered by the U.S. government's bar-ring the bank from collecting money for silk delivered to the United States before the freeze—would permanently lock up Japan's main holding of blocked dollars. It was clear that oil cargoes would never sail. This casting away of hope immediately preceded Tokyo's decision to demand financial relief, explicit in time and very substantial in amount, countered by American mus-ings of barter concessions much below Japanese needs.

Specific Demands for Freezing Relief

As resource stockpiles dwindled, and with the military's reluctant consent, Togo proposed "Plan A," an offer reciting kinder words about free trade in China but standing firm on the Axis pact and rejecting troop withdrawals for twenty-five years. As expected, Hull rebuffed it. Togo followed with "Plan B," an interim truce. Japan would evacuate Indochina if the United States kept its nose out of China, resumed trade promptly at pre-freeze levels, supplied oil in abundance, and prodded the Dutch to supply more.[4] The army insisted on amending Plan B so that "the United States will promise to supply Japan with the petroleum it needs." On 14 November the generals defined their terms: The United States must sell a tonnage of oil equivalent to 42 million barrels per year (converted here at 7 barrels per metric ton), including 10.5 million barrels of avgas, and ensure another 14 million barrels from the East Indies. If the Dutch did not agree, Japan would occupy the Indies. If the United States did not comply one week after signing an agreement, war would begin. Togo and Tojo scaled down the extravagant demands to 28 million barrels of U.S. oil, still a wildly improbable figure 34 percent greater than the annual rate of U.S. sales in January–July 1941. The amount was 259 percent greater than the 7.8 million barrel annual quota based on 1935–36 that Washington had contemplated in August for possible trade resumption. Avgas had been effectively embargoed since December 1939. Nomura did not present the exorbitant demand because Hull's response to Togo's first plan intervened.[5]

In November special ambassador Saburo Kurusu arrived to assist Nomura, whose English was not the best. As presented to Hull on 20 November, Plan B proposed evacuation of Indochina, American noninterference in China matters, restoring pre-freeze trade, including an undefined volume of oil, and helping obtain Indies resources. Considering the plan "preposterous," Hull pondered a response, urged by the military services to buy time for defense preparations and by China and England not to go soft.[6] On 18 October Hull had mused to Lord Halifax, the British ambassador, about a minor swap of silk for cotton—not oil—in exchange for a promise of a status quo in the Pacific. Anxious to avoid a rupture, the Japanese envoys suggested another humble accommodation: small quantities of U.S. rice and oil for Japan, far less than its full requirements, with guarantees that none would go to its armed forces. Hull was willing to think about it. Roosevelt informed Winston Churchill that the United States might thaw the freeze slightly on quasi-barter terms, strictly for civilian goods, for a three-month trial. The United States would license exports of food products, ships' bunker fuel, pharmaceuticals, raw cotton worth up to six hundred thousand dollars per month, and some petroleum for civilian needs while encouraging the Dutch to supply more. Yet the United States would not unfreeze Japan's dollars. Instead, it would buy Japanese products, two-thirds of which was to be raw silk—about 5 percent of the pre-freeze rate of silk purchases—just sufficient to finance the U.S. exports and to service Japanese bonds owned by Americans.[7] But the gesture, overtaken by the onrushing crisis, was never offered to Japan.

For six crucial days in November Hull played with notions of a modus vivendi ("manner of living"), a standstill of three months during which Japan would abandon southern Indochina, limit forces in the north, and commence peace discussions with China. In return the United States would unfreeze some Japanese dollars and resume some exports, although export controls in effect "for reasons of national defense" would remain. It would encourage the British and Dutch to act similarly. Between 20 and 26 November, Hull reviewed a slew of proposals and modifications from administration officials that watered down his proposal. Acheson's boastful report of the excellent results of the financial freeze arrived on his desk (chapter 17). By 24 November Hull's draft conceded a barter-type exchange of raw silk for oil and other goods, amounts not specified, but no release of blocked dollars.

The eviscerated modus vivendi was never offered to the Japanese. Allied scouting planes spotted a troop convoy heading for Thailand and Malaya. Landings there were sure to provoke war. On 26 November Hull's definitive response, approved by FDR, retreated all the way back to stiff-necked demands for the four principles and unlinking from Germany. Tojo deemed it an ultimatum.[8] When six Japanese aircraft carriers sortied from the Kurile Islands, Washington sent a war warning to Pearl Harbor and other bases. An imperial conference of 1 December gave up on negotiations and decided irretrievably that the empire would attack. On 4 December the southern invasion force sailed for Malaya from Hainan Island. On the sixth Roosevelt made a futile personal appeal for peace to Emperor Hirohito. On 7 December Japan attacked Pearl Harbor. The two nations were at war.

EPILOGUE

Bankruptcy and War Crimes

I n common English usage, "bankruptcy" is a synonym for "impoverishment." Japan was cast into international bankruptcy, a condition of absolute illiquidity, by the U.S. financial weapon. The choke hold of the relentless freeze rendered its dollars and gold worthless for national survival.

It was a strange sort of bankruptcy. Japan's reserve of gold and dollars exceeded $200 million in late 1941, enough to buy, for example, four years of U.S. oil at pre-freeze shipment rates, yet it was rendered useless. Thereafter Japan piled $60 million of new gold and $15 million of silver into the useless reserve every year until it suspended mining of precious metals in 1944. Japan had invested in gold mines, collected gold ornaments, and nurtured dollar-earning exports.[1] It had husbanded its reserve for future purchases of resources for its war economy, inflicting "the curse of gold" on its people by a "wholesale attack on the standard of living." At the end of the war, although the economy was in a shambles, the government of Japan was awash in gold amounting to twice its hoard in 1941. After the surrender the gold and silver in the Bank of Japan and other government vaults was sequestered by MacArthur's occupation forces. As to Japan's frozen dollars, they were never returned.[2]

A contemporary journalist summed it up. He could not have known that for four years, U.S. Treasury and Federal Reserve analysts had predicted Japan would soon exhaust its assets and necessarily abandon its aggressive policies. However, he wrote, "Japanese leaders exerted every possible effort . . . to avoid this outcome. They succeeded. . . . Gold production was stimulated. . . . A vast foreign exchange reserve was maintained." Although U.S. forecasts of empty vaults proved false, Japan was plunged into the international bankruptcy they predicted because of a stroke of a pen in Washington.[3]

Two views, one American and one Japanese, illustrate the attitudes about Japan's bankruptcy on the eve of war.

When Dean Acheson arrived at the State Department in January 1941 he rediscovered the prodigious powers of Section 5(b) of the 1917 Trading with the Enemy Act. He and colleagues of like mind promoted its deployment against Japan, then twisted a cautious squeeze designed "to bring Japan to its senses, not its knees" into strangulation. Acheson, an officer of the department charged with peaceful solutions through diplomacy, boasted to Cordell Hull on 22 November 1941 that financial crippling had proven far more devastating to Japan than embargoes. The freeze administrators thwarted Japan from removing its dollars from U.S. control as it had been doing for a year. Their actions slashed U.S. exports to zero despite Japan's valid export licenses for oil, and other licenses it would have been entitled to for cotton, lumber, and foodstuffs. Nor could Japan pay the mineral-rich nations of North and South America or the Dutch Indies, which demanded dollars, while the sterling bloc joined in the freeze. U.S. markets abruptly closed to Japan. Washington refused to allow Japanese trading companies to receive dollars, even if paid into their blocked accounts, hastening the ascendancy of nylon, which devastated silk farmers and demolished Japan's largest renewable flow of dollars.[4]

Through Japanese Eyes

In Japanese eyes the bankruptcy was a lethal threat, an assault on the nation's very existence. After the war, Koichi Kido, lord keeper of the privy seal and adviser to Emperor Hirohito, delivered an eloquent statement through his American defense counsel, William Logan Jr., before the International Military Tribunal for the Far East. (Kido was found guilty of war crimes and sentenced to life imprisonment but was released in 1955.)

Kido styled his defense "Japan Was Provoked into a War of Self-Defense." Allied charges of war crimes defined aggression as "a first or unprovoked attack or act of hostility." Kido argued that strangling an island nation dependent on foreign resources was a method of warfare more drastic than physical force because it aimed at undermining national morale and the well-being of the entire population through starvation. A nation, he concluded, had the right to decide when economic and financial blockade was an act of war that placed its survival in jeopardy. Kido thereby harked back to the dawn of international law three centuries earlier when jurists held that refusal to sell to another nation might well be a valid casus belli under extraordinary circumstances such as starvation.

The defense added, "We know of no parallel case in history where an economic blockade . . . was enforced on such a vast scale with such deliberate, premeditated, and coordinated precision. . . . Responsible leaders at that time sincerely and honestly believe[d] that Japan's national existence was at stake." Because sanctions "threatened Japan's very existence and if continued would have destroyed her," the "first blow was not struck at Pearl Harbor." Indeed, Lojan continued, the "Pacific War was not a war of aggression by Japan. It was a war of self defense and self preservation."[5]

Unfortunately for Japan, its leaders chose a war that brought upon it far more economic devastation than any sanctions, along with great loss of life and untold misery. Although struggling along under bankruptcy without going to war was a dreary prospect, a third course was open to Japan: renouncing imperial aggression in return for thawing of the freeze. One may wonder, what if Japan had endured the freeze long enough to ascertain that Germany could not win and had then abandoned the Axis, perhaps even joined the Allied side as it had in 1914? It would have prospered mightily by selling ships, machinery, and other goods to the Allies. It would have emerged after the war as the strongest regional power, with a world-class navy, an overflowing treasury, and a zeal for industrial modernization, just as colonial empires in Asia were crumbling. It might have shored up China against communism. A cooperative Japanese commercial "empire" in East Asia, economically buoyant and trading internationally on a grand scale a generation sooner, could have changed the course of history in the twentieth century and beyond.

APPENDIX 1

The U.S. Oil Shortage that Never Was

In July 1941 President Franklin D. Roosevelt cited a shortage of oil products on the U.S. East Coast as an important rationale for halting oil sales to Japan, even though Japan drew oil solely from California and that oil could not be shipped to the Atlantic. Harold Ickes, the petroleum coordinator, along with his deputy Ralph Davies and a hastily recruited team of experts from the industry, evaluated the diversion to Lend-Lease service of fifty U.S. tankers, comprising 20 percent of the fleet that delivered most of the oil consumed in the northeastern states. The diversion would result in a shortfall of liquids there amounting to 20 percent, that is, 350,000 to 400,000 barrels per day. Because gasoline was the largest volume product, and because Ickes insisted that nonessential driving could be easily curtailed, he demanded a reduction of gasoline consumption, initially of 10 percent in August versus July, with larger cuts to follow. Trucks, buses, and taxis were exempted, which ultimately would result in a 33 percent reduction for private passenger cars. Refineries in the region were ordered to cut deliveries to retail gasoline stations. The stations were told to close on nights and Sundays. But Ickes's importunings were ineffective. Alarmed motorists filled their tanks and hoarded gasoline.[1]

The U.S. Senate appointed a special committee to investigate, chaired by Senator Francis Maloney of Connecticut. (The House also named a merchant marine committee to investigate.) In late August and early September the Maloney committee convened to hear witnesses. Ralph Davies testified on behalf of Ickes, who was traveling. He backtracked half way on his agency's estimates, conceding that half the fancied East Coast shortfall of 353,000 barrels per day could be overcome by the end of 1941. Deep loading and other tanker efficiencies, recommissioning idle ships, and employing barges had already upped deliveries by 70,000 barrels per day. Ten thousand railroad tank cars were to be pressed into service to haul another 73,700 barrels per day; the railroads agreed to cut their freight rates in half (although still far higher than tanker rates). He hoped 175,000 barrels per day would be delivered gradually by Great Lakes tankers, reversing of regional pipeline flows to supply inland parts of the Northeast, conservation, and coal substitution. Davies humbly apologized for his sneer that inventories in northeastern storage tanks were "sludge." Nevertheless, he persisted, restriction of gasoline for motorists, by formal or informal rationing, would be necessary throughout 1941 so that tankers could haul winter heating oil. Eventually, new tankers and a pipeline from Texas would permanently solve the problem.[2]

The Maloney committee also heard from angry retail gasoline operators. Rationing based on July's sales, as Ickes wanted, ignored patterns of large summertime need in resort areas and lower need in cities. The American Automobile Association declared that pleasure driving was vastly exaggerated, and that 77 percent of auto trips were for business or commuting.[3]

John J. Pelley, head of the Association of American Railroads, belittled the shortage. He assured the senators that 20,000 tank cars (out of a U.S. fleet of 125,000, excluding 29,000 that hauled liquid foods and chemicals) were standing idle because of the growth of ocean haulage over recent years.[4] A car could haul 200 barrels on a twenty-day Texas–New York round trip, equivalent to 10 barrels delivered per day. Thus 20,000 idle cars could move 200,000 barrels per day to the East Coast, more than Davies' feared 175,000-barrel extended shortage. Even 250,000 barrels per day by rail was feasible, he told the amazed senators, by shortening turnaround times and hitching together mile-long trains of 100 cars. The debate degenerated into arguments about the meaning of "idle": Was a car idle if it stood empty for just a day or two? And were there enough locomotives? It became clear that the railroads were anxious not only for freight business but also to kill a proposed Texas–New York pipeline that was stalled for lack of an allocation of steel.[5]

On 11 September 1941 the Maloney committee accepted the railroaders' boast. It delivered a blistering criticism of Ickes for falsely threatening a shortage and creating alarm and confusion. Ickes's "frightening picture" was really "a 'shortage' in a large surplus—and not a shortage of products, or a lack of facilities to transport them." While not quite accusing Ickes of promoting a war scare, the senators commended the industry's efforts and unanimously urged an end to rationing and calming the public's "mild form of hysteria."[6]

Harold Ickes felt personally insulted. Boiling mad, the petroleum coordinator demanded to be heard when the Maloney committee reconvened on 1 and 2 October 1941. His staff had sent telegrams to 188 companies that owned or leased railroad tank cars to inquire how many they could offer for East Coast oil service. The responses indicated that there were only 5,192 cars available in the entire United States. Pelley's 20,000 cars had been wildly misrepresented, Ickes declared, and his mischief incalculable. He persisted in his plans for even more stringent rationing of gasoline as the autumn approached. Davies had warned that 50 percent cuts for private autos would be necessary. Lifting restrictions would be "stupid."[7]

Two weeks later Harold Ickes suddenly changed his mind. A delegation of oil company executives headed by William S. Farish, president of Standard Oil of New Jersey, had come to him to request cancellation of rationing plans because there would be no transportation shortage. The reason was that the British were about to release most of the shuttle tankers. Prime Minister Winston Churchill had told Parliament that losses to submarines had been far less severe than feared. The oil executives politely suggested that if Ickes persisted in rationing he ought to come up with a different explanation. Davies meekly said it must be true if Farish said so. He advised his boss to beat a retreat from heavy-handed rationing set for late October.[8]

The imaginary shortage evaporated almost overnight. Edwin W. Pauley, a wealthy oilman and Democratic party confidante (and a later secretary of the navy) traveled to London for a study of the United Kingdom oil situation. On his return he went directly to a lengthy conference with Roosevelt. The administration then announced that forty tankers would return to domestic service by the end of November 1941. The Lend-Lease Administration directed British oil buying to Caribbean countries, freeing still more U.S. tankers. November deliveries lifted East Coast fuel inventories 5 percent above a year earlier. Empty vessels were docking at Gulf Coast ports ahead of schedule. On 1 December shippers cut coastwise tanker rates 20 percent. Expensive rail transportation, having peaked at 143,000 barrels per day, abruptly ceased. As winter approached even Ickes found the situation "satisfactory." He churlishly confided to his diary that he always knew there was gasoline enough for "every desire" and that he was merely trying to avoid winter hardships.[9]

A tantalizing question is whether Britain actually needed any U.S. tankers in 1941. British civilians were tightly rationed. Campaigns in the Mediterranean consumed less oil than expected. Britain had expanded its tanker fleet by acquiring or leasing bottoms from Nazi-occupied nations. In 1939 the British Empire operated 445 tankers. It built 30 more in 1940–41 and obtained use of about half the 375 tankers of Norway, Holland, and a few other countries. Sinkings in the Atlantic through 1941 cost 117 tankers (75 empire and 41 others), and a few were lost in other oceans. In 1941, therefore, the United Kingdom controlled about 30 percent more tonnage than before the war. Although convoying lengthened turnaround times by 20 to 30 percent, not every route was convoyed and the shiplines had abandoned many long-haul peacetime routes. In the second half of 1941 losses in the Atlantic dropped sharply due to air patrols from Iceland and the UK, enabling the British to rebuild depleted stocks with Lend-Lease oil. They admitted to Pauley that before Lend-Lease a lack of dollars forced them to buy from sterling area companies in the Persian Gulf via the Cape of Good Hope route. Possibly they had underestimated the shipping relief of shorter Lend-Lease voyages. Or perhaps they wished to maximize their "free ride" of the U.S. shuttle haulage half way to England.[10]

Throughout 1941 California was able to produce far more oil than it could ship. Although southern and central parts of the state were amply serviced by pipelines, acute shortages arose in service to regions from northern California to Alaska due to requisitions of tankers to serve Britain and the Soviet Union. Only twenty-five hundred railroad cars were on hand in the far West. In October the refineries cut intakes of crude oil for lack of storage tanks. The shrinking market due to transportation deficiencies and the halt of sales to Japan (which had loaded the oil in its own tankers) induced the industry's Conservation Committee to further restrict crude liftings, from 640,000 barrels per day in July to 613,000 in November and December 1941 with further cuts to follow.[11] Roosevelt's citing of an East Coast shortage as a rationale for denying to Japan California's oil products, which could not be shipped to the Atlantic, had no basis in reality.

APPENDIX 2

Details of the OSS/State Department Study of Japanese Foreign Trade

Arthur B. Hersey titled his study for the Office of Strategic Services and the Department of State "The Place of Foreign Trade in the Japanese Economy; an analysis of the external trade of Japan proper between 1930 and 1943 focusing on possible or probable postwar development." He comprehensively analyzed Japan's external trade with both the yen bloc and the rest of the world in three representative prewar years: 1930, 1936, and, to a lesser extent, 1938.[1] His goal was to outline a possible range of conditions of Japan's economy about five years after the end of World War II to assist U.S. planners contemplating postsurrender and occupation policies. The methodology was complex. To link actual past to hypothetical future years Hersey converted physical units (pounds, bales, square yards, calories, etc.) to a common denominator of "constant yen," a proxy for physical units that also allowed him to adjust erratic prices of internationally traded goods into more comparable units.[2]

During the war many economists expected a return of the global Depression after a brief postwar boom. Hersey believed Japan's future in international trade to be especially bleak. Its appetite for imports of minerals, industrial crops, machinery, and even foodstuffs was almost unbounded. But its capacity to import would be limited to the hard currency it could earn from exporting goods and services and from gold mining. (He considered foreign loans unlikely.) In the 1930s Japanese exports had expanded rapidly, but the benefits to the people had been circumscribed for several reasons. A rising share of exports went to the yen bloc, which could neither pay in hard currency nor deliver the most needed commodities. While foreign countries erected barriers against Japanese goods, the terms of trade (relative world prices) worsened after 1930. No foreign loans were available due to disorganized financial markets in America and Europe and active discouragement of lenders by those governments because of Japan's aggressions.

"The core of the analysis," Hersey wrote, was a classification of Japan's imports (typically 90 percent raw and semiprocessed materials and foods and 10 percent manufactures) into two categories: commodities required by factories that manufactured products for export and commodities for final consumption within Japan. The latter, labeled "retained imports," comprising 59 to 68 percent of all imports in the 1930s, contributed directly to the standard of living. Another 25 percent of imports were materials for processing and resale abroad, primarily raw cotton for textiles, wood pulp and salt for rayon, and metals, chemicals, and fuels for other manufactures. A final 8 percent of imports were offsets to exports of a similar nature, swapped, in effect, because Japan both bought and sold in various grades and processed forms, wheat, sugar, fish, coal, and fertilizer.[3]

Japan's greatest dilemma in the 1930s, Hersey believed, had been deterioration of the "barter terms of trade," that is, weak export prices and high import prices. Japan had to run harder to stay in the same place internationally. For consistency he recast the data into indexes of "constant yen" at 1930 terms of trade. (He also calculated 1936 and 1938 terms of trade although they were of less relevance to his conclusions.) Hersey selected 1930 as a "best case" year, similar to the relatively prosperous 1920s, and the last equilibrium year of Japan's international trade before the turmoil of world depression, yen devaluation, the Manchurian adventure, and foreign trade discrimination. In 1930 Japan's upscale products enjoyed high prices abroad, notably raw silk and silk fabrics, premium seafoods, fine pottery, and other consumer luxuries, while prices of raw cotton and most other imported agricultural and forestry products were low. (Japan did not yet import oil, metals, or minerals on a large scale in 1930, and not much machinery.)[4]

A terms-of-trade index is not the same as the familiar domestic price index. It is a ratio of *relative* prices, that is, an export price index divided by an import price index. Hersey calculated data for twenty internationally traded product classes that he aggregated into eight groups: food; fertilizer and fodder; coal and petroleum; metals and minerals; cotton, wool, and pulp for rayon; lumber and paper pulp; and manufactured goods. He assigned to the terms of trade in 1930 an arbitrary index number of 100. The index for any other year, actual or predicted, was that year's export price index divided by its import price index. A resulting index above 100 meant a favorable trend for Japan, and vice versa for numbers below 100. Although any prediction was "pure guesswork," Hersey admitted, a postwar Japan enjoying 1930 terms of trade could fare adequately in the world, though not richly. "It is doubtful," he opined, "whether Japan's terms of trade will under any circumstances be more favorable than they were in the 1920s and 1930."

Hersey examined the improvements of the Japanese standard of living before the war. Economists had been awed by a surge of retained imports—79 percent higher in 1936 and 86 percent higher in 1938 compared with 1930—but the benefit to ordinary Japanese families was somewhat illusory. Yen devaluation, worsening terms of trade, and a massive switch to importing and stockpiling of industrial and strategic goods left the rise of retained imports for the benefit of the public at only 14 percent, barely more than population growth of 9 and 12 percent respectively since 1930. Yet the Japanese standard of living had undeniably improved, by about 10 percent per capita. Food consumption per capita was thought to be unchanged; the rising population was fed from rising domestic farm output through intensive fertilization. Gains in nonfood goods and services ranged from 20 percent to more than 30 percent per capita. As with food, the gains were mostly achieved by surges in production from domestic resources, notably chemicals, electrical energy, and paper, and by the effect of rayon pulp (10 percent of textiles cost) substituting for raw cotton (50 percent of textile cost). The experience implied that if postwar Japan could import consumer needs for its populace at the 1930 rate in real terms per capita, reduction of the standard of living would be tolerable, although disappointing for a population used to improving conditions.[5]

For his "highly tentative" postwar models of trade and living standards Hersey adopted the hypothetical year "1950" to represent a date a few years after the war when physical reconstruction would be largely completed, production of most domestic-sourced goods recovered, and crop yields normal. Population growth was a crucial assumption. Japan's population had risen steadily at about 1 million per year, from 64.4 million in 1930 to 72 million in 1938. Expecting continuation of that rate, Hersey expected a population increase to 81 or 82 million in "1950," after adjusting for war casualties and repatriation of Japanese émigrés from Asia.[6] For a country that historically found difficulty in feeding itself, millions of extra mouths would intensify the dilemma of maintaining living standards in the face of weakened exports.

Three adjustments have been made here to adapt Hersey's data from "1950" to represent Japan in, say, 1942, under a freeze but not at war with the Allies. First, the population differences between the periods of seven to eight million people are neutralized by converting trade to per capita values. Second, yen are converted to dollars at appropriate exchange rates. Third, his eight commodity groups are simplified into two: consumer commodities and other.

Japan's postwar future was clouded by an anticipated vicious cycle of trade: uncertain markets, adverse prices, and technological changes (notably the substitution of nylon, reducing raw silk exports by an assumed 50 percent)[7] resulting in a shortage of hard currency to buy raw materials for factories that produced for export. The uncertainties were profound. Rather than guess at world appetite for Japan's specialized goods, Hersey found it easier and surer to calculate imports essential for survival of an impoverished populace. He therefore set imports as the independent variable and assumed two levels of "retained" and other imports. He then "reverse engineered" his models to determine the exports necessary to fund the purchasing abroad. Japan's exporting capability became the dependent variable.

Hersey developed two scenarios of the Japanese standard of living in "1950" by arbitrarily assuming two levels of nutrition, expressed as daily calories per person, which set an upper limit on non-food imports. Case A assumed the 2,250 calories prevailing in 1930, which had not increased much if any in the following ten years. Assuming, however, that Japan's capacity to harvest crops and fish had topped out by 1941, a larger share of its limited postwar earnings would necessarily have to pay for imported food, fertilizer, and fishing boat fuel. Imports of materials for clothing, shelter, and infrastructure would have to be severely constrained by government priority rules, leaving little or nothing for other consumer goods such as foodstuff varieties. The procedure resulted in reduced postwar living standards of 25 to 33 percent depending on the details assumed.[8]

Case B envisioned a horrendous outcome for the Japanese people because of an exporting capacity so enfeebled that not even basic nourishment and health could be maintained. Hersey arbitrarily assumed a 20 percent reduction in nutrition below Case A, to 1,800 calories per person per day. Food and fertilizer needs would overwhelm other import priorities. Only minor imports could be financed for other consumer needs and urgent infrastructure. Retained imports per capita would slump 67 percent below 1930.[9]

Hersey also calculated terms of trade for 1936, the last peacetime year and a "worst case" year for Japan. Raw silk prices had fallen disastrously. Textiles and other wares were restricted by U.S. tariffs and quotas and by British imperial preference. Although exports of chemicals and mechanical products—bicycles, sewing machines, industrial machinery—held up better, Japan mostly sold them to the empire for yen. Meanwhile, prices of imported commodities were propped up by dominant suppliers such as U.S. government supports of cotton. (Strategic metals and fuels remained relatively cheap but were minor items of import before the war in China.) Relative to a 1930 index of 100, export prices in 1936 dropped to 95 whereas import prices soared to 129. Japan then had to sell 33 percent more goods to buy the same basket of imports. Because Hersey assumed the value of other imports as equal to Japan's residual buying power after meeting food and fertilizer needs, the large difference between 1930 and 1936 terms of trade dictated a necessity of much larger exports, but did not alter his Case A and B models of "1950." For example, Case A, calibrated to the 1936 terms of trade, required 55 percent more exports versus the 1930 terms of trade model, $1.62 billion versus $1.05 billion, to achieve the same standard of living established by Hersey's assumptions. (Hersey did not itemize exports in detail as he did for imports because of extreme uncertainty over the products Japan could sell, and to which countries, after the war.) Despite Japanese censorship of data from 1936 onward, Hersey calculated a somewhat improved 1938 terms of trade index but did not rely on it because distortions caused by the war in China, commodity stockpiling, and a renewed U.S. depression that lowered the cost of Japanese imports rendered it irrelevant to his vision of "1950."[10]

NOTES

Prologue: War Plan Orange

1. Edward S. Miller, *War Plan Orange: The U.S. Strategy to Defeat Japan, 1897–1945* (Annapolis, Md.: Naval Institute Press, 1991), 2–8, and chap. 14.

Sources and Technical Notes

1. The U.S. Library of Congress catalog lists 115 books in English under "Pearl Harbor Attack." Many address the diplomatic prelude rather than the attack itself. A few espouse conspiracy theories.

2. National Archives and Records Administration (NARA), *Holocaust-Era Assets: A Finding Aid to Records at the National Archives at College Park, Maryland* (Washington, D.C.: NARA, 1999). The files are in Office of Assistant Secretary for International Affairs, RG 56, NA (hereafter cited as OASIA), and Records of the Federal Reserve System, RG 82, NA. Secretary of the Board of Governors of the Federal Reserve System to National Archives, Agreement to Transfer Records and accompanying letter, 23 January 1997; and Greg Bradsher to author, e-mail, 26 January 2007, both in author's files.

3. *Record* 3, no. 4 (May 1997); William W. Stiles, Secretary of the Board of Governors to Assistant Archivist for Records Services, National Archives, declassifications agreement and letter, 23 January 1997, in author's files.

4. *Prologue* 2, no. 4 (Winter 1992): 415.

5. See chapter 16, note 16.

Introduction: Bankruptcy

1. Jonathan Utley, "Upstairs, Downstairs at Foggy Bottom: Oil Exports and Japan, 1940–41," *Prologue: The Journal of the National Archives*, Spring 1976, 24.

Chapter 1. Trading with the Enemy

1. "Franklin D. Roosevelt's 'Quarantine' Speech," *Documents for the Study of American History*, http://www.vlib.us/amdocs/texts/fdrquarn.html (accessed 8 December 2006); press conference, 6 October 1937, American Presidency Project web site, http://www.presidency.ucsb.edu (accessed 2 December 2006).

2. Emeric De Vattel, *The Law of Nations; or Principles of the Law of Nature Applied to the Conduct and Affairs of Nations and Sovereigns* (New York: Berry and Rogers, 1787), chap. 8, para. 90.

3. Louis Martin Sears, *Jefferson and the Embargo* (New York: Octagon Books, 1927).

4. House, Committee on Interstate and Foreign Commerce, *Hearings on H.R. 4704, Trading with the Enemy*, 65th Cong., 1st sess., 29–31 May 1917 (Washington, D.C.: GPO, 17).

5. William C. Redfield, Secretary of Commerce, testimony, in ibid., 29 May 1917.

6. Dr. Edward E. Pratt, Chief, Bureau of Foreign and Domestic Commerce, testimony, in ibid., 29 May 1917.

7. William C. Redfield, testimony, in ibid., 29 May 1917.

8. The bill also upheld contracts whereby U.S. fire insurance companies hedged excess risks with German reinsurance companies, and royalty payments for German patents so as to allow U.S. manufacture of Salvarsan, a German· medicine for venereal diseases that afflicted many American draftees.

9. Senate, Subcommittee on Commerce, *Hearings on H.R. 4960*, Sen. Joseph E. Ransdell presiding, 65th Cong., 1st sess., 23 July–2 August 1917 (Washington, D.C.: GPO, 1917). Includes text of House bill.

10. McAdoo came close to winning the Democratic nomination for president in 1924.

11. William G. McAdoo, Secretary of the Treasury, testimony, Senate, Subcommittee on Commerce, *Hearings on H.R. 4960*.

12. William C. Redfield, Secretary of Commerce, testimony, in ibid., 13 August 1917.

13. *Who Was Who in America*, Vol. 1.366 (Chicago: Marquis Who's Who, 1966). *Washington Post*, 2 January 1914, 1, 7 July 1914, 2, 1 April 1917, SM10, 1 December 1918, 19, 6 March 1919, 6. *Wall Street Journal*, 27 April 1915, 8. Milton C. Elliott, General Counsel, Federal Reserve Board, testimony, in ibid., 27 July, 17 August 1917; House, Committee on Ways and Means, *Conference Report: House Report No. 155 to Accompany H.R. 4960*, 65th Cong., 1st sess., 21 September 1917 (Washington, D.C.: GPO, 1917); see especially "Statement of the Managers on the Part of the House," appended to the report, citing amendment 18(b).

14. Congress, *Trading with the Enemy Act: To Define, Regulate, and Punish Trading with the Enemy, and for Other Purposes*, Act Ch. 106, 40 Stat. 411, 6 October 1917, Section 5(b) (Washington, D.C.: GPO, 1917).

15. House, Subcommittee on International Economic Policy and Trade of the Committee on International Relations, *Emergency Controls on International Economic Transactions,* Hearings before the Subcommittee on International Economic Policy and Trade of the Committee on International Relations, House of Representatives*, 95th Cong., 1st sess. (Washington, D.C.: GPO, 1977); House, Subcommittee on International Economic Policy and Trade of the Committee on International Relations, *Hearings on H.R. 1560 and H.R. 2382 and Markup of Trading with the Enemy Reform Legislation*, 95th Cong., 1st sess., 29, 30 March, 19, 26 April, 5 May, 2, 8, 9, 13 June 1977 (Washington, D.C.: GPO, 1977).

16. Charles Huberich, *The Law Relating to Trading with the Enemy* . . . (New York: Baker Voorhis, 1918).

17. Exceptions were disposals of seized German assets in the United States and settlement of claims with other countries that extended into the 1930s and in some court cases beyond World War II.

18. President Richard Nixon ended the prohibition order, but law-abiding Americans and U.S. businesses never profited from the rise of gold from an official price of thirty-five dollars to several hundred dollars per ounce that citizens of foreign countries later enjoyed in the 1970s.

19. In 1940–41 Section 5(b) provided the authority for Roosevelt to freeze U.S. assets of conquered countries and eventually those of Germany and Japan, and to impose controls of domestic consumer credit. After the war it formed the legal basis for President Harry Truman's intervening in a steel strike, Lyndon Johnson's controls on Americans investing abroad, and several presidents' limiting of trade with communist and other disapproved countries. Some executive orders cited an emergency, and some did not bother. In the wake of the 1970s Watergate scandal, Congress grew restless about "emergency" powers. In 1976 the Senate Subcommittee on International Trade and Commerce recounted the extraordinary number of national emergencies that presidents had declared: "A majority of the people of the United States have lived all their lives under emergency government." Senator Jonathan B. Bingham, chairman, had learned to his dismay that invocations of 5(b) since December 1950 had relied on an "unlimited emergency" declared by Truman when Chinese forces swarmed into Korea to fight U.S. troops. Appalled by cabinet officials' stumbling

justifications of "Alice in Wonderland" actions, he sputtered, "Your position is incredible." In 1977 Congress enacted the International Economic Powers Act (IEEPA), which reconfirmed presidential power to invoke controls over foreign financial transactions and to freeze U.S. assets of foreign countries, firms, and individuals if he found "any unusual and extraordinary threat" from abroad, but not declarations of a national emergency·for any reason he fancied. He was to consult with Congress if time permitted and in any case to report every six months to allow Congress time to write legislation. The president was empowered to assign any government agency as administrator, ending the automatic ascendancy of the Treasury Department. The reforms eliminated unintended nuisances by exempting ordinary travel expenses and the import and export of information in any format. Most important, it eliminated the right to invoke controls over purely domestic transactions during peacetime. Through 2005 the United States has invoked the IEEPA more than fifty times, against nations and, especially since 2000, against terrorists and terrorist organizations. Yet Section 5(b) lives on. The Jimmy Carter administration pleaded for its indefinite survival so that presidents could act instantaneously and sweepingly in a war emergency, and because more than four hundred government actions that rested upon it would have been jeopardized. In 1976 the TWEA was abbreviated and renamed the War Powers Act. A president now may invoke its draconian powers, including controls over domestic financial transactions, only in case of an emergency involving an actual war, declared or undeclared. Power has not been easily surrendered.

Chapter 2. The 1930s: Financial Power Slumbering

1. Harold G. Moulton with Juinichi Ko, *Japan: An Economic and Financial Appraisal* (Washington, D.C.: AMS Press, 1931), Appendix A.

2. Commerce Department, Bureau of Foreign and Domestic Commerce, *The United States in the World Economy; the International Transactions of the United States During the Interwar Period*, prepared by Hal B. Lary (Washington, D.C.: GPO, 1943), charts. Japan suspended payments during World War II and the postwar occupation but eventually paid every penny of prewar debt, the last of it in 1970.

3. Senate, Committee on Finance, *Hearings: Sale of Foreign Bonds or Securities in the United States Pursuant to S. Res. 19*, 72nd Cong., 1st sess. (Washington, D.C.: GPO, 1932), Pursuant to S. Res. 19, esp. testimony of Thomas W. Lamont, 18 December 1931, 12–13, and Otto Kahn, 4 January 1932, 359–61.

4. House, Committee on Foreign Affairs, *Prohibition of U.S. Loans to Japan Due to Japanese War Activities in Violation of the Kellogg-Briand Pact*, 7 March 1932, microfiche, CIS 72 HFo-T.23, Library of Congress; *Congressional Record*, 9 March 1945, 1932, 5587.

5. "Inter-Allied Debts," *Encyclopaedia Britannica* 12:462–67. As recently as the 1980s the annual report of the U.S. secretary of the treasury reported the war debts, which had more than doubled due to unpaid accrued interest.

6. U.S. Attorney General, "Opinion Upon the Act to Prohibit Financial Transactions with Any Foreign Government in Default on Its Obligations to the United States," *American Journal of International Law* 29, no. 1 (January 1935): 160–67; Ray Tucker, "Johnson's Johnson Act," *Scribner's Commentator*, February 1941, 7–12.

7. Japan had not borrowed abroad during World War I. It had loaned about $120 million to tsarist Russia that the Soviet government declined to repay. The Johnson Act prevented allied borrowings from U.S. investors in World War II. After the war its terms were vitiated by exempting governments that subscribed to the IMF and World Bank, thus reopening U.S. capital markets to most nations, except the Soviet bloc until the end of the Cold War. Annex C to NSC 5808/1, *The Johnson Act* (18 U.S.C. 955), 13 April 1954, electronic database, Library of Congress Declassified Documents Reference System.

8. Congress, Joint Resolution Extending and Amending Public Resolution Numbered 67, 74th Cong., 2nd sess., 29 February 1936, in *Public Laws of the United States of America*, vol. 49, pt. 2, 1152–53.

9. Herbert Feis, *The Road to Pearl Harbor: The Coming of the War Between the United States and Japan* (Princeton, N.J.: Princeton University Press, 1950), 11–12.

10. Ibid., 13–16.

11. John Morton Blum, *From the Morgenthau Diaries* (Boston: Houghton Mifflin, 1965), 1:74 and passim; *American National Biography Online*, http://www.anb.org/articles/07/07-00652.html (accessed 4 May 2006). Morgenthau's secretary, Henrietta Klotz, saved minutes of meetings and documents, filling over eight hundred volumes of diaries, indispensable to historians of the era.

12. Civil Service Commission, *Official Register of the United States* (Washington, D.C.: GPO, 1930–42); Blum, *From the Morgenthau Diaries* 1:160–61; Viner: *New York Times*, 26 December 1933, 17, 31 March 1934, 21, 20 April 1938, 4, 24 September 1938, 5; White: *American National Biography Online* and *New York Times*, 18 August 1948, 1; Taylor: Blum, *From the Morgenthau Diaries* 1:487–89; Knoke: *New York Times*, 15 October 1931, 41, 29 February 1936, 23, 9 January 1937, 24.

13. A. Lochead to Morgenthau, Japanese Balances in New York, 14 December 1937, Box 21, File Japan Foreign Exchange Position, OASIA.

14. Richard D. McKinzie, "Oral History Interview with Bernard Bernstein," 23 July 1975, Harry S. Truman Library, Independence, Mo., online at http://www.trumanlibrary.org/oralhist/bernsten.htm (accessed 1 January 2005).

15. Ibid.

16. Meeting Re Possible Control of Japan's Credits and Purchasing Channels in United States, 17 December 1937, in Henry Morgenthau Jr., *The Morgenthau Diaries*, Robert E. Lester, project coordinator, microfilm, 250 rolls (Bethesda, Md.: University Publications of America, 1995–97) (hereafter cited as *Morgenthau Diaries*), Roll 28.

17. Ibid.

18. Ibid., 17 December 1937.

19. Ibid., 18 December 1937.

20. Miller, *War Plan Orange*, 213.

Chapter 3. Hanging by a Silken Thread

1. The literature on silk is voluminous. Listed below are those relevant to the pre-1939 years. For later years, see chapter 12. For Japan the bedrock source is Japan Statistical Association, *Historical Statistics of Japan*, 5 vols. (Tokyo: Japan Statistical Association, 1987) (annual figures, 1868 to post–World War II), vols. 1 and 2 for sericulture and manufacturing, vol. 3 for international trade. *Japan Year Book* (later *Japan and Manchukuo Year Book*) (Tokyo: Japan Year Book Office, 1905–41) is also useful. Narratives on sericulture, manufacture, and exports appear in most standard works in English about emergence of the Japanese economy. Useful studies include William W. Lockwood Jr., "Japanese Silk and the American Market," *Far Eastern Survey*, 12 February 1936, 31–36; Kenzoo Hemmi, "Primary Product Exports and Economic Development: The Case of Silk," in *Agriculture and Economic Growth: Japan's Experience*, ed. Kazushi Ohkawa, Bruce F. Johnston, and Hiromitsu Kaneda (Princeton, N.J.: Princeton University Press and Tokyo University Press, 1970); Tessa Morris-Suzuki, "Sericulture and the Origins of Japanese Industrialization," *Technology and Culture*, January 1992, 101–21; Kym Anderson, "The Perspective of Japan in Historical and International Perspective," in *New Silk Roads: East Asia and World Textile Markets*, ed. Kym Anderson (Cambridge: Cambridge University Press, 1992). *Silk* magazine (see below) published articles on Japanese sericulture. Export finance is described in Raw Silk Importers, Incorporated, "Memorandum of Raw Silk Distribution in U.S.A. Market," 15 September 1941, submitted by Japanese Embassy to State Department, File 894.6552/24, Roll 16, State Department microfilm series LM-68, RG 59, NA.

The U.S. government studied the domestic silk business extensively (works cited in this note are Washington, D.C.: GPO unless otherwise noted). The Commerce Department, Bureau of the Census published elaborate censuses of manufactures: *Silk Manufacture* or *Silk and Silk Goods*, 1900, 1909, 1914, 1919, 1921, 1925, 1927; *Silk and Rayon Goods*, 1931, 1933, 1935 (included in *Cotton Manufactures and Rayon and Silk*, 1937); *Hosiery and Knit Goods*, 1914; *Clothing*, 1914; and *Wearing Apparel*, 1921, 1923, 1925, 1927. Exports and imports are in Commerce Department, Bureau of Foreign and Domestic Commerce, *Foreign Commerce and Navigation of the*

United States, annual (Washington, D.C.: GPO, 1893–1942). Older data is in Tariff Commission, *Historical Statistics of the United States on CD-ROM: Colonial Times to 1970*, 1986 [1975] series U295-316. Hearings were held by House, Committee on Ways and Means, Schedule 12, *Silk and Manufactures of*, 70th Cong., 2nd sess., February 1929. The Tariff Commission published detailed studies of the domestic industry and foreign competition: *Silk and Manufactures of Silk*, Schedule L, 1918; *Silk, Silk Yarns and Threads, and Silk Pile Fabrics*, 1921; *Broad-Silk Manufacture and the Tariff*, 1926; *Textile Imports and Exports, 1891–1927*, 1929; *Economic Analysis of Foreign Trade of the United States in Relation to the Tariff*, 1933; and *Annotated Tabular Survey* [1928–36]: *Japanese Trade Studies*, 1945. The National Recovery Administration, Division of Review, published *The Silk Textile Industry*, Evidence Study No. 37, mimeograph (Washington, D.C., 1935).

U.S. history is in Shichiro Matsui, *The History of the Silk Industry in the United States* (1927; reprint, New York: Howes, 1930). Books on silk manufacture include Leo Duran, *Raw Silk: A Practical Hand-Book for the Buyer* (New York: Silk Publishing, 1913, 1921) and Isabel B. Wingate, *Textile Fabrics and Their Selection*, 6th ed. (Englewood Cliffs, N.J.: Prentice Hall, 1970). By far the most useful periodicals are *Silk* (earlier *Silk Reporter*), 1877–1932, and *Silk and Rayon Digest* (monthly), 1933–37, which covered every aspect of the silk trade, including prices. For rayon, see William Haynes, *Cellulose: The Chemical that Grows* (Garden City, N.Y.: Doubleday, 1953).

Books and articles on women's outerwear fashions, often dedicated to one era or decade, are too numerous to list. They are readily found in library catalogs under headings of fashion, dress, or costume. A notable nineteenth-century work is National Council of Women of the United States, "Symposium on Women's Dress," *Arena*, September 1892, 488–506, Microfilm 05422, Roll 93, Library of Congress. Specialized works are Claudia B. Kidwell and Margaret C. Christman, *Suiting Everyone: The Democratization of Clothing in America* (Washington, D.C.: Smithsonian Institution Press, 1974); Elizabeth Ewing, *Dress and Undress: A History of Women's Underwear* (New York: Drama Book Specialists, 1978); and the special focus of Valerie Steele in *Fashion and Eroticism: Ideals of Feminine Beauty from the Victorian Era to the Jazz Age* (New York: Oxford University Press, 1985) and *Women of Fashion: Twentieth Century Designers* (New York: Rizzoli International, 1991).

The history of hosiery is in Milton N. Glass, *History of Hosiery, from the Piloi of Ancient Greece to the Nylons of Modern America* (New York: Fairchild Publications, 1955); Johannis Dirk de Haan, *The Full-Fashioned Hosiery Industry in the U.S.A.* (The Hague: Mouton, 1957). Technical works include *From Raw Silk to Silk Hosiery*, monograph (New York: Charles Chipman and Sons, 1920); Holeproof Hosiery Company, *Better Hosiery: The Story of Holeproof* (Milwaukee: Holeproof, 1924); Edward Max Schenke, *The Manufacture of Hosiery and Its Problems* (New York: National Association of Hosiery Manufacturers, 1935); Max C. Miller, *Knitting Full Fashioned Hosiery* (New York: McGraw-Hill, 1937); and Irene Miller, *Buying and Selling Hosiery* (New York: Fairchild Publications, 1949). Useful trade journals include the monthly *Hosiery Retailer*, later the *Hosiery Age*, 1922–31; the National Association of Hosiery Manufacturers' *Special News Letter*, a weekly published in Charlotte, North Carolina, 1923–66; the National Association of Hosiery Manufacturers' *Quarterly Statistical Bulletin of the Hosiery Industry*, New York, 1934–39, with excellent statistics; and *Underwear and Hosiery Review*, 1935–41 (East Stroudsberg, Pa.: Knit Goods Publishing), especially "The Story of Hosiery Fashions from 1918 to 1938," January 1938, 90–113; "Hosiery Saleswoman's Handbook," September 1938, 52–73; and "To Sell Hosiery Successfully . . . ," October 1939, 34–55.

2. Haru Matsukata Reischauer, *Samurai and Silk* (Cambridge: Belknap Press, 1986), 157.

3. Silk knitting terminology was confusing. Gauge indicated the number of needles on a knitting bar of standard length; high-gauge machines knitted finer yarns into sheer fabric. Denier indicated the weight of a standard length of yarn, so a low denier meant a sheer knit. It is simplest to describe stocking yarns by the number of silk threads twisted together, as in six thread, three thread, and so forth, the fewest threads yielding the finest yarns and sheerest hosiery.

4. *Japan Year Book*, 1937.

5. National Association of Hosiery Manufacturers, *Quarterly Statistical Bulletin of the Hosiery Industry*, 1939 Review.

6. Interdepartmental Committee on Silk, "The Economic Vulnerability of the United States in Raw Silk and Silk Waste," March 1941, Studies Prepared for the Office of the Administrator of Export Control (AEC), prepared by Ruth E. K. Peterson, Entry 44, Boxes 1–2, Records of the Tariff Commission, RG 81, NA (hereafter cited as Records of the Tariff Commission).

7. Ibid.

Chapter 4. Japan's Failed Quest for Dollars through Manufacturing

1. Japan Statistical Association, *Historical Statistics of Japan*, vol. 3.

2. Ibid.; Tariff Commission, "United States Imports for Consumption of the Principal Commodities Imported from Japan," mimeograph from typescript, Washington, July 1941; copy in New York Public Library, call no. TLH 1941, catalogue book 254-1-2, and Library of Congress call no. HF3127.A4, 1941b.

3. History and surveys of the Japanese cotton textile industry include Tariff Commission, *Information Survey on the Japanese Cotton Industry and Trade* (Washington, D.C.: GPO, 1921); Tariff Commission, *Cotton Cloth: Report to the President on the Differences in Costs of Production of Cotton Cloth in the United States and in the Principal Competing Country*, Report No. 112, 2nd ser. (Washington, D.C.: GPO, 1936); Tariff Commission, Records of Investigation Under Sections 332, 336, and 337 of the Tariff Act of 1930, 1929–66, Records of the Tariff Commission: Box 63, Cotton Cloth 1935–36; Box 60, Velveteens 1936; Box 58, Velveteens c. 1938; and Box 4, Long Staple Cotton 1933–34; Tariff Commission, *Cotton Textiles*, Special Industry Analysis No. 34, Japanese Trade Studies, prepared for the Foreign Economic Administration, September 1945, Boxes 1–2, Entry 43, Records of the Tariff Commission; Keizo Seki, *The Cotton Industry of Japan* (Tokyo: Japan Society for the Promotion of Science, 1956). Reports on Japan's imports of raw cotton include American Consul, Osaka, "Japan Cotton Situation—Review and Outlook," 17 August 1940, File 868.1101, Roll 14, State Department microfilm series LM-68, RG 59, NA; Interdepartmental Committee on Raw Textile Fibers and Cordage, "The Economic Vulnerability of Japan in Raw Cotton," 5 April 1941, Reports on the Economic Vulnerability of Japan, 1941–43, Entry 44, Boxes 1–2, Records of the Tariff Commission.

4. Commerce Department, Bureau of the Census, *Census of Manufactures: Cotton Manufactures*, 1919–35 (Washington, D.C.: GPO, 1920–36); *Census of Manufactures: Cotton Manufactures and Rayon and Silk Manufactures*, 1937, 1939; Commerce Department, *Foreign Commerce and Navigation of the United States*.

5. Tariff Commission, *Recent Developments in the Foreign Trade of Japan, Particularly in Relation to the Trade of the United States* (Washington, D.C.: GPO, 1936), 3–9, 14–19, 25–49, 54–71; Tariff Commission, *Cotton Cloth*; Osamu Ishii, "Cotton-Textile Diplomacy: Japan, Great Britain and the United States, 1930–1936" (Ph.D. diss., Rutgers University, 1977); Warren S. Hunsberger, *Japan and the United States in World Trade* (New York: Harper & Row, 1964), passim; Teijiro Uyeda, *The Recent Development of Japanese Foreign Trade with Special Reference to Restrictive Policies of Other Countries and Attempts at Trade Agreements* (Tokyo: Japanese Council Institute of Pacific Relations, 1936).

6. Tariff Commission, "United States Imports for Consumption of the Principal Commodities"; Tariff Commission, "United States Imports from Japan and Their Relation to the Defense Program and to the Economy of the Country," typescript, Washington, September 1941, copy in New York Public Library, call no. TLH 1941, catalogue books 254-1-2 and 254-2-2 (with annual details, 1935–40 and 1937–40, respectively); Japan Statistical Association, *Historical Statistics of Japan*, vol. 3; Interdepartmental Committee on Raw Textile Fibers and Cordage, "Economic Vulnerability of Japan in Raw Cotton."

7. Tariff Commission, *Computed Duties and Equivalent Ad Valorem Rates on Imports into the United States from Principal Countries, Calendar Years 1929, 1931, and 1935*, W.P.A. Statistical Project 265-31-7000, Richmond, Va., 1937.

8. C. R. Harler, *The Culture and Marketing of Tea* (London: Humphrey Milford, 1933); William H. Ukers, *All About Tea* (New York: Tea and Coffee Trade Journal, 1935); James Norwood

Pratt, *The Tea Lover's Treasury* (San Francisco: 101 Productions, 1982); Shin'ya Sugiyama, *Japan's Industrialization in the World Economy, 1859–1899: Export Trade and Overseas Competition* (Atlantic Heights, N.J.: Athlone Press, 1988), chap. 5.

9. Tariff Commission, "United States Imports for Consumption of the Principal Commodities" and "United States Imports from Japan"; Interdepartmental Committee on Chemicals, Fertilizers and Related Products, "The Economic Vulnerability of Japan in Menthol," "The Economic Vulnerability of Japan in Peppermint Oil," "The Economic Vulnerability of Japan in Agar-Agar," "The Economic Vulnerability of Japan in Natural Camphor, Crude and Refined," "The Economic Vulnerability of Japan in Pyrethrum Flowers," and "The Economic Vulnerability of Japan in Creosote Oil," April 1941, Reports on the Economic Vulnerability of Japan, 1941–43, Entry 44, Boxes 1–2, Records of the Tariff Commission.

10. Tariff Commission, *Computed Duties*; Commerce Department, Bureau of Foreign and Domestic Commerce, *Trade of the United States with Japan in 1938* (Washington, D.C.: GPO, April 1939); Tariff Commission, "United States Imports for Consumption of the Principal Commodities" and "United States Imports from Japan"; Interdepartmental Committee on Fishery Products, "The Economic Vulnerability of Japan in Fish, Shellfish and Fish Livers," 15 April 1941.

11. House, Committee on Ways and Means, *Hearings, Tariff Readjustment*, 70th Cong., 2nd sess., February 1929, testimony of hat makers, importers, and unions, 6359–98, February 1929 (hereafter cited as House, Committee on Ways and Means, *Hearings*); Tariff Commission, *Computed Duties*; Tariff Commission, "United States Imports for Consumption of the Principal Commodities" and "United States Imports from Japan"; Interdepartmental Committee on Miscellaneous Products, "The Economic Vulnerability of Japan in Miscellaneous Products," 25 April 1941.

12. Tariff Commission, *Cost of Production of Slide Fasteners and Parts Thereof; Report to the President, with Appendix Proclamation by the President*, Report No. 113, 2nd ser. (Washington, D.C.: GPO, 1936); Tariff Commission, *Computed Duties*; Tariff Commission, "United States Imports for Consumption of the Principal Commodities" and "United States Imports from Japan."

13. Tariff Commission, Planning Committee, recommendation re electric light bulbs, with related correspondence, 7 July 1933, Box 20, RG 81; Tariff Commission, *Computed Duties*; Tariff Commission, "United States Imports for Consumption of the Principal Commodities" and "United States Imports from Japan."

14. Sidney Ratner, *The Tariff in American History* (New York: Van Nostrand, 1972); Congress, *Tariff Act of 1930*, 71st Cong., 2nd sess., in *United States Statutes at Large*, vol. 46, ch. 497 (Washington, D.C.: GPO, 1930); Senate, *Economic Analysis of Foreign Trade of the United States in Relation to the Tariff*, Report of the Tariff Commission in Response to Senate Resolution 325, 72nd. Cong., 2nd sess., Doc. 180 (with large statistical compendium of tariff rates for 1929, 1931 and 1932, annotated) (Washington, D.C.: GPO, 1933); Tariff Commission, *Recent Developments in the Foreign Trade of Japan*.

15. Statements of U.S. pottery producers and of David Walker representing Morimura Brothers, importers, vol. 2, *Earths, Earthenware and Glassware*; and Statement of Japanese merchants forwarded by Secretary of State Stimson at oral request of Japanese ambassador to Senate committee, 25 July 1929, vol. 18, *Foreign Communications* (hereafter cited as Statement of Japanese merchants), both in Senate, Committee on Finance, *Hearings, Tariff Act of 1929*, 71st Cong., 1st sess., June 1929 (Washington, D.C.: GPO, 1929) (hereafter cited as Senate, Committee on Finance, *Hearings*); Tariff Commission, *Computed Duties*; Tariff Commission, "United States Imports for Consumption of the Principal Commodities" and "United States Imports from Japan"; Interdepartmental Committee on Nonmetallic Minerals and Manufactures, "The Economic Vulnerability of Japan in Pottery" and "The Economic Vulnerability of Japan in Glass and Glassware," April 1941.

16. Statement of B. W. Doyle representing Pyroxylin Plastics Manufacturers' Association, Senate, Committee on Finance, *Hearings*, vol. 1, *Chemicals, Oils and Paints* (hereafter cited as Senate, Statement of B. W. Doyle); Tariff Commission, *Synthetic Camphor: The Relation of Domestic Production of Synthetic Camphor to Domestic Consumption* (Washington, D.C.: GPO, 1935);

Interdepartmental Committee on Chemicals, Fertilizers and Related Products, "Economic Vulnerability of Japan in Natural Camphor, Crude and Refined."

17. John K. Winkler, *Five and Ten: The Fabulous Life of F. W. Woolworth* (1940; reprint, Freeport, N.Y.: Books for Libraries, 1970); Statement of Japanese merchants; Statement of A. Q. Smith of Woolworth, Senate, Committee on Finance, *Hearings*, vol. 15, *Sundries* (hereafter cited as Statement of A. Q. Smith).

18. Statement of B. W. Doyle representing the Pyroxylin Plastics Manufacturers Association and other interests including American Brush Manufacturers Association, House, Committee on Ways and Means, *Hearings*, vol. 1 (hereafter cited as House, Statement of B. W. Doyle), and Senate, Statement of B. W. Doyle, vol. 1; Statement of Japanese merchants; Tariff Commission, *Tooth and Other Toilet Brushes and Backs and Handles*, Report no. 81 (Washington, D.C.: GPO, 1934); Tariff Commission, *Computed Duties*; Tariff Commission, "United States Imports for Consumption of the Principal Commodities" and "United States Imports from Japan."

19. Tariff Commission, *Sun Goggles*, Report to the President, 14 December 1934, Box 11, Locator 6-24-5, Records of the Tariff Commission; *Sun Glasses or Sun Goggles*, Report 103, ser. 2 (Washington, D.C.: GPO, 1935); Senate and House, Statement of B. W. Doyle; Tariff Commission, *Computed Duties*; Tariff Commission, "United States Imports for Consumption of the Principal Commodities" and "United States Imports from Japan."

20. Statements of Fred W. Tauber, Celluloid Group of the National Council of Importers and Traders, House, Committee on Ways and Means, *Hearings*, vol. 1; A. C. Gilbert, Toy Manufacturers Association and the Doll Association, House, Committee on Ways and Means, *Hearings*, vol. 14, and Senate, Committee on Finance, *Hearings*, vol. 14; Briefs of the Toy Group of the National Council of American Importers and Traders, Toy Manufacturers of the U.S., and Doll Manufacturers Association, House, Committee on Ways and Means, *Hearings*, vol. 14; House and Senate, Statement of B. W. Doyle; Statement of A. Q. Smith; Statement of Japanese merchants; Tariff Commission, *Dolls and Toys of Pyroxylin Plastic*, Box 78, Files 1932–1935, Locator 6-20-1, Records of the Tariff Commission; Commerce Department, Bureau of the Census, *Census of Manufactures: Toys and Sporting and Athletic Goods*, 1935, 1939 (Washington, D.C.: GPO, 1937, 1940); Tariff Commission, *Toys*, Special Industry Analysis No. 8, Japanese Trade Studies, March 1945, Box 2, Entry 43, Records of the Tariff Commission; Tariff Commission, *Computed Duties*; Tariff Commission, "United States Imports for Consumption of the Principal Commodities" and "United States Imports from Japan."

Chapter 5. Anticipating Japan's Bankruptcy, 1937–1940

1. Herbert Feis, Economic Adviser, "Japan's Ultimate Foreign Exchange Resources," 20 September 1937, Box 21, File Japan Foreign Exchange Position, OASIA.

2. Titles and service years of most individuals are in Civil Service Commission, *Official Register of the United States*, 1937–41 (Washington, D.C.: GPO, 1937–41); and *Congressional Directory* (Washington, D.C.: GPO, 1937–41).

3. *New York Times*, 24 October 1937, 64; *Washington Post*, 30 January 1968, B3.

4. *New York Times*, 24 October 1937, 64, and 19 June 1946, 41.

5. *New York Times*, 19 June 1946, 41, 2 December 1952, 1, and 6 June 1980, D15; Wikipedia, http://en.wikipedia.org/wiki/Frank_Coe (accessed 30 May 2006). When Morgenthau retired in 1946, Secretary John W. Snyder cleared out most New Deal appointees. Coe left so fast to join White at the IMF that "high officials . . . did not know he had gone." The House Un-American Activities Committee investigated Coe in 1948 on charges of spying for Soviet Russia, and the Senate again in 1952. He invoked the Fifth Amendment against self incrimination and resigned his IMF post. In 1958 he moved to Red China with his family and served the Mao government. He died there in 1980. Harry Dexter White, who faced similar accusations, died in 1948 (chapter 8, note 42).

6. *American Men and Women of Science: The Social and Behavioral Sciences*, 12th ed. (New York: Jacques Cattell Press, 1973), vol. 1.

7. *New York Times*, 22 October 1938, 23.

8. *Dictionary of American Biography*, Supplement 5, 1951–55, American Council of Learned Societies, 1977, electronic document, Biography Resource Center, Library of Congress; *New York Times*, 2 April 1953, 27.

9. *Marquis Who's Who* (Chicago: Marquis Who's Who, 2006), electronic document, Biography Resource Center, Library of Congress. Knapp later received the Decorated Order of the Rising Sun for postwar work at the World Bank and State Department.

10. On line at http://www.ny.frb.org/aboutthefed/GHarrisonbio.html (accessed 10 June 2006).

11. *Dictionary of American Biography*, Supplement 10,1976–80, electronic document; *New York Times*, 29 February 1936, 23.

12. *New York Times*, 15 October 1931, 41, 9 January 1937, 24, 26 January 1937, 29, and 29 February 1936, 23; transcript of meeting, 17 December 1937, *Morgenthau Diaries*, Roll 28.

13. *New York Times*, 12 October 1941, 38; *Marquis Who's Who*, electronic document, Biography Resource Center, Library of Congress; *American Men and Women of Science: The Social and Behavioral Sciences*, vol. 1.

14. *American Men and Women of Science: The Social and Behavioral Sciences*, vol. 1.

15. *New York Times*, 8 May 1991, D22; *American Men and Women of Science: The Social and Behavioral Sciences*, vol. 1.

16. *New York Times*, 21 May 1991.

17. Many of the young experts went on to distinguished careers. Collado was named the first U.S. executive director of the International Monetary Fund, and ultimately became a senior executive of Standard Oil Company of New Jersey, now Exxon Mobil. Moore stayed on as research chief at the New York Fed, subsequently consulting for Latin American governments. Tamagna advised various U.S. agencies during the war; he ultimately rose to chief of international finance and policy at the Federal Reserve Board of Governors. At the Treasury, Kamarck became chief of the International Finance Division and after the war was the director of development of the World Bank.

18. *American National Biography Online*; Feis, *Road to Pearl Harbor*.

19. *Who Was Who in America*, vol. 3 (Chicago: Marquis Who's Who, 1966).

20. Accompanying letter from Col. J. M. Churchill, Acting Assistant COS, G-2, 6 April 1940, file 894.50/119-1/2, Roll 11, State Department microfilm series LM-68, RG 59, NA; meeting, 10 October 1940, *Morgenthau Diaries*, vol. 2, Roll 26; Pehle: *New York Times*, 19 June 1946, 41.

21. E. F. Lamb to Knoke, Japan: International Assets, 28 December 1938, File Japan International Position 1937–46, Box 50, International Subject Files, 1907 to 1974, International Finance Division and predecessors 1907–1974, Records of the Federal Reserve Board, RG 82, NA (hereafter cited as FRB).

22. O. E. Moore, "The Effect of the War with China," 18 August 1939, Box 50, File Japan International Position 1937–46, FRB.

23. G. F. Luthringer, "Japanese Gold and Foreign Exchange Resources at the End of 1939," 23 January 1940, File 894.51, Roll 11, State Department microfilm series LM-68, RG 59, NA; W. H. Rozell to Knoke, Japanese Dollar Expenditures, 24 February 1940, Box 50, File Japan International Position 1937–46, FRB.

24. Norman E. Towson, "The Economic Position of Japan: Current Estimate," 26 March 1940; and Stanley K. Hornbeck, Adviser on Political Relations, 30 April 1940, both in File 894.50-119-1/2, Roll 11, State Department microfilm LM-68, RG 59, NA.

25. Moore, "Effect of the War with China."

26. Haas to Morgenthau, Japan's Foreign Exchange Resources, 13 December 1937; Lamb to Knoke, Japan: International Assets, 28 December 1938; Towson, "Economic Position of Japan," 26 March 1940.

27. FDR to the Acting Secretary of the Treasury, 5 August 1939, OASIA; BB (probably Bernard Bernstein), Memorandum to the President, 5 August 1939, Box 21, File Japan Gold and Silver, OASIA.

28. Edward S. Miller, "Japan's Other Victory: Overseas Financing of the War," in *The Russo-Japanese War in Global Perspective: World War Zero*, edited by John W. Steinberg, Bruce W. Men-

ning, David Schimmelpenninck van der Oye, David Wolff, and Shinji Yokote (Leiden, Netherlands: Brill, 2005), 466–78.

29. Moulton with Ko, *Japan*, appendix; unsigned, Some Pertinent Data on Restrictions on Japanese Trade, 1937, Box 21, File Japanese Foreign Funds Control Program, OASIA.

30. Laurence Phillips Dowd, "Japanese Foreign Exchange Policy 1930–1940" (Ph.D. diss., University of Michigan, 1952), chaps. 2–3.

31. Unsigned, Japan: Our Gold Import Point, Japan: Our Gold Export Point, 26 May 1933, Box 50, File International Japan Gold 1928–1954, FRB.

32. Gold and silver were and are traded in troy ounces about 10 percent heavier than the familiar avoirdupois ounces. There are 12 troy ounces in a troy pound and 32.15 per kilogram.

33. Haas to Morgenthau, Japan's Foreign Exchange Resources, 13 December 1937; E.G. Collado to Knoke, Japanese Gold Stocks, 16 December 1937, Box 50, File International Japan Gold 1928–1954, FRB.

34. O. E. Moore to Knoke, Japanese Gold Production and Reserves, 29 February 1940, Box 50, File International Japan Gold 1928–1954, FRB.

35. White (signed by Haas) to Morgenthau, Restricting Areas in Which Japan Could Sell Her Gold, 9 October 1937, Box 21, File Japan Gold and Silver, OASIA; W. H. Rozell and F. M. Tamagna to Knoke, Japan's Gold and Dollar Assets, 31 March 1941, Box 50, File International Japan Gold 1928–1954, FRB.

36. Rozell, Yokohama Specie Bank Reports, 28 August 1940, Box 50, File Japan Banking—Yokohama Specie Bank, FRB (hereafter cited as Yokohama Specie Bank Reports).

37. Allan Sproul, memorandum, 23 June 1937, Box 21, File Japan Gold and Silver, OASIA.

38. Commerce Department, Bureau of Foreign and Domestic Commerce, *The Balance of International Payments of the United States in 1937* (Washington, D.C.: GPO, 1938); Haas to Morgenthau, Japan's Foreign Exchange Resources, 13 December 1937; E. G. Collado to Knoke, Japanese Exchange Balances—Japan's Present International Position, 20 October 1937; FT (prob. Frank T. Tamagna), Japan's International Position, 28 August 1940, Box 50, File Japan International Position 1937–46, FRB; Moore to Knoke, Japanese Gold Production and Reserves, 29 February 1940; unsigned, Survey of the Gold Fund Special Account, August 1945, and J. Tenenbaum to Friedman, Japanese Gold Production and Operation of Gold Fund Special Account, 2 January 1946, Box 21, File Japan Gold and Silver, OASIA.

39. Unsigned, Relations with Foreign Banks, 20 January 1936, Box 69, File International Foreign Accounts General 1927–1954 (1), FRB; unsigned table, Japan Official Gold Stocks, 29 September 1938, Box 50, File Japan General, FRB; H. D. White to Morgenthau, Recent Changes in Japan's Foreign Exchange Resources, 28 October 1938, Box 21, File Japan Foreign Exchange Position, OASIA; Lamb to Knoke, Japan: International Assets, 28 December 1938; Luthringer, "Japanese Gold and Foreign Exchange Resources"; unsigned table, Net Imports of Gold to the United States from Japan, c. 13 January 1942, Box 50, File Japan International Gold 1928–1954, FRB; Commerce Department, *United States in the World Economy*, charts.

40. Towson, "Economic Position of Japan," 26 March 1940; A. M. Kamarck to White, Preliminary Memorandum on Japanese Foreign Exchange Resources, 31 October 1940, Box 21, File Japan Foreign Exchange Position, OASIA.

41. Rozell to Knoke, Japanese Dollar Expenditures, 24 February 1940.

42. Haas to Morgenthau, Japan's Foreign Exchange Resources, 13 December 1937; unsigned table, Japan Official Gold Stocks, 29 September 1938; Tamagna, Japan's International Position, 28 August 1940.

43. Feis, "Japan's Ultimate Foreign Exchange Resources"; unsigned table, Japan Official Gold Stocks, 29 September 1938; Lamb to Knoke, Japan: International Assets, 28 December 1938; P. S. Brown to White, Japan's Stock of Gold, 19 January 1940; unsigned, Gold Shipments, 29 October 1940; WHT (prob. W. H. Taylor), Japan: Gold Production in Ounces by Areas and Total Value, 31 January 1941, File Japan Gold and Silver; and Tenenbaum to Friedman, Japanese Gold Production and Operation, 2 January 1946, all in Box 21, OASIA; Moore to Knoke, Japanese Gold Production and Reserves, 29 February 1940; Commerce Department, Bureau of Domestic and

Foreign Commerce, *Manchurian Gold Mining Experiences Poor Year in 1939* (Washington, D.C.: GPO, 4 March 1940); "Gold Production Subsidy Increased," *Far Eastern Financial Notes* 2, nos. 5 (March 1940) and 11 (June 1940); Tamagna to Knoke, Japan's Undisclosed Gold Stock, 10 September 1940, File International Japan Gold; and J. B. Knapp, "Japanese Gold Production," 13 February 1941, File International Japan Gold 1928–54, both in Box 50, FRB; Supreme Commander Allied Powers (SCAP), Natural Resources Section, *Gold and Silver in Japan*, Report No. 128, prepared by Robert Y. Grant, Tokyo, June 1950.

44. P. S. Brown to White, Japan's Production and Supply of Gold in 1937, c. January 1938, Box 21, File Japan Gold and Silver, OASIA.

45. Moore to Knoke, Japanese Gold Production and Reserves, 29 February 1940; unsigned, Gold Shipments, 29 October 1940, and U.S. Embassy, Tokyo, to Secretary of State, No. 5416, Japan's Gold Position, 28 February 1941, both in File 894.51/714, Roll 14, State Department microfilm series LM-68, RG 59, NA; SCAP, *Gold and Silver in Japan*, 112.

46. Moore to Knoke, Japanese Gold Production and Reserves, 29 February 1940.

47. Brown to White, Japan's Production and Supply of Gold in 1937, c. January 1938; Brown to White, Japan's Stock of Gold 19, January 1940; Moore to Knoke, Japanese Gold Production and Reserves, 29 February 1940; Commerce Department, *Manchurian Gold Mining*; P. Mihalik to Knoke, Japanese Gold Reserves, 7 May 1940, Box 50, File International Japan Gold 1928–1954, FRB; Tamagna to Knoke, Japan's Undisclosed Gold Stock, 10 September 1940; George A. Nakinson, First Secretary of U.S. Embassy, Tokyo, to Secretary of State, Japan's Gold Position, 22 November 1940, Box 21, File Japan Gold and Silver, OASIA; W. H. Taylor to White, Japanese Foreign Exchange Reserves, 7 February 1941, Box 21, File Japan Foreign Exchange Position, OASIA.

48. Brown to White, Japan's Production and Supply of Gold in 1937, c. January 1938; Moore to Knoke, Japanese Gold Production and Reserves, 29 February 1940; Commerce Department, *Manchurian Gold Mining*; unsigned, Gold Shipments, 29 October 1940.

49. Brown to White, Japan's Production and Supply of Gold in 1937, c. January 1938; Moore to Knoke, Japanese Gold Production and Reserves, 29 February 1940.

50. Knapp, "Japanese Gold Production"; SCAP, *Gold and Silver in Japan*, 23.

51. SCAP, *Gold and Silver in Japan*, tables 7 and 8.

52. Taylor to White, Japanese Foreign Exchange Resources, 7 February 1941; H. D. White to Morgenthau, Japanese Foreign Exchange Resources, 7 February 1941, Box 21, File Japan Foreign Exchange Position, OASIA.

53. Tenenbaum to Friedman, Japanese Gold Production and Operation, 2 January 1946; SCAP, *Gold and Silver in Japan*.

54. Feis, "Japan's Ultimate Foreign Exchange Resources"; E. G. Collado to Knoke, Japan: Silver Statistics, 28 January 1938, Box 50, File Japan General 1932–1941, FRB; Ernest A. Tuppar, Division of Foreign Trade Statistics, Department of Commerce to Frank Dietrich, Treasury Department, 29 January 1938, Box 21, File Japan Gold and Silver, OASIA; E. G. Collado to Knoke, Japan: Increase in Fiduciary Note Issue Limit, Withdrawal of Subsidiary Silver Coin, 25 February 1938, Box 50, File Japan General 1922–1941, FRB; Moore, "Effect of the War with China"; SCAP, *Gold and Silver in Japan*.

55. Haas to Morgenthau, Japan's Foreign Exchange Resources, 13 December 1937; Brown to White, Japan's Production and Supply of Gold in 1937, c. January 1938; Lamb to Knoke, Japan: International Assets, 28 December 1938; Brown to White, Japan's Stock of Gold, 19 January 1940; Luthringer, "Japanese Gold and Foreign Exchange Resources"; Moore to Knoke, Japanese Gold Production and Reserves, 29 February 1940; Tamagna to Knoke, Japan's Undisclosed Gold Stock, 10 September 1940; U.S. Embassy, Tokyo, to Secretary of State, Japan's Gold Position, 28 February 1941; Tenenbaum to Friedman, Japanese Gold Production and Operation, 2 January 1946.

56. Moore to Knoke, Japanese Gold Production and Reserves, 29 February 1940.

57. Brown to White, Japan's Stock of Gold, 19 January 1940.

58. Unsigned, Japan Foreign-Currency Holdings Reported (Trans-Pacific, 14 February 1935), Box 21, File Japan Foreign Exchange Position, OASIA; Feis, "Japan's Ultimate Foreign Exchange

Resources"; Collado to Knoke, Japanese Exchange Balances, 20 October 1937; unsigned (probably H. D. White), "How Effective Could the 'Quarantine' Be Made," c. autumn 1937, Box 21, File Japan Foreign Funds Control Program, OASIA; Haas to Morgenthau, Japan's Foreign Exchange Resources, 13 December 1937; H. D. White and A. Lochead, "Estimate of Japanese Assets in the United States as of 15 December 1937," n.d., *Morgenthau Diaries*, Roll 28; unsigned, Some Pertinent Data on Restrictions on Japanese Trade; Lamb to Knoke, Japan: International Assets, 28 December 1938; W. H. Rozell to Knoke, Japanese Investment in the United States and American Investments in Japan, 11 September 1940, Box 50, File Japan General 1922–1941, FRB; W. H. Rozell to Knoke, Japanese Investments in the United States, 3 February 1941, Box 94, File Loans and Investments—Foreign Deposits in U.S. 1926–41 (1), FRB; Taylor to White, Japanese Foreign Exchange Reserves, 7 February 1941; White to Morgenthau, Japan's Foreign Exchange Position, 25 February 1941, Box 2, File Japan's Foreign Exchange Position, OASIA.

59. Great Britain, for example, requisitioned its subjects' U.S. and Canadian stocks and bonds to finance munitions purchases before the advent of Lend-Lease aid.

60. Collado to Knoke, Japanese Exchange Balances, 20 October 1937; Haas to Morgenthau, Japan's Foreign Exchange Resources, 13 December 1937; unsigned, Some Pertinent Data on Restrictions on Japanese Trade; Lamb to Knoke, Japan: International Assets, 28 December 1938.

61. Collado to Knoke, Japanese Exchange Balances, 20 October 1937; White and Lochead, "Estimate of Japanese Assets"; Rozell to Knoke, Japanese Investments in the United States, 3 February 1941; Treasury Department, *Census of Foreign-Owned Assets in the United States* (Washington, D.C.: GPO, 1945), 15ff, 63–83; Office of Alien Property Custodian, *Report for the Period March 11, 1942 to June 30, 1943* (Washington, D.C.: GPO, 1943); Office of Alien Property Custodian, *Report for the Fiscal Year Ending June 30, 1944* (Washington, D.C.: GPO, 1944); Office of Alien Property Custodian, *Report for the Fiscal Year Ending June 30, 1946* (Washington, D.C.: GPO, 1946).

62. After the war the Specie Bank reported sterling deposits worth only $3 million.

63. Even restraints on buying of Japanese silver (which was of a purity desirable for photographic film) by U.S. refineries, as suggested by Senator Key Pittman, might undermine faith in gold, it was believed. R. S. Brown to White, Should We Continue to Purchase Japanese Silver? 17 January 1940, and F. Dietrich to Silver File, 23 January 1940, both in Box 21, OASIA.

64. White (signed by Haas) to Morgenthau, Restricting Areas, 9 October 1937, FDR to the Acting Secretary of the Treasury, 5 August 1939; Bernstein, Memorandum to the President, 5 August 1939; Brown to White, Should We Continue to Purchase Japanese Silver? 17 January 1940; Dietrich to Silver File, 23 January 1940; White to Morgenthau, Senator Pittman's letter on Treasury purchases of silver from Japan, 25 January 1940, Box 21, File Japan Gold and Silver, OASIA.

65. W. H. Rozell to McKeon, Yokohama Specie Bank Reports, 3 August 1940, Box 50, File Japan Banking—Yokohama Specie Bank, FRB.

Chapter 6. Birth of an Embargo Strategy: The Alternative to Bankrupting Japan

1. Senate, Joint Resolution 173, 74th Cong., 1st sess., 31 August 1935, in *United States Statutes at Large*, vol. 49, pt. 1 (Washington, D.C.: GPO, 1936), 1081–85; Joseph C. Green, Executive Secretary, Minutes of the Meeting of the National Munitions Control Board, 24 September 1935; President of the United States, Proclamation: Enumeration of Arms, Ammunition, and Implements of War, 25 September 1935, File National Munitions Control Board Designation, Box 82, Central Files 1917–1956, OASIA; President of the United States, Proclamation, 5 October 1935, in *American Journal of International Law* 30, no. 1, Supplement: Official Documents (January 1936): 63–65; Stuart L. Weiss, "American Foreign Policy and Presidential Power: The Neutrality Act of 1935," *Journal of Politics* 30, no. 3 (August 1968): 672–95.

2. Senate, Joint Resolution 51, 75th Cong., 1st sess., 1 May 1937, in *United States Statutes at Large*, vol. 50, pt. 1 (Washington, D.C.: GPO, 1937), 121–28; James Wilford Garner, "The United States Neutrality Act of 1937," *American Journal of International Law* 31, no. 3 (July 1937): 385–97; Frederick C. Adams, "The Road to Pearl Harbor: A Reexamination of American

Far Eastern Policy, July 1937–December 1938," *Journal of American History* 58, no. 1 (June 1971): 73–92; Michael A. Barnhart, *Japan Prepares for Total War: The Search for Economic Security, 1919–1941* (Ithaca, N.Y.: Cornell University Press, 1987), 119–22; Feis, *Road to Pearl Harbor*, 41.

3. Correspondence among Chinese Ambassador Want, Secretary of State Hull, and U.S. Ambassador to Japan Joseph C. Grew, 1–12 June 1938; memoranda by Joseph C. Green, Chief of the Office of Arms and Munitions Control, and Charles W. Yost, Assistant Chief, to Hull, 13–26 June 1938, 618–22, and State Department to British Embassy, 9 November 1938, 625–26, all in State Department, *Foreign Relations of the United States: Diplomatic Papers* (Washington, D.C.: GPO, 1938) (hereafter cited as *FRUS*); Acting Secretary of State, statement, 3 June 1938; Yost to 148 Persons and Companies Manufacturing Airplane Parts, 1 June 1938, *FRUS*; State Department, Office of Research and Intelligence, D.C. *Papers Relating to the Foreign Relations of the United States and Japan, 1931–41* (Washington, D.C.: GPO, 1943) (hereafter cited as *FRUS Japan*), 2:201–2; Benjamin J. Williams, "The Coming of Economic Sanctions in American Practice," *American Journal of International Law* 37, no. 3 (July 1943): 388–89; Feis, *Road to Pearl Harbor*, 19n3, 44n7; Jerome B. Cohen, *Japan's Economy in War and Reconstruction*, International Secretariat of the Institute of Pacific Relations (Minneapolis: University of Minnesota Press, 1949). Aircraft statistics in Commerce Department, *Foreign Commerce and Navigation of the United States*, 1936–42.

4. Treaty and protocol signed at Washington on 21 February 1911 and related ratifications, in Charles I. Bevans, *Treaties and Other International Agreements of the United Sates of America 1776–1949*, Department of State Publication 8615 (Washington, D.C.: GPO, 1972), 9:416–22; T. A., Division of Trade Agreements to Hull, Possible Termination of Commercial Treaty with Japan, 30 July 1938; George C. Sprague, attorney, to Osaka Syosen Kaisha, Treaty of Commerce and Navigation of 1911 Between Japan and the United States, 15 August 1939, File 894.512/53, RG 59, NA; Correspondence among Hull, Grew, Eugene H. Doorman, Henry Grady, Japanese Ambassador Kensuke Horinouchi, and others, 7 July 1939–1 September 1940, *FRUS, The Far East*, 1939, 3:560–635, 1940, 4:630–636.

5. FDR, address recommending revision of the Neutrality Law, 21 September 1939, online at http://www.ibiblio.org/pha/7-2-188/188-14.html (accessed 6 October 2002), Paper 14; Barnhart, *Japan Prepares*, 21, 41; Feis, *Road to Pearl Harbor*, 40–45; *Encyclopaedia Britannica* 1945, 22:848–49.

6. State Department, press release, 15 December 1939, and Hull to Horinouchi, 6 and 27 January 1940, both in *FRUS Japan* 2:202–6; Barnhart, *Japan Prepares*, 119–21, 152, 179–85; Feis, *Road to Pearl Harbor*, 44n7.

7. Interdepartmental Committee on Non-Ferrous Metals and Manufactures, study prepared for the Office of the Administrator of Export Control, Report No. IO 4-2, *Industrial Objectives, Japan, Aluminum and Magnesium*, 25 Aug 1941; Foreign Economic Administration, Board of Economic Warfare, Enemy Branch, *Preliminary Survey of Japanese Aluminum*, 18 Oct 1942; Office of Strategic Services (OSS), Research and Analysis Branch, R. and A. No. 2155, *Japanese Aluminum Production and Fabrication*, 31 May 1944; L. C. Raymond, Tariff Commission, *Special Industry Analysis No. 2, Aluminum*, prepared for the Liberated Areas Branch, FEA, January 1945; SCAP, General Headquarters, Economic and Scientific Section, Statistics and Research Division, *The Aluminum Industry of Japan*, Special Report No. 9, 3 April 1946, File 407-100 Aluminum, Boxes 21–23; War Department, Headquarters, Army Service Forces, *Civil Affairs Handbook: Japan: Section 6, Natural Resources*, Manual M-354-6, 22 July 1944, File 401-200 (A), Box 10, all in ONI, Japan Monographs 1939–47, RG 38, NA; Commerce Department, *Foreign Commerce and Navigation of the United States*, 1936–42.

8. Interdepartmental Committee on Industrial Objectives, "Japan, Aluminum and Magnesium," 25 Aug 1941; Cohen, *Japan's Economy*, 158–60.

9. Robert H. Ridgway and H. W. Davis, "Molybdenum, Tungsten, and Vanadium," in Interior Department, Bureau of Mines, *Minerals Yearbook*, annual (Washington, D.C.: GPO, 1939–42); Commerce Department, *Foreign Commerce and Navigation of the United States*, 1936–42.

10. State Department, press release, 20 December 1939, Horinouchi to Hull, and Hull to Horinouchi, memo, 6 January 1940, all in *FRUS Japan* 2:203–7; *Encyclopaedia Britannica* 15:827;

American Chemical Society, "The Houdry Process," Washington, 1999, online at http://acsweb-content.acs.org/landmarks/landmarks/hdr/index.html (accessed 2 November 2002); Bruce A. Finlayson, University of Washington, "The Fluidized Bed Reactor Page," on line at http://faculty.washington.edu.fanlayso/Fluidized_Bed/FBR_Intro/history_fbr.htm (accessed 3 November 2002); Barnhart, *Japan Prepares*, 180–82. The holy grail was a true antiknock fuel of 100 octane. British production arrived in time to win the Battle of Britain, but U.S. production of 100-octane fuel did not come on line until May 1942.

11. Robert F. Maddox, "Senator Harley M. Kilgore and Japan's World War II Business Practices," *West Virginia History* 55 (1996): 127–142, on line at http://www.wvculture.org/history/journal_wvh/wvh55-6.html (accessed 2 November 2002).

Chapter 7. Export Controls, 1940 to Mid-1941

1. War Department Industrial College of the Armed Forces, "History," on line at http://www.ndu.edu/ICAF/history/index.htm (accessed 25 October 2006); *Industrial Mobilization for War: History of the War Production Board and Predecessor Agencies, 1940–1945* (New York: Greenwood Press, 1969), 1:18–21, 68–70; William L. Langer and S. Everett Gleason, *The Undeclared War, 1949–1941* (New York: Harper and Brothers, 1953), 180–90.

2. Congress, *An Act to Expedite the Strengthening of the National Defense*, H.R. 9850, 76th Cong., 3rd sess., 2 July 1940, in *Public Laws of the United States of America*, vol. 49, pt. 1 (Washington, D.C.: GPO, 1941), 712–14.

3. Senate, Joint Resolution 173, 1081–85; Green: *Washington Post*, 11 August 1931, 8, and 19 September 1934, 1; *New York Times*, 18 July 1935, 4, 18 August 1935, 7, 22 September 1935, 1, and 14 January 1940, 34; Yost: *New York Times*, 22 September 1935, 1, and 23 May 1981, 21. Yost went on to a distinguished postwar career as ambassador to three Third World countries, and in 1969–71 as the American delegate to the United Nations.

4. Feis, *Road to Pearl Harbor*, 74; FEA, Records Analysis Division, "Pre-Pearl Harbor Organization," File FEA Administrative History Pearl Harbor Organization, Box 13, Entry 145, RG 169, NA.

5. *National Cyclopedia of American Biography*, vol. F, *1939–1942* (New York: James T. White, 1942), 514–15; *Who Was Who in America* 3:467; *New York Times*, 25 November 1968, 47; extract from War Department, Industrial College of the Armed Forces, "History."

6. *Industrial Mobilization for War* 1:71–73; NARA, *Federal Records of World War II* (Washington, D.C.: GPO, 1950), 1:149.

7. State Department, "Application for License to Export Articles and Materials (Other than Arms, Ammunition, and Implements of War and Tin-Plate Scrap) Designated by the President as Necessary to the National Defense Pursuant to Section 6 of the Act of Congress Approved July 2, 1940," Box 4863, File Frozen Credits 1940–44, RG 59, NA.

8. Roosevelt, Proclamation 2413 with Regulation, 2 July 1940; Proclamation 2417 with Regulations, 26 July 1940; Proclamation 2433, 12 September 1940; Proclamation 2449, 10 December 1940; Proclamation 2451, 20 December 1940; Proclamation 2453 and EO 8631,10 January 1941; Proclamation 2456 and EO 8668, 4 February 1941; Proclamation 2461 and EO 8594, 25 February 1941; Proclamation 2464 and 2465, EO 8702 and 8703, 4 March 1941; Proclamation 2468, 27 March 1941; Proclamation 2476, 14 April 1941; and Proclamation 2488, 28 May 1941, all in *FRUS Japan* 2:211–18. Press releases are also included for most items.

9. Japanese Embassy to U.S. Department of State, 3 August 1940; Department of State to Japanese Embassy, 6 August 1940; Roosevelt, Proclamation 2433, 12 September 1940, all in *FRUS Japan* 2:218–20; Feis, *Road to Pearl Harbor*, 93; Irvine H. Anderson Jr., "The 1941 *De Facto* Embargo Oil of Japan: A Bureaucratic Reflex," *Pacific Historical Review*, May 1975, 207–12; Barnhart, *Japan Prepares*, 190–91; Roland H. Worth Jr., *No Choice but War: The United States Embargo Against Japan and the Eruption of War in the Pacific* (Jefferson, N.C.: McFarland, 1995), 30–33.

10. In the 1960s and 1970s the world steel industry converted again, to basic oxygen and electric furnace processes.

11. Tariff Commission, *Iron and Steel: A Survey of the Iron and Steel Industries and International Trade of the Principal Producing and Trading Countries . . .*, Report No. 128, 2nd ser. (Washington, D.C.: GPO, 1938), 61–63, 75–77, 125–139, 279–300, 381–93; Interior Department, *Minerals Yearbook*, 1932–42, chapters on iron and steel; Interior Department, Bureau of Mines, *Mineral Resources of Japan*, Foreign Minerals Survey vol. 2, no. 5 (Washington, D.C.: GPO, October 1945); Interdepartmental Committee on Iron and Steel, "The Economic Vulnerability of Japan in Iron, Steel and Ferro-Alloys," Reports on the Economic Vulnerability of Japan, 1941–43, Entry 44, Boxes 1–2, Records of the Tariff Commission; War Department, *Civil Affairs Handbook: Japan*; Office of Intelligence Coordination and Liaison (OCL), *The Place of Foreign Trade in the Economy of Japan: An Analysis in Two Volumes of the External Trade of Japan Proper between 1930 and 1943 Focusing on Possible or Probable Post-war Developments*, Intelligence Research Report OCL-2815 (Washington, D.C.: GPO, 1943–46), vol.1, pt. 2, 234–63; U.S. Strategic Bombing Survey (USSBS), Basic Materials Division, *Coal and Metals in Japan's War Economy*, Report No. 36 (Washington, D.C.: GPO, 1946); Cohen, *Japan's Economy*, 118–19, 48.

12. Equivalent calculations by the author.

13. Senate, Subcommittee of the Committee on Military Affairs, *Hearings: A Bill to Provide for the Protection and Preservation of Domestic Sources of Scrap and Steel*. 75th Cong., 3rd sess., 4 April 1938 (Washington, D.C.: GPO, 1938), 77–179; Interior Department, Bureau of Mines, *Consumption of Ferrous Scrap and Pig Iron in the United States*, Reports of Investigation 3329 (1935), 3366 (1936), 3420 (1937–38) (Washington, D.C.: GPO, 1935–38); thereafter scrap survey in chapters on iron and steel in Interior Department, *Minerals Yearbook*; Jack Gutstadt, *Scrap Iron and Steel: An Outline of the Many Ramifications and Developments of a Major Industry Together with Statistics, Formulas, and Other Similar Data* (Chicago: Jack Gutstadt, 1939); Edwin Charles Barringer, *The Story of Scrap* (Washington, D.C.: Institute of Scrap Iron and Steel, 1954). Exports by U.S., regional, and total are in Commerce Department, *Foreign Commerce and Navigation of the United States*, 1936–42.

14. Feis, *Road to Pearl Harbor*, 11–12.

15. Barnhart, *Japan Prepares*, 189.

16. Ibid, 91; Feis, *Road to Pearl Harbor*, 49, 92–94.

17. Roosevelt, Proclamation 2417 with Regulations, 26 July 1940, *FRUS Japan*, 216–17; Jonathan G. Utley, *Going to War with Japan, 1937–1941* (Knoxville: University of Tennessee Press, 1985), 105–7; Feis, *Road to Pearl Harbor*, 101–8; Yost to Maxwell, 10 September 1940, Boxes 271–72, File 400.3295, Entry 98, FEA, Office of the Administrator of Export Control, Central File (Area) "Japan," RG 169, NA.

18. White House, press release, 26 September 1940; Regulations Governing Exports, 30 September 1940; Embassy of Japan to Department of State, 7 October 1940; Japanese Ambassador to Secretary of State, 8 October; Secretary of State, memorandum, 8 October 1940; and State to Japanese Embassy, 23 October 1940, all in *FRUS Japan* 2:223–29. The Tripartite Treaty is available online at http://www.yale.edu/lawweb/avalon/wwii/triparti.htm.

19. Yost to Maxwell, 10 September 1940; Roosevelt, Proclamation No. 2449, EO 8607, State Department press release, 10 December; Embassy of Japan to Department of State, 21 December 1940; Department of State to Japanese Embassy, 10 January 1941, *FRUS Japan* 2:232–38; Barnhart, *Japan Prepares*, 190–91; Feis, *Road to Pearl Harbor*, chap. 14. In 1915 Japan forced some of its "Twenty-One Demands" on China by a treaty that would have reduced it to an economic colony. U.S. protests of violation of the Open Door free trade policy were unavailing. Meanwhile, Japan's shiplines were profitably taking over Pacific trade routes abandoned by the warring powers, and its shipyards were booming with orders for ships assembled from imported American steel plates. When the United States entered the war in 1917 it restricted steel exports, a severe blow to Japan. Viscount Kikujiro Ishii came to Washington to confer with Secretary of State Robert Lansing. The Lansing-Ishii Notes of 2 November 1917 reaffirmed the Open Door but conceded Japan's "special interests" in China due to "propinquity." The United States resumed steel shipments, for which Japan agreed to sell or lease to it an equivalent tonnage of ships. Japan delivered only a handful of ships before the Armistice. The Lansing-Ishii agreement was withdrawn in 1923. Burton F. Beers,

Vain Endeavor: Robert Lansing's Attempts to End the American-Japanese Rivalry (Durham, N.C.: Duke University Press, 1962); William J. Williams, "American Steel and Japanese Ships: Transpacific Trade Disputes During World War I," unpublished paper, Colorado Springs, Colo., in author's files.

20. Interior Department, *Minerals Yearbook*; Interdepartmental Committee on Iron and Steel, "Economic Vulnerability of Japan in Iron, Steel and Ferro-Alloys"; OCL, *Place of Foreign Trade*, vol. 1, pt. 2, 234–63; USSBS, *Coal and Metals*; Barnhart, *Japan Prepares*, 239, 255–58, 263–70; James William Morley, ed., *The Final Confrontation: Japan's Negotiations with the United States, 1941* (New York: Columbia University Press, 1994), 239, 255–58, 263–70.

21. Commerce Department, *Foreign Commerce and Navigation of the United States*, 1936–42; *An Act . . .* , White House Press Release, 2 July 1940, in President of the United States, Press Releases, mimeograph, Washington, 1933, call no. E740.5.A3, Library of Congress; A Review of Licenses for Tools to Japan with View of Recommending Revocation, 1 October 1940; reports on machine tool loadings and licenses, 10 and 11 October 1940, File 164 Japan, Box 271; Machinery, Summary of Information, 7 April 1941, File 412.3 Japan, Box 272, Central File (Area) "Japan," all in Office of the Administrator of Export Control, RG 169, NA; Assistant Secretary of State Berle, memorandum, 19 and 30 November; Secretary of State to Morishima, 9 and 17 December 1940, *FRUS Japan* 2:211–16, 229–32; Barnhart, *Japan Prepares*, 184–85.

22. Roosevelt, Proclamation 2453, EO 8631, 10 January; Proclamation 2456, EO 8669, 4 February; Proclamation 2461, EO 8693, 25 February; Proclamations 2463–2465, EOs 8702–8703, 4 March; Proclamation 2468, 27 March; Proclamation 2476, 14 April; Proclamation 2488, State Department press release, 28 May 1941; State Department, *Bulletin* 4:84, 1 February 1941, 128; and *Bulletin* 4:85, 8 February 1941, 158, all in *FRUS Japan* 2:239–63. Various agencies, recommendations for licensing, 13 articles, 12 February 1941; phosphates, 20 and 31 March 1941, 8 April 1941; cotton linters, 3 April 1941; and toluol and specialty metals, 23 April 1941, all in Files 164 Japan and 411.820 Japan, Box 271, Central File (Area) "Japan," Office of the Administrator of Export Control, RG 169, NA.

23. Maxwell to Acheson, with memorandum criticism of export licensing arrangements, 21 April 1941, File 811.20(d) Regulations/4987, Box 2683; Leonard H. Price, Division of Controls, to Green, 9 July 1941, Box 3677, File 811.20(d) Regulations/3909, RG 59, NA; FEA, "Pre-Pearl Harbor Organization"; Feis, *Road to Pearl Harbor*, 142.

24. FEA, "Pre-Pearl Harbor Organization."

25. Major T. S. Riggs, Assistant to Administrator of Export Control, to Acheson, Extent of Control Report, 23 July 1941, Box 3677, File 811.20(d) Regulations/3874, RG 59, NA; Major John E. Russell, Chief, Programs Section, Percentage of United States Exports Now Under Control, 29 August 1941, File Planning Division, Box 77, Entry 97, Central File, Office of the Administrator of Export Control RG 169, NA.

Chapter 8. The Japanese Financial Fraud in New York

1. See chapter 2.

2. "Yokohama Specie Bank," *Japan: An Illustrated Encyclopedia* (Tokyo: Kodansha, 1993).

3. Rozell to McKeon, Yokohama Specie Bank's Reports, 3 August 1940, Box 50, File Japan Banking-Yokohama Specie Bank, FRB.

4. McKeon, untitled memorandum, 7 August 1940, Box 20, File Japan Banks and Banking, vol. 1, OASIA.

5. Rozell to McKeon, Yokohama Specie Bank's Reports, 3 August 1940; Rozell to McKeon, 10 August 1940, Yokohama Specie Bank Reports.

6. McKeon to L. Werner Knoke, untitled, 10 August 1940, Box 20, File Japan Banks and Banking, vol. 1, OASIA.

7. McKeon to Knoke, untitled, 10 August 1940; J. B. Knapp to Morse, International Capital Movements—Japanese Revisions, 27 August 1940, Box 50, File Japan Banking YSB, FRB.

8. Rozell, Yokohama Specie Bank Reports, 28 August 1940, Box 50, File Japan Banking YSB, FRB.

9. Knapp to Morse, International Capital Movements—Japanese Revisions, 27 August 1940, Box 50, File Japan Banking YSB, FRB.

10. Frank M. Tamagna to Board of Governors, Japan's International Position, 28 August 1940. In 1946 this report about the hidden account was sent to the Justice Department for use in the Tokyo war crimes trials as an illustration of the duplicity of Japanese leaders planning for an aggressive war. The report was not introduced at the trials. Handwritten notation: "Certified copy given Justice Dept. 5/28/46 for use in Tokyo trials."

11. Commerce Department, *Balance of International Payments*, 1937, 61.

12. Donald Moggridge, ed., *The Collected Writings of John Maynard Keynes* (Cambridge: Macmillan/Cambridge Press for the Royal Economic Society, 1979), 23:1–10; Robert Skidelsky, *John Maynard Keynes: Fighting for Freedom* (New York: Viking, 2001), 74–76.

13. Tamagna, Japan's International Position, 28 August 1940; Charles H. Coe to Harry Dexter White, The Incomplete Reporting of Foreign Assets and Liabilities by the Yokohama Specie Bank of New York, 9 October 1940, Box 20, File Japan Banks and Banking, vol. 1, OASIA.

14. Knapp to Morse, International Capital Movements, 27 August 1940.

15. Coe to White, Incomplete Reporting of Foreign Assets and Liabilities, 9 October 1940.

16. Edward H. Foley Jr., General Counsel, to Morgenthau, 23 September 1940, *Morgenthau Diaries*, vol. 2, Roll 28.

17. Meeting, 10 October 1940, *Morgenthau Diaries* 2:26.

18. EO No. 8389, 10 April 1940, as amended; Regulations under Executive Order No. 8389, as Amended, State Department, *Documents Pertaining to Foreign Funds Control*, 16 August 1941, Box 4683, File Frozen Credits 1940–41, RG 59, NA. This forty-six page compendium includes approximately ninety orders, rulings, decisions, circulars and general licenses issued from 10 April 1940 through 16 August 1941.

19. Office of Alien Property Custodian, *Report for the Period March 11, 1942 to June 30, 1943*.

20. Coe to White, Incomplete Reporting of Foreign Assets and Liabilities, 9 October 1940.

21. Meeting, 10 October 1940, *Morgenthau Diaries* 2:26.

22. Kamarck to White, Preliminary Memorandum, 31 October 1940.

23. Tamagna to Knoke, Japan's Undisclosed Gold Stock, 10 September 1940.

24. Kamarck to White, Preliminary Memorandum, 31 October 1940.

25. George A. Nakison, First Secretary of U.S. Embassy, Tokyo to Secretary of State, Japan's Gold Position, 22 November 1940, Box 21, File Japan Gold and Silver, OASIA.

26. J. Edgar Hoover, Director, Federal Bureau of Investigation, to Morgenthau, 29 November 1940, *Morgenthau Diaries* 2:30.

27. Wiley to Morgenthau, enclosing memorandum on Foreign Exchange Control to submit to the secretary of state, 2 December 1940, *Morgenthau Diaries* 2:30.

28. Feis, *Road to Pearl Harbor*, 141–44; Jacob Viner to Morgenthau, Memorandum for the Secretary of State, 3 December 1940, *Morgenthau Diaries* 2:39.

29. Viner, Mr. Wiley's draft of memorandum for the Secretary of State on general exchange control, with attachment, 3 December 1940; Wiley to Morgenthau, 4 December, 1940, *Morgenthau Diaries* 2:31.

30. Entries of 30 December 1940 and 6 January 1941 in *Morgenthau Diaries*, cited in Feis, *Road to Pearl Harbor*, 143n20, 144n22.

31. Confidential memo, Brig. Gen. Sherman Miles, Acting Assistant Chief of Staff, G-2 to Chief of Staff No. 30, Freezing of Japanese Funds in America, 24 October 1940, *Morgenthau Diaries* 2:27.

32. Viner, Mr. Wiley's draft of memorandum, 3 December 1940; Wiley to Morgenthau, 2 and 4 December 1940; Feis, *Road to Pearl Harbor*, 227n3.

33. Rozell to Knoke, Japanese Investments in United States and American Investment in Japan, 11 September 1940, Box 50, File Japan General 1922–1941, FRB.

34. Notes of meeting, 9 October 1940, *Morgenthau Diaries* 2:26.

35. H. E. Hesse to White, 6 December 1940, Box 20, File Japan Banks and Banking, vol. 1, OASIA.

36. Merle Cochran, Morgenthau Meeting, 10 October 1940, *Morgenthau Diaries* 2:26.

37. Kamarck to White, Cooperation of the Bank of America with the Japanese, 12 December 1940, Box 20, File Japan Banks and Banking vol. 1, OASIA.

38. Coe to White, Incomplete Reporting of Foreign Assets and Liabilities, 9 October 1940; Hesse to White, 6 December 1940.

39. Meeting, October 15, 1940, *Morgenthau Diaries* 2:26.

40. Rozell to Knoke, Japan's Financial Position vis-à-vis the United States, 23 January 1941, Box 50, File Japan Finance 1922–51 (1), Federal Reserve Bank of New York (hereafter cited as FRBNY).

41. Taylor to White, Japanese Foreign Exchange Resources, 7 February 1941.

42. The name of Harry Dexter White conjures up the postwar accusations that he assisted Soviet espionage before and during World War II, perhaps even spied for the Russians. His case has been addressed in several books and innumerable articles. White, a brilliant economist, had joined the Treasury in 1934 and risen as Morgenthau's admired aide and brains-truster to head the Division of Monetary Research. In 1944 he led the U.S. delegation in conferences that designed the World Bank and the International Monetary Fund. In the 1990s the federal government released "Venona" decrypts of Soviet messages confirming that he passed information to Moscow. It is unclear whether White acted on behalf of Soviet interests in 1941 in shaping U.S. financial policy toward Japan. Vitali Pavlov, a former KGB (Soviet state security) official in an article and a later a book written during the post–Cold War information thaw of the 1990s, described "Operation Snow" (a play on White's name). Pavlov wrote that he contacted White under diplomatic cover in a restaurant in Washington in late April 1941, urging him to promote U.S. actions to draw Japanese ambitions for conquest away from Siberia and toward a confrontation in the Pacific, perhaps including a war with the United States, so that the USSR would not have to fight on two fronts when Hitler attacked.

There is no evidence that the Soviets influenced White's recommendation of February 1941 to freeze Japan's assets immediately. White's one alleged meeting with Vitaly Pavlov occurred in April 1941. The flight of Japan's money from New York was reason enough for urgency. Both Morgenthau and White then lost interest in Japan as they focused on Lend Lease. After February White's input on the subject of freezing Japanese assets largely disappeared from the records. His voice was notably absent in late July when the freeze was discussed with Roosevelt, decided upon, and implemented. White was not appointed as the Treasury's representative on the powerful three-man policy board that determined the severity of the freeze. He was passed over in favor of Edward H. Foley Jr., the Treasury Department's senior lawyer—and not even an assistant secretary—leaving command of what became the draconian total freeze to Dean Acheson in the State Department. The momentum toward launching financial war against Japan was an American phenomenon, not Soviet inspired. Later in 1941 White drew up a utopian scheme for peace in Asia through withdrawal of the U.S. fleet from the Pacific, Japanese evacuation from China matched by Soviet troops backing away from Manchuria, non-aggression pacts, huge American economic aid and loans to both Japan and China, and sale by Japan of three-fourths of its military production to the United States at cost plus. The paper languished until Morgenthau forwarded it to Hull and Roosevelt on 17 November 1941, long after the freeze of Japan's assets. On 26 November Hull incorporated for the president a watered-down version of the wildly unrealistic scheme as a possible basis for diplomatic settlement. White's fantasy of buying off Japan was the antithesis of Pavlov's alleged prodding to inflame it to war. It came, of course, to naught. Sources: Vitaly Pavlov, "The Time Has Come to Talk About Operation Snow," Novosti Razvedki I Kontrrazvedki (News of Intelligence and Counterintelligence), No. 11-12, Moscow, 1995, translation kindly provided by Dr. John Haynes, Library of Congress; Jerrold Schechter and Leona Schechter, *Sacred Secrets*:

How Soviet Intelligence Operations Changed American History (Washington, D.C.: Brassey's, 2002), chap. 2.

43. Taylor to White, Japanese Foreign Exchange Resources, 7 February 1941; White to Morgenthau, Japan's Foreign Exchange Position, 25 February 1941.

44. White to Morgenthau, Japan's Foreign Exchange Position, 25 February 1941.

45. Taylor to White, Japanese Gold Movements and Dollars [sic] Balances in the United States, January to March 1941, 21 March 1941, Box 21, File Japan Gold and Silver, OASIA.

46. White to Morgenthau, 3 April 1941, *Morgenthau Diaries* 2:44.

Chapter 9. An Aborted Financial Freeze, Early 1941

1. Three others held that title: Adolf A. Berle Jr., Breckenridge Long, and G. Howland Shaw. All were junior to Secretary Cordell Hull and Undersecretary Sumner Welles.

2. Dean Acheson, *Present at the Creation: My Years in the State Department* (New York: Norton, 1969), 16–35; Robert A. Divine, "Acheson, Dean Gooderham," *American National Biography Online*; James Chace, *Acheson: The Secretary of State Who Created the American World* (New York: Simon & Schuster, 1998), 84–87.

3. R. R. Stout, 1st Lt., to Maxwell, 15 February 1941, Notes on Meeting of 6 February 1941 in Maxwell's office, File Binder, "Economic Warfare Planning OAEC," Files 336.11–350.05, Box 184, FEA, Office of the Administrator of Export Control, Entry 97, Central File, RG 169, NA (hereafter cited as File Binder, "Economic Warfare Planning, OAEC").

4. The CEDC was to consist of an odd combination of the secretaries of the State and Treasury Departments, the attorney general, the federal loan administrator, and somebody from the Office of Production Management. It would advise the president, congress and other agencies, and set policy for a stunning array of regulatory activities: financial including asset freezing, export control including direction of the ECA, defense procurement for foreign countries (presumably including Lend-Lease), and shipping requisitions. Financial controls would be applied immediately to Germany, Italy, and the European neutrals, but not Japan. In an administrative tangle, the Treasury would administer all operations but could not alter the ECA's licensing procedures without State's approval. The State Department would have a sort of veto power on issues that affected foreign relations—presumably everything. The attorney general would bring indictments against violations of foreign controls that detrimentally affected defense. In a final bit of obfuscation, all actions of the secretary of the treasury and the attorney general were to be "conclusively presumed" to be in accord with the policies of State and the CEDC.

5. Schwarz to Morgenthau, 14 February 1941; Hull to FDR, Memorandum on the Freezing of Foreign Funds, 14 February 1941; Treasury staff conference, 14 February 1941, a.m.; Shea, draft executive order; and Foley to Morgenthau, all in *Morgenthau Diaries*, vol. 1, Roll 40; Blum, *From the Morgenthau Diaries* 2:332–37.

6. Foley, Memorandum for the Secretary's Diary, 18 February 1941; Morgenthau to Foley and Pehle, 21 February 1941; and Foley and Pehle to Morgenthau, 21 February 1941, all in *Morgenthau Diaries*, vol. 2, Rolls 40–41; Blum, *From the Morgenthau Diaries* 1:457n.

7. Morgenthau to Gaston, 3 March 1941, *Morgenthau Diaries* 2:42.

8. Acheson, *Present at the Creation*, 27–30; Langer and Gleason, *Undeclared War*, chap. 9.

9. Grew to Secretary of State, 10 March 1941, *FRUS* 5:794–95; internal memo, Division of Far Eastern Affairs, State Department, 12 March 1941, file 894.5034, State Department microfilm series LM-68, RG 59, NA.

10. Carlton Savage biography, Savage Endowment for International Relations and Peace, http://oip.uoregon.edu/savage/bio.php (accessed 20 July 2006); *Washington Post*, 26 May 1990, B6; *New York Times*, 17 January 1936, 8, 2 August 1938, 17, and 7 June 1939, 7. In 1943 Savage prepared a publication of diplomatic papers, *War and Peace*, concerning the events leading up to World War II.

11. Savage considered alternative schemes, cosmetically less strident but yielding roughly similar results. For example, an executive order might freeze the assets of every country, then license transactions for all except Japan; or require licensing of all foreign transactions but grant unre-

stricted licenses to all nations except Japan; or revoke with respect to Japan alone the unrestricted global exchange license of 1934.

12. Savage to Welles, 24 March 1941, with draft executive order attached, File 894.5151/242, Roll 15, State Department microfilm LM-68, RG 59, NA. Savage had been reassigned from the historian's office and named an assistant to Assistant Secretary Breckenridge Long, and later as an aide to Assistant Secretary Adolf A. Berle Jr. Long was an aging lawyer and politician who returned to department headquarters in 1940 after assignments abroad. His involvement with the world emergency involved control of immigrant visas for refugees. Berle was a lawyer of wide government experience, a charter member of FDR's "brain trust," and best known as an author of seminal book on corporate control of the economy, "a Bible of the New Left"; his later biographer titled his book *Liberal*. It seems unlikely that either Long or Berle would have sponsored Carlton Savage's draft freeze order. He forwarded it to Welles at the request of Herbert Feis, economic adviser.

13. Acheson, *Present at the Creation*, 23.

14. Chandler Morse to Hewes, Thoughts on Methods of Economic Warfare, 10 January 1941, and Staley to Hewes, 30 January 1941, both in File Binder, "Economic Warfare Planning OAEC."

15. Morse to Hewes, Thoughts on Methods of Economic Warfare, 10 January 1941; Staley to Hewes, 30 January 1941; and Ralph Turner to Hewes, 4 April 1941; H. Lary, Japan's Vulnerability to Financial Pressure, 4 March 1941, Far Eastern Regional Studies (lists of), File General Correspondence, Projects Section Foreign Funds, E88, Box 700, Administrator of Export Control, RG 169, NA.

16. Hewes to Maxwell, US-UK Cooperation, 31 March 1941; and Hewes to Bernstein, 4 April 1941, both in File Binder, "Economic Warfare Planning OAEC."

17. Hewes to Ralph Turner, Techniques for the Study, 8 April 1941, File "A Plan for Administering the Preclusive Purchasing of World Commodities"; Warren S. Hunsberger, "Loans as an Instrument of Economic Warfare (Studies in the Technique of Economic Warfare)," File Economic Warfare by Loans, both in Box 698, General File of Chief, Export Section, Administrator of Export Control, RG 169, NA.

Chapter 10. Japan's Vulnerability in Strategic Resources

1. F. H. Miles Jr., Colonel, Office of the Commandant of the Army Industrial College to Maxwell, 23 September 1940; Maxwell to Secretary of War, 1 October 1940; and Secretary of War to Maxwell, 7 October 1940, all in File Binder, "Economic Warfare Planning OAEC."

2. NARA, *Federal Records of World War II* 1:150ff.

3. Advisory Commission to the Council of National Defense to the President, memo, 27 November 1940, File Binder, "Economic Warfare Planning OAEC."

4. *Who Was Who in America*, vol. 3; *Washington Post*, 3 February 1941, 7.

5. *American Men and Women of Science: Economics, 1974* (New York: R. R. Bowker, 1974); *New York Times*, 28 September 1954, 19.

6. *Who Was Who in America and World Notables, 1977–81* (Chicago: Marquis Who's Who, 1981), vol. 7.

7. *Washington Post*, 28 December 1934, 5.

8. Thomas Hewes, draft letter Maxwell to FDR, 17 December 1940, File Binder, "Economic Warfare Planning OAEC."

9. R. R. Stout, 1st Lt., to Maxwell, notes on meeting of 6 February 1941 in Maxwell's office, 14 February 1941; Hewes to Maxwell, US-UK Cooperation, 31 March 1941; Lee, cable from London to AEC with copies to secretaries of war, navy, and treasury re: British organization for economic warfare, 29 April 1941; and Hewes to Maxwell, Prompt Initiation of Economic Pressure, 2 May 1941, all in File Binder, "Economic Warfare Planning OAEC."

10. R. L. Maxwell, Administrator, to Chairman, U.S. Tariff Commission, 20 December 1940, File: Projects General, Box 700; Louis S. Ballif, Chief Sundries Div., U.S. Tariff Commission to Chandler Morse, AEC, "The International Use of Economic Pressure as an Instrument of

National Policy," 17 February 1941, File: Commodities, Report Correspondence, Box 699; Far Eastern Regional Studies, File: General Correspondence, n.d., Box 700, 26 February to 19 July 1941; and Administrator of Export Control, all in Entry 88, RG 169, NA.

11. Louis S. Ballif to Hewes, "Assistance of Existing Government Agencies in Economic Warfare," 13 December 1940, File Binder, "Economic Warfare Planning OAEC."

12. Minutes of the First Meeting of the Steering Committee of the Export Control Commodity Studies, 24 February 1941, File: Commodity Committees, General File of Chief, Export Section, Box 698, Entry 88, Administrator of Export Control, RG 169, NA.

13. Joint letter from Stark and Marshall, 4 April 1941, in WPD 4402-6, cited in War Department, Office of the Chief of Military History, "Planning the Defeat of Japan: A Study of Total War Strategy," unpublished monograph, prepared by Lt. Col. Henry C. Morgan, 1961, 96; Maxwell to CNO and COS, Economic Warfare Committee on Far Eastern Trade, 17 March 1941, and Stark and Marshall to Maxwell, Economic Warfare Committee on Far Eastern Trade—Policy Affecting Army and Navy Representatives, 17 March 1941, both in File Binder, "Economic Warfare Planning OAEC."

14. The number is approximate. Some studies were supplemented or updated later in 1941 and during the war.

15. Morse to Moser, Chairman of Far East Research Unit, Additional Research Projects, 11 March 1941, File: Current Projects Unit Genl File, 1941, Box 700; Chandler Morse to all members of the Steering Committee and committee chairmen, Form of Commodity Reports, 15 March 1941; unsigned, Projects Section to Commodity Chairman, Special Reports on Possibilities for Preclusive Purchasing, 19 March 1941; Hewes to Maxwell, Handling of Reports to Projects Section from Interdepartmental Commodity Committees, 3 April 1941, File: Commodity Committees, all in General File of Chief, Exports Section, Administrator of Export Control, FEA, Entry 88, Box 698, RG 169, NA.

16. Transmittal letter with list or reports of Economic Vulnerability of Japan, 11 April 1941, File: Commodities, Report Correspondence, Box 699, General File of Chief, Export Section, Administrator of Export Control, FEA, Entry 88, RG 169, NA. This lists most of the studies. In August, after the freeze and full embargo was imposed, a few vulnerability studies were further updated.

17. Richard Sanger to Hewes, transmittal of reports to General Maxwell, 9 May 1941, and Commerce Department to Morse, 26 May 1941, both in File: Commodities, Report Correspondence, Box 699, General File of the Chief, Projects Section, Administrator of Export Control, Entry 88, RG 169, NA. A full set of the vulnerability studies is in Boxes 698–700. Another set is in Reports on the Economic Vulnerability of Japan 1941–43, Boxes 1–2, Entry 44, Records of the Tariff Commission.

18. Administrator of Economic Control (Brig. Gen. R. L. Maxwell) to Chief of Staff [Marshall] and Chief of Naval Operations [Stark], and many other addressees, "Coordinated Plan of Economic Action in Relation to Japan," draft in 2 vols., 1 May 1941; transmittal letters to various officials and letters of acknowledgment, c. 6 to 13 May 1941, are found in Boxes 271–72, File 350.05, Central File (Area) "Japan," Office of the Administrator of Export Control, RG 169, NA. Some of the prewar studies, including the Coordinated Plan, cannot be located. The ECA, reorganized several times, evolved into an enormous wartime bureaucracy under other names. It was disestablished by executive order on 15 September 1941, after the financial freeze was imposed on Japan. Its functions were subsumed into an Office of Export Control under an Economic Defense Board, also created in 1941 to strengthen international economic relations. After Pearl Harbor it was renamed the Board of Economic Warfare. In 1943 its functions were transferred to a new Office of Economic Warfare which in turn was superseded by the Foreign Economic Administration within the Office of Emergency Management (OEM). The collection of these agencies' records at the National Archives measures 2,598 cubic feet, of which those of the ECA and its successors handling export controls constitute 201 linear feet.

19. Hewes to Maxwell, Prompt Initiation of Economic Pressure, 2 May 1941.

20. Interdepartmental Committee on Iron and Steel, "Economic Vulnerability of Japan in Iron, Steel and Ferro-Alloys." The interdepartmental committee reports in notes 20–36 are all in Boxes 698-700, General File of the Chief, Projects Section, Administrator of Export Control, RG 169, NA.

21. Interdepartmental Committee on Non-Ferrous Metals and Manufactures, "Economic Vulnerability of Japan in Copper."

22. Interdepartmental Committee on Nonmetallic Minerals and Manufactures, "The Economic Vulnerability of Japan in Abrasives," 1 April 1941.

23. Interdepartmental Committee on Chemicals, Fertilizers and Related Products, "The Economic Vulnerability of Japan in Carbon Black," 7 April 1941.

24. Interdepartmental Committee on Raw Textiles, Fibers and Cordage, "The Economic Vulnerability of Japan in Miscellaneous Vegetable Fibers," 5 April 1941.

25. Interdepartmental Committee on Nonmetallic Minerals and Manufactures, "The Economic Vulnerability of Japan in Bauxite and Fluorspar," 2 April 1941.

26. Interdepartmental Committee on Chemicals, Fertilizers and Related Products, "The Economic Vulnerability of Japan in Methanol, Butanol and Acetone," 7 April 1941. A study on dynamite and other explosives amounted to one page because Japan was self-sufficient and U.S. exports were embargoed.

27. Interdepartmental Committee on Petroleum, "The Economic Vulnerability of Japan in Petroleum," April 1941.

28. Interdepartmental Committee on Nonmetallic Minerals and Manufactures, "The Economic Vulnerability of Japan in Bauxite and Fluorspar," 2 April 1941.

29. Interdepartmental Committee on Iron and Steel, "The Economic Vulnerability of Japan in Ferro-Alloys," April 1941.

30. Interdepartmental Committee on Iron and Steel, "The Economic Vulnerability of Japan in Iron, Steel and Ferro-Alloys."

31. Interdepartmental Committee on Nonmetallic Minerals and Manufactures, "The Economic Vulnerability of Japan in Asbestos," 7 April 1941.

32. Interdepartmental Committee on Nonmetallic Minerals and Manufactures, "The Economic Vulnerability of Japan in Quartz Crystals," 2 April 1941.

33. Interdepartmental Committee on Nonmetallic Minerals and Manufactures, "The Economic Vulnerability of Japan in Mica," 2 April 1941.

34. Interdepartmental Committee on Miscellaneous Products, "The Economic Vulnerability of Japan in Miscellaneous Products," 25 April 1941.

35. Interdepartmental Committee on Nonmetallic Minerals and Manufactures, "The Economic Vulnerability of Japan in Graphite," 2 April 1941.

36. Interdepartmental Committee on Nonmetallic Minerals and Manufactures, "The Economic Vulnerability of Japan in Optical Glass," 1 April 1941. Interdepartmental Committee on Raw Textiles, Fibers and Cordage. "The Economic Vulnerability of Japan in Miscellaneous Vegetable Fibers," 5 April 1941.

37. State Department Far Eastern Division (Jones), Japan: Economic Estimate, 27 May 1941, file 89450/154, Roll 11, State Department microfilm series LM-68, RG 59, NA.

Chapter 11. The Vulnerability of the Japanese Economy and People

1. Secondary works on Japan's consumer economy, especially food and fertilizer, include historical statistics: Cohen, *Japan's Economy*; Hunsberger, *Japan and the United States in World Trade*; William W. Lockwood, *The Economic Development of Japan: Growth and Structural Change 1868–1938* (Princeton, N.J.: Princeton University Press, 1954); and W. J. Macpherson, *The Economic Development of Japan c. 1868–1941* (Cambridge: Macmillan, 1987). U.S. prewar reports other than the vulnerability studies include Far Eastern Division, State Department (Jones), Japan Economic Estimate, 27 May 1941, File 894.50/154, Roll 11, State Department microfilm series LM-68, RG 59, NA.

Wartime U.S. studies were largely based on prewar data: War Department, Headquarters, Army Service Forces, *Civil Affairs Handbook: Japan*, 22 July 1944; Office of Naval Intelligence, ONI Japan Monographs, File 401-200 (A), Box 10, Section 6, Natural Resources, RG 38, NA; Navy Department, Office of Chief of Naval Operations, *Civil Affairs Guide: Far Eastern Nutritional Relief (Japanese Culture)*, 15 August 1944, OPNAV 13-18, Box 18, File Agriculture-Food-General, RG 38, NA; OCL, *Place of Foreign Trade*, vol. 1, pt. 2, 160-231, tables II-1 to II-16.

Postwar studies include accurate prewar information: SCAP, General Headquarters, *Japanese Food Situation*, 1 May 1946, Box 18, Japanese Monograph Series, RG 38, NA; USSBS, Over-All Economic Effects Division, *The Effects of Strategic Bombing on Japan's War Economy*, December 1946, 53–54, 188, 195–96, 235–37; USSBS, Manpower, Food and Civilian Supplies Division, *The Japanese Wartime Standard of Living and Utilization of Manpower*, January 1947, 1–16, 99–104; *Chemicals in Japan's War*, 1946, appendix. Prewar statistics are available in Japan Statistical Association, *Historical Statistics of Japan*. U.S. exports in Commerce Department, *Foreign Commerce and Navigation of the United States*.

2. At the time of Commodore Perry's arrival Japan's population was larger than that of the United States and of any European country except Russia. It ranked third in the world behind China and India.

3. The imperial policy also had a cultural dimension. The Japanese, then as now, preferred short-grained, glutinous "Japonica" rice grown in the temperate home islands and Korea. Although "Indica" rice of tropical southeast Asia cost only half, and by 1939 only one third as much as Japonica, only the poorest citizens tolerated "inferior" Indica rice, scarcely preferable to coarse field grains. During a visit by the author in the 1990s a domestic rice shortage forced the government to mandate blending of domestic rice with 10 percent California Japonica and 6 percent Thailand Indica. Rather than blend, the food markets tied together three plastic bags of appropriate sizes. The California rice was tolerated but consumers threw away the little bags of Indica.

4. Jerome B. Cohen, *Economic Problems of Free Japan* (Princeton, N.J.: Center of International Studies, Princeton University, 1952), 7–8.

5. Ibid., 16.

6. *Encyclopaedia Britannica* 1941, 12:901.

7. State Department, *Japan Economic Estimate*, 27 May 1941, 3.

8. OCL, *Place of Foreign Trade*, vol. 1, pt. 2, 182–205.

9. Reference works on fertilizers including crop responses: Ministry of Economic Warfare, "Japan: Supplies of Fertilizers in 1942 in Relation to Food Production," London, 30 December 1941, Records of the U.S. Department of State Relating to the Internal Affairs of Japan 1940–1944, decimal files 894, File 894.659/FERTILIZER/2, Roll 13, State Department microfilm series LM-68, RG 59, NA; SCAP, General Headquarters, Natural Resources Section, *Fertilizers in Japan; a Preliminary Report*, Report 55, prepared by Maj. G. L. W. Swanson and Mr. Tanada, Tokyo, 10 September 1946; Kazushi Ohkawa, Bruce F. Johnston, and Hiromitsu Kaneda, eds., *Agriculture and Economic Growth: Japan's Experience* (Princeton, N.J.: Princeton University Press and University of Tokyo Press, 1970); John J. Doyle, *The Response of Rice to Fertilizer*, FAO Agricultural Studies 70 (Rome: Food and Agricultural Organization of the United Nations, 1966); Moyle Strayhorn Williams and John W. Couston, *Crop Production Levels and Fertilizer Use* (Rome: Food and Agricultural Organization of the United Nations, 1962); O. P. Engelstad, ed., *Fertilizer Technology and Use*, 3rd ed. (Madison, Wisc.: Soil Science Society of America, 1985); Isaburo Nagai, *Japonica Rice: Its Breeding and Culture* (Tokyo: Yokendo, 1959); Kym Anderson and Rod Tyers, "Japanese Rice Policy in the Interwar Period: Some Consequences of Imperial Self Sufficiency," *Japan and the World Economy* 4 (1992): 102–27.

10. Around 1900 the only accessible source of nitrogen was sodium nitrate mined in the deserts of northern Chile, which in 1903 supplied 67 percent of world nitrogen demand. But sodium nitrate was inefficient in wet paddies, and required dollars Japan could ill afford. In the gaslight era industrial countries produced ammonium sulfate containing 20 percent nitrogen as a byproduct of "town gas" from coal baked in ovens, reacted with sulfuric acid. In 1905 Japan com-

menced manufacture of ammonium sulfate from domestic coal, using iron-sulfur pyrites for acid. However, demand for coproduct town gas and solid coke residue did not grow fast enough. Around the time of World War I chemists learned to fix atmospheric nitrogen by combining air with hydrogen gas obtained from passing steam over incandescent coke, and conversion to ammonium sulfate. Japan adopted the process but still imported 62 percent of its need in 1928.

11. Germany ranked first. The United States, ranked second, relied mainly on its huge coke industry and on imports.

12. Interdepartmental Committee on Chemicals, Fertilizers and Related Products, "The Economic Vulnerability of Japan in Fertilizers," "The Economic Vulnerability of Japan in Ammonium Sulfate," and "The Economic Vulnerability of Japan in Sodium Nitrate and Other Nitrates," 7 April 1941, all in Boxes 698–700, General File of the Chief, Projects Section, Administrator of Export Control, RG 169, NA.

13. USSBS, *Coal and Metals*, 147–54, 158; *Chemicals in Japan's War*, appendix, 10–25; *Japanese Wartime Standard of Living*, 11–12.

14. Nineteenth-century agronomists observed the benefits of phosphates in crushed animal bones (and human bones from graveyards according to legend) and in guano, ancient bird excrement on a few dry Pacific islands that were mined out in a few years. Japan was deficient in livestock bones. Green manures supplied some, but fish, soybean cake, and fuel ashes were not rich in phosphates.

15. State Department, *Japan Economic Estimate*, 27 May 1941; OCL, *Place of Foreign Trade* 1:192–97, 2:57, tables II-9, II-10; USSBS, *Chemicals in Japan's War*, 83–84, and appendix, 47–48; *Japanese Wartime Standard of Living*, 12; *Effects of Strategic Bombing*, 155–57, 193.

16. Interdepartmental Committee on Chemicals, Fertilizers and Related Products, "Economic Vulnerability of Japan in Phosphate Rock," 8 April 1941; Interior Department, Bureau of Mines, "Mineral Resources of Germany's Former Colonial Possessions," *Foreign Minerals Quarterly* 2, no. 3 (July 1939).

17. Bertrand L. Johnson and K. G. Warner, "Phosphate Rock," in Interior Department, *Minerals Yearbook*, 1937–41.

18. Interdepartmental Committee on Chemicals, Fertilizers and Related Products, "The Economic Vulnerability of Japan in Phosphate Rock."

19. USSBS, *Japanese Wartime Standard of Living*, 12; USSBS, *Coal and Metals*, 155, 157, 193.

20. International Potash Institute, *Japanese Potassium Symposium* (Berne, Switz.: Second Japanese Potassium Congress, 1958); Stanley A. Barber, Robert D. Munson, and W. B. Dancy, "Production, Marketing, and Use of Potassium Fertilizers," in *Fertilizer Technology and Use*, 2nd ed., ed. R. A. Olson (Madison, Wisc.: Soil Society of America, 1971).

21. J. H. Hedges, "Potash," in Interior Department, *Minerals Yearbook*, 1937, 1938, 1939, 1941; OCL, *Place of Foreign Trade*, vol. 1, pt. 2, 182–205, tables II-11, II-12; Interdepartmental Committee on Chemicals, Fertilizers and Related Products, "Economic Vulnerability of Japan in Potash"; correspondence, 1 November 1940, 5 February, and 2 May 1941, Boxes 271–72, Files 428.3 Japan, Central File (Area), Office of the Administrator of Export Control, RG 169, NA; Robinson Newcomb, "Potash Scarce," *Far Eastern Survey*, 20 November 1940, 272. In an offer of barter trade in September 1941, Japan sought to acquire six thousand tons of manure salts, second in value to oil on its shopping list. See chapter 17.

22. USSBS, *Effects of Strategic Bombing*, 235–37.

23. Interdepartmental Committee on Fishery Products, "Economic Vulnerability of Japan in Fish, Shellfish and Fish Livers"; OCL, *Place of Foreign Trade*, vol. 1, pt. 2, 169–72, tables II-3, II-4; USSBS, *Japanese Wartime Standard of Living*, 14.

24. OCL, *Place of Foreign Trade*, vol. 1, pt. 2, 172, tables II-1, II-2; Navy Department, *Civil Affairs Guide*; USSBS, *Japanese Wartime Standard of Living*, 16; "World Food Needs Benefit Average Soybean Producers," *Farm Week*, 1 September 1967.

25. Interdepartmental Committee on Fats and Oils, "The Economic Vulnerability of Japan in Fats and Oils," 31 March 1941; OCL, *Place of Foreign Trade*, vol. 1, pt. 2, 172–73; USSBS, *Coal*

and Metals, 194–95; Navy Department, *Civil Affairs Guide,* 9, 16; USSBS, *Chemicals in Japan's War,* appendix, 83. Mitsubishi placed large orders for lard in March and April despite a 4 March executive order requiring licensing of edible oils because shortages were appearing. On 25 July, the day before the dollar freeze, it sold at a loss sixty-five carloads on the West Coast.

26. OCL, *Place of Foreign Trade,* vol. 1, pt. 2, 167–69; USSBS, *Japanese Wartime Standard of Living,* 16; USSBS, *Coal and Metals,* 238.

27. Commerce Department, Bureau of Foreign and Domestic Commerce, Commerce Reports, weekly, 30 September 1939, 878; State Department, Naval Attaché, Tokyo, *Japan's Soda Industry and Its Dependence on Imported Salt,* 16 September 1940, File 894.659/23, Roll 13, State Department microfilm series LM-68, RG 59, NA; OCL, *Place of Foreign Trade,* vol. 1, pt. 2, 284–89 and tables II-26 to II-28; War Department, *Civil Affairs Handbook,* 22 July 1944; State Department, Office of Research and Intelligence, *Situation Report: Japan, the Status of the Japanese Textile Industry,* pt. 2, *Rayon,* 24 May 1946, file 3479.1, Box 19, ONI Japan Monographs; Interdepartmental Committee on Forest Products and Manufactures, "The Economic Vulnerability of Japan in Forest Products and Manufactures," 29 March 1941; Interdepartmental Committee on Chemicals, Fertilizers and Related Products, "The Economic Vulnerability of Japan in Salt," 7 April 1941, "The Economic Vulnerability of Japan in Soda Ash (Calcined Sodium Carbonate)," 8 April 1941, and "The Economic Vulnerability of Japan in Caustic Soda (Sodium Hydroxide)," 7 April 1941; USSBS, *Chemicals in Japan's War,* appendix, 85; USSBS, *Coal and Metals,* 146, 194; "Rayon Fiber," fibersourcehome, http://www.fibersource.com/f-tutor/rayon.htm (accessed 8 October 2005). Japan obtained caustic soda by processing soda ash (sodium carbonate, Na_2CO_3) with ammonia or by electrolysis. Soda ash, in turn, was manufactured from common salt (sodium chloride, NaCl).

28. OCL, *Place of Foreign Trade,* vol. 1, pt. 2, 276–81, tables II-24, II-28; Seki, *Cotton Industry of Japan;* Interdepartmental Committee on Raw Textile Fibers and Cordage, "Economic Vulnerability of Japan in Raw Cotton"; Tariff Commission, *Cotton Textiles,* 2, cited in Cohen, *Japan's Economy;* USSBS, *Coal and Metals,* 230–31; *Japanese Wartime Standard of Living,* 116, 118.

29. Interdepartmental Committee on Hides and Skins, "The Economic Vulnerability of Japan in Hides and Skins, Leather and Leather Manufactures, and Furs, Special Report on Hides and Skins, Leather and Leather Manufactures, and Furs," 27 June 1941; Special Report on the Possibilities for Preclusive Purchasing of Hides and Skins, 21 March 1941; Interdepartmental Committee on Chemicals, Fertilizers and Related Products, "The Vulnerability of Japan in Vegetable Tanning Materials," 7 April 1941; OCL, *Place of Foreign Trade,* vol. 1, pt. 2, 319–22, table II-30; USSBS, *Japanese Wartime Standard of Living,* 41–42, 119–20.

30. Interdepartmental Committee on Rubber, "The Vulnerability of Japan in Rubber," 6 March 1941; OCL, *Place of Foreign Trade,* vol. 1, pt. 2, 313–16, table II-30; Tariff Commission, Footwear, Rubber Soled, investigations under 1930 Act, 1931–35, Records of the Tariff Commission; USSBS, *Japanese Wartime Standard of Living,* 41–42, 119–20.

31. Interdepartmental Committee on Forest Products and Manufactures, "Vulnerability of Japan in Forest Products and Manufactures"; OCL, *Place of Foreign Trade,* vol. 1, pt. 2, 299–306, table II-29; War Department, *Civil Affairs Handbook,* 22 July 1944; "Japan Needs Wood," *Far Eastern Survey,* 26 February 1941, 32.

32. Interdepartmental Committee on Chemicals, Fertilizers and Related Products, "The Economic Vulnerability of Japan in Gum Rosin," 7 April 1941, and "The Economic Vulnerability of Japan in Borax," 7 April 1941. This committee also submitted reports on several minor vegetable products.

33. OSS, Central Information Division, name and subject card indexes to Series 16, Country: Japan, 117583C, Boxes 297–303, Entry 2.12, January 1946, RG 226, NA; Commerce Department, *Foreign Commerce and Navigation of the United States,* 1936–42; Grew to Hull, 20 January 1940, *FRUS,* vol. 4.

Chapter 12. The Vulnerability of Japanese Exports to the United States

1. Official statistics from Commerce Department, *Foreign Commerce and Navigation of the* *United States*; Tariff Commission, "United States Imports from Japan"; Commerce Department, Bureau of the Census, *Census of Manufactures: Cotton Manufactures and Rayon and Silk Manufactures*, 1939 (Washington, D.C.: GPO, 1940); Japan Statistical Association, *Historical Statistics of Japan*, vol. 3 (comparative analyses by the author); *Underwear and Hosiery Review*, May, November 1939; de Haan, *Full-Fashioned Hosiery Industry*, 42–44; Earl Constantine, President, National Association of Hosiery Manufacturers, correspondence and discussions with State Department officials, including Donald Hiss, Stanley Hornbeck, and Henry Grady, 15, 17, and 23 February 1940, Files 611.9431 and 694.11, Roll 9, Records Relating to U.S. Commercial Relations with Japan 1929–1949, RG 59, NA; E. I. du Pont de Nemours and Company, "Nylon," online at http://heritage.dupont.com/touchpoints/tp_1935-2/depth.shtml (accessed 18 October 2006).

2. Interdepartmental Committee on Silk, "Economic Vulnerability of the United States in Raw Silk and Silk Waste," W. S. Hunsberger, Silk, 11 April 1941, File 423 Silk Japan, Entry 98, Records of the FEA Administrator of Export Control, RG 169, NA.

3. FEA, Far Eastern Committee, Projects Section, "Preliminary, Summary Report on Silk: Japan and the United States," 27 April 1941, prepared by Wirth Ferger, Box 698, General File of Chief, Projects Section, Entry 88, Office of Administrator of Export Control, RG 169, NA. In August 1941 Du Pont lifted licensing restrictions against blending with nylon. The U.S. government mandated blending for the few silk stockings still in production and urged at least 50 percent blending of other yarns, even for nylons.

4. Tariff Commission, "United States Imports from Japan."

5. Interdepartmental Committee on Silk, "Economic Vulnerability of the United States in Raw Silk and Silk Waste"; FEA, "Preliminary, Summary Report on Silk: Japan and the United States"; Tariff Commission, "United States Imports from Japan," 174–75; Acheson to Hull, 13 September 1941, File 894.6552/23, Roll 16, State Department microfilm series LM-68, RG 59, NA. In September military needs were deemed secret.

6. Interdepartmental Committee on Silk, "Economic Vulnerability of the United States in Raw Silk and Silk Waste"; Lt. Col. John G. Burr to Chief of Ordnance, War Department, The Possibility of the Use of Raw Silk for Powder Bags, 22 May; and Office of the Chief of Ordnance to Administrator of Export Control, 27 May 1941, both in File Commodities—Reports Correspondence, Box 699, General Files—Projects, Administrator of Export Control, RG 169, NA; Tariff Commission, "United States Imports from Japan," 181–85.

7. Commerce Department, *Foreign Commerce and Navigation of the United States*, 1935–41; Japan Statistical Association, *Historical Statistics of Japan*, vol. 3.

8. In the United States both silk and nylon went to war. American women wore shiny stockings of heavy six-thread rayon or cotton, or they applied suntan lotion and drew mock seams up the backs of their legs with eyebrow pencil. The Japanese uprooted the mulberry trees to free up land for growing food. After the surrender MacArthur's occupation staff found about eight million pounds of raw silk in bales, less than two months of average prewar exports. They tried to auction it to American mills to raise occupation support funds, but received few bids at low prices. When full-fashioned hosiery production resumed in America nylon took the entire market. By 1955 silk stockings disappeared from shops. Seamless nylons in turn yielded to spandex-nylon pantyhose during and after the miniskirted 1960s. Japan today does not produce silk except for the weaving of a few ceremonial articles. China supplies the relatively small world demand for a fiber, now a novelty, valued for its natural imperfections in casual vogues that have displaced the lavish elegance of bygone days.

9. Interdepartmental Committee on Fishery Products, "Vulnerability of Japan in Fish, Shellfish and Fish Livers"; Tariff Commission, "United States Imports from Japan," 25–65.

10. Interdepartmental Committee on Miscellaneous Products, "Vulnerability of Japan in Miscellaneous Products"; Tariff Commission, "United States Imports from Japan," 194–97.

11. Interdepartmental Committee on Nonmetallic Minerals and Manufactures, "Vulnerability of Japan in Pottery"; Tariff Commission, "United States Imports from Japan," 203–14.

12. Interdepartmental Committee on Miscellaneous Products, "Vulnerability of Japan in Miscellaneous Products"; Tariff Commission, "United States Imports from Japan," 215–34.

Chapter 13. The Vulnerability of Japan in Petroleum

1. Oil volumes were, and still are, commonly expressed in barrels of forty-two U.S. gallons. Seven barrels weigh about one short ton of two thousand pounds, depending on the crude or refined liquid product. Data were often expressed in barrels produced, consumed, or transported per day.

2. Commerce Department, Bureau of Foreign and Domestic Commerce, *Fuel and Power in Japan*, Trade Information Bulletin No. 821 (Washington, D.C.: GPO, January 1935); Commerce Department, *Foreign Commerce and Navigation of the United States*; Navy Department, "Report on Petroleum Situation of Japan," 12 March 1941, prepared by Lt. Cdr. A. H. McCollum, USN, File 894.6363/383, Records of the U.S. Department of State Relating to the Internal Affairs of Japan 1940–1944, File 894, State Department microfilm series LM-68, RG 59, NA; Interdepartmental Committee on Petroleum, "Economic Vulnerability of Japan in Petroleum"; FEA, Special Areas Branch, Far East Enemy Division, *Prewar and Wartime Civilian Fuel and Lighting Consumption in Japan Proper*, July 1944, File 401-200, Japan, Box 9, ONI, Japan Monographs 1939–47, RG 38, NA; War Department, *Civil Affairs Handbook: Japan*; USSBS, Oil and Chemicals Division, *Oil in Japan's War* (Washington, D.C.: GPO, February 1946); Irvine H. Anderson Jr., *The Standard-Vacuum Oil Company and United States East Asian Policy, 1933–1941* (Princeton, N.J.: Princeton University Press, 1975).

3. Interior Department, *Minerals Yearbook*, 1936–42, chapters on petroleum.

4. Ibid.; Anderson, *Standard-Vacuum Oil*; Interdepartmental Committee on Petroleum, "Economic Vulnerability of Japan in Petroleum."

5. Stanley K. Hornbeck to Hull, 11 January 1941, File 894.6363/378, State Department microfilm series LM-68, RG 59, NA; Anderson, *Standard-Vacuum Oil*.

6. G-2 of Headquarters, Eighth Corps Area, Confidential informant, reliable, 29 November 1940; Rejection of Appeal by Tide Water Associated Oil Co.; and Yost (State) to Maxwell, sending report by Assistant Secretary of the Treasury Herbert E. Gaston, 9 May 1941, all in File 463.7 Japan, Box 272, Central File (Area), Office of the Administrator of Export Control, RG 169, NA.

7. Correspondence between Division of Controls, State Department, and Export Control Administration re: steel drums, 20 November 1940, 19, 21, 24 February, 8 May, 21 June 1941, and re: dismantled tanks, 29 April 1941, all in File 457.1 Japan, Central File (Area), Office of the Administrator of Export Control, RG 169, NA. In World War II steel drums were vital for fueling planes at advanced bases. Japanese aircraft carriers in the Pearl Harbor attack carried drummed fuel.

8. White to Ullman, Export Control—Shipments to Japan, 28 January 1941, *Morgenthau Diaries*, vol. 2, Roll 36; Japan: United States Principal Exports to, Monthly and Five Months 1941, c. 17 August 1941, Table VII-8-1, Area File 041.221 Japan, FEA, RG 169, NA. Per-barrel figures calculated by the author.

9. Joseph C. Green, Division of Controls to A-A, Memorandum, 19 July 1941, Box 3677, File 811.20 (D) Regulations/3884 1/2 PS/MNP, RG 59, NA. Figures converted to barrels by the author.

10. Welles, telegram to all Collector of Customs, 30 July 1941, File 911.20 (D) Regulations/3882A, Box 3677, Department of State Regulations [of Export Controls] 811.20(D), RG 59, NA.

11. Unless otherwise noted, following information is from Navy Department, "Report on Petroleum Situation of Japan"; Interdepartmental Committee on Petroleum, "Economic Vulnerability of Japan in Petroleum."

Chapter 14. Momentum for the Financial Freeze, May–July 1941

1. Grew to Secretary of State, 15 November 1940, *Morgenthau Diaries*, vol. 2, Roll 29; F. W. Tamagna to Knoke, Japanese Dollar Balances, 29 November 1940, Box 94, File Loans and Investments Foreign Deposits in U.S. (1), International Finance Division and Predecessors 1907–1974, FRB.

2. J. B. Knapp to Gardner, Bank of Brazil to hold official dollar accounts of Japan and Portugal, 26 November 1940; and W. H. Rozell, Transfer of Japanese Funds from New York to Brazil, 5 May 1941, both in Box 50, File Japan General 1922–1941, FRB.

3. White to Morgenthau, Japan's Foreign Exchange Position, 25 February 1941; Rozell to Knoke, Japanese Funds in New York, 16 March 1941, Box 50, File Japan General 1922–1941, FRB.

4. Japan Statistical Association, *Historical Statistics of Japan*, vol. 3.

5. Rozell to Knoke, N.Y. Account of Netherlands Purchasing Commission, 24 May 1941, File Loans and Investments Foreign Deposits in U.S. (1), Box 94; Tamagna to Knoke, 13 June 1941, Transfers of Dollar Funds from Java Bank to Yokohama Specie Bank, 13 June 1941, File Java Banking; and Transfers of Dollar Funds from Java Bank to Yokohama Specie Bank, 16 July 1941, File Japan Banking, Box 51, all in Records of the Federal Reserve Board of Governors, International Finance Division and Predecessors 1907–1974, FRB; Secretary of the Treasury to Secretaries of State, War and Navy, May–December Japanese Withdrawals of Funds from U.S., n.d. 1941, File 894.51/719, Records of the U.S. Department of State Relating to the Internal Affairs of Japan 1940–1944, Roll 14, State Department microfilm series LM-68, RG 59, NA.

6. Meeting at State Department with Aetna Insurance Company, 17 May 1941; Louis Pink, New York State Insurance Commissioner to Herbert Feis, 17 October, 20 December 1940, 16 May 1941; and Feis to Pink, 28 December 1940, 27 May, 9 July 1941, all in File 894.51, Roll 14, State Department microfilm series LM-68, RG 59, NA.

7. Dietrich to Silver File, January 23, 1940; Acheson to Bankers Trust Company, 20 June 1941, File 894.51/735, State Department microfilm series LM-68, RG 59, NA.

8. *New York Times*, 18 June 1941, 11, 3 July 1941, 31; FRBNY, *Monthly Review*, June and July 1941.

9. J. Edgar Hoover to Russell L. Maxwell, 21 May 1941; Maxwell to Hoover 26 May 1941; and Office of Stanley Hornbeck, re: Treasury report, 13 May, 1941, all in File 463.7 Japan, Box 272, Central File (Area), Office of the Administrator of Export Control, RG 169, NA.

10. White to Ullman, Export Control, Table VII-8-1. June and July are inferred from Commerce Department, *Foreign Commerce and Navigation of the United States*, 1941.

11. Sumner Welles, Acting Secretary of State, Memorandum of Conversation; and British Embassy to the Department of State, 14 July 1941, both in *FRUS*, 1941, 5:826–27.

12. Feis, *Road to Pearl Harbor*, 204. The declaration also triggered presidential powers such as requisitioning merchant ships.

13. State Department, *Documents Pertaining to Foreign Funds Control.*

14. Treasury Department, *Census of Foreign-Owned Assets*, 5.

15. Ibid., vii, 1–13.

16. Two ships ran the blockade during the fall of 1941. Operations continued in 1942 but thereafter diminished as the naval noose tightened and largely ended in 1944 due to sinkings.

17. Charles W. Yost, Assistant Chief Division of Controls, 9 April 1941, *FRUS*, 1941, 5:808–9; Joseph C. Green, Division of Controls to A-A, 19 June 1941, and Maxwell to Acheson, 30 June 1941, both in File 811.20 Regulations, State Department microfilm series LM-68, RG 59, NA. Months of supply calculated by author.

18. These events are related in detail in the many diplomatic histories of the coming of war. Among the most relevant to this narrative are Barnhart, *Japan Prepares*; Utley, *Going to War with Japan*; and Feis, *Road to Pearl Harbor*.

19. Welles, Memorandum of Conversation, and Hornbeck, memorandum of conversation, 16 July 1941, both in *FRUS*, 1941, 5:826–32.

20. Feis, *Road to Pearl Harbor*, 229.

21. E. H. Foley Jr. to Morgenthau, 21 July 1941, *Morgenthau Diaries*, vol. 2, Roll 55.

22. Harold R. Stark, Chief of Naval Operations to FDR, 21 July 1941, enclosing Turner memo of same date; and Acheson, Memorandum of Conversation, 23 July 1941, both in *FRUS*, 1941, 5:835–42; Feis, *Road to Pearl Harbor*, 239–41.

23. Feis, *Road to Pearl Harbor*, 247.

24. Utley, "Upstairs, Downstairs at Foggy Bottom," 24.

25. Hornbeck, Memorandum by the Adviser on Political Relations, 19 July 1941, *FRUS*, 1941, 5:832–33.

26. Green to A-A, 19 July 1941; Utley, "Upstairs, Downstairs at Foggy Bottom," 24. Utley cites memoranda of Edward Foley of 19, 21 July in *Morgenthau Diaries*.

27. Commerce Department, *Foreign Commerce and Navigation of the United States*, 1935–41.

28. Green to A-A, 19 July 1941.

29. Calculations by the author.

30. Welles to Grew, 1 August 1941, *FRUS*, 1941, 5:851.

31. Commerce Department, *Foreign Commerce and Navigation of the United States*, 1935–41; Principal Exports . . . Five Months 1941, c. 17 August 1941, Table VII-8-1. Inferred quotas calculated by the author.

32. Foley to Morgenthau, 21 July 1941, *Morgenthau Diaries*, vol. 2; Utley, "Upstairs, Downstairs at Foggy Bottom," 24.

33. Memo from Undersecretary to Morgenthau, Cabinet Meeting, 24 July 1941; and D. H. Bell to E. H. Foley Jr., 24 July 1941, both in *Morgenthau Diaries*, vol. 2; Utley, "Upstairs, Downstairs at Foggy Bottom," 24.

34. Meeting of Welles, Acheson, and Treasury officials, 25 July 1941, *Morgenthau Diaries*, cited in Utley, "Upstairs, Downstairs at Foggy Bottom," 24; Stark to FDR, 21 July 1941, *FRUS*, 1941, 5:835–36.

35. Meeting of Welles, Acheson, and Treasury officials, 25 July 1941, *Morgenthau Diaries*, vol. 2, Roll 56. Jonathan Utley notes that decisions at this conference were confirmed between Acheson and Canadian and British diplomats; "Upstairs, Downstairs at Foggy Bottom," 24.

36. Feis, *Road to Pearl Harbor*, 244–45.

37. *New York Times*, 26 July 1941, 5.

38. Rozell to Knoke, Yokohama Specie Bank's Reports, 23 July 1941, Yokohama Specie Bank Reports; Liquidation of Dollars by Japan, 15 July 1941, Box 50, File Japan General 1922–41, FRB.

39. FRBNY to Treasury, 23 July 1941, File 894.51/733, State Department microfilm series LM-68, RG 59, NA.

40. Feis, Economic Affairs, 25 July 1941, Box 4861-4863, File 840.51 Frozen Credits/2737, RG 59, NA.

41. State Department, re FBI advice, 1 August 1941, State Department microfilm series LM-68, RG 59, NA; Hornbeck to Hiss, 2 August 1941, File Frozen Credits July 26 to December 21, 1941; Office of Alien Property Custodian, *Report for the Fiscal Year Ending June 30, 1946*.

42. Office of Alien Property Custodian, *Report for the Period March 11, 1942 to June 30, 1943*.

43. See chapter 8.

44. Commerce Department, *Foreign Commerce and Navigation of the United States*, 1941; Japan Statistical Association, *Historical Statistics of Japan*, Table 10-5-a; Tenenbaum to Friedman, Japanese Gold Production and Operation, 2 January 1946.

45. Calculations by the author.

46. White to Morgenthau, Japan's Foreign Exchange Position, 25 February 1941.

Chapter 15. The Fictitious U.S. Oil Shortage

1. The following articles in *Oil and Gas Journal*: unsigned, 8 May 1941, 33; 15 May 1941, 20–21, 26; 29 May 1941, 14–15; 12 June 1941, 18, 20; Norman H. Stanley, "Industry May Avert Severe Cut in East Coast Supplies," 3 July 1941, 8–9, 24; unsigned, "Ways Explored to Replace Capacity of 50 Tankers," 10 July 1941, 26–27, 31, 34, 42; unsigned, 17 July 1941, 14, 17; 24 July 1941, 22; 7 August 1941, 9, 14, 19; 14 August 1941, 24, 28, 31, 80; 21 August 1941, 25–26, 30, 74; 28 August 1941, 24–25, 30; 4 September 1941, 16–17; 11 September 1941, 15; 18 September 1941, 60–61; 25 September 1941, 30–31, 115; 2 October 1941, 16, 22; 9 October 1941, 20, 24; 16 October 1941, 28, 30; P. L. Stockman, "Adequate New Reserves Found [in California] to Offset This Year's Output"; A. H. Bell, "Voluntary Crude-Oil Curtailment in California Effective," 30 October 1941, A46, A94; unsigned, "Tanker Diversion and Japanese Embargo Cut California Exports," 30 October 1941, A89–90; 30 October 1941, A109; and 6 November 1941, 81; Commerce Department, *Foreign Commerce and Navigation of the United States*; Interior Department, *Minerals Yearbook*.

2. Senate, Committee on Military Affairs, *Report of Proceedings: Hearings Held Before the Committee*, 77th Cong., 1st sess., 22 April 1941 (Washington, D.C.: GPO, 1941); Senate, Special Committee to Investigate Gasoline and Fuel-Oil Shortages Pursuant to S.Res. 156, *Hearings*, 77th Cong., 1st sess. (hereafter cited as Senate, Special Committee, *Hearings*), pt. 1, 28–29 August, 3–6, 9, 19 September 1941; pt. 2, 1–2 October 1941; Senate, Special Committee, *Hearings*, 11 September 1941.

3. *Oil and Gas Journal*, 29 May, 3, 10 July, 7 August, and 11 September 1941; Catherine B. A. Behrens, *Merchant Shipping and the Demands of War* (London: HMSO, 1955), 190–97; H. Duncan Hall, *North American Supply* (London: HMSO, 1955); D. J. Payton-Smith, *Oil: A Study of War-time Policy and Administration* (London: HMSO, 1971), xvii, 129, 146–53, 162–63, 178–81, 195–211, 243–45, 375–79, 488–89.

4. "Ways Explored," *Oil and Gas Journal*, 10 July 1941.

5. Payton-Smith, "Notes on Weights and Measures," in *Oil*, xvii; *Oil and Gas Journal*, 11 September 1941, 17.

6. T. H. Watkins, "Ickes, Harold LeClair," *American National Biography Online*; *New York Times*, 4 February 1942, 1; Blum, *From the Morgenthau Diaries* 2:344, 349–53, 358; Harold L. Ickes, *The Secret Diary of Harold L. Ickes* (New York: Simon and Schuster, 1954), 3:392, 456.

7. *Oil and Gas Journal*, 18 September 1941, 61.

8. Davies testimony, Special Committee, *Hearings*, pt. 1, 28 August 1941, 1–52.

9. Ickes, *Secret Diary* 3:96, 537, 543–60, 567–68; Feis, *Road to Pearl Harbor*, 206–7; Brig. Gen. Russell L. Maxwell, 24 February, 21 June 1941 (handwritten note re: FDR), Box 72, File 457.1 Japan, Entry 98, Central File (Area), Office of the Administrator of Export Control, RG 169, NA.

10. *Oil and Gas Journal*, various dates, May–July 1941, esp. 3 and 10 July 1941.

11. Exhibit, Report of W. Alton Jones, Special Committee, *Hearings*, pt. 2, 286–87; Statement of John J. Pelley, President of the Association of American Railroads, 3 September 1941, pt. 1, 81–112; Statement of Josiah W. Bailey, President, American Automobile Association, 24 August 1941, pt, 1, 73–79; *Oil and Gas Journal*, 10 July 1941, 26–27, 42.

12. *Oil and Gas Journal*, 24 July 1941, 22.

13. Maxwell Hamilton, memorandum, 22 July 1941, 834, and Welles to FDR, 31 July 1941, 846–48, both in *FRUS*, 1941, vol. 5.

14. Stark to Hull, enclosing memo to FDR, 22 July 1941, *FRUS*, 1941, 5:835; Feis, *Road to Pearl Harbor*, 237.

15. Radio Bulletin No. 176, issued by the White House, 25 July 1941, in Feis, *Road to Pearl Harbor*, 236–37.

Chapter 16. Freeze: The Crucial Month of August 1941

1. President of the United States, Press Releases; also in Foley to Morgenthau, 25 July 1941, *Morgenthau Diaries*, vol. 2, Roll 56; Feis, *Road to Pearl Harbor*, 238.

2. Feis, *Road to Pearl Harbor*, 242–43; *New York Times*, 26 July 1941, 4; Utley, "Upstairs, Downstairs at Foggy Bottom," 25.

3. EO 8832, 26 July 1941, and related orders and licenses, State Department, *Documents Pertaining to Foreign Funds Control*; Undersecretary to Morgenthau, cabinet meeting, 24 July 1941, *Morgenthau Diaries*, vol. 2, Roll 56.

4. Feis, *Road to Pearl Harbor*, 247. The committee of Acheson, Foley, and Shea was sometimes referred to in documents as the Interdepartmental Policy Committee, or just the Policy Committee, when establishing regulations and rules, and as the FFCC when it passed judgment on specific transactions. The practice varied informally.

5. *New York Times*, 26 July 1941, 4, 5, 12; 27 July 1941, 4, 18, 19, 41; 29 July 1941, 4; 30 July 1941, 4; and 2 August 1941, 21; Cochran to Morgenthau, 26 July 1941, *Morgenthau Diaries*, vol. 2, Roll 56.

6. Treasury Department, *Census of Foreign-Owned Assets*; Blum, *From the Morgenthau Diaries* 2:341.

7. General Licenses 54 to 66, 26 July 1941, State Department, *Documents Pertaining to Foreign Funds Control*.

8. YSB Seattle branch, telegrams and letters to head office Tokyo, to other YSB branches, and to correspondent banks, 26 July–16 August 1941, notebook "S13," Office of Alien Property Custodian, Box 30, Entry 190, Yokohama Specie Bank Treasury Papers 1940–42, Records Relating to World War II, Seized Records of Japanese Banks, RG 131, NA; Welles to U.S. Embassy Chungking, *Morgenthau Diaries*, vol. 2, Roll 56.

9. Application for License (blank), Box 4683, File Frozen Credits 1940–41, RG 59, NA.

10. YSB Seattle branch, files, and notebook registers of applications for licenses to transfer funds, various dates, 26 July–1 October 1941, Box 30, Office of Alien Property Custodian, Yokohama Specie Bank Treasury Papers 1940–42.

11. Jones to Acheson, 8 August 1941; National Council of American Importers to Hornbeck, 11 August 1941; Acheson to Iguchi, 15 August 1941; and Miller to Acheson, 20 September 1941, all in *FRUS*, 1941, vol. 5; Japanese Financial Commission to Acheson, 25, 28 August, 8 September 1941; Jameson to Hiss, 27 August 1941; Jones, Far Eastern Division, American-owned Transit Cargo in Japan, 4 September 1941; George Atcheson Jr. to Hecht, 9 October 1941; and Acheson to Bacher of U.S. Chamber of Commerce, 23 October 1941, all in Box 3359, File 800.8890, RG 59, NA.

12. George F. Luthringer to Acheson, Suggested Policy with Respect to the Control of United States–Japanese and Philippine-Japanese Trade Under Executive Order no. 8389, as Amended, 30 July 1941, *FRUS* 1941, 5:844–45.

13. Welles to FDR, 31 July 1941 (with footnote: "President Roosevelt approved the recommendations, with the notation 'SW OK. FDR'"), *FRUS*, 1941, 5:846–48; Utley, "Upstairs, Downstairs at Foggy Bottom," 25–26; Barnhart, *Japan Prepares*, 230–32; Feis, *Road to Pearl Harbor*, 247–48.

14. Acheson to Hull, Trade with Japan, 22 September; and Nomura to Hull 3 October 1942, both in *FRUS*, 1941, 5:881–84, 892.

15. Henry Gass to Harry Dexter White, Japanese Unblocked Foreign Exchange Assets, 11 August 1941, Box 4866, File 840.51 Frozen Credits 1940–1944, RG 59, NA.

16. Ibid.; W. H. Rozell to Knoke, Yokohama Specie Bank's Reports, 23 July 1941, Yokohama Specie Bank Reports. The value of the official yen in Shanghai was estimated at eleven cents on 18 August 1941, and military yen occupation currency at twelve cents, based on cross-rates of the Chinese yuan. By 1944 the yen was estimated to be worth only five to seven cents due to inflation. Commerce Department, Bureau of Domestic and Foreign Commerce, "The Role of the Bank of Japan in the Japanese War Effort," mimeograph, Washington, D.C., 1944, call no. HG3326.U5, Library of Congress; *Oriental Economist*, December 1941, 618.

17. Gass to White, Japanese Unblocked Foreign Exchange Assets, 11 August 1941.

18. Welles to Collectors of Customs, 1 August 1941, *FRUS*, 1941, 5:850.

19. Acheson to Welles, 16 August 1941, *FRUS*, 1941, 5:859; and MMH (Hamilton) re *Shiriya*, 8 August 1941, Box 4864, File 840.51 Frozen Credits/3337, RG 59, NA.

20. Hull (initialed by Acheson) to Collector of Customs, Los Angeles, telegram, 11 August 1941, *FRUS*, 1941, 5:850.

21. Acheson, Memorandum of Conversation (with Iguchi), 15 August 1941, File 840.51 Frozen Credits/3302; A.U. Fox, Memorandum, 19 August 1941; Donald Hiss to Miller, c. 21 August 1941; Jones to Acheson, 22 August 1941, File 840.51 Frozen Credits/3476; and Yost, memorandum, 4 September, and addendum, 5 September 1941, File 840.51 Frozen Credits/3336, all in Boxes 4861–4865, RG 59, NA.

22. Federal Reserve bank examiners assisted, In both eras the treasury cooperated with export controllers, the Commerce Department in World War I and the ECA and State's Division of Controls in 1940–41, but there was no precedent for sharing the licensing of financial transactions with any other agencies or cabinet departments.

23. For origins of the FFCC, see chapter 9. For biographies of individuals see index. An Acheson biographer states he was chairman of the FFCC, but there is no record of this. Chace, *Acheson*, 85. Acheson, as later secretary of state under Roosevelt and Truman, is recognized as one of the most important statesman of American history for his internationalist policies during the early Cold War as a supporter of the Marshall Plan and military alliances. He wrote several books, including a Pulitzer Prize–winning autobiography. Inquiries to the Harry Truman Library in Missouri which holds Acheson's papers for his period as secretary of state, and to the Sterling Memorial Library at Yale University which holds his personal papers, indicated that there is nothing of further interest about the freeze of Japanese assets in 1941 in those collections. The others' careers were less distinguished. Foley served in the army in World War II, returned to the treasury as head of a contracts settlements division, and rose to undersecretary under Truman. He left government in 1953 to establish a law firm that specialized in tax matters, and raised funds for democratic politicians. Shea did not rise in rank at the Justice Department. After the war he assisted his former boss Jackson as an assistant prosecutor at the Nuremberg war crimes trials. He cofounded a Washington law firm and spent four decades in litigation and antitrust work.

24. Utley, "Upstairs, Downstairs at Foggy Bottom," 24.

25. Anderson, *Standard-Vacuum Oil*, 178–79; Barnhart, *Japan Prepares*, 231; Feis, *Road to Pearl Harbor*, 246–48; Utley, *Going to War with Japan*, 155–56; Utley, "Upstairs, Downstairs at Foggy Bottom," 26–27; Langer and Gleason, *Undeclared War*, 655.

26. Utley, "Upstairs, Downstairs at Foggy Bottom," 28.

27. Acheson, *Present at the Creation*, chaps. 3 and 4.

Chapter 17. Barter and Bankruptcy

1. The idea of a high-level committee arose in part from proposals and counterproposals during the first half of 1941 in which the Treasury, the ECA, and the Interdepartmental Policy Committee each argued that it should take charge of export control, subject to policy guidance from an advisory committee. The ECA's proposal suggested the vice president as "director." A major element of the 1941 reorganizations was subordinating the agency dealing with allocation of materials to the civilian economy with the Office of Production Management (OPM), which allocated materials for military needs. *Industrial Mobilization for War*, vol. 1; Bureau of the Budget, Office of Administrative Records, Records Analysis Division, *The United States at War: Development and Administration of the War Program by the Federal Government* (Washington, D.C.: GPO, 1946), 65–67, 71–86, 89–91; OEM, *United States Government Manual* (Washington, D.C.: GPO, c. 1945), 98–99A.

2. *Who Was Who in America*, vol. 5.

3. Bureau of the Budget, *United States at War*, 86.

4. Ralph Turner to Col. Charles McKnight, Chief, Projects Section, Meeting with Vice-President Wallace on 19 August, 21 August 1941, File Binder, "Economic Warfare Planning OAEC," Box 184, FEA, Office of the Administrator of Export Control, Entry 97, Central File, RG-169, NA.

5. Bureau of the Budget, *United States at War*, 67.

6. Acheson, Memorandum of Conversation, 15 August 1941, *FRUS*, 1941, 5:857–58.

7. Haruo Iguchi, "An Unfinished Dream: Yoshisuke Ayukawa's Economic Diplomacy Toward the U.S., 1937–1940," Kyoto, Doshisha University, Sophia Education and Research Center for Education Services, Sophia University Institute for American and Canadian Studies web site, http://www.info.sophia.ac.jp/amecana/Journal/16-2.htm (accessed 18 January 2006).

8. Desvernine to Hull, Desvernine to Wallace, 5 September 1941, File 894.6552/22, Internal Affairs of Japan 1940–1944, Roll 16, State Department microfilm series LM-68, RG 59, NA.

9. Raoul E. Desvernine, *Democratic Despotism* (New York: Dodd, Mead, 1936), 112–23; Frederick Randolph, "The American Liberty League, 1934–1940," *American Historical Review* 56, no. 1 (October 1950): 19–33; *Washington Post*, 3 June 1996, B3; *New York Times*, 24 August 1935, 3; 6 May 1938, 33; 26 August 1941, 30; 16 November 1941, F3; and 3 June 1966, 38.

10. R. R. Stout, to Maxwell, notes on meeting, 14 February 1941, File Binder, "Economic Warfare Planning OAEC"; George F. Luthringer to Acheson, Suggested Policy re: Trade under E.O. 8389 as Amended, 30 July 1941; Welles to FDR, 31 July 1941, *FRUS*, 1941, 5:844–48.

11. Ragnar Nurske, League of Nations, *International Currency Experience*, Geneva 1944, in *International Finance*, ed. Mira Wilkins (New York: Arno, 1978), 177–83; "Clearing Accounts," online at http://www.bankinghistory.de/Bulletin/EABH-web (accessed 1 September 2003); "Dollar Pooling in the Sterling Area," *American Economic Review* 44, no. 4 (September 1954): 559–76; Richard S. Sayers, *Financial Policy, 1939–1945* (London: HMSO, 1956), 232–41; F. M. Tamagna to Knoke, Transfers of Dollar Funds from Java Bank to Yokohama Specie Bank, 13 June 1941, File Java Banking, Box 51, International Subject Files, 1907 to 1974, International Finance Division and Predecessors 1907–1974, FRB.

12. Noel Hall to Acheson, The Freezing Order and Japan, 12 August; and untitled 18 August 1941, both in Box 4854, File 840.51 Frozen Credits/3478, /3479, RG 59, NA.

13. Lubricating oils, although one-third of the value of petroleum-related purchases in 1941, were not on the list.

14. Desvernine to Wallace, 5 September 1941, with tables attached.

15. Calculations by the author.

16. Acheson to Hull, 13 September 1941; Acheson, Memorandum of Conversation, Japanese Silk and Barter Proposal, 18 September 1941, File 894.6522/23 and 124, RG 59, NA.

17. Hull to Attorney General, 23 January 1943, File 894.6552/26, RG 59, NA; Ambassador Nomura, Dispatch to Tokyo, 19 September 1941, in Donald M. Goldstein and Katherine V. Dillon, eds., *The Pacific War Papers: Japanese Documents of World War II* (Washington, D.C.: Potomac Books, 2004), 136–234.

18. Acheson, Memorandum of Conversation, 18 September 1941; Miller to Acheson, 20 September 1941; and Acheson to Miller, 20 September 1941, all in File 840.51 Frozen Credits/3546, RG 59, NA.

19. Ambassador Nomura, two dispatches to Tokyo, 19 September 1941, in Goldstein and Dillon, *Pacific War Papers*. These messages makes clear that high Japanese authorities knew of the Desvernine mission and supported it.

20. Nomura, dispatch to Tokyo, 5 December 1941, in Goldstein and Dillon, *Pacific War Papers*.

21. Attorney General to Hull, 28 December 1942; Hull to Attorney General, 23 January 1943; and Salisbury, Far Eastern Affairs to Hull, 22 September 1943, all in File 894.6552/9, Roll 16, Department of State microfilm series LM-68, RG 59, NA; Congressional Research Service, "Conducting Foreign Relations Without Authority: The Logan Act," online at http://www.pennhyill.com/foreign policy (accessed 1 September 2003); Raoul E. Desvernine, summaries of *Wake Up*

America broadcasts on ABC Blue Network, 1943–46, GOLDIndex, http://www.radioindex.com (accessed 29 August 2003); Drew Pearson, "The Washington Merry-Go-Round," *Washington Post*, 10 December 1945, 5.

22. Miller to Acheson, 20 September 1941.

23. Nomura to Hull, two oral messages, 3 October 1941, *FRUS*, 1941, 5:892.

24. "Japanese Embassy to Treasury, oral, 9 October 1941, *FRUS*, 1941, 5:895–96; "U" to Welles, 17 October 1941, and Edward G. Miller, Memorandum for the Files, 24 October 1941, both in Box 4868, File 840.51 Frozen Credits/4184–4185, RG 59, NA.

25. Joseph W. Ballantine, Memorandum of Conversation, 3 October 1941, *FRUS*, 1941, 5:891–92; Acheson to Hamilton, handwritten, 24 October 1941, File 840.51 Frozen Credits/4185, RG 59, NA.

26. Acheson, *Present at the Creation*, 26–27.

27. See notes to Appendix 1, this volume.

28. Welles, Memorandum of Conversation, 2 August 1941, *FRUS*, 1941, 5:852.

29. Jones, Application by a Japanese cotton firm in the United States to change its business from export trade to domestic trade, 7 October; and MMH, reply, 14 October 1941, both in File 840.51 Frozen Credits/4182, RG 59, NA.

30. E. T. Wailes to Hiss, 25 August 1941, "Regulations" File 1941 811.20(D)/4425; Yokohama Specie Bank (Seattle Branch), "Application(s) for a License to Engage in a Foreign Exchange Transaction, Transfer of Credit, Payment, Export or Withdrawal from the United States, or the Earmarking of Gold or Silver Coin or Bullion or Currency, or the Transfer, Withdrawal or Exportation of, or Dealing in, Evidences of Indebtedness or Evidences of Ownership of Property," filed with the Federal Reserve Bank of San Francisco, and notarized affidavits of residency and ownership, c. 26 July to 7 December 1941, Box 30, Office of Alien Property Custodian, Yokohama Specie Bank Treasury Papers 1940–42, RG 131, NA.

31. Acheson, untitled memorandum, 18 August; Grew to Secretary of State, 22 August; and Secretary of State to Grew, 5 September 1941, all in *FRUS*, 1941, 5:861–64, 871–72.

32. Adrian S. Fisher, Memorandum of Conversation, 23 October; application for release of funds for port expenses of the SS *Tatuta Maru* and SS *Taiyo Maru*, 23 October; and licenses for obtaining fuel and supplies in Honolulu for SS *Tatuta Maru*, 24 October 1941, all in File 840.51 Frozen credits/FW4223, FW4868, RG 59, NA.

33. Looseleaf notebook S.13, Box 30, Yokohama Specie Bank License Papers 1940–42, Box 30, Entry 190, Seized Records of Japanese Banks, Alien Property Custodian, RG 131, NA.

34. Donald Hiss, Chief Foreign Funds Control Division, to the *Iron Age*, 3 December 1941, File 840.51 Frozen Credits/4354, RG 59, NA.

35. E. G. Miller to Fisher, 25 August 1941, enclosing Memorandum of Nishiyama, Financial Counselor of the Japanese Embassy, 20 August 1941, forwarded to Acheson, File 840.51 Frozen Credits/3546, RG 59, NA.

36. Feis to Acheson, 19 September; and G. L. Luthringer, Interest Payments Due on Japanese Dollar Bonds in the Near Future, 23 September 1941, both in File 840.51 Frozen Credits/3787, RG 59, NA.

37. C. Ashwood, National Bank Examiner, Comptroller of the Currency, Yokohama Specie Bank, New York, meeting with T. Nishiyama, 14 October, with forwarding letters to Pehle and Acheson 18 October 1941, File 840.51 Frozen Credits/3714, RG 59, NA; W. P. Folger, Chief National Bank Examiner to Delano, 21 October 1941, Box 20, File Japan Banks and Banking, vol. 1, OASIA.

38. Miller to Acheson, 5 September 1941, *FRUS*, 1941, 5:869–70.

39. Feis to Acheson, 19 September 1941.

40. C. Ashwood, National Bank Examiner, meeting with Nishiyama and Nishi, 14 October 1941; and correspondence and phone conversations between comptroller of the currency, Bernstein, Fox, Miller, and Fox re: Yokohama Specie Bank West Coast branches, 20 and 21 October 1941, all in File 840.51 Frozen Credits/4448, RG 59, NA.

41. *New York Times*, 29 November 1941, 4.

42. Office of Alien Property Custodian, *Report for the Period March 11, 1942 to June 30, 1943* and *Report for the Fiscal Year Ending June 30, 1944*.

43. *New York Times*, 1 December 1944, 33; 3 June 1955, 23; 30 September 1955, 38; 11 April 1967, 24; and *Wall Street Journal*, 20 April 1946, 4.

44. President, Yokohama Specie Bank, to Minister of Finance; Reorganization Plan of the Yokohama Specie Bank, 22 March 1946; and Ministry of Finance of the Japanese Government to Economic and Scientific Section, GHQ, 9 April 1946, all in Box 20, File Japan Banks and Banking Foreign, vol. 1, OASIA; *Japan: An Illustrated Encyclopedia* (Tokyo: Kodansha, 1993), 99.

45. Acheson to Secretary of State, Present Effect of the Freezing Control in the Economic Control as Exercised Upon Japan, 22 November 1941, *FRUS*, 1941, 4:903–4.

Chapter 18. Calamity: The Economy under Siege

1. Gary Clyde Hufbauer, Jeffrey J. Schott, and Kimberly Ann Elliott, *Economic Sanctions Reconsidered*, vol. 1, and *History and Current Policy* and vol. 2 *Supplemental Case Histories*, both 2nd ed. (Washington, D.C.: Institute for International Economics, 1990).

2. Frank S. Williams, Strictly Confidential Fortnightly Background Report, October 27–November 8, 1941, endorsed by Grew, 10 November 1941; Congress, Joint Committee on the Investigation of the Investigation of the Pearl Harbor Attack, *Hearings*, 79th Cong., 1st sess., 39 vols. (Washington, D.C.: GPO, 1946), 20:4051–57, online at http://www.ibiblio.org/pha/pha.

3. White to Morgenthau, 1 October 1941, *Morgenthau Diaries*, 447:48–49, as reprinted in *Morgenthau Diary (China)*, vol. 1, U.S. Senate, Internal Security Subcommittee on the Judiciary (Washington, D.C.: GPO, 1965), 472.

4. Williams, Strictly Confidential Fortnightly Background Report, 10 November 1941; Grew to Department of State, 3 December 1941, *PHA* 14:1049–51. Some of Grew's reports cited in this chapter, apparently paraphrased, appear in Joseph C. Grew, *Ten Years in Japan* (New York: Simon and Schuster, 1944), chap. 5.

5. Memorandum for the Chief of Naval Operations, 21 October 1941, *PHA* 15:1845.

6. Morley, *Final Confrontation*, 159–69 and Appendix 5.

7. Ibid., 175, 289–96; Barnhart, *Japan Prepares*, 246.

8. White to Morgenthau, untitled, 1 October 1941; Williams, Strictly Confidential Fortnightly Background Report, September 15–27, 1941, *PHA* 20:4041–49; Brigadier-General Sherman Miles, Army G-2, Memorandum for the Chief of Staff, 5 September 1941, *PHA* 14:1353; Grew to Department of State, Report of Conditions During the Month of August 1941, *PHA* 20:4051–52; OP 16-F to Chief of Naval Operations, 21 October 1941, *PHA* 15:1845.

9. Barnhart, *Japan Prepares*, 239, 246–48, 255–58; Morley, *Final Confrontation*, 159–69, 289–96, Appendix 5; Worth, *No Choice but War*, chaps. 7–8.

10. Grew to Department of State, Report of Conditions During the Month of July 1941, cited in Worth, *No Choice but War*, 175–77; White to Morgenthau, 1 October 1941; Williams, Strictly Confidential Fortnightly Background Report, October 27–November 8, 1941, 10 November 1941; Miles, Memorandum for Chief of Staff, 5 September 1941.

11. Morley, *Final Confrontation*, 159–169, 289–93, 326, Appendix 5.

12. *American Men and Women of Science: Economics 1974*, 234; American Economic Association, Directory of Members, *American Economic Review*, October 1974, 173; National Archives, *Guide to Federal Records in the National Archives of the United States*, Records of the National Emergency Council, RG 44.3, NA, http://www.archives.gov/research/guide-fed-records/groups/044.html#44.3 (accessed 24 October 2006).

13. OCL, *Place of Foreign Trade*, includes vol. 1, pt. 1, xvii, 1–158, issued 29 August 1946; vol. 1, pt. 2, 159–362, issued September 1946; and vol. 2 (statistical summary and charts) xii, 1–128, issued January 1946. The OSS was the ancestor of the Central Intelligence Agency, established in 1947. William W. Lockwood, an economics professor and author on Japan's economy, called it "a

valuable study" as late as 1954. Lockwood, *Economic Development of Japan*, 314. Jerome Cohen, a professor of economics at the City College of New York, criticized the study because it did not address the motivations for prewar Japanese trade-control measures and thus "hinders an attempt to understand the problem as the Japanese then saw it." Cohen, *Japan's Economy*, 12n27. Lockwood and Cohen had access to 1937–41 data after the war that was unavailable to Hersey until nearly the end of the study. Cohen's point is irrelevant for applying the study to this chapter, which is intended as a speculation on how U.S. authorities might have evaluated the impact of the dollar freeze on Japan if continued for a few years.

14. OCL, *Place of Foreign Trade*, vol. 1, pt. 1, i–vi, 1–42, 67–108; vol. 1, pt. 2, 159–351; vol. 2.

15. Ibid., vol. 1, pt. 1, 21–28, 110–11.

16. Ibid., vol. 1, pt. 1, 43–66 91–97 109–145; vol. 1, pt. 2 177–81, 205–12, 231–33, 254–63, 272, 294–98, 308–10, 344–45, 352–59.

17. "China Food," International Institute for Applied Systems Analysis (IIASA), http://www.iiasa.ac.at/ Research/LUC/ChinaFood/data/diet/diet_1.htm (accessed 24 October 2006).

18. OCL, *Place of Foreign Trade*, vol. 1, pt. 2, 165–71.

19. Ibid., vol. 1, pt. 1, 64.

20. Ibid., vol. 1, pt. 1, 61–66 (Asiatic diet, 64), 114–15, 134–37, 143, app. 145–48, 152–53, tables I-20, I-21 I-22; vol. 1, pt. 2, 177–81, 208–12, 231–33, 254–64, 272–74, 294–98, 305–6, 309–10, 319, 322, 327–28, 336–37, 339, 341, 344–45, 348–49, 352–59.

21. Ibid., vol. 1, pt. 1, 95–101.

Chapter 19. Futility: The Final Negotiations

1. The U.S. Library of Congress lists 115 books in English under "Pearl Harbor Attack," several dealing with the diplomatic and military preludes rather than the attack itself (and a few espousing conspiracy theories). The principal published documentary sources are *FRUS*, 1941, vol. 5; *FRUS Japan*; Congress, Joint Committee on the Investigation of the Investigation of the Pearl Harbor Attack, *Hearings*; and Defense Department, *The "Magic" Background of Pearl Harbor* (Washington, D.C.: GPO, 1978). General works include Cordell Hull, *The Memoirs of Cordell Hull* (New York: Macmillan, 1948); Feis, *Road to Pearl Harbor*; Langer and Gleason, *Undeclared War*; Roberta Wohlstetter, *Pearl Harbor: Warning and Decision* (Stanford, Calif.: Stanford University Press, 1962); Dorothy Borg and Shumpei Okamato, eds., *Pearl Harbor as History: Japanese-American Relations 1931–1941*, Studies of the East Asia Institute (New York: Columbia University Press, 1973); Gordon W. Prange with Donald M. Goldstein and Katherine V. Dillon, *At Dawn We Slept: The Untold Story of Pearl Harbor* (New York: Viking, 1991); and Akira Iriye, *Pearl Harbor and the Coming of the Pacific War* (Boston: Bedford/St. Martin's, 1999). Works that focus on the freeze and embargo in the negotiations include Utley, *Going to War with Japan*; Barnhart, *Japan Prepares*; and Worth, *No Choice but War*. On the Japanese side, see Morley, *Final Confrontation*; and Goldstein and Dillon, *Pacific War Papers*, 136–234.

2. State Department officers contributed advice, but Ambassador Grew in Tokyo was relegated to incidental adviser and message carrier. Neither the secretaries of war and the navy nor their uniformed chiefs, who tended to favor a softer line to gain time for building up defenses, participated in direct negotiations, nor did other cabinet-level officials, although some operated as advisers and go-betweens. Consultations within the government were eclectic, ranging from sideline discussions to full cabinet meetings. Intelligence agencies provided Roosevelt, Hull, and a very few others with deciphered messages between Tokyo and its ambassadors. Historians have differed on whether code breaking helped U.S. negotiators or hindered them due to misunderstandings and poor translations. In Japan, Prime Minister Prince Fumimaro Konoe was an expansionist. Shortly before the freeze the foreign ministry passed from the quirky, pro-Axis Yosuke Matsuoka to the relatively moderate Admiral Teijiro Toyoda who was more wiling to negotiate. However, the Army and Navy held the balance of power because a general and an admiral served as mandatory members of the cabinet so either could bring down a government by resigning. Pol-

icy was set in liaison conferences, often lasting hours, conducted among the Army and Navy officers, in cabinet conferences including at least the prime minister and foreign minister and service chiefs, and ultimately imperial conferences before Emperor Hirohito and his household advisers.

3. Morley, *Final Confrontation*, 175ff, 243.

4. Ibid., 261–65, Appendix 9.

5. Ibid., 262 316; Barnhart, *Japan Prepares*, 254–59.

6. Barnhart, *Japan Prepares*, 235, 260; *FRUS*, 1941, 4:642–44; Hull, *Memoirs* 2:1070.

7. Joseph P. Lash, *Roosevelt and Churchill, 1939–1941* (New York: Norton, 1976), 457, 466–69.

8. Barnhart, *Japan Prepares*, 235; Morley, *Final Confrontation*, 305, 317–20.

Epilogue: Bankruptcy and War Crimes

1. Estimates by the author. In March 1941 the Bank of Japan reported $117 million of gold in its vaults. Mine production through July was about $20 million. Another $23 million is attributed so scrap gold purchases, residual holdings in the Gold Fund Special Account and gold held by other government agencies assumed from postwar data, minus industrial use. In February 1941 the FRBNY had estimated that Japan held about $205 million of gold, an exaggeration probably due to an older statement of the Bank of Japan and overestimating gold production. Liquid dollar assets of the Yokohama Specie Bank and other Japanese banks in the United States were about $40 million as reported by the Office of Alien Property Custodian, more or less depending on settlements of domestic liabilities ultimately allowed by the APC. Just before the freeze virtually all strategic products except oil had been embargoed, but Japan probably could not have purchased more than the recent $50 million of U.S. oil (annual rate) due to tanker shortages. Purchases of nonstrategic civilian products from America, some subject to licensing but likely to be allowed due to abundance such as cotton, lumber, pulp, phosphate, foodstuffs, pharmaceuticals, and some chemicals, had been about $25 million per year. Against this potential $75 million of U.S. supplies, Japan was exporting $150 million to the United States (although the $100 million of raw silk was sure to decline due to nylon's inroads). Purchases from other dollar countries were curtailed by American and British preemptive buying of raw materials. As Kurt Bloch, a reporter for the *Far Eastern Survey*, noted, "Japan's financial difficulty abroad is no longer finding means of paying for foreign goods, but rather finding foreign goods for which available means of payment can be used. . . . At present, Japan's gold problem may not differ greatly from that of the United States," an ironic statement because the United States had no need of gold for international transactions as all nations would gladly have accepted unlimited amounts of dollars. BB, Memorandum to the President, 5 August 1939. Kurt Bloch, "Japan on Her Own," *Far Eastern Survey*, 3 November 1941, 244–49.

2. In 1945 an accounting submitted to the occupation forces reported that the Bank of Japan, the mint, and other government agencies held approximately $461 million in gold bullion and coin, $134 million of which was said to be held on earmark for the account of Thailand and French Indochina for goods purchased from them during the war. Government agencies also held $49 million in silver bullion and coins and $4 million in currencies, primarily U.S. and British. The Yokohama Specie Bank reported its overseas branches owned $10 million in U.S. dollars and $4 million in sterling, which of course had been frozen, $20 million of Swiss, Swedish, and Portuguese currency accounts, and minor holdings of South American currency accounts. The government also held $28 million (prewar value) of German marks, yen, military yen, and local currencies of the colonies and of occupied China and conquered areas, nominally worth hundreds of millions of dollars but all of dubious value. Jenkins to I. S. Friedman and Coe, Gold Bullion and Other Foreign Exchange Assets in Japan, 16 October 1945; Division of Monetary Research, Tokyo Reports on gold, silver, platinum, currency, etc., owned by Japanese Government or Bank of Japan, 1 November 1945, File Japan Foreign Exchange Position; Survey of the Gold Fund Special Account, c. August 1945; Tenenbaum to Friedman, Japanese Gold Production and Operation, 2 January 1946; J. Tenenbaum to Jenkins, Foreign Exchange Assets of the Yokohama Specie Bank, 1 March 1946, Box 20, File Japan Banks and Banking, vol. 1, OASIA.

3. Bloch, "Japan on Her Own."

4. Acheson to Secretary of State, Present Effect of the Freezing Control in the Economic Control as Exercised Upon Japan, 22 November 1941, *FRUS*, 1941, 4:903–4.

5. R. John Pritchard, commentator International Military Tribunal for the Far East, *The Tokyo Major War Crimes Trial: The Records of the International Military Tribunal for the Far East* (New York: Edward Mellen Press, 1998), 90:43159–62.

Appendix 1. The U.S. Oil Shortage that Never Was

1. See chapter 15 for the period prior to the financial freeze.

2. Ralph H. Davies, Acting Petroleum Coordinator for National Defense, testimony, pt. 1, 28 August, 1–52; letter from Davies, 4 September, 165–67; and Davies statement, 9 and 10 September 1941, 272–347, 356–80, all in Special Committee, *Hearings*.

3. Special Committee, *Hearings*, pt. 1, 29 August, 73–79; 8 September 1941, 215–39.

4. Ralph Budd, a transportation advisor to the Council of National Defense, calculated 29,000 idle cars. Statement, Special Committee *Hearings*, pt 1, 4 September 1941.

5. John J. Pelley, President of the Association of American Railroads, Statement and Testimony, 3 September, Special Committee, *Hearings*, pt. 1, 81–112; letter from Pelley, 5 September 1941, 191–214; Statement and Testimony, 2 October, Special Committee, *Hearings*, pt. 2, 605–38.

6. Special Committee, Report No. 576, *Gasoline and Fuel-Oil Shortages: Preliminary Report*, 11 September 1941.

7. Harold L. Ickes, Petroleum Coordinator for National Defense, Statement and Testimony of 1 October 1941, Special Committee, *Hearings*, pt. 2, 383–593; Ickes, *Secret Diary*, 622–23.

8. Ickes, *Secret Diary*, 630–32; Statement of Admiral Emory S. Land, Chairman, Maritime Commission, 29 August 1941, Special Committee, *Hearings*, pt. 1, 53–73; Senator Francis Maloney, comment, 1 October 1941, Special Committee, *Hearings*, pt. 2, 574–75; *Economist*, 26 July 1941, cited in Special Committee, *Hearings*, pt. 1, 28 August 1941, 354–55.

9. *Oil and Gas Journal*, 30 October, 9, 12, 18 1941; 6 November 1941, 59; 20 November 1941, 18; and 4 December 1941, 16; Ickes, *Secret Diary*, 631–32. Pelley's claims were ultimately justified. In April 1942, when German U-boats were sinking many tankers off the Atlantic and Gulf coasts, the railroads moved six hundred thousand barrels per day to the East Coast, a volume almost 50 percent of the prewar rate of total supply for the region.

10. Payton-Smith, *Oil*, 129, 162–63, 178–81, 195–211, 375–79, Appendixes IV, VI; *Oil and Gas Journal*, 9 October, 1941, 24.

11. *Oil and Gas Journal*, 4 August 1941, 28, 80; 21 August 1941, 26; 11 September 1941, 14–15; 2 October 1941, 16; 6 November 1941, 59, 66; 4 December 1941, 20.

Appendix 2. Details of the OSS/State Department Study of Japanese Foreign Trade and Finance

1. For description of the study, see chapter 18, note 13.

2. OCL, *Place of Foreign Trade*, vol. 1, pt. 1, iii.

3. Ibid., iv; vol. 1, pt. 2, tables II-32 to II-34.

4. Ibid., vol. 1, pt. 1, iii; 11–21.

5. Ibid., 2–21.

6. Ibid., 110–11.

7. Ibid., 121.

8. Ibid., 43–66, 91–97, 109–145; vol. 1, pt. 2 177–81, 205–12, 231–33, 254–63, 272, 294–98, 308–10, 344–45, 352–59.

9. Ibid., vol. 1, pt. 1, 61–66, 114–15, 134–37, 143, app. 145–48, 152–53, tables I-20, I-21, I-22; vol. 1, pt. 2, 177–81, 208–12, 231–33, 254–64, 272–74, 294–98, 305–6, 309–10, 319, 322, 327–28, 336–37, 339, 341, 344–45, 348–49, 352–59.

10. Ibid., vol. 1, pt. 1, 67–87.

BIBLIOGRAPHY

United States Government Documents and Records

Administrator of Export Control (AEC). Classified Central File (Area) and Central File Area "Japan," July1940 to June 1942, Entry 97. RG 169, NA.
————. Chief, Export Section. General File, Entry 88. RG 169, NA.
————. Enemy Branch. Records of the Military Products Section. Far East Enemy Division. Finding Aid PI 29, Entry 50. RG 169, NA.
————. Far Eastern Committee. Projects Section. "Preliminary, Summary Report on Silk: Japan and the United States." 27 April 1941. Prepared by Wirth Ferger. General File of Chief, Projects Section, Entry 88, Box 698. RG 169, NA.
————. Planning Division. Central File, Entry 97. RG 169, NA.
————. Projects Section. General Files of the Chief, Entry 98. RG 169, NA.
————. List of Far Eastern Studies, February–July 1941. RG 169, NA.
————. List of Reports Prepared as of 15 Dec 1941. RG 169, NA.
Advisory Commission to the Council of National Defense. *Minutes of the Advisory Commission to the Council of National Defense, June 12, 1940 to October 22, 1941.* Historical Reports on War Administration, War Production Board. Washington, D.C.: GPO, 1946.
Bureau of the Budget. Office of Administrative Records. Records Analysis Division. *The United States at War: Development and Administration of the War Program by the Federal Government.* Washington, D.C.: GPO, 1946.
Civilian Production Administration Board. *Industrial Mobilization for War: History of the War Production Board and Predecessor Agencies, 1940–1945.* Vol. 1. Supervised by George W. Auxier, Board Historian. Washington, D.C.: GPO, 1947. Reprint, New York: Greenwood Press, 1969.
Civil Service Commission. *Official Register of the United States.* Washington, D.C.: GPO, 1930–42.
Commerce Department. Bureau of Foreign and Domestic Commerce. *The Balance of International Payments of the United States in 1937, 1938.* Washington, D.C.: GPO, 1938, 1939.
————. Commerce reports. Weekly. Washington, 1937–40.
————. *Foreign Commerce and Navigation of the United States.* Annual. Washington, D.C.: GPO, 1893–1942.
————. *Fuel and Power in Japan.* Trade Information Bulletin No. 821. Washington, D.C.: GPO, January 1935.
————. *Manchurian Gold Mining Experiences Poor Year in 1939.* Washington, D.C.: GPO, 4 March 1940.
————. "The Role of the Bank of Japan in the Japanese War Effort." Mimeograph. Washington, D.C., 1944. Call no. HG3326.U5. Library of Congress.

————. *Trade of the United States with Japan in 1938.* Washington, D.C.: GPO, April 1939.

————. *The United States in the World Economy; the International Transactions of the United States During the Interwar Period.* Prepared by Hal B. Lary. Washington, D.C.: GPO, 1943.

————. Bureau of the Census. *American Business; Retail Distribution: Variety Store Chains and Department Store Chains, 1933.* Washington, D.C.: GPO, 1935.

————. *Census of Manufactures: Clothing, 1914.* Washington, D.C.: GPO, 1915.

————. *Census of Manufactures: Cotton Manufactures,* 1919, 1921, 1923, 1925, 1927, 1929, 1931, 1933, 1935. Washington, D.C.: GPO, 1920, 1922, 1924, 1926, 1928, 1930, 1931, 1934, 1936.

————. *Census of Manufactures: Cotton Manufactures and Rayon and Silk Manufactures,* 1937, 1939. Washington, D.C.: GPO, 1938, 1940.

————. *Census of Manufactures: Hosiery and Knit Goods, 1914.* Washington, D.C.: GPO, 1915.

————. *Census of Manufactures: Silk and Rayon Goods,* 1931, 1933, 1935. Washington, D.C.: GPO, 1932, 1934, 1936. Included in *Census of Manufactures: Cotton Manufactures and Rayon and Silk,* 1937.

————. *Census of Manufactures: Silk Manufacture* or *Silk and Silk Goods,* 1900, 1909, 1914, 1919, 1921, 1925, 1927. Washington, D.C.: GPO, 1901, 1910, 1915, 1920, 1922, 1926, 1928.

————. *Census of Manufactures: Toys and Sporting and Athletic Goods, 1939.* Washington, D.C.: GPO, 1940. Toys and related goods are in *Census of Manufactures Summary Report,* 1937, 1940.

————. *Census of Manufactures: Toys, Games and Children's Wheeled Goods, 1935.* Washington, D.C.: GPO, 1936.

————. *Census of Manufactures: Wearing Apparel,* 1921, 1923, 1925, 1927. Washington, D.C.: GPO, 1922, 1924, 1926, 1928.

————. *Historical Statistics of the United States on CD-ROM: Colonial Times to 1970.* Washington, D.C.: GPO, 1976.

————. *Statistical Abstract of the United States.* Annual. Washington, D.C.: GPO, 1930–46.

————. Office of Coordinator of International Trade Statistics. *Evidences of Economic Pressure in Japan, December 6, 1941.* File 502-300, Japan Exports, Office of Naval Intelligence, Monograph Files, Japan 1939–46, Box 48. RG 38, NA.

————. Regional Information Division. *Position of the United States in Japan's Trade.* Washington, D.C.: GPO, 26 January 1940.

Congress. *An Act to Expedite the Strengthening of the National Defense.* H.R. 9850. 76th Cong., 3rd sess., 2 July 1940. In *Public Laws of the United States of America,* vol. 40, pt. 1.

————. *Congressional Directory.* Washington, D.C.: GPO, 1937–41.

————. *Neutrality Act 1935.* 74th Cong., 1st sess. In *Public Laws of the United States of America Passed by the Seventy-Fourth Congress, 1935–1936,* pt. 1, 1081–85. Washington, D.C.: GPO, 1936.

————. *Neutrality Act 1936.* 74th Cong., 1st sess. In *Public Laws of the United States of America Passed by the Seventy-Fourth Congress, 1935–1936,* pt. 1, 1152–53. Washington, D.C.: GPO, 1936.

————. *Neutrality Act 1937.* 75th Cong., 1st sess. In *Public Laws of the United States of America Passed by the Seventy-Fifth Congress, 1st Sess., 1937,* pt. 1, 121–28. Washington, D.C.: GPO, 1937.

————. *Tariff Act of 1930.* 71st Cong., 2nd sess. In *United States Statutes at Large,* vol. 46, ch. 497. Washington, D.C.: GPO, 1930.

————. *Trading with the Enemy Act: To Define, Regulate, and Punish Trading with the Enemy, and for Other Purposes.* Act Ch. 106, 40 Stat. 411. 6 October 1917. Washington, D.C.: GPO, 1917.

————. Congressional Research Service. "Conducting Foreign Relations Without Authority: The Logan Act." Online at http://www.pennhyill.com/foreign policy (accessed 1 September 2003).

————. House. Committee on Foreign Affairs. *Prohibition of U.S. Loans to Japan Due to Japanese*

War Activities in Violation of the Kellogg-Briand Pact. 7 March 1932. Microfiche. CIS 72 HFo-T.23. Library of Congress.

———. Committee on International Relations. Subcommittee on International Trade and Commerce. *Trading with the Enemy: Legislative and Executive Documents Concerning Regulation of International Transactions in Time of Declared National Emergency.* Washington, D.C.: GPO, 1976.

———. Committee on Interstate and Foreign Commerce. *Hearings on H.R. 4704, Trading with the Enemy.* 65th Cong., 1st sess., 29–31 May 1917. Washington, D.C.: GPO, 1917.

———. Committee on Ways and Means. *Conference Report: House Report No. 155 to Accompany H.R. 4960.* 65th Cong., 1st sess., 21 September 1917. Washington, D.C.: GPO, 1917.

———. *Hearings, Tariff Readjustment.* 70th Cong., 2nd sess., February 1929. Schedule 1, *Chemicals, Oils and Paints.* Schedule 2, *Earths, Earthenware and Glassware.* Schedule 12, *Silk and Manufactures of; Sundries; Various Items.* Washington, D.C.: GPO, 1929.

———. Joint Committee on the Investigation of the Pearl Harbor Attack. *Hearings.* 79th Cong., 1st sess. 39 vols. Washington, D.C.: GPO, 1946. On line at http://www.ibiblio.org/pha/pha.

———. Joint Resolution 51. 75th Cong., 1st sess., 1 May 1937. In *United States Statutes at Large,* vol. 50, pt. 1. Washington, D.C.: GPO, 1937.

———. Joint Resolution 173. 74th Cong., 1st sess., 31 August 1935. In *United States Statutes at Large,* vol. 49, pt. 1. Washington, D.C.: GPO, 1936.

———. Joint Resolution Extending and Amending Public Resolution Numbered 67. 74th Cong., 2nd sess., 29 February 1936. In *Public Laws of the United States of America,* vol. 49, pt. 2, 1152–53.

———. Subcommittee on International Economic Policy and Trade of the Committee on International Relations. *Emergency Controls on International Economic Transactions, Hearings before the Subcommittee on International Economic Policy and Trade of the Committee on International Relations, House of Representatives.* 95th Cong., 1st sess. Washington, D.C.: GPO, 1977.

———. *Hearings on H.R. 1560 and H.R. 2382 and Markup of Trading with the Enemy Reform Legislation.* 95th Cong., 1st sess., 29, 30 March, 19, 26 April, 5 May, 2, 8, 9, 13 June 1977. Washington, D.C.: GPO, 1977.

———. Senate. *Economic Analysis of Foreign Trade of the United States in Relation to the Tariff.* Report of the Tariff Commission in Response to Senate Resolution 325. Document 180. 72nd Cong., 2nd sess. Washington, D.C.: GPO, 1933.

———. Committee on Finance. *Hearings: Sale of Foreign Bonds or Securities in the United States Pursuant to S. Res. 19.* 72nd Cong., 1st sess. Washington, D.C.: GPO, 1932.

———. *Hearings, Tariff Act of 1929.* 71st Cong., 1st sess., June 1929. Washington, D.C.: GPO, 1929.

———. Committee on Military Affairs. *Report of Proceedings: Hearings Held Before the Committee.* 77th Cong., 1st sess., 22 April 1941. Washington, D.C.: GPO, 1941.

———. Special Committee to Investigate Gasoline and Fuel-Oil Shortages Pursuant to S.Res.156. *Hearings.* 77th Cong., 1st sess. Pt. 1, 28–29 August, 3–6, 9, 19 September 1941. Pt. 2, 1–2 October 1941. Washington, D.C.: GPO, 1941.

———. *Preliminary Report.* 77th Cong., 1st sess., 11 September 1941.Washington, D.C.: GPO, 1941.

———. Subcommittee of the Committee on Military Affairs. *Hearings: A Bill to Provide for the Protection and Preservation of Domestic Sources of Scrap and Steel.* 75th Cong., 3rd sess., 4 April 1938. Washington, D.C.: GPO, 1938.

———. Subcommittee on Commerce. *Hearings on H.R. 4960.* Sen. Joseph E. Ransdell presiding. 65th Cong., 1st sess., 23 July–2 August 1917. Washington, D.C.: GPO, 1917.

———. Subcommittee on the Committee on Finance. *Hearings: Tariff Act of 1929.* 71st Cong., 1st sess. Schedule 1, *Chemicals, Oils and Paints.* Schedule 2, *Earths, Earthenware and Glassware.* Schedule 15, *Sundries.* Washington, D.C.: GPO, 1929.

Defense Department. *The "Magic" Background of Pearl Harbor*. Washington, D.C.: GPO, 1978.

Federal Reserve Bank of New York (FRBNY). *Annual Report*. New York: FRBNY, 1931–46.

———. *Monthly Review*. New York: FRBNY, 1940–43.

Federal Reserve Board of Governors. International Finance Division and Predecessors 1907–1974. International Subject Files, 1907 to 1974. RG 82, NA. Declassified 1 April 1997 under EO 12958. See the *Record* 3, no. 5 (May 1997). The Federal Reserve Board of Governors decided to turn over these records to the National Archives rather than segregate those relevant only to the Holocaust and to permit pre-1967 records to be opened to the public immediately (and later records thirty years after created). The board also transferred records of the Federal Reserve Bank of New York that "relate to the activity in accounts for foreign governments or international institutions." See William W. Wiles, Secretary of the Board of Governors, to Michael J. Kurtz, Assistant Archivist for Records Services, NARA, 23 January 1997, copy in author's files.

Foreign Economic Administration (FEA). Economic Intelligence Division. Board of Economic Warfare. 1942–1944, Sources of Economic Information Exploited in WWII, Seized Enemy Alien Files, 1944–45. RG 169, NA.

———. Planning Division. Projects Section. List of Reports Prepared as of 15 Dec 1941. RG 169, NA.

———. Records Analysis Division. "Pre Pearl Harbor Organization" [of the FEA and other economic warfare agencies]." N.d. (probably during World War II). File: FEA Administrative History Pearl Harbor Organization, History Monographs Prepared by Division, Entry 145. RG 169, NA.

———. Special Areas Branch. "Japanese Machine Tools Industry." 1 February 1944. Japan Tools: Machine, Box 38, File 409-500. ONI Monograph Files, Japan 1939–46. RG 38, NA.

———. Far East Enemy Division. "Prewar and Wartime Civilian Fuel and Lighting Consumption in Japan Proper." July 1944. Box 9, File 401-200, Japan. ONI, Japan Monographs 1939–47. RG 38, NA.

Interdepartmental Committee Reports on the Vulnerability of Japan.

Reports of the various interdepartmental committees on the economic vulnerability of Japan were prepared for the Office of the Administrator of Export Control (AEC). Reports on the Economic Vulnerability of Japan, 1941–43, Boxes 1–2, Entry 44, Records of the Tariff Commission. RG 81, NA. Also in General File of the Chief, Projects Section, AEC, Boxes 698–700. RG 169, NA.

Interdepartmental Committee on Chemicals, Fertilizers and Related Products. "The Economic Vulnerability of Japan in Agar-Agar."

———. "The Economic Vulnerability of Japan in Ammonium Sulfate."

———. "The Economic Vulnerability of Japan in Borax."

———. "The Economic Vulnerability of Japan in Carbon Black."

———. "The Economic Vulnerability of Japan in Caustic Soda."

———. "The Economic Vulnerability of Japan in Chemical Fertilizers and Related Products."

———. "The Economic Vulnerability of Japan in Chinchona Bark and Quinine."

———. "The Economic Vulnerability of Japan in Creosote Oil."

———. "The Economic Vulnerability of Japan in Dynamite and Other Explosives."

———. "The Economic Vulnerability of Japan in Fertilizers."

———. "The Economic Vulnerability of Japan in Gum Rosin."

———. "The Economic Vulnerability of Japan in Menthol."

———. "The Economic Vulnerability of Japan in Methanol, Butanol and Acetone."

———. "The Economic Vulnerability of Japan in Natural Camphor, Crude and Refined."

———. "The Economic Vulnerability of Japan in Nux Vomica."

———. "The Economic Vulnerability of Japan in Peppermint Oil."

———. "The Economic Vulnerability of Japan in Phosphate Rock."

———. "The Economic Vulnerability of Japan in Potash."

———. "The Economic Vulnerability of Japan in Pyrethrum Flowers."

———. "The Economic Vulnerability of Japan in Salt."

————. "The Economic Vulnerability of Japan in Soda Ash."

————. "The Economic Vulnerability of Japan in Sodium Nitrate and Other Nitrates."

————. "The Economic Vulnerability of Japan in Vegetable Tanning Materials."

Interdepartmental Committee on Fats and Oils. "The Economic Vulnerability of Japan in Fats and Oils."

Interdepartmental Committee on Fishery Products. "The Economic Vulnerability of Japan in Fish, Shellfish and Fish Livers."

Interdepartmental Committee on Forest Products. "The Economic Vulnerability of Japan in Forest Products and Manufactures."

Interdepartmental Committee on Hides and Skins. "The Economic Vulnerability of Japan in Hides and Skins, Leather and Leather Manufactures, and Fur."

Interdepartmental Committee on Iron and Steel. "The Economic Vulnerability of Japan in Iron, Steel and Ferro-Alloys."

Interdepartmental Committee on Miscellaneous Products. "The Economic Vulnerability of Japan in Miscellaneous Products."

Interdepartmental Committee on Non-Ferrous Metals and Manufactures. "The Economic Vulnerability of Japan in Copper."

Interdepartmental Committee on Nonmetallic Minerals and Manufactures. "The Economic Vulnerability of Japan in Abrasives."

————. "The Economic Vulnerability of Japan in Asbestos."

————. "The Economic Vulnerability of Japan in Bauxite and Fluorspar."

————. "The Economic Vulnerability of Japan in Glass and Glassware."

————. "The Economic Vulnerability of Japan in Graphite."

————. "The Economic Vulnerability of Japan in Mica."

————. "The Economic Vulnerability of Japan in Miscellaneous Products."

————. "The Economic Vulnerability of Japan in Optical Glass."

————. "The Economic Vulnerability of Japan in Pottery."

————. "The Economic Vulnerability of Japan in Quartz Crystals."

Interdepartmental Committee on Petroleum. "The Economic Vulnerability of Japan in Petroleum with Special Report on Vulnerability of Japan to Attack on Petroleum."

Interdepartmental Committee on Raw Textiles, Fibers and Cordage. "The Economic Vulnerability of Japan in Miscellaneous Vegetable Fibers."

————. "The Economic Vulnerability of Japan in Raw Cotton."

Interdepartmental Committee on Rubber. "The Economic Vulnerability of Japan in Rubber."

Interdepartmental Committee on Silk. "The Economic Vulnerability of the United States in Raw Silk and Silk Waste."

Interior Department. Bureau of Mines. *Consumption of Ferrous Scrap and Pig Iron in the United States*. Reports of Investigation 3329, 3366, and 3420. Washington, D.C.: GPO, 1935–38.

————. *Iron and Steel Scrap in California and Nevada*. Prepared by George Casper Branner. Washington, D.C.: GPO, 1960.

————. "Mineral Resources of Germany's Former Colonial Possessions." *Foreign Minerals Quarterly* 2, no. 3 (July 1939).

————. *Mineral Resources of Japan*. Foreign Minerals Survey. Vol. 2, no. 5. Washington, D.C.: GPO, October 1945.

————. *Minerals Yearbook*. Annual. Washington, D.C.: GPO, 1939–42.

International Military Tribunal for the Far East (IMTFE). "Documents Accepted by the Tribunal (Index)." Washington, 1946–48. Entry 13. RG 238, NA.

————. "Documents Rejected by the Tribunal (Index)." Washington, 1946–48. Entry 15. RG 238, NA.

————. *The Tokyo Major War Crimes Trial: The Records of the International Military Tribunal for the Far East*. R. John Pritchard, commentator. New York: Edward Mellen Press, 1998. Original documents in Tokyo War Crimes Trials, RG 331, NA.

National Archives and Records Administration (NARA). *Federal Records of World War II*. Washington, D.C.: GPO, 1950.

———. "Funding Foreign Policy: General Records of the Department of the Treasury Pertaining to American Foreign Policy." By Kenneth Heger. *Record*, May 1998, 26–27.

———. *Guide to Federal Records in the National Archives of the United States*. Records of the National Emergency Council. RG 44.3, NA. Online at http://www.archives.gov/research/guide-fed-records/groups/044.html#44.3 (accessed 24 October 2006).

———. *Holocaust-Era Assets: A Finding Aid to Records at the National Archives at College Park, Maryland*. Washington: NARA, 1999. online at http://www.archives.gov/research/holocaust/index.html (accessed 3 April 2005).

National Recovery Administration. Division of Review. *The Silk Textile Industry*. Evidence Study No. 37. Mimeograph. Preliminary draft. Washington, 1935.

National Security Council. *The Johnson Act* (18 U.S.C. 955). Annex C to NSC 5808/1. 13 April 1954. Electronic database. Library of Congress Declassified Documents Reference System.

Navy Department. Office of Chief of Naval Operations. *Civil Affairs Guide: Far Eastern Nutritional Relief (Japanese Culture)*. 15 August 1944. OPNAV 13-18. Box 18, File Agriculture-Food-General. RG 38, NA.

———. Office of Naval Intelligence. Japan Monograph Series. Asia and the Pacific. Japan, 1939–1946, Records of the Chief of Naval Operations, Section 6, Natural Resources. RG 38, NA.

———. *Regular Japanese Shipping Routes, Change #3*. January 1941. Box 48, File 502-100, Japan Exports, Office of Naval Intelligence, Monograph Files, Japan 1939–46. RG 38, NA.

———. "Report on Petroleum Situation of Japan." 12 March 1941. Prepared by Lt. Cdr. A. H. McCollum, USN. Microfilm. File 894.6363/383. State Department microfilm series LM-68. RG 59, NA.Office of Alien Property Custodian. Records Relating to World War II, Seized Records of Japanese Banks, Entry 190, Yokohama Specie Bank Treasury Papers 1940–42. RG 131, NA. Records seized from foreign banks and corporations were restricted from public use until fifty years after seizure (1992). See NARA, "Records of the Office of Alien Property," *Guide to Federal Records in the National Archives of the United States, Records of the Office of Alien Property, Section 131.1*, online at http://search.arcives.gov.

———. *Report for the Fiscal Year Ending June 30, 1944*. Washington, D.C.: GPO, 1944.

———. *Report for the Fiscal Year Ending June 30, 1946*. Washington, D.C.: GPO, 1946.

———. *Report for the Period March 11, 1942 to June 30, 1943*. Washington, D.C.: GPO, 1943.

Office of Emergency Management (OEM). *United States Government Manual*. Washington, D.C.: GPO, c. 1945.

Office of Intelligence Coordination and Liaison (OCL). *The Place of Foreign Trade in the Economy of Japan: An Analysis in Two Volumes of the External Trade of Japan Proper between 1930 and 1943 Focusing on Possible or Probable Post-war Developments*. Intelligence Research Report OCL-2815. Prepared by Arthur B. Hersey. Washington, D.C.: GPO, 1943–46. Call no. HF3826.U5 1946. Library of Congress.

Office of the Special Advisor to the President on Foreign Trade. "A Balance of International Accounts of the United States with Special Reference to the Items in Each Account and the Methods Used in Estimating Them." Typescript. Washington, D.C., 1934. Call No. HG 388.3.U7.U6 1934. Library of Congress.

Office of Strategic Services (OSS). *Civil Affairs Handbook: Japan: Section 6, Natural Resources*. Prepared for Headquarters, Army Service Forces. ASF Manual M-354-6. 22 July 1944. Box 10, File 401-200 (A). ONI, Japan Monographs, RG 38, NA.

———. Central Information Division. Name and subject card indexes to Series 16, Country: Entry 2.12, Japan, 117583C, January 1946. RG 226, NA.

———. Research and Analysis Branch. *Comments on Estimates of Minimum Japanese Import Requirements*. 30 November 1944. Call no. UB 250 .U33 no. 2725. Library of Congress.

————. "Financial Programs of Japan in Japan and Occupied Areas." Extracts from Radio Tokyo (shortwave) and affiliated stations from December 1941 to May 1, 1944. Honolulu, 1944. Call no. UB 250 .U33 no. 2629. Library of Congress.

————. Food Situation in Japan. Mimeograph. Washington, 5 July1945. Call no. UB 250 .U33 no. 3214. Library of Congress.

————. Japanese Aluminum Production and Fabrication. R. and A. No. 2155, 31 May 1944. RG 226, NA.

————. Japanese Needs for Imports from Outside the Areas Japan Controls. Washington, D.C.: GPO, 1944. Call no. UB250 .U33 no. 2626. Library of Congress.

President of the United States. "Press Releases." Mimeograph. Washington, D.C., 1933. Call no. E740.5.A3. Library of Congress.

State Department. "Commerce and Navigation, Treaty [with Japan] and Protocol Signed at Washington February 21, 1911." 37 Stat. 1504. Treaty Series 558. In Treaties and Other International Agreements of the United States of America, 1776–1949, comp. Charles I. Bevans, 416–22. Dept. of State Publication 8615. Washington, D.C.: GPO, 1972.

————. Documents Pertaining to Foreign Funds Control. 16 August 1941. Box 4863, File Frozen Credits 1940–41. RG 59, NA.

————. Foreign Relations of the United States: Diplomatic Papers. 1937–41. Washington, D.C.: GPO, 1938–42.

————. Division of Controls. Decimal Files. Frozen Credits 1940–44. 840.51. RG 59, NA.

————. Decimal Files. Regulations [of Export Controls]. 811.20(D). RG 59, NA.

————. Decimal Files. "Shipping Files." 800.8890. RG 59, NA.

————. Naval Attaché, Tokyo. Japan's Soda Industry and Its Dependence on Imported Salt. 16 September 1940. File 894.659/23, Roll 13. State Department microfilm series LM-68. RG 59, NA.

————. Office of Research and Intelligence. Papers Relating to the Foreign Relations of the United States and Japan, 1931–41. Washington, D.C.: GPO, 1943.

————. Records of the Internal Affairs of Japan 1940–1944. Decimal files 894. State Department microfilm series LM-68. RG 59, NA.

————. Situation Report: Japan, the Status of the Japanese Textile Industry. Pt. 2, Rayon. 24 May 1946. Box 19, File 3479.1. ONI, Japan Monographs. RG 38, NA.

————. Far Eastern Division. Japan Economic Estimate. 27 May 1941. File 894.50/154, Roll 11. State Department microfilm series. RG 59, NA.

————. Purport Lists for the Department of State Decimal File 1910–1944. Microfilm series M973. Washington: NARA, 1976.

————. Records Relating to Political Relations Between the United States and Japan, 1930–1939. RG 59, NA.

————. Records Relating to U.S. Commercial Relations with Japan 1910–1949. Decimal Files 611.94 and 694.11. 17 rolls. State Department microfilm series LM-158. RG 59, NA.

————. Treaties and Other International Agreements of the United Sates of America 1776–1949. Publication 8615. Prepared by Charles I. Bevans. Washington, D.C.: GPO, 1972.

Supreme Commander Allied Powers (SCAP). General Headquarters. Economic and Scientific Section. Statistics and Research Division. The Aluminum Industry of Japan. Special Report No. 9. 3 April 1946. Boxes 21–223, File 407-100 Aluminum. ONI, Japan Monographs 1939–47. RG 38, NA.

————. Natural Resources Section. Fertilizers in Japan; a Preliminary Report. Report 55. Prepared by Maj. G. L. W. Swanson and Mr. Tanada. Tokyo, 10 September 1946. Call no. HC 461 .58 no. 55. Library of Congress.

————. Fertilizer Practices in Japan; a Preliminary Report. Report 93. 30 September 1947. Call no. HC 461 .58 no. 93. Library of Congress.

————. *Gold and Silver in Japan*. Report 128. Prepared by Robert Y. Grant. Tokyo, June 1950. Library of Congress.

————. *Japanese Food Situation*. Prepared for the Honorable Herbert Hoover and Members, Famine Relief Committee. 1 May 1946. Copy in Box 18, Japan Monograph Series. RG 38, NA.

————. *Sericulture in Japan*. Report 76. 25 April 1947. Call no. HC 461 .58 no. 76. Library of Congress.

Tariff Commission Reports

The files for Tariff Commission reports are in Records of Investigation Under Sections 332, 336, and 337 of the Tariff Act of 1930, 1929–66. RG 81, NA. Description of records by NARA created in 1992. See *Prologue* 2, no. 4 (Winter 1992): 415. (Postwar the Tariff Commission was renamed the U.S. International Trade Commission.)

————. *Aluminum*. Special Industry Analysis No. 2. Prepared for the Liberated Areas Branch, FEA. January 1945. Prepared by L.C. Raymond. Boxes 21–23, File 407-100 Aluminum. ONI, Japan Monographs 1939–47. RG 38, NA.

————. *An Analysis of the Trade Between Japan and the United States*. Prepared in Response to Senate Resolution 334. 72nd Cong., 2nd sess. Confidential, mimeographed. Washington, D.C.: GPO, March 1934.

————. *Annotated Tabular Survey* [of 1928–36]. *Japanese Trade Studies*. Washington, D.C.: GPO, 1945.

————. *Broad-Silk Manufacture and the Tariff*. Washington, D.C.: GPO, 1926.

————. *Changes in Import Duties Since 1930*. Washington, D.C.: GPO, 1936.

————. *Computed Duties and Equivalent ad Valorem Rates on Imports into the United States from Principal Countries, Calendar Years 1929, 1931, and 1935*. W.P.A. Statistical Project 265-31-7000. Richmond, Va., 1937.

————. *Cost of Production of Slide Fasteners and Parts Thereof; Report to the President, with Appendix Proclamation by the President*. Report No. 113, 2nd ser. Washington, D.C.: GPO, 1936.

————. *Cotton Cloth: Report to the President on the Differences in Costs of Production of Cotton Cloth in the United States and in the Principal Competing Country* [Japan]. Report No. 112, 2nd ser. Washington, D.C.: GPO, 1936.

————. *Cotton Textiles*. Special Industry Analysis No. 34. Japanese Trade Studies. Prepared for the Foreign Economic Administration. September 1945. Boxes 1–2, Entry 43, Records of the Tariff Commission. RG 81, NA.

————. *Dolls and Toys of Pyroxylin Plastic*. Files 1932–1935, Records of the Tariff Commission. RG 81, NA.

————. *Economic Analysis of Foreign Trade of the United States in Relation to the Tariff*. Washington, D.C.: GPO, 1933.

————. *Electric Lamps*. Files 1933, Records of the Tariff Commission. RG 81, NA.

————. *Footwear, Rubber Soled*. Investigations under 1930 Act. Washington, D.C.: GPO, 1931–35.

————. *Information Survey on the Japanese Cotton Industry and Trade*. Washington, D.C.: GPO, 1921.

————. *Iron and Steel and Reciprocal Trade Agreements*. Washington, D.C.: GPO, January 1941.

————. *Iron and Steel: A Survey of the Iron and Steel Industries and International Trade of the Principal Producing and Trading Countries* . . . Report No. 128, 2nd ser. Washington, D.C.: GPO, 1938.

————. *Pottery: Household Table and Kitchen Articles of Earthenware and of China, Porcelain and Other Vitrified Wares*. Report to the president. Mimeograph. 10 April 1945. Box 1, Locator 6-24-4, Records of the Tariff Commission. RG 81, NA.

————. *Recent Developments in the Foreign Trade of Japan, Particularly in Relation to the Trade of the United States*. Washington, D.C.: GPO, 1936.

————. *Silk and Manufactures of Silk.* Schedule L. Washington, D.C.: GPO, 1918.

————. *Silk, Silk Yarns and Threads, and Silk Pile Fabrics.* Washington, D.C.: GPO, 1921.

————. *Slide Fasteners.* Files, 1933–35. RG 81, NA.

————. *Sun Glasses or Sun Goggles.* Report 103, ser. 2. Washington, D.C.: GPO, 1935.

————. *Sun Goggles.* Report to the President. 14 December 1934. Washington, D.C.: GPO, 1935.

————. *Synthetic Camphor: The Relation of Domestic Production of Synthetic Camphor to Domestic Consumption.* Washington, D.C.: GPO, 1935.

————. *Textile Imports and Exports, 1891–1927.* Washington, D.C.: GPO, 1929.

————. *Tooth and Other Toilet Brushes and Backs and Handles.* Report No. 81. Washington, D.C.: GPO, 1934.

————. *Toys.* Special Industry Analysis No. 8. Japanese Trade Studies. March 1945. Records of the Tariff Commission. RG 81, NA.

————. *Two Centuries of Tariffs: The Background and Emergence of the United States Tariff Commission.* Prepared by John M. Dobson. Washington, D.C.: GPO, 1976.

————. "United States Imports for Consumption of the Principal Commodities Imported from Japan." Mimeograph from typescript. Washington, July 1941. Copy in New York Public Library, call no. TLH 1941, catalogue book 254-1-2, and Library of Congress, call no. HF3127.A4, 1941b.

————. "United States Imports from Japan and Their Relation to the Defense Program and to the Economy of the Country." Typescript. Washington, September 1941. Copy in New York Public Library, call no. TLH 1941, catalogue book 254-2-2.

Treasury Department. *Census of Foreign-Owned Assets in the United States.* Washington, D.C.: GPO, 1945.

————. Central International Files 1917–1956. RG 56, NA.

————. General Records International Affairs 1926–1970. RG 56, NA.

————. Office of Assistant Secretary for International Affairs (OASIA). 1936–72. RG 56, NA. During World War II was renamed Office of the Assistant Secretary in Charge of Monetary Research and Foreign Funds Control. Declassified 1 April 1997 under EO 12958. See *Prologue*, March 1997, 24.

U.S. Strategic Bombing Survey (USSBS). Basic Materials Division. *Coal and Metals in Japan's War Economy.* No. 36. Washington, D.C.: GPO, 1946.

————. Oil and Chemicals Division. *Chemicals in Japan's War.* Nos. 49 and 50. Washington, D.C.: GPO, 1946.

————. *Oil in Japan's War.* Nos. 51 and 52. Washington, D.C.: GPO, February 1946.

————. Over-All Economic Effects Division. *The Effects of Strategic Bombing on Japan's War Economy.* No. 53. Washington, D.C.: GPO, December 1946.

War Department. Army. Military Intelligence Division. *Power Production in Japan.* G-2 Report, Japan, I.G. No. 4460. New York, 2 December 1941. Box 12, Office of Naval Intelligence Monograph Files, Japan 1939–46, File 401-400, Electricity (War). RG 38, NA.

————. Chief of Staff. G2. "The Economic Position of Japan: Current Estimate." 26 March 1940. Prepared by Lt. Norman E. Towson, MI-reserve. 894.50/119 1/2, Roll 11. State Department microfilm series LM-68. RG 59, NA.

————. Headquarters, Army Service Forces. *Civil Affairs Handbook: Japan: Section 6, Natural Resources,* and *Japan Forest Resources.* Manual M-354-6, Civil Affairs. 22 July 1944. Box 10, File 401-200 (A). ONI, Japan Monographs 1939–47. RG 38, NA.

————. Industrial College of the Armed Forces. "History." online at http://www.ndu.edu/ICAF/history/index.htm (accessed 25 October 2006).

————. Office of the Chief of Military History. "Planning the Defeat of Japan: A Study of Total War Strategy." Unpublished monograph. Prepared by Lt. Col. Henry C. Morgan. 1961.

Books, Articles, Essays, and Other Published Works, and Documents Other than U.S. Government

Acheson, Dean G. *Present at the Creation: My Years in the State Department.* New York: Norton, 1969.

Adams, Frederick C. "The Road to Pearl Harbor: A Reexamination of American Far Eastern Policy, July 1937–December 1938." *Journal of American History* 58, no. 1 (June 1971): 73–92.

American Academy of Political and Social Science. "America and Japan: A Survey of Current Relations Between the United States and Japan, with Their Background and Implications." *Annals* (Philadelphia), May 1941.

American Chemical Society. "The Houdry Process." Washington, 1999. online at http://acsweb-content.acs.org/landmarks/landmarks/hdr/index.html (accessed 2 November 2002).

American Economic Association. Directory of Members. *American Economic Review,* October 1974.

American Men and Women of Science: Economics, 1974. New York: R. R. Bowker, 1974.

American Men and Women of Science: The Social and Behavioral Sciences. 12th ed. New York: Jacques Cattell Press, 1973.

American National Biography Online. http://www.anb.org/articles.

Anderson, Irvine H., Jr. "The 1941 *De Facto* Embargo Oil of Japan: A Bureaucratic Reflex." *Pacific Historical Review,* May 1975, 201–31.

———. *The Standard-Vacuum Oil Company and United States East Asian Policy, 1933–1941.* Princeton N.J.: Princeton University Press, 1975.

Anderson, Kym, ed. *New Silk Roads: East Asia and World Textile Markets.* Cambridge: Cambridge University Press, 1992.

———. "The Perspective of Japan in Historical and International Perspective." In Kym, *New Silk Roads.*

Anderson, Kym, and Rod Tyers. "Japanese Rice Policy in the Interwar Period: Some Consequences of Imperial Self Sufficiency." *Japan and the World Economy* 4 (1992): 103–21.

Ayusawa, Iwao. "Elements of Stability: A Japanese View." *Annals of the American Academy of Political and Social Science,* May 1941, 24–27.

Barber, Stanley A., Robert D. Munson, and W. B. Dancy. "Production, Marketing, and Use of Potassium Fertilizers." In *Fertilizer Technology and Use.* 2nd ed., edited by R. A. Olson. Madison, Wisc.: Soil Society of America, 1971.

Barnhart, Michael A. *Japan and the World Since 1868.* International Relations and the Great Powers Series. London: Edward Arnold, 1995.

———. *Japan Prepares for Total War: The Search for Economic Security, 1919–1941.* Ithaca, N.Y.: Cornell University Press, 1987.

Barringer, Edwin Charles. *The Story of Scrap.* Washington: Institute of Scrap Iron and Steel, 1954.

Beers, Burton F. *Vain Endeavor: Robert Lansing's Attempts to End the American-Japanese Rivalry.* Durham, N.C.: Duke University Press, 1962.

Behrens, Catherine B. A. *Merchant Shipping and the Demands of War.* London: HMSO, 1955.

Bell, A. H. "Voluntary Crude-Oil Curtailment in California Effective." *Oil and Gas Journal,* 30 October, A46, A94.

Bloch, Kurt. "Japan on Her Own." *Far Eastern Survey,* 3 November 1941, 244–49.

———. "Japan's Problem Reversed." *Far Eastern Survey,* 30 June 1941, 135–36.

———. "Japan's War Economy." *Annals of the American Academy of Political and Social Science,* May 1941, 17–23.

Blum, John Morton. *From the Morgenthau Diaries.* Vols. 1 and 2. Boston: Houghton Mifflin, 1965.

Blumenthal, Tuvia. "The Japanese Shipbuilding Industry." In Patrick with Meissner, *Japanese Industrialization,* 129–60.

Boone, Andrew R. "Motorships of the Silk Fleet Sail World's Greatest Sea Race." *Popular Science Monthly* 126 (April 1935): 14–15, 105–6.

Borg, Dorothy. *The United States and the Far Eastern Crisis of 1933–1938: From the Manchurian Incident Through the Initial State of the Undeclared Sino-Japanese War*. Harvard East Asian Series. Cambridge: Harvard University Press, 1964.

Borg, Dorothy, and Shumpei Okamato, eds. *Pearl Harbor as History: Japanese-American Relations, 1931–1941*. Studies of the East Asia Institute. New York: Columbia University Press, 1973.

Boulding, Kenneth E., and Alan H. Gleason. "War as an Investment: The Strange Case of Japan." In *Economic Imperialism: A Book of Readings*, edited by Kenneth E. and Tapan Mukerjee Boulding. Ann Arbor: University of Michigan Press, 1972.

Bowman, Mary Margaret Coughlin. "Presidential Emergency Powers Related to International Economic Transactions: Congressional Recognition of Customary Authority." *Vanderbilt Journal of Transnational Law* 11, no. 3 (Summer 1978): 515–34.

Boyce, Robert. "Economics." In *The Origins of World War Two*, edited by Robert Boyce and Joseph A. Maiolo, 249–72. Basingstoke, UK: Palgrave Macmillan, 2003.

———. "World Depression, World War: Some Economic Origins of the Second World War." In *Paths to War: New Essays on the Origins of the Second World War*, edited by Robert Boyce and Esmonde M. Robertson, 55–95. New York: St. Martin's Press.

Boyden, Bruce. "Domestic Pressures and Sanctions Against Japan, 1939–1940." 1992. online at http://www.omnivore.org.bruce/papers/e70.pdf (accessed 5 January 2003).

Butow, Robert J. C. *Tojo and the Coming of War*. Stanford, Calif.: Stanford University Press, 1961.

Carpet and Rug Institute. "Rayon Fiber." online at http://www.fibersource.com/f-tutor/rayon.htm (accessed 8 October 2005).

Chace, James. *Acheson: The Secretary of State Who Created the American World*. New York: Simon & Schuster, 1998.

Chida, Tomohei. *The Japanese Shipping and Shipbuilding Industries: A History of Their Modern Growth*. Atlantic Heights, N.J.: Athlone Press, 1990.

"ChinaFood." International Institute for Applied Systems Analysis (IIASA) web site, http://www.iiasa.ac.at/Research/LUC/ChinaFood/data/diet/diet_1.htm (accessed 24 October 2006).

Christians, William F., and Otis P. Starkey. "The Far East as a Source of Vital Raw Materials." *Annals of the American Academy of Political and Social Science*, May 1941, 80–85.

Clare, George. *The ABC of Foreign Exchanges*. London: Macmillan, 1936.

Cohen, Jerome B. *Japan's Economy in War and Reconstruction*. Minneapolis: University of Minnesota Press, 1949.

———. *Japan's Postwar Economy*. Center of International Studies, Princeton University. Bloomington: Indiana University Press, 1958.

Constantino, Maria. *Fashions of a Decade: The 1930s*. New York: Facts on File, 1992.

Crowley, James B. *Japan's Quest for Autonomy: National Security and Foreign Policy, 1930–1938*. Princeton, N.J.: Princeton University Press, 1966.

de Haan, Johannis Dirk. *The Full-Fashioned Hosiery Industry in the U.S.A.* The Hague: Mouton, 1957.

Desvernine, Raoul E. *Democratic Despotism*. New York: Dodd, Mead, 1936.

———. Summaries of *Wake Up America* broadcasts on ABC Blue Network, 1943–46. GOLDIndex, http://www.radioindex.com (accessed 29 August 2003).

De Vattel, Emeric. *The Law of Nations; or Principles of the Law of Nature Applied to the Conduct and Affairs of Nations and Sovereigns*. New York: Berry and Rogers, 1787.

Dictionary of American Biography. Supplement 5, 1951–55. American Council of Learned Societies, 1977. Electronic document. Biography Resource Center, Library of Congress.

———. Supplement 10, 1976–80. New York: Charles Scribner's Sons, 1995. Electronic document. Biography Resource Center, Library of Congress.

Divine, Robert A. "Acheson, Dean Gooderham." *American National Biography Online*, http://www.anb.org/articles/07/07-00002.html (accessed 4 May 2006).

"Dollar Pooling in the Sterling Area." *American Economic Review* 44, no. 4 (September 1954): 559–76.

Dore, Ronald, and Radha Sinha. *Japan and World Depression, Then and Now: Essays in Memory of E. F. Penrose.* New York: St. Martin's Press, 1967.

Douglas, Henry H. "America Finances Japan's 'New Order.'" *Amerasia* 4, no. 5 (July 1940): 221–24.

Dowd, Laurence Phillips. "Japanese Foreign Exchange Policy 1930–1940." Ph.D. diss., University of Michigan, 1952. Ann Arbor: UMI, 1994.

Doyle, John J. *The Response of Rice to Fertilizer.* FAO Agricultural Studies 70. Rome: Food and Agricultural Organization of the United Nations, 1966.

Duran, Leo. *Raw Silk: A Practical Hand-Book for the Buyer.* New York: Silk Publishing, 1913, 1921.

E. I. du Pont de Nemours and Company. "Nylon." online at http://heritage.dupont.com/touch-points/tp_1935-2/depth.shtml (accessed 18 October 2006).

Encylcopaedia Britannica. Chicago: Encyclopaedia Britannica, 1945.

Engelstad, O. P., ed. *Fertilizer Technology and Use.* 3rd ed. Madison, Wisc.: Soil Science Society of America, 1985.

European Association for Banking and Financial History. "Clearing Accounts." online at http://www.bankinghistory.de/Bulletin/EABH-web (accessed 1 September 2003).

Ewing, Elizabeth. *Dress and Undress: A History of Women's Underwear.* New York: Drama Book Specialists, 1978.

Fanno, Marco. *Normal and Abnormal International Capital Transfers.* Studies in Economic Dynamics 1. Minneapolis: University of Minnesota Press, 1939.

Federico, Giovanni. *An Economic History of the Silk Industry, 1830–1930.* Cambridge Studies in Modern Economic History 5. Cambridge: Cambridge University Press, 1997.

Feis, Herbert. *Petroleum and American Foreign Policy.* Commodity Policy Studies, vol. 3, Food Research Institute, Stanford University, Monograph 3. New York: American Enterprise Association, March 1944.

———. *The Road to Pearl Harbor: The Coming of the War Between the United States and Japan.* Princeton, N.J.: Princeton University Press, 1950.

Finlayson, Bruce A. "The Fluidized Bed Reactor Page." University of Washington, http://faculty/washington.edu.fanlayso/Fluidized_Bed/FBR_Intro/history_fbr.htm (accessed 3 November 2002).

"Frank Coe." Wikipedia, http://en.wikipedia.org/wiki/Frank_Coe (accessed 30 May 2006).

"Franklin D. Roosevelt's 'Quarantine' Speech." *Documents for the Study of American History.* Marchex, Inc., http://www.vlib.us/amdocs/texts/fdrquarn.html (accessed 8 December 2006).

From Raw Silk to Silk Hosiery. Monograph. New York: Charles Chipman and Sons, 1920.

Fujise, Hiroshi. *Japan's Historical Position in the World Trade 1900–1940.* International Economic Conflict Discussion Paper. Nagoya, Japan: Economics Research Center, Nagoya University, 1982.

Garner, James Wilford. "The United States Neutrality Act of 1937." *American Journal of International Law* 31, no. 3 (July 1937): 385–97.

Glass, Milton N. *History of Hosiery, from the Piloi of Ancient Greece to the Nylons of Modern America.* New York: Fairchild Publications, 1955.

"Gold Production Subsidy Increased." *Far Eastern Financial Notes* 2, nos. 5 (March 1940) and 11 (June 1940).

Goldsmith, Raymond William. *The Financial Development of Japan, 1868–1977.* New Haven, Conn.: Yale University Press, 1983.

Goldstein, M., and Katherine V. Dillon, eds. *The Pacific War Papers: Japanese Documents of World War II.* Washington, D.C.: Potomac Books, 2004.

Goralski, Robert, and Russell W. Freeburg. *Oil and War: How the Deadly Struggle for Fuel in WWII Meant Victory or Defeat.* New York: William Morrow, 1987.

Gordon, David Livingston, and Royden Dangerfield. *The Hidden Weapon: The Story of Economic Warfare*. London: Harper and Brothers, 1947. Reprinted in *The Politics and Strategy of World War II*, general ed. Manfred Jonas. New York: DeCapo Press, 1976.

Grew, Joseph C. *Ten Years in Japan*. New York: Simon & Schuster, 1944.

Gutstadt, Jack. *Scrap Iron and Steel: An Outline of the Many Ramifications and Developments of a Major Industry Together with Statistics, Formulas, and Other Similar Data*. Chicago: Jack Gutstadt, 1939.

Hall, H. Duncan. *North American Supply*. London: HMSO, 1955.

Handley, Susannah. *Nylon: The Story of a Fashion Revolution*. Baltimore: Johns Hopkins University Press, 1999.

Harler, C. R. *The Culture and Marketing of Tea*. London: Humphrey Milford, 1933.

Harrington, Mary Keenan. "Reagan v. Wald and the Grandfather Clause of the Trading with the Enemy Act: A Lesson in Explicit Vagueness." *Pace Law Review* 5, no. 3 (Spring 1985): 693–733.

Haskell, Ira J. *Hosiery Thru the Years*. Lynn, Mass.: Carole Mailing Service, 1956.

Haynes, William. *Cellulose: The Chemical that Grows*. Garden City, N.Y.: Doubleday, 1953.

Hemmi, Kenzoo. "Primary Product Exports and Economic Development: The Case of Silk." In Ohkawa, Johnston, and Kaneda, *Agriculture and Economic Growth*.

Herzberg, James R. "American Economic Policies Towards Japan, 1931–1941." Ph.D. diss., University of Texas at Austin, 1977. Ann Arbor: UMI, 1994.

———. *A Broken Bond: American Economic Policies Towards Japan, 1931–1941*. New York: Garland, 1988.

Herzog, James H. *Closing the Open Door: American-Japanese Diplomatic Negotiations, 1936–1941*. Annapolis: Naval Institute Press, 1973.

———. "Influence of the United States Navy in the Embargo of Oil to Japan, 1940–1941." *Pacific Historical Review* 35, no. 3 (August 1966): 317–28.

Hijikata, Seibi. *History of Finances*. Modern History of Japanese Civilization 6. Tokyo: Toyo Keizai Shinposha, 1940. Translation sent by Prof. Yasuhiko Doi, 1995.

Holeproof Hosiery Company. *Better Hosiery: The Story of Holeproof*. Milwaukee: Holeproof, 1924.

Hollerman, Leon. *Japan's Dependence on the World Economy: The Approach Toward Economic Liberalization*. Princeton, N.J.: Princeton University Press, 1967.

Howe, Christopher. *The Origins of Japanese Trade Supremacy*. Chicago: University of Chicago Press, 1996.

Huberich, Charles. *The Law Relating to Trading with the Enemy . . .* New York: Baker Voorhis, 1918.

Hufbauer, Gary Clyde, Jeffrey J. Schott, and Kimberly Ann Elliott. *Economic Sanctions Reconsidered: History and Current Policy*. 2nd ed., and *Supplemental Case Histories*. Washington, D.C.: Institute for International Economics, 1990.

Hull, Cordell. *The Memoirs of Cordell Hull*. New York: Macmillan, 1948.

Hunsberger, Warren S. *Japan and the United States in World Trade*. Published for the Council on Foreign Relations. New York: Harper & Row, 1964.

Ickes, Harold L. *The Secret Diary of Harold L. Ickes*. New York: Simon & Schuster, 1954.

Iguchi, Haruo. "An Unfinished Dream: Yoshisuke Ayukawa's Economic Diplomacy Toward the U.S., 1937–1940." Kyoto: Doshisha University. Sophia Education and Research Center for Education Services, Sophia University Institute for American and Canadian Studies, http://www.info.sophia.ac.jp/amecana/Journal/16-2.htm (accessed 18 January 2006).

Ike, Nobutake, ed. *Japan's Decision for War: Records of the 1941 Policy Conferences*. Stanford, Calif.: Stanford University Press, 1967.

Ikeda, Michiko. "Protectionism and Discrimination Against Japan's Foreign Trade, 1926–1937." Ph.D. diss., Harvard University, 1989. Ann Arbor: UMI, 1994.

Industrial Mobilization for War: History of the War Production Board and Predecessor Agencies, 1940–1945, New York: Greenwood Press, 1969.

International Potash Institute. *Japanese Potassium Symposium*. Berne, Switz.: Second Japanese Potassium Congress, 1958.

Iriye, Akira. *The Origins of the Second World War in Asia and the Pacific*. New York: Longman, 1987.

———. *Pearl Harbor and the Coming of the Pacific War*. Boston: Bedford/St. Martin's, 1999.

Ishii, Osamu. "Cotton-Textile Diplomacy: Japan, Great Britain and the United States, 1930–1936." Ph.D. diss., Rutgers University, 1977.

Janeway, Eliot. "Japan's New Need: American Steels, Machines and Oils." *Asia* 38, no. 6 (June 1938): 338–40.

Japan: An Illustrated Encyclopedia. Tokyo: Kodansha, 1993.

Japan Ministry of Commerce and Industry. Bureau of Commerce. Section on Foreign Trade. *Exports and Imports of Japan Proper, 1940 & 1941*. Tokyo, 1945. MIS 225487, Box 48, File 502-200 Japan Imports. ONI, Monograph Files. RG 38, NA.

"Japan Needs Wood." *Far Eastern Survey*, 26 February 1941.

"Japan's Plans for World War II." *International Review of Military History* 38 (1978): 199–267.

Japan Statistical Association. *Historical Statistics of Japan*. 5 vols. Tokyo: Japan Statistical Association, 1987.

Japan Year Book (later *Japan and Manchukuo Year Book*). Tokyo: Japan Year Book Office, 1905–41.

Kidwell, Claudia B., and Margaret C. Christman. *Suiting Everyone: The Democratization of Clothing in America*. Washington: Smithsonian Institution Press, 1974.

Kindleberger, Charles P. *The World in Depression, 1929–1939*. History of the World Economy in the Twentieth Century Series. London: Allen Lane/Penguin Press, 1973.

Langer, William L., and S. Everett Gleason. *The Undeclared War, 1939–1941*. New York: Harper and Brothers, 1953.

Lasker, Bruno, and W. L. Holland, eds. *Problems of the Pacific, 1931*. Chicago: University of Chicago Press, 1932.

———. *Problems of the Pacific, 1933: Economic Conflict and Control*. Chicago: University of Chicago Press, 1934.

Laubner, Ellie. *Fashions of the Roaring '20s*. Atglen, Pa.: Schiffer, 1996.

League of Nations. Economic and Financial Committee. *International Currency Experience*. Series of Publications II.A.4 1944. Geneva: League of Nations, 1944. Reprint, New York: Arno Press, 1978.

———. *Report on Exchange Control*. Series C.232 M.131 1938 IIA. Geneva: League of Nations, 1938.

———. Economic, Financial and Transit Department. *Trade Relations Between Free-Market and Controlled Economies*. League of Nations Series Publications. Prepared by Jacob Viner. Geneva: League of Nations, 1943.

———. *Quantitative Trade Controls, Their Causes and Nature*. Geneva: League of Nations, 1943.

Libby, Justin H. "Rendezvous with Disaster: There Never Was a Chance for Peace in American-Japanese Relations, 1941." *World Affairs* 158, no. 3 (Winter 1996): 137–47.

Lockwood, William W., Jr. "American-Japanese Trade: Its Structure and Significance." *Annals of the American Academy of Political and Social Science* 215 (May 1941): 86–92.

———. *The Economic Development of Japan: Growth and Structural Change 1868–1938*. Princeton, N.J.: Princeton University Press, 1954.

———. *The Foreign Trade Policy of the United States*. New York: Institute of Pacific Relations, 1936.

———. "Japanese Silk and the American Market." *Far Eastern Survey*, 12 February 1936, 31–36.

———. "Trade and Trade Rivalry Between the United States and Japan." In *Problems of the Pacific, 1936*. Proceedings of the Sixth Conference of the Institute of Pacific Relations, 15–29 August 1936, 211–62. Chicago: Chicago University Press, 1937.

Macpherson, W. J. *The Economic Development of Japan c. 1868–1941*. Cambridge: Macmillan, 1987.

Maddox, Robert F. "Senator Harley M. Kilgore and Japan's World War II Business Practices." *West Virginia History* 55 (1996). online at http://www.wvculture.org/history/journal_wvh/wvh55-6.html (accessed 2 November 2002).

Marquis Who's Who. Chicago: Marquis Who's Who, 2006. Electronic document. Biography Resource Center, Library of Congress.

Marshall, Jonathan. *To Have and Have Not: Southeast Asian Raw Materials and the Origins of the Pacific War*. Berkeley and Los Angeles: University of California Press, 1994.

Matsui, Shichiro. *The History of the Silk Industry in the United States*. 1927. Reprint, New York: Howes, 1930.

McClenahan, William Moore, Jr. "Orderly Competition: American Government, Business and the Role of Voluntary Export Restraints in United States–Japan Trade, 1934–1972." Ph.D. diss. George Washington University, 1993. Ann Arbor: UMI, 1994.

McKinzie, Richard D. "Oral History Interview with Bernard Bernstein." 23 July 1975. Harry S. Truman Library, Independence, Mo., http://www.trumanlibrary.org/oralhist/bernsten.htm (accessed 1 January 2005).

Medlicott, William Norton. *The Economic Blockade*. Edited by W. K. Hancock. History of the Second World War: United Kingdom Civil Series. London: HMSO and Longmans, Green, 1952.

Metzler, Mark. "American Pressure for Financial Internationalization in Japan on the Eve of the Great Depression." *Journal of Japanese Studies* 28, no. 2 (Summer 2002): 277–300.

Miller, Edward S. "Japan's Other Victory: Overseas Financing of the War." In *The Russo-Japanese War in Global Perspective: World War Zero*, edited by John W. Steinberg, Bruce W. Menning, David Schimmelpenninck van der Oye, David Wolff, and Shinji Yokote, 466–78. Leiden, Netherlands: Brill, 2005.

———. *War Plan Orange: The U.S. Strategy to Defeat Japan, 1897–1945*. Annapolis, Md.: Naval Institute Press, 1991.

Miller, Irene. *Buying and Selling Hosiery*. New York: Fairchild Publications, 1949.

Miller, Max C. *Knitting Full Fashioned Hosiery*. New York: McGraw-Hill, 1937.

Ministry of Economic Warfare. "Japan: Supplies of Fertilizers in 1942 in Relation to Food Production." London, 30 December 1941. 894.659/FERTILIZER/2, Roll 13. State Department microfilm series LM-68. RG 59, NA.

Mitani, Taichiro. *Japan's International Financiers and World Politics*. British Association of Japanese Studies. *Proceedings* 5 (1980): 29–53, 209–12.

Mitchell, W. L., and Kate Mitchell, eds. *Problems of the Pacific, 1936*. Institute of Pacific Relations. Chicago: University of Chicago Press, 1937.

Mitsubishi Economic Research Bureau, Tokyo. *Japanese Trade and Industry: Present and Future*. London: Macmillan, 1936.

Moggridge, Donald, ed. *The Collected Writings of John Maynard Keynes*. Vol. 23. Cambridge: Macmillan/Cambridge Press, 1979.

Morgenthau, Henry, Jr. *The Morgenthau Diaries*. Robert E. Lester, project coordinator. Microfilm. 250 rolls. Bethesda, Md.: University Publications of America, 1995–97.

Morley, James William, ed. *Dilemmas of Growth in Prewar Japan*. Conference on Modern Japan, Studies in the Modernization of Japan. Papers of the Sixth and Final Seminar. Princeton, N.J.: Princeton University Press, 1971.

———. *The Final Confrontation: Japan's Negotiations with the United States, 1941*. New York: Columbia University Press, 1994.

Morris-Suzuki, Tessa. "Sericulture and the Origins of Japanese Industrialization." *Technology and Culture*, January 1992, 101–21.

Moulton, Harold G., with Juinichi Ko. *Japan: An Economic and Financial Appraisal*. Washington: AMS Press, 1931.

Nagai, Isaburo. *Japonica Rice: Its Breeding and Culture*. Tokyo: Yokendo, 1959.

Nagaoko, Shinjiroo. "Economic Demands on the Dutch East Indies." In *The Fateful Choice: Japan's Advance into Southeast Asia, 1939–1941*, edited by James William Morley. New York: Columbia University Press, 1980.

Nakamura, Takafusa. *Economic Growth in Prewar Japan*. Translated by Robert A. Feldman. New Haven, Conn: Yale University Press, 1971.

National Council of Women of the United States. "Symposium on Women's Dress." *Arena*, September 1892, 488–506. Microfilm 05422, Roll 93. Library of Congress.

National Cyclopedia of American Biography. Vol. F, *1939–1942*. New York: James T. White, 1942.

Newcomb, Robinson. "American Economic Action Affecting the Orient." *Annals of the American Academy of Political and Social Science*, May 1941, 133–39.

———. "Potash Scarce." *Far Eastern Survey*, 20 November 1940.

Nippon Steel Corporation. *History of Steel in Japan*. Tokyo: Nippon Steel, 1973.

Norman, E. H. *Japan's Emergence as a Modern State*. New York: Institute of Pacific Relations, 1940.

Nurske, Ragnar. *International Currency Experience*. Geneva: League of Nations, 1944. In Mira Wilkins, advisory ed., *International Finance*, 177–83. New York: Arno, 1978.

Ohkawa, Kazushi. *Growth Rate of the Japanese Economy Since 1878*. Tokyo: Kinokuniya Bookstore, 1957.

Ohkawa, Kazushi, Bruce F. Johnston, and Hiromitsu Kaneda, eds. *Agriculture and Economic Growth: Japan's Experience*. Princeton, N.J.: Princeton University Press and University of Tokyo Press, 1970.

Ohkawa, Kazushi, Miyohei Shinohara, and Larry Meisner, eds. *Patterns of Japanese Economic Development: A Quantitative Appraisal*. New Haven, Conn.: Yale University Press, 1979.

Okada, Maj. Gen. Kikusaburo. "Prewar Material Potential and the Resolve to Fight the United States and Britain." Translated by Military Intelligence Section Allied Translator and Interpreter Section, General Staff. In *War in Asia and the Pacific, 1937–1949*, edited by Donald S. Detwiler and Charles B. Burdick. New York: Garland, 1980.

Patrick, Hugh, in collaboration with Larry Meissner, eds. *Japanese Industrialization and Its Social Consequences*. Berkeley and Los Angeles: University of California Press, 1976.

Payton-Smith, D. J. *Oil: A Study of War-time Policy and Administration*. London: HMSO, 1971.

Penrose, E. F. "Japan's Basic Economic Situation." *Annals of the American Academy of Political and Social Science*, May 1941, 1–6.

Prange, Gordon W., with Donald M. Goldstein and Katherine V. Dillon. *At Dawn We Slept: The Untold Story of Pearl Harbor*. New York: Viking, 1991.

Pratt, James Norwood. *The Tea Lover's Treasury*. San Francisco: 101 Productions, 1982.

Randolph, Frederick. "The American Liberty League, 1934–1940." *American Historical Review* 56, no. 1 (October 1950): 19–33.

Ratner, Sidney. *The Tariff in American History*. New York: Van Nostrand, 1972.

Raw Silk Importers, Inc. "Memorandum of Raw Silk Distribution in U.S.A. Market." New York, 15 September 1941. File 894.6552/24. State Department microfilm series LM-68. RG 59, NA.

Reischauer, Haru Matsukata. *Samurai and Silk*. Cambridge, Mass.: Belknap Press, 1986.

Roosevelt, Franklin D. Address recommending revision of the Neutrality Law, 21 September 1939, Paper 14. online at http://www.ibiblio.org/pha/7-2-188/188-14.html (accessed 6 October 2002).

———. Press Conference. 6 October 1937. American Presidency Project. online at http://www.presidency.ucsb.edu (accessed 2 December 2006).

———. "A Proclamation: By the President of the United States of America." *American Journal of International Law* 30, no. 1, Supplement: Official (January 1936): 63–65.

Sagan, Scott D. "From Deterrence to Coercion to War: The Road to Pearl Harbor." In *The Limits of Coercive Diplomacy*, 2nd ed., edited by Alexander L. George and William E. Simons, 57–90. Boulder, Colo.: Westview Press, 1994.

———. "The Origins of the Pacific War." *Journal of Interdisciplinary History* 18, no. 4 (Spring 1988): 839–922.

Savage Endowment for International Relations and Peace. "Carlton Savage." online at http://oip.uoregon.edu/savage/bio.php (accessed 20 July 2006).

Sayers, Richard S. *Financial Policy, 1939–1945*. London: HMSO, 1956.

Schenke, Edward Max. *The Manufacture of Hosiery and Its Problems*. New York: National Association of Hosiery Manufacturers, 1935.

Schumpeter, Elizabeth Boody. *The Problem of Sanctions in the Far East*. New York: Japan Institute, 1940.

———. "The Yen Bloc: Program and Results." *Annals of the American Academy of Political and Social Science*, May 1941, 29–35.

———, ed. *The Industrialization of Japan and Manchukuo, 1930–1940*. New York: Macmillan, 1940. .

Sears, Louis Martin. *Jefferson and the Embargo*. New York: Octagon Books, 1927.

Seavey, James Matthews. "Neutrality Legislation in the United States." Ph.D. diss., Law School of Georgetown University, 1939.

Seki, Keizo. *The Cotton Industry of Japan*. Tokyo: Japan Society for the Promotion of Science, 1956.

Shepherd, Jack. "Japan's Southward Advance—Economic and Political." *Annals of the American Academy of Political and Social Science*, May 1941, 44–53.

Shinjo, Hiroshi. *History of the Yen: 100 Years of Japanese Money-Economy*. Research Institute for Economics and Business Administration, Kobe University. Kobe, Japan: Tenri Printing, 1962.

Skidelsky, Robert. *John Maynard Keynes: Fighting for Freedom, 1937–1946*. New York: Viking, 2001.

Stanley, Norman. "Industry May Avert Severe Cut in East Coast Supplies." *Oil and Gas Journal*, 3 July 1941, 8–9, 24.

Steele, Valerie. *Fashion and Eroticism: Ideals of Feminine Beauty from the Victorian Era to the Jazz Age*. New York: Oxford University Press, 1985.

———. *Fetish: Fashion, Sex and Power*. New York: Oxford University Press, 1996.

Sternberg, Fritz. "Japan's Economic Imperialism." *Social Research*, September 1945, 328–49.

Stockman, P. L. "Adequate New Reserves Found [in California] to Offset This Year's Output." *Oil and Gas Journal*, 30 October 1941, A46, A94.

Sugiyama, Shin'ya. *Japan's Industrialization in the World Economy, 1859–1899: Export Trade and Overseas Competition*. Atlantic Heights, N.J.: Athlone Press, 1988.

Suzuki, Norihisa. *A History of Japanese Finance*. Tokyo: Kenkyusha Press, 1938.

Takahashi, Inoguchi, and Daniel I. Okimoto, eds. *The Political Economy of Japan: The Changing International Context*. Stanford, Calif.: Stanford University Press, 1988.

Tamaki, Norio. *Japanese Banking: A History, 1859–1959*. Studies in Monetary and Financial History. Cambridge: Cambridge University Press, 1995.

"Tanker Diversion and Japanese Embargo Cut California Exports." *Oil and Gas Journal*, 30 October 1941, A89–90, A109.

Taoka, George M. "The Role of the Bank of Japan in the Administration of the Economic and Financial Controls of the Government During National Emergencies with Special Emphasis on the Sino-Japanese War and the World War II Periods." Ph.D. diss., Columbia University, 1955. Ann Arbor: UMI, 1994.

"Tripartite Treaty." Yale Law School. Avalon Project, http://www.yale.edu/lawweb/avalon/wwii/tri-parti.htm (accessed 5 July 2006).

Tucker, Ray. "Johnson's Johnson Act." *Scribner's Commentator*, February 1941, 7–12.

Ukers, William H. *All About Tea*. New York: Tea and Coffee Trade Journal, 1935.

U.S. Attorney General. "Opinion Upon the Act to Prohibit Financial Transactions with Any Foreign Government in Default on Its Obligations to the United States." *American Journal of International Law* 29, no. 1 (January 1935): 160–67.

Utley, Jonathan G. *Going to War with Japan, 1937–1941*. Knoxville: University of Tennessee Press, 1985.

————. "Upstairs, Downstairs at Foggy Bottom: Oil Exports and Japan, 1940–41." *Prologue: The Journal of the National Archives,* Spring 1976, 17–28.

Uyeda, Teijiro. *The Recent Development of Japanese Foreign Trade with Special Reference to Restrictive Policies of Other Countries and Attempts at Trade Agreements.* Tokyo: Japanese Council, Institute of Pacific Relations, 1936.

Watkins, T. H. "Ickes, Harold LeClair." *American National Biography Online,* http://www.anb.org/articles (accessed 4 May 2006).

"Ways Explored to Replace Capacity of 50 Tankers." *Oil and Gas Journal,* 10 July 1941, 26–27, 31, 34, 42.

Weiss, Stuart L. "American Foreign Policy and Presidential Power: The Neutrality Act of 1935." *Journal of Politics* 30 no. 3 (August 1968): 672–95.

Who Was Who in America. Vols. 1 and 3. Chicago: Marquis Who's Who, 1966.

Who Was Who in America and World Notables, 1977–81. Vol. 7. Chicago: Marquis Who's Who, 1981.

Wilkins, Mira. "American-Japanese Direct Foreign Investment Relationships, 1930–1952." *Business History Review* 16, no. 1 (Spring 1982): 497–517.

————. *The History of Foreign Investment in the United States, 1914–1945.* Cambridge: Harvard University Press, 2004.

Williams, Benjamin J. "The Coming of Economic Sanctions in American Practice." *American Journal of International Law* 37, no. 3 (July 1943): 386–96.

Williams, Moyle Strayhorn, and John W. Couston. *Crop Production Levels and Fertilizer Use.* Rome: Food and Agricultural Organization of the United Nations, 1962.

Williams, William J. "American Steel and Japanese Ships: Transpacific Trade Disputes During World War I." *Prologue* 25, no. 3 (Fall 1993): 249–56.

Wingate, Isabel B. Wingate. *Textile Fabrics and Their Selection.* 6th ed. Englewood Cliffs, N.J.: Prentice Hall, 1970.

Winkler, John K. *Five and Ten: The Fabulous Life of F. W. Woolworth.* Freeport, N.Y.: Books for Libraries, 1970.

Wohlstetter, Roberta. *Pearl Harbor: Warning and Decision.* Stanford, Calif.: Stanford University Press, 1962.

Women of Fashion: Twentieth Century Designers. New York: Rizzoli International, 1991.

"World Food Needs Benefit Average Soybean Producers." *Farm Week,* 1 September 1967.

Worrell, Estelle Ansley. *American Costume, 1840–1920.* Harrisburg, Pa.: Stackpole Books, 1979.

Worth, Ronald H., Jr. *No Choice but War: The United States Embargo Against Japan and the Eruption of War in the Pacific.* Jefferson, N.C.: McFarland, 1995.

Wray, William D. *Japan's Economy: A Bibliography of Its Past and Present.* New York: M. Wiener, 1989.

Wright, Philip Green. *The American Tariff and Oriental Trade.* Chicago: University of Chicago Press, 1931.

————. "The Bearing of Recent Tariff Legislation on International Relations." *American Economic Review* 23, no. 1 (March 1933): 16–26.

Yamazawa, Ippei. *Economic Development and International Trade: The Japanese Model.* Translated by Ippei Yamazawa. Honolulu: East-West Center, Resources Systems Institute, 1990.

Yamazawa, Ippei, and Yuzo Yamamoto. "Trade and Balance of Payments." In Ohkawa, Shinohara, and Meisner, *Patterns of Japanese Economic Development,* 134–56.

Yasuba, Yasuhichi. "Did Japan Suffer from a Shortage of Natural Resources Before World War II?" *Journal of Economic History* 36, no. 3 (September 1996): 543–60.

Yergin, Daniel. *The Prize: The Epic Quest for Oil, Money and Power.* New York: Simon & Schuster, 1991.

Newspapers and Periodicals

American Modiste. Various dates, nineteenth and twentieth centuries.
Designer and the Woman's Magazine. Various dates, nineteenth and twentieth centuries.
Economist (London). 1935–42.
Hosiery Retailer (later *Hosiery Age*). 1922–31.
New York Times. ProQuest Historical Newspapers, http://www.proquest.com.
Oil and Gas Journal. 1939–41.
Oriental Economist. 1940–41.
Quarterly Statistical Bulletin of the Hosiery Industry. 1934–39.
Silk (previously *Silk Reporter*). 1877–1932.
Silk and Rayon Digest. 1933–37.
Special News Letter. National Association of Hosiery Manufacturers. 1923–66.
Underwear and Hosiery Review. 1935–41.
Wall Street Journal. ProQuest Historical Newspapers, http://www.proquest.com.
Washington Post. ProQuest Historical Newspapers, http://www.proquest.com.

INDEX

ABOUT THE AUTHOR

Edward S. Miller is a prize-winning historian and author on American naval and strategic history. His book *War Plan Orange: The U.S. Strategy to Defeat Japan, 1897–1945*, published by the Naval Institute Press, received wide acclaim from senior cabinet and military leaders and the press. He was named author of the year by the Institute in 1992. The work earned five history prizes, including the Theodore and Franklin D. Roosevelt Prize in Naval History, and was also published in Japanese.

Bankrupting the Enemy, like the author's previous book, draws on newly declassified sources of a crucial historical era. It brings together Miller's interests in national strategy and finance, the latter stemming from a thirty-year career that culminated as Chief Financial Officer of a major international mining and energy corporation. He also served as director of U.S.-Japanese joint ventures in metal production. His knowledge of resource economics was furthered by his appointment in 1982 by President Ronald Reagan as Vice President-Finance of the U.S. Synthetic Fuels Corporation in Washington, D.C., where he was responsible for assessing the financial viability of multi-billion-dollar synthetic oil and gas projects.

Miller received his BA from Syracuse University, Phi Beta Kappa, and did graduate studies at NYU and the Harvard Business School. He served two years in the Army Finance Corps in the 1950s.